# LATE LATIN
# AND
# EARLY ROMANCE

**ARCA** Classical and Medieval Texts, Papers and Monographs 8
(ISSN 0309-5541)
General Editors: Francis Cairns · Robin Seager


PUBLICATION OF THIS VOLUME WAS ASSISTED BY A
GENEROUS GRANT FROM THE BRITISH ACADEMY

# LATE LATIN
# AND
# EARLY ROMANCE
in Spain and Carolingian France

ROGER WRIGHT

 FRANCIS CAIRNS

*Published by*
Francis Cairns
The University, P.O. Box 147, Liverpool L69 3BX
Great Britain

First published 1982

*British Library Cataloguing in Publication Data*

Wright, Roger
    Late Latin and Early Romance in Spain and
    Carolingian France. — (ARCA classical and medieval
    texts, papers and monographs, ISSN 0309-5541; 8)
    1. French language — to 1500
    2. Spanish language — to 1500
    3. Latin language, Medieval and modern
    I. Title      II. Series
    447'.01     PC2814
    ISBN 0-905205-12-X

Printed in Great Britain by Redwood Burn Ltd, Trowbridge, Wiltshire

# CONTENTS

Contents

Contents

## PREFACE

A very large number of colleagues have helped me in the preparation of this book. In particular I wish to thank Glyn Burgess, Klaus-Dietrich Fischer, Jonathan Foster, Margaret Gibson, the late Harold Hall, Richard Hitchcock, Derek Lomax, Nigel Vincent, Max Wheeler, the patient staff of the Inter-Library Loan Office of Liverpool University Library, and the many members of tolerant audiences that have commented on one (or more) of the nineteen conference papers delivered since 1974 to test the ideas elaborated in this book. I am also very grateful to Sandie Murphy for typing the manuscript.

Liverpool, February 1982

# INTRODUCTION

This book examines the implications of a single hypothesis: that
"Latin", as we have known it for the last thousand years, is an invention
of the Carolingian Renaissance.

At first sight, this idea may seem eccentric. Latin is, after all, by
definition, the speech used in the Roman Empire, and written Latin, at
least, seems to have been essentially the same ever since. The normal
modern view of the medieval period has been that, broadly speaking,
the educated spoke Latin and everybody else spoke whatever vernacular
was normal in their community; that Latin remained the same, and
vernacular existed alongside it.

When applied to communities in which the vernacular was some
variety of Old Romance, this established theory does not appeal to the
historical linguist. Old Romance is a chronological development from
the Latin of the Roman Empire, and it is not *a priori* likely that any
variety of language can stand still for a millennium in one part of the
community while the rest of that community gradually evolves the
vernacular in the normal manner. All languages change; that seems to be
an empirical fact. What the historical linguist prefers to envisage in
Romance communities is merely that over the years the spoken
language developed in different ways in different places, without any
pockets of total resistance, until eventually the different areas of the
Old Romance world evolved their varieties of speech so much that
orthographical reforms had to be undertaken.

The problem with this view is that it apparently conflicts with
documentary evidence. Written Latin from every century survives on
manuscript. In and after the twelfth-century Renaissance, there can be
no doubt that Latin was taught, learnt, read, written, and at times
spoken, as a conceptually distinct language from medieval Catalan,
Portuguese, Sicilian, etc. At that point there are two languages in any
one literate Romance community, Latin and the local vernacular. A
thousand years earlier, within the Roman Empire, there had been one

language (Latin). This one language had the sociolinguistic and geographical variation normal in any widely-spread speech community. So when did the distinction begin to be felt between "Latin" and "Romance"? The usual answer to that question suggests that the separation into coexisting, distinct norms had already happened by the end of the Western Roman Empire in the fifth century. This assumption is often vague rather than explicit. Philological evidence shows incontrovertibly what would be expected anyway, that the "Proto"-Romance speech of the end of the Empire had evolved considerably from the speech of the first century A.D.; the simultaneous existence in the fifth century of an old-fashioned Latin is not so incontrovertible but is usually taken for granted.

Such coexistence of educated, archaizing speech with normal regional vernaculars as is usually postulated for Early Medieval Romance communities is attested elsewhere. The varieties of Modern Greek and of Arabic are often cited as parallels to the Latin-Romance distinction characteristic of at least the later Middle Ages. Yet the preservation of Classical Arabic and of Katharevousa depends on a conscious, detailed, continuous and consistent process of education and training such as is hard to postulate for the whole of Romance Europe in the Early Middle Ages. If this is a sound analogy, we shall have to seek the start of the Latin-Romance distinction at some point when a conscious decision to change the nature of linguistic education in this way can plausibly be postulated in a historical context. The immediate candidate for such a turning-point is the period of reform around the year 800 A.D. in the realms of the Emperor Charlemagne; the suggestion offered in this book is that an integral part of the educational reforms of that time included the introduction of "Medieval Latin", originally as a method of reading texts aloud distinct from ordinary vernacular Romance.

This theory implies that before the advent of these reforms into a community there was no contemporary distinction between "Latin" and "Romance". Everyone used styles of their local vernacular, however well or badly educated they were. It is normal in any area and in any language for educated people such as lawyers, priests, poets and linguists to have a larger vocabulary and use complicated syntax more often than their neighbours; these are ordinary features of style variation and sociolinguistic patterning that occur in all communities and need cause no surprise here. Learning to write involved the techniques for reproducing on parchment outdated inflexional morphology (such as *-m*, *-bus*, *-abit*) and a spelling system not closely suited to the evolved Romance. Seventh-century French [vjɛɾdʒə] or [viɾdʒə], for example, might be spelt VIRGEN, VIRGINEM, VIRGINE or VIRGINI, in the same way as Modern French [ʃɑːt] can be spelt *chante, chantes* or *chantent*. The old written standard had to be followed by the few who wished to write, with the result that the written texts of the Early Middle Ages look *prima facie* as if their authors spoke more or less the same language as Plautus or Pliny. The old vocabulary, grammar and spelling could be picked up from books. Old pronunciation, however, cannot be picked up directly from books.

Pronunciation is thus the key issue in this case. Only when a consistently archaizing "Latin" pronunciation norm starts being consciously used in a Romance community is the ground prepared for a complete conceptual distinction between two separate languages, rather than the preexisting collection of varying styles that is normally found within one language.

If we look to see whether the hypothesis of the introduction of a new, but archaic, pronunciation norm during the Carolingian reforms is plausible, we discover that it is. The court scholars had the task of raising the level of Church education, including the introduction of a standardized manner of performing the Roman liturgy. To this end was prepared an authorized text of the Bible; Alcuin's *De Orthographia* (dealing with both spelling and pronunciation) was compiled at about the same time, 796-800 A.D. It seems probable that a standardized method of reading texts aloud was decreed, which involved the oral production of a specified sound for every written symbol in the text. This new pronunciation caused VIRGINEM to be read (in theory) as [virginem] or (in practice) as [viɾdʒinem]; this system of giving every letter a sound has been that used in reading Latin ever since. All scholars accept that this has been the case since c.800; the novelty of the view presented here lies in the suggestion that this had not happened before in any Romance-speaking community; that the result of the reform was suddenly to create a distinction between two coexisting pronunciation norms. Were such a reform applied in Modern English, *Wright* would be read as [wɾɪght] (or [wɾixt]) rather than [ɾait], etc.

At first the reform applied only to reading aloud. One of its consequences was the invention of a system of writing Old French elaborated for the purpose of specifying intelligible vernacular reproduction of texts such as oaths, sequences or sermons.

The implications of this theory are considerable. It requires reexamination of topics central to the study of Medieval Latin language and literature, of all the Medieval Romance languages and literatures, of

Romance Philology, of historical linguistics, and of medieval European history. This book attempts to cover all these aspects insofar as they relate to the central theme, but no individual section claims to be a complete study of its subject. The focus is maintained on the relationship between Latin and Romance. For the sake of space, not all the Romance area will be investigated in detail in this volume. Spain will take the centre of the stage for the latter part of this book; it is there that the theory requires the greatest reevaluation of accepted views. The Roman liturgy only came to Spain (outside Catalonia) in 1080 A.D., some three centuries after its promulgation in France, and came to be used generally only in the thirteenth century. If Medieval Latin was indeed invented for use initially only with the reformed Roman liturgy, it should not have existed in Spain before that date. Various areas of early medieval Spain (Visigothic Spain, Moslem Spain, León, the Rioja) produced extensive writing in what is at first glance "Latin"; it is proposed here that the texts are compatible with the hypothesis that their originators spoke Old Spanish and that the texts are the written modes of that Old Spanish. It turns out that established facts (as opposed to accepted wisdom) concerning Spanish culture from c.600 to c.1250 are not incompatible with the perspective proposed here, and in many cases are explained, more satisfactorily than they have been hitherto, by the theory that Medieval Latin was in Spain a revolutionary innovation after 1080 rather than a miraculous survival from the very distant past.

# 1

# LATE LATIN, EARLY ROMANCE AND HISTORICAL LINGUISTICS

**The Traditional View**

A widely accepted theory concerning Late Latin and Early Romance is that both coexisted as spoken languages during the centuries between the end of the Roman Empire and the twelfth-century Renaissance[1]. The evidence for this is supposed to be both textual and philological. The textual evidence, of the surviving written works of this period, will be considered in the next chapter. The philological and linguistic evidence will be considered in this chapter.

This "two-norm" theory is phrased in different ways. The common factor is that scholars consider, broadly speaking, that throughout these years there is a significant distinction that can be made between the speech of the educated, who spoke some kind of "Latin", and the speech of the uneducated, who spoke their local evolved vernacular. The following representative quotations, here presented in chronological order, show how entrenched this belief has become.

Rice (1909: 7), discussing postulated loanwords from educated Latin into the vernacular, stated simply that:

> The forms of early Old French loanwords prove beyond all doubt that a conservative form of language, based on the spelling of the time and on oral tradition, must have existed in both the seventh and eighth centuries.

Menéndez Pidal (1926: para.109) declared flatly that:

> Latin was in the early centuries ... the language of elevated communication between all educated people; it was thus the only, or at least the main, norm of good speech. Romance was merely colloquial; only the uneducated had Romance as their sole means of expression. (My translation)

---

1. This chapter draws on previous published work of mine; in particular Wright 1976a, 1976b, and 1980.

Alfred Ewert (1933: para.500):

... the clerks carried into their pronunciation of Latin many of the features of the vulgar tongue ...

Mildred Pope's influential handbook similarly assumed that Latin and Romance were distinct when she stated that (1934: 229):

In Gallo-Roman, particularly in Early Gallo-Roman, the clerks carried over into their pronunciation of Latin the tendencies that were most strongly affecting the speech of the time, and the words borrowed at this epoch ordinarily reflect these developments.

E. Löfstedt (1959: 3):

There could be no sharper contrast than that between the conservative character of officialdom's language and the tendencies of popular speech.

Norberg has studied Medieval Latin with greater sympathy than most other scholars, but he too has been sure that pre-Carolingian Latin and vernacular are conceptually distinguishable (1968: 29):

Merovingian Latin has above all been profoundly influenced by the spoken language.

Lüdtke had the idea of rephrasing this supposed bilingualism in pre-Carolingian times into the sociolinguistic concept of diglossia (1968: para.5.1.3; for "diglossia" see Ferguson 1959):

... a gap is formed between the vernacular language, naturally learnt, continually evolving, and the language of culture ... the gap between the two languages must have been getting deeper and wider and the diglossia ever more obvious.

The most influential of all the North American Romance philologists, R.A. Hall, described the relationship between Latin and Romance in the following way (1974: 106) — suitable for the Late Middle Ages, but here projected back to the immediate post-Imperial centuries:

LATIN AS A SECOND LANGUAGE. The antinomy between Romance and Latin did not imply, as has often been thought, that the latter ceased to be spoken, and survived only as a "dead" language used exclusively for writing and reading ... Latin was the regular language of instruction, discussion, and debate, in elementary and advanced learning, in the church, in law-courts, and in the offices of lawyers and notaries. It also served as a lingua franca for learnèd persons, not only in their written correspondences, but in their personal contacts with each other at home or on their travels.

Bustos Tovar was even prepared to envisage a three-fold distinction in seventh-century Spain (1974: 67):

While in very educated circles they would have continued to speak a Latin learnt at school ... similar to that written by St. Julian or

St. Isidore, on another level, without such specialized study, they would have spoken a Romance-affected Latin similar to what later became the popular Leonese Latin. On a lower level they would have used Old Romance.

Macpherson had no qualms about the distinction (1975: 94-5):

> Until well into the medieval period Latin continued to be the common language of cleric, lawyer, administrator, natural philosopher and man of letters; Church Latin and written Latin exerted a continuous influence on the spoken language ... The popular phonetic development of a word may be arrested or modified at some stage in its development by the pronunciation of the more educated classes.

Bynon was prepared to assert (1977: 249-50):

> There can be no doubt that both the dignitaries of the Church and educated people in general used Latin as the normal means of communication throughout the area from a very early period.

The idea continues to flourish in the 1980s. Lapesa's widely-used and now much-revised *History of the Spanish Language* still declares that ecclesiastical pronunciation was different from the ordinary vernacular (1980: 110):

> Some words have existed uninterruptedly in speech, free from the memory of their literary form and abandoned to the course of phonetic evolution ... others have not undergone a phonetic development unencumbered with learnèd reminiscences ... VIRGINE or ANGELUS ... in preaching and in religious ceremonies were pronounced in a way that may not have been exactly pure Latin but was essentially respectful of the Latin; people's ears became accustomed to the ecclesiastical pronunciation, whose influence prevented the usual phonetic tendencies from running their course: VIRGINE became *virgen*, not *verzen*, and ANGELUS *ángel*, not *año* or *anlo*.

There is, then, a consensus concerning the plausibility of the distinction between some kind of spoken "Latin" and the vernacular. In future chapters, however, the evidence in support of this dichotomy will be examined and found not to be substantial; it needs to be made clear here in advance that the view being argued against is indeed very widely held and believed, rather than being a mere straw man. Almost everyone who has studied the linguistic state of Romance communities in the centuries from 400 to 800 seems to accept that Latin and Romance speech both existed at the time, and some believe that they coexisted in earlier times as well (e.g. Leonard 1980, Pulgram 1975; cp. Janson 1981, reviewing Pulgram).

The argument in favour of this view seems to be (i) an instinctive feeling that "Latin" must have survived alongside Romance in the Early

Middle Ages, if only because there it is, incontrovertibly, in the Later Middle Ages, allied to (ii) the discovery, well-argued and by now indisputable, that many of the linguistic developments from Imperial Latin to Romance began long before the end of the Roman Empire. A few scholars have briefly rebelled against this idea; e.g. Janson (1979: 13), "Proto-Romance is Latin and Latin is Proto-Romance"; but the implications of this identification have yet to be explored.

### Learnèd Vocabulary

Around the turn of this century, philological attention was turning to words borrowed from Latin into French; Berger's study (1899) began a trend taken up by e.g. Paris (1909). Words taken into Old French from Latin in the Middle Ages are often identifiable because they have not evolved phonetically in the way that a comparable "popular" form would have done; a standard example is Fr. *fragile*, borrowed from Latin, with the *g* representing a consonant, as opposed to O.Fr. *fraile* (Mod. *frêle*), a popularly evolved form with the *-agi-* group regularly simplified to *-ai-* without a consonant (cp. MAGISTER > *maître*). The earliest French texts written in an orthography that attempts to correspond to the evolved phonetic forms are set down in the ninth century, at which point the coexistence in France of two ways of writing and pronouncing a word can be regarded as established knowledge. This distinction between Latin and Romance was at that time assumed not to be something new in the ninth century but to have been in existence for many centuries already. Yet we know anyway that the pronunciation of Latin was reformed in c.800 A.D.; the systematic learnèd-uneducated distinction, in phonetics as in orthography, can only be regarded as surely attested with the Strasbourg Oaths (842). The discovery of "learnèd" vocabulary was a real discovery but the conclusion that these unevolved "Latinate" forms had existed in such a form in anyone's speech before the ninth century was logically unwarranted. When Le Coultre made an acute analysis of Alcuin's *De Orthographia* in 1905, he claimed that Alcuin was describing Latin as traditionally spoken, and never considered the idea that this official "Latin" pronunciation might have been something new that had not existed in France previously.

Despite the uncertain basis of the argument, the supposedly proven existence of unevolved archaizing learnèd pronunciation, in the years between the Roman Empire and the emergence of written Romance in new spelling systems, came to be treated in Romance philology as established fact. This assumption had the consequence that any word which seemed not to have evolved enough, according to the discoverable regularities of sound change, became a candidate for being described, on this evidence alone, as a "learnèd" word. Whereupon the existence of such an educated unevolved layer of phonetics in pre-Carolingian Romance came to be seen as apparent confirmation of the two-norm theory. The argument is thus circular: the theory of learnèd vocabulary depends on the Latinate layer, and the theory of a Latinate layer largely depends on the learnèd forms.

Yet the historical and textual evidence (to be examined in subsequent chapters) is compatible with a simpler hypothesis: that this Latinate pronunciation norm, which gave each written letter a separate sound, was established in a Romance community for the first time by the Carolingian Reforms of c.800 A.D. It is worth looking to see if the philological data that are supposed to support the two-norm theory can be explained in other ways with the procedures of historical linguistics. If so, the existence of borrowings from Latin can be accepted as plausible only after the advent of the new "Latinate" pronunciation into any community. The traditional theory can be thus supported for the years after 800 in France and 1080 in Spain, but words containing "Latinate" phonetic features cannot be regarded as evidence of the "Latin" social dialect in preceding centuries. The circularity of the traditional argument can thus be broken, and the hypothesis advanced that the only speech styles that existed in any Romance community before these reforms belonged to the evolving Old Romance vernacular of that community, and nothing else.

### The Identification of the "Learnèd" Word

The words traditionally identified as "learnèd" are those that appear to be exceptions to the general regularities of phonetic change; they have not evolved as much as phonetically analogous words usually did, and the view is generally held that this is specifically due to the predominant use of these words by the educated classes in society, who used "Latin" rather than Romance. For example, the original consonant cluster -NS- usually loses the [n] : MENSAM >Sp. *mesa*, MENSEM > Sp. *mes*. The [n], however, is still there in the descendents of PENSO in its sense of to "think"; Sp. *pienso*, Ital. *penso*, Fr. *pense*, etc. Similarly, philological orthodoxy states that words beginning originally with FL- palatalize in Spanish into [ʎ]: FLAMMAM > *llama*. The [fl-] is still there, however, in *flor*, from FLOREM. Spanish *pienso* and *flor*, therefore, regularly feature on the lists of learnèd vocabulary such as that in

Bustos Tovar (1974: 482-83, 607-08), as words whose supposed phonetic retardation is due to their use by the educated.

The identification of those words that are supposed to have been used predominantly by the Latinate thus depends on the prior establishment of which developments are to be regarded as "regular". The regularities of sound change are sometimes called "laws", but they are not generally applicable in the same sense that the rules of grammar are. We can tell, for example, that in English there is a phonetic rule that adds [s] to the singular form of a noun to form a plural, or to a verb to form the third person singular present, when that noun or verb form ends in an unvoiced consonant (other than a sibilant). Neologisms such as the transatlantic verb *deescalate* (*Nixon deescalates U.S. involvement*) or the noun *raincheck* (*they took rainchecks*) form the third person singular present and plural form respectively in this manner. This suggests that native speakers have some kind of a "rule" in their heads that [-s] is added to words in such circumstances whether or not they have heard or used the words before. In such cases, where it is plausible to suggest that there are rules which speakers follow, it is reasonable to claim that any word which does not conform to this pattern is some kind of "exception". *Children*, for example, is a survivor from an age in which the rule of English was different, and it is thus legitimately characterized as an "exception" in the modern language. Sound changes, however, cannot be postulated as existing within the speakers' heads. The simultaneous availability of two variants might be known to a speaker, but the evidence does not support the idea that "Latin [-ns-] > Spanish [-s-]" had the same kind of psychological reality as "[bɪt] + plural = [bɪts]". Sound laws are statistical truths discovered afterwards by scholars; at the time of their operation they appear as cases of variation or as competition of forms, and unless the native speakers are etymologists they do not base their own practice on any knowledge of which form is the older and which is the newer.

### Geographical Regularity

It is worth considering, then, why any particular sound change comes to be thought of as "normal" or "regular" at all. There are many factors in play, but the basic ones are geographical and statistical.

It is regarded as normal and regular for CA- at the start of original Latin words to develop to *ch(a)-* in France ([ʃa]): for example, CANTANT > *chantent*, CATTUM > *chat*; or, in a free syllable, to *che*: CARUM > *cher*. It is also regarded as normal and regular for CA- at the start of these words not to develop at all in Castille; CANTANT > Sp. *cantan*, CARUM > *caro*. The presence of neither of these developments has caused the other to be considered by philologists to be exceptional or irregular, because the regularities concerned can be neatly allocated to different sides of linguistic boundaries, and hence the divergence is considered of no significance, as if it were believed that the political divisions of nineteenth-century Europe had been instinctively followed by the sixth-century inhabitants of Romania. In this manner, two different resolutions of the same original etymon have been considered to be both normal or regular. On the other hand, scholars have not usually thought such variants to be similarly regular if both occur in the same area. The inevitability of the sound law, remorselessly altering every word whose phonetic configuration brought it into the scope of that law, as the nineteenth-century grammarians are popularly believed to have envisaged it, only applied within geographical units. The same development could be regular in one valley but irregular in another. From the point of view of the early scholars of the subject, most of whom were specialists in the Romance of Northern France, this geographical proviso was an essential assumption. Without it, the logical application of the theory that the educated were supposed to use archaic forms could have been most unfortunate: Sardinia, in general, is the area whose speech seems to have evolved least from Latin, and Northern France the area whose speech, in general, seems to have evolved most, but they would hardly have wanted to conclude that early medieval Sardinia was the most educated and literate part of Romania.

This avoidance of the logical conclusions of accepting the two-norm theory was half-noticed, and sometimes rationalized away with another bold assumption, that increased intellectual activity leads to language change. Entwistle (1962: 72) expressed this in the following characteristically neat manner:

> It is the languages which have the most active intellectual background that show the most rapid changes.

There is little serious evidence to support this view either. Even in Early Romance it is untenable, since although Merovingian France seems to have been more active intellectually than contemporary Sardinia, it was considerably less active intellectually than Visigothic Spain, whose language also, in general, seems to have evolved less than Northern French. But even if it were tenable as an *a priori* linguistic principle it would conflict logically with the two-norm theory; the educated élite, supposedly responsible for lack of evolution and Latinate speech habits, and the active intellectuals, supposedly responsible for rapid evolution and vernacular speech habits, are the same people.

This confusion is heightened by yet a third belief, that remote illiterate dialects are usually more archaic in their speech than the educated norm. Some scholars seem to have quite cheerfully believed this at the same time as the two-norm theory, which is based on the contrary assumption, that the educated élite are usually more archaic in their speech than the illiterate rustics. There are, of course, archaic features preserved in some rustic dialects. There are, of course, also evolved features attested only in rustic dialects. Neither case seems to suggest to modern linguists that there is any link at all either way between comparative literacy and comparative archaism of speech in different geographical areas.

Scholars have avoided the problems caused by these mutually incompatible assumptions partly by vagueness, partly by ignoring them, but also by separating different geographical areas into different study areas. There is, therefore, no problem about having the evolution of CANTO > *chante* described as "regular" in one place and that of CANTO > *canto* described as "regular" in another; different places are said to have different languages, even in the sixth century. What has been definitely regarded as a problem, however, given this geographical slant on the question of regularity, is the coexistence in the same place of apparently different developments from the same kind of etymon. *Chante* is no problem to the philologist who is only considering CANTO > *canto* in Castille; but the different Castilian development of a different word in the same place, such as CATTUM > *gato*, is considered problematic, "sporadic", "irregular".

### Statistical Regularity

Once the decision had been taken (subconsciously, in the main) that it was sensible to parcel out the field of Romance Philology into geographical units of study, the decision concerning which developments are to be regarded as "regular" was normally made on a statistical basis. Concerning the development in Spain of initial CA-, for example, 150 medieval entries in Corominas' briefer etymological dictionary (1961) show no change – e.g. CAPRAM > *cabra*, CAPUT > *cabo*, CAPITALEM > *caudal*, CASTELLUM > *castillo*, Greek κατά > *cada*, etc. – whereas 20 entries show the development of initial [ka] to [ga]; *gato* < CATTUM, *galápago* < *CALAPACCUM, *gamella* < CAMELLAM (cp. B. Löfstedt 1959: 52-3), *gamuza* < CAMOCEM, *gañote* formed off *caña*, *garapiñar* < *CARPINIARE, *garrucha* < *carrucha*, *garúa* < *CALUGINEM,

*garulla* < *CARULIAM*, *garza* < Celtic *KARKIA*, *gavilla* formed off
CAVUM, *gazmoño* formed off CADMIA, *gazpacho* perhaps formed off
CASPA, *gazuza* formed off *cazar*, *gamarra* formed off CAMUM. (There
are also several Arabisms: *gafa* < qaf'a, *gasa* < qazz, *gabán* < gabâ,
*garrafa* < qarâb, *gaznate* < *gannât. Arabisms do not always have this
effect: e.g. *alcázar, alcalde, cadí, cadozo, candil*.) The latter development, of [ka] > [ga], is thus quite widespread.

The voicing of [ka] to [ga] is statistically more common if the
[ka] is preceded by a vowel: e.g. VACARE > *vagar*, PACANT > *pagan*,
SECAT > *siega*, etc. These statistics are awkward to assess in view of the
number of distinct morphological forms that might or might not be
included, but it seems reasonable to suggest that taking all positions into
account [ga] < [ka] might be as common as [ka] unchanged; however,
the regularity is usually assessed (for good reasons) on the basis of word-
position and phonetic environment, and there is no doubt that statistically in standard Castilian Spanish it is "regular" for word-initial [ka-]
not to change and for post-vocalic [-ka] to voice to [-ga]. In this way,
for purely statistical reasons, *cantan* and *siega* are both said to develop
"regularly", even though they develop differently, whereas *gato*, etc.
and e.g. *foca* < PHOCA, are "exceptions" to be explained in some further
way, despite the same results being "regular" in *siega* and *cantan* respectively. (*Foca* is a fifteenth-century borrowing from educated Latin.)

CANTO > *canto* is a statistically "regular" result in every respect. CA > *ca* is regular; -NT- > -*nt*- is "regular", once we regard the
normal development of -NTI + vowel > -*nz* ([ntj > nts > nθ]) as a
separate case (e.g. CANTIONEM > *canción*); -O > -*o* in the first person
singular is "regular", once we frame a separate rule for monosyllables
(SUM > *soy*, STO > *estoy*, VADO > *voy*, DO > *doy*). *Canto* is thus
"regular" vernacular, not ascribed to "Latinate" speakers, despite the
fact that it is for practical purposes phonemically and phonetically the
same as the Latin CANTO. Accordingly, mere similarity to the Latin is
not the criterion for being thought a learnèd word whose retardation is
attributable to educated use; the criterion is that of greater similarity to
the Latin than to words evolved from phonetically analogous origins.
*Pienso* < PENSO, for example, is said to be "culto", even though the
stressed [e] has diphthongized in the vernacular manner; it is statistically more common for the -N- to disappear from -NS-, as in *mesa* <
MENSAM, *tiesa* < TENSAM, etc. with the result that *pienso*, although it
has evolved a non-Latinate diphthong, is officially a learnèd word, and
*canto*, although it has hardly evolved at all, is allowed to have existed
in the vernacular.

The case of *flor* is instructive. It is arguable whether even the statistics support the common description of *flor* as a "cultismo". There seem to be six original Latin words with initial FL- that survived in the early medieval vernacular. Of those six, four have preserved the initial cluster: *flaco* < FLACCUM, *fleco* < *flueco* < FLOCCUM, *flojo* < FLUXUM, *flor* < FLOREM[2]. One has palatalized the cluster to [ʎ]: *llama* < FLAMMAM. The other has reduced the cluster to a simple [l]: *lacio* < FLACCIDUM. Comparing FL- with CA-, it might have been expected that FL- > *fl*- would be considered the "regular" shape of vernacular forms, with *llama* and *lacio* being considered "sporadic" and in need of further *ad hoc* rationalization. This has indeed been the treatment given to *lacio*. Malkiel perceived a problem here (1963-64: 159); aware that according to prevailing orthodoxy FLACCIDUM "ought" to have become [ʎatsjo], with an initial palatal [ʎ], he accepted the view that the form once existed as the standard, with the subsequent [ʎ] > [l] explained as a desire to dissimilate palatals in the light of the following [j]. (*Llacio* is attested as a variant.) This attempt to explain a development of [f-] > [ø] through a debatably general palatalization followed by depalatalization is possible; but it may not be necessary, even though it has convinced Macpherson (1975: 136) and Dworkin (1978: 609). F- > ø is in fact the statistically normal resolution of F- before a vowel (FACIT > *hace*, FILIAM > *hija*, etc.). *Llama* might seem to be similarly sporadic, but in fact it has been called "regular", because FL- was grouped for analytical purposes with other initial clusters of unvoiced consonant plus [l]. Initial PL- and CL- offer us sufficient examples of palatalization, such as *llorar* < PLORARE, *lleno* < PLENUM, *llave* < CLAVEM, for it to be statistically true that, for all initial unvoiced consonant + [l-] clusters, [ʎ] is the regular evolved form.

Choosing a different brief and a different field of operations thus produces a different pattern of regularity; within FL- words, *flor*, *flaco*, *fleco* and *flojo* are "regular"; within F- words, *lacio* is "regular"; within unvoiced C + [l]- words, *llama* is "regular". The choice of the grammarians has fallen on the latter; *llama* is patted on the head for

---

2. The case of *fleco* is confused by the existence of the rare word *lleco*. If both come from FLOCCUM, as Corominas suggests, then *fleco*/*lleco* will be a pair of doublets; doublets are discussed below. But the existence of Medieval Latin *frecus/frocus/froccus*, with the same meaning as *lleco* ("uncultivated land"), suggests that this word, probably of Germanic origin, could be the source. Since the etymology is unclear, and the first sure attestation of *lleco* is in Covarrubias' dictionary (1611), I have felt justified in omitting it from this section.

meek obedience, and the others have seemed to require special explanation. In this case and others, it might seem to have been quite haphazard which form was said to be regular, although in practice the possibility of assigning unchanged forms to "culto" speech may have made the choice of the evolved form as the "regular" one more likely. Once the assignation is made it is seen as indisputable. Corominas took it as firm, for example, and was moved to speculate on the apparent fact that *flor*, *fleco*, *flaco* and *flojo* seemed to have been confined to the educated. Under *flojo* (1954-57: II,541b) he declared that "the conservation of the FL- group is due to the moral aspect of the word, which accounts for the triumph of the pronunciation of the educated classes, as happened in *flor*, *flaco* and other similar words." This attempt at an explanation is unconvincing. Were it not for the *fl-* phenomenon, would we consider "flower" (*flor*), "thin" (*flaco*), "fringe" (*fleco*), "feeble" (*flojo*) to be essentially more moral concepts than "flames" (*llamas*)? The flames of hell suggest not. Even if they are, what evidence is there that uneducated groups never discuss morality? Morality is surely a feature of the conversation of all, even if not of the behaviour, and evaluative terminology is a linguistic universal in any group. In cases such as this, Corominas seems to expect his readers to visualize the monks of Early Medieval Spain as being so determined to resist the postulated general Castilian change of initial FL- > [ʎ] that they refuse to call flowers by anything other than the Latinate *flor*; while having no particular reservations about losing the final [-e] of the spoken form, nor, indeed, about changing the gender from the Latin masculine to the Castilian feminine. (At the same time, the Italian monks successfully preserved the original gender, but were happy to palatalize into *il fiore*, so morality too has geographically distinct linguistic consequences, it seems.) How, subsequently, were these monks so successful at the task of encouraging the other 99% of the population to ignore the development that is supposedly taking place unanimously in their speech, and say *flor* rather than their natural *\*llor*? Why do the same monks say *llama* without a qualm? Monasteries had fires, the outside world had flowers, and the scenario is not plausible.

Corominas' brave attempt to explain the absurd consequences of his predecessors' views is surely untenable. The postulate, however, that *fl-* words need some kind of special explanation, survives. Malkiel explained the supposed "cultismo" of *flor* as arising "since generic terms are frequently *cultismos*" (1963-64: 29-31); this idea comes from Lapesa (1980: para.25.3), but is hardly to be taken seriously. "Flower"

is no more a generic concept than is "man" or "fish"; *hombre* <
HOMINEM and *pez* < PISCEM are hardly Latinate. *Fleco* is also developed to a greater extent than the vernacular regularity would
foresee: FLOCCUM > *flueco* is fair enough, but *flueco* > *fleco*, phono-
tactically explicable through the awkwardness of [flwe], is over-evolved.
Were this really a word confined to the supposedly archaizing literate,
*\*floco* would seem more consistent. Malkiel, however, "granted in
principle the existence of a significant learnèd transmission of these
clusters" (1963-64: 157), so even when the attribution of learnèdness is
as statistically dubious as it is with *fl-* Malkiel felt unable to dispute it.

One voice has been raised against it. Badía Margarit (1972) has
diffidently declared his belief that the [ʎ] was a late evolution, and that
such obviously non-learnèd words as *claro* < CLARUM were either
words that had not succumbed by the time of standardization in the
late thirteenth century or words borrowed from a non-Castilian dialect
(since PL-, CL- > [ʎ] is exclusively Castilian). Badía's suggestion has
been ignored, even by the scholar in whose honour it was offered.
There are many such cases in which a reconsideration of the statistical
basis of the attribution of "regularity" shows that a form might as
plausibly be considered "regular" as "irregular", and in which any
postulated "rules" have many exceptions.

It is not the intention here to explain all such variations, but in
the case of *flor* it can be simply done along traditional lines. Even if we
accept FL- > [ʎ] as the "rule", we can make *flor* "regular" by adding a
rider that the palatalization never operated in such a way as to produce
monosyllables. As a statement of fact, it is true that in Castilian there
are no monosyllables beginning with [ʎ] and there probably never have
been. Latin ILLOS, for example, palatalized to *ellos* [eʎos] in tonic
positions, but reduced to *los* rather than *\*llos* in atonic positions; this
suggests there was a distaste for such a form, even perhaps a morpheme
structure rule. Being monosyllabic is acceptable as a respectable conditioning factor for change; for example, the retention of final nasal
consonants is confined to monosyllables (QUEM > *quien*, CUM > *con*,
but NUMQUAM > *nunca*). Had Menéndez Pidal included this rider, the
idea that only the educated were moral or generic enough to talk about
flowers would not have needed to rise. It is not my purpose here to claim
to have explained *flor* by this rider, for there seems to me to be nothing
to explain, but the possibility of such an explanation is an example of
the way in which, if we wish them to, irregular forms can be made
"regular" by a stroke of the legislative pen. The assignation of regularity
or irregularity is not always a simple process or even a meaningful one.

The supposedly anomalous forms, such as *pienso* and *flor*, have thus only been identified as such on the basis of the prior establishment of the "rules". In Spain, the rules were engraved on tablets of stone under the title of *Manual de Gramática Histórica Española* (Menéndez Pidal 1904). Any recalcitrance to those rules became a sufficient reason for the word in question to be placed among the ranks of "cultismos" or "semicultismos", learnèd words confined to or influenced by the "Latinate" élite. This attribution could be taken to extremes. The case of *engendrar*, for example, takes the theory of "cultismo" into the realms of mild absurdity. Latin INGENERARE has undergone at least eight identifiably "regular" sound changes in its development to Modern Spanish *engendrar*, viz: the change of the initial "short" [i] to [e] ; the loss of the internal atonic [e] ; the subsequent insertion of a [d] , which is legitimately regardable as "regular", for the [nr] cluster was unstable in Old Spanish (it sometimes survived (*honra*), sometimes reversed (GENERUM > *yerno*), but often acquired the [d] , as in the future forms of *poner* and *tener*, *pondré*, *tendré* (which coexisted in O. Sp. with *porné*, *terné*) ); the loss of the final [e] in approximately the twelfth century; the change of Latin [g] to Old Spanish [dʒ] before a front vowel (as in Modern Italian *genero*); the deaffrication of the [dʒ] to [ʒ] in the late Middle Ages; the unvoicing of the [ʒ] to [ʃ] in the Renaissance period; the subsequent backing of this voiceless fricative to [x] . It might thus be thought to be not obviously an archaizing Latinate form. But the theory was held that in Old Spanish the affricate [dʒ] ought to have been reduced to a palatal [j] before a front vowel, as indeed happened in e.g. GELUM > *hielo*, GERMANUM > *iermano* > *hermano*, GENERUM > *yerno*; nor do the forms with stress on the stem diphthongize (*engendra*, not *\*engiendra*). As a result, *engendrar* is stigmatized as being retarded and learnèd (cp. Bustos Tovar, 1974: 444). This may not be justified. There are no cases at all that I can see of Latin -NGE- becoming [nje] in a pretonic syllable; *hielo* and *yerno* have tonic vowels that diphthongized anyway, and the instability of the pretonic [j] in the transient [jermano] — which was never the standard form, soon becoming Sp. *hermano* (and Port. *irmão*) — is another symptom of the medieval Castilian tendency I have discussed elsewhere to avoid diphthongs in pretonic position (Wright 1976c). It is hard to be certain, but there seem to have been only three cases of -NGE- > [nje] even in a Latin tonic syllable; *quinientos* < QUINGENTOS, O.Sp. *punniente* < PUNGENTEM, *cinientes* < CINGENTES (disregarding affixes such as in *tañendo* < TANGENDO; Menéndez Pidal 1926: para.49). In addition, there is in INGENERARE the morpheme boundary after IN-, which is able to inhibit other changes (e.g. INSIGNARE > *enseñar*, not *\*eseñar*), and the whole situation with -NG- plus front vowel is fluid; we have, for example, IUNGERE > O.Sp. *unzir* (O.Sp. [dz]), GINGIVAM > *encía* ([ts]), TANGIT > *tañe* ([ɲ]), and other resolutions to show that "regularity" in this case is hardly discoverable at all (see Malkiel 1975a). Such confusion could well inhibit diphthongization; criticism of the form for not undergoing the "regular" change may be misplaced[3].

*Engendrar* is an extreme case. Many of the supposed "culto" forms have little firm basis for such an attribution, however, and the label has merely hindered their rational examination. Even so, there are forms for which surprise at their archaism is legitimate; the status of exceptions in historical linguistic theory needs to be examined in connection with them.

### Types of Change

Some sound changes are "isolative" ones that apply in all phonetic circumstances. The Proto-Romance merger of originally long and short [a] is one such. Completely isolative changes probably do not occur in Early Romance; Latin stressed or countertonic [u] > [y] in French, as in *tu, nul, durer*, has been said to be isolative, but the presence of stress is a conditioning factor even here. For practical purposes, Early Romance developments can be regarded as "conditioned" changes, ones that applied in some phonetic circumstances but not in others.

This, for example, explains how the loss of [n] in *mesa* < MENSAM can be described as "normal". In general, Latin [n] does not normally disappear, neither initially – e.g. NATAM > *nada* – nor intervocalically – e.g. TENERE > *tener* – nor in a cluster – e.g. DENTEM > *diente*. Its loss is, however, statistically regular under the phonetic condition of having a following [s], so it is reasonable to draw up the regularities [n] > ø / _ [s] (and [k] > [ɣ] / V _ V).

The relationship between isolative and conditioned change is not clear, although they may well be connected. Wang (1969), for example, wondered whether even long-established conditioned changes may be isolative changes that have not yet spread as far as they will.

---

3. GENERUM > *yerno* ("son-in-law") may have chosen [j] and [rn] at the same time as *engendrar* chose to avoid [j] and adopt [ndr]; the two words being given opposing choices in the current free variations ([dʒ-] and [j-]; [rn] and [ndr]) in order to avoid confusion of "son-in-law" and the central morpheme of *engendrar*. Cp. the variants *gente ~ yente*; and Malkiel (1979) on *hasta* and *hacia*.

Maybe all examples of Latin [ka] will be Spanish [ga] in a millennium or two, as all positions of Latin /b/ seem to have become eventually Spanish /β/ (Penny 1976). Krishnamurti (1978) has taken the cue and cheerfully described a change that has now been going for twenty centuries and could last for as many more.

There is one general point concerning conditioned change that is of particular relevance to the words under examination in this chapter; the fact that after the conditioned change has operated, the old sound will usually survive as a phonetic entity in those contexts unaffected by the conditions. The only exception to this could be the suffering by a phoneme of more than one conditioned change simultaneously in such a way that no contexts are left unaffected; this situation is possible but most unlikely. For example, Latin [t] became Spanish [d] and then [ð] intervocalically, became [ts] and then [θ] before [j], and disappeared word-finally; even so, it survives initially, and even intervocalically as the simplification of some consonant clusters in which it was originally the second part (e.g. *gota* < GUTTAM, *escrito* < SCRIPTUM), and the phoneme itself is as vital as ever even if relatively fewer words contain it now than two millennia ago. This means that, in general, if any form, for any reason, does survive unaltered a change which we might otherwise expect it to undergo, the form may stick out like a sore thumb to modern philologists, but speakers of the time, even synchronic phonologists of the time, are unlikely to think of it as peculiar at all. *Pensar*, for example, is immediately obvious to the modern philologist as being a remarkable exception to the [ns] > [s] "rule"; but the [n] and the [s] are in themselves very common sounds of Early Romance, and even the cluster [ns] has moral support from forms such as *cansar* (< CAMPSARE). If we permit ourselves to ignore the morpheme boundaries that sometimes blocked the change, and involve the same sounds, the support from analogous forms is quite large (e.g. *enseñar* < INSIGNARE, *consolar* < CONSOLARI). Accordingly, there need have been no prolonged or tense struggle for survival on the part of such a sound as the [n] in *pensar*. Whatever the reasons for its survival, the form itself would not have seemed peculiar or undesirable at all within the superseding phonological system. So far as I know, noone thought *pensar* in any way to be a strange word until the philologists decided it was last century. If there is a sensible reason for a word's not undergoing a conditioned change, not changing is a simple goal for the word to achieve; "exceptions" within historical linguistics are not usually "exceptions" within the synchronic phonological structure of the language.

If then, for some reason, speakers prefer not to develop a word in the same way as most analogous words, there is rarely a synchronic reason for it not to remain unchanged. As the next section shows, there is reason to suppose that some words are less amenable to a change than are others, for reasons that are at times discernible but do not normally have anything at all to do with the relative literacy of different strata of society.

### Lexical Diffusion

Wang's 1969 article arose from the problems that can confront a word that is being subjected to two changes at the same time; if the changes are incompatible — for example, if the application of each change removes the condition for the other — it is impossible, with the best will in the world, for a word to evolve in a regular way. A Romance example is Latin LIMPIDUM "clear, attractive" > Spanish *limpio* "clean", *lindo* "pretty". Unless Corominas (1954-57) and Dworkin (1978: 607) were right in thinking that Spanish *lindo* descends from LEGITIMUM[4], — in Portuguese *lindo* the case is stronger — we can see that both result from "regular" changes; between two unstressed vowels, [d] regularly disappears — cp. *tibio* < TEPIDUM, *recio* < RIGIDUM; between two consonants it is regular for atonic [i] to disappear — cp. *linde* < LIMITEM — and if three consonants thereby cluster the middle one disappears and the others assimilate — cp. *once* < UNDECIM. *Limpio* is the result of the first change, which removes the second consonant, with the consequence that the conditions for the second change do not apply; *lindo* is the result of the second change, which removes the vowel, with the consequence that the conditions for the first change do not apply. The two words share the semantic content of LIMPIDUM in a sensible manner, and the incompatibility is resolved.

This general idea (with Chinese evidence, in the main) led Wang to consider whether some morphemes are more keen to change than

---

4. Corominas decided that the stressed [i] of LIMPIDUM "ought" to have opened to [e], despite the indisputable provenance of *limpio* from LIMPIDUM, the evidence of the exact opposite in *tibio* < TEPIDUM, and the form *linde* from LIMITEM. LEGITIMUM > *lindo* involves several unattested and debatable steps, and we would expect to find many Medieval variants (cp. MET-IPSIMUM > *meismo, mesmo, mismo*, etc), which we find in Portuguese but not in Spanish. Dworkin remarked (wrongly) that "most Hispanists reject the equation LIMPIDU > *lindo*"; phonetically this etymon is still surely the most likely, but the Spanish semantics may well have been affected by LEGITIMUM or its Portuguese descendants, and the form of Ptg. *lindo* may have been affected by Sp. *lindo*.

others. The traditional theory of sound change assumed that the progress of a change operated the same way at the same time in every relevant word, but this was never more than an assumption; a simple look at changes in progress has shown without any doubt that often, perhaps always, some relevant morphemes undergo a change before others[5]. If this is true, as it seems to be, then the problem of accounting for "archaic" unevolved forms that survive in speech could be redefinable as the problem of deciding why certain words should find themselves at the beginning, and others at the end, of the queue for the application of that change. If the change fails to reach every item, those at the end of the queue will be left unaltered, and as we saw in the last section there are unlikely to be dreadful phonological consequences of this.

The idea of a queue has subsequently been elevated into a theoretical school, that of "Lexical Diffusion". Chen attacked those who use "dialect borrowing" as a panacea for any problem; he pointed out (1972: 462) "the inadequacy, both methodological and factual, of a facile recourse to interdialectal borrowing as an 'explanation' of irregular sound changes." This recourse is at least feasible if the dialects concerned are indisputably known to exist; inventing hypothetical dialects from which to borrow otherwise inexplicable forms, such as inventing a spoken Latin distinct from Early Romance in Early Medieval Europe, would seem even less adequate as a way of shunting aside cases of ostensibly insufficient evolution. Chen and Wang then joined forces to attack the traditional preference for ignoring exceptions (1975: 256):

> The neogrammarians were rightly perceptive of the significance of the over-all regularity of phonological processes, since there was no a-priori reason why sound laws should operate with such remarkable uniformity ... the neogrammarians often blamed the exceptions on such culprits as dialect mixture and analogy. Cross-dialectal interferences are certainly present in most real linguistic situations; but more often than not, linguists have used dialect mixture as an excuse for not producing evidence of a substantive nature.

This theory now has an established place within historical linguistics; most scholars, including many specialists in dialectology, accept that sound change in practice often affects some words later than others. "For dialectologists, the theory of Lexical Diffusion is credible in a way that the structuralist and generativist hypotheses are

---

5. In 1980 BBC English, the [ɑ] > [æ] change that seems to be slowly occurring seems to have affected the morpheme *trans-* ([træns]) but not *plant* ([plɑːnt]): hence *transplant* often has two different vowels ([trɑnsplɑːnt]).

not . . ." (Chambers and Trudgill 1980: 176). Not all scholars consider this to be particularly important, and until we can gather why words change in the order they do it is not particularly illuminating. The theory does not imply, as some of its critics apparently think it does (e.g. Harlow 1975-76), that the order is random. It has hardly been applied to Romance at all yet; Wang (1977) edited a collection of articles on various phenomena in different languages, none of which are Romance. Wang himself is centrally concerned with Chinese, and, despite using occasional data supplied by Malkiel, has no interest in Latin or Romance; but the comments above on "dialect mixture" apply well to Early Romance, in which the traditionally postulated surviving "Latin" has been one such dialect to be wheeled on when the "rules" have too many recalcitrants.

"Lexical Diffusion", as a simple statement of the fact that in many sound changes words do not all change at once, is probably the dominant view by now. Chen even suggested (1972: 473) that it is so obvious that the burden of proof rests on its opponents; one of these would have been Saussure, who regarded change as affecting sounds irrespective of the words they happen to be used in, but the evidence is not obviously on his side. The lexicon is apparently destined to assume a much greater importance in linguistic theory of the 1980s than in that of the 1960s (e.g. Bresnan et al. 1978), and the theory of lexical diffusion is merely one aspect of a wider realignment. Meanwhile, with regard to our problem of phonetically retarded "learnèd" words that seem to have existed in speech before the Carolingian reforms, lexical diffusion has permitted us to suggest that these words might merely be words that were at the end of the queue, which the change never reached. Why words should go to the end of the queue is the question that needs to be answered next.

### Strengthening and Phonaesthetics

The idea that some words seem deliberately not to want to undergo a change that is otherwise general in the language is not in itself new. For example, as a general point, Zonneveld (1978: 261) suggested that "it may become plausible to at least entertain the idea of a sound change being competed against by its own converse", as hyper-correction; and within Romance Posner (1974: 106-09) has implied such a reaction in her comments on the strange phenomenon of the occasional "strengthening" or doubling of some intervocalic Latin con-sonants that refrain from voicing, comparing for example the voicing of the [-t-] in Latin TOTAM to *toda* in Spain, predictably, with its gemination to *tutta* in Italy and preservation as an unvoiced consonant in Catalonia (*tota*) and Northern France (*toute*). Posner suggests that in France, at least, TOTA saw the change coming in words already affected (e.g. VITA, NATA, in which [-t-] voiced and eventually disappeared, > *vie*, *née*) and shied away in horror; "one must assume that intervocalic surds have been reinforced, so that there is no longer an input to the voicing rule" (1974: 108).

We can hardly claim that every regional dialect which fails to undergo a change suffered in the dialect of a cognate neighbour has positively resisted such a change; but the sporadic strengthening of some words in the face of a change, when they seem to have deliberately disqualified themselves from the conditions of that change, can only have occurred if the theory of lexical diffusion holds, or else by the time TOTA saw what had happened to NATA it would be too late. The theory does not explain why it happened, but it does explain how it was possible at all. French *toute* is in fact a more interesting case than Italian *tutta*, since so few Tuscan forms did eventually voice, and some Italian words geminated − under different stress conditions − without the threat of such a change (e.g. FEMINA > *femmina*). (Wanner and Cravens 1980 also reject the usual "facile recourse to dialect mixture" to explain the voiced forms in Tuscan.)

One non-phonetic reason which might lead a word to prefer not to change, and hide at the back, is what Samuels called "phonaesthetics" (1972: paras 3.10, 5.4 and 7.2) and others have called "sound symbolism". One example discussed by Samuels concerns the English change of *er* to *ar* as has happened in such words as *clerk*. An exception to this was the word *swerve*, which remained as it was; the possibility of phonaesthetics arises here because the central sequence may have some kind of psychological connection with meanings of circular movement, as in *twirl*, *whirl* or *whirr*. A variant of this can concern onomatopoeic words, whose motivation might run the risk of being lost after the change. Dworkin (1975: 468) has suggested that the mildly surprising decision to choose variants with the inter-vocalic consonant *g* ([ʒ], now [x]) in Spanish *rugir* (to roar) < RUGIRE and *mugir* (to moo) < MUGIRE, compared with e.g. *ruido* < RUGITUM, could be attributable to the desire to preserve suitably loud consonants in such words (although the existence of English *moo* shows that this is not an overwhelming tendency). This might also apply to *maullar*, "miaow", since the possible [aw] > [o] development would have lessened its felinity. This word first appears in Spanish orthography in the *Glosario del Escorial* (2484, CATELO *por mahullar como gato*) of c.1400, but it undoubtedly existed earlier; for example, it appears (spelt MEOLARE) in a delightful list of animal noises compiled in tenth- or twelfth-century Moslem Toledo (Castro 1936; Díaz y Díaz 1976b: 154). Such strictly onomatopoeic words may seem to have a greater motive for recalcitrance than the psychological phonaesthesia of *swerve*; neither would have sufficient strength to resist the steamroller effect of the neo-grammarian sound laws, but both can be seen as plausible reasons for the words concerned being further to the back of a diffusion queue than other words unaffected by such considerations.

Archaism and reluctance to change is not the only consequence that has been envisaged for phonaesthetic considerations; Malkiel (1980b) has even suggested, tongue apparently not in cheek, that the excessive assimilation in the opening of the initial vowel of Sp. *maravilla* < MIRABILIA, where the most closed Latin vowel, [ī], became the most open Spanish vowel, [a], is due to what he calls "phonosymbolism": marvels leave their witnesses open-mouthed. Any explanation is perhaps better than none! Sound symbolism is taken by Samuels further than it might be thought plausible to take it, but if all we are looking for are the reasons for the order within a queue we already have reasons to believe exists, even the most minor considerations might turn out to be relevant.

### Homonymy

#### a) Clash

Romance philology made one of its rare contributions to linguistic theory when the dialect geographers proposed that some strange phenomena could be attributed to a desire to avoid homonymic clash. When two words are destined to become indistinguishable if the ordinary evolutions were to occur, it often happens that one or both of the words either disappears or evolves in an unpredictable manner. The standard and original example concerns Gascon farmyards, where CATTUS "cat" and GALLUS "cock" were both destined to lead to Gascon *gat*; but that form is now confined to "cat", with the "cock" being referred to with a variety of different words entirely (cp. Ullmann 1967: chap.7). Such cases of the disappearance of one of the lexical units are sufficiently well attested for homonymy to be plausibly offered as the reason. Within Spanish, this is visible in such cases as AUT > *o*, UBI > *o* > ø; ET > *y*, IBI > *y* > ø; FENUCULUM > *hinojo*, GENU-CULUM > *hinojo* > ø (except in the unambiguous phrase *de hinojos*, "on one's knees"). UBI has been replaced by *donde* < DEUNDE, IBI by *allí* < AD ILLIC, and GENUCULUM by *rodilla* < ROTAM + the diminutive (cp. ROTAM > *rueda* "wheel").

It has been occasionally argued that prospective homonymy is a reason for lack of evolution, on the assumption that this prospect could be sufficient to keep the word back in the first place. But it has in the event proved difficult to find incontrovertible examples in which a homonymic clash has prevented a change from happening at all. Speakers cannot foresee a clash before it arrives, nor hear it until it has been uttered. The above Spanish examples in fact confirm that although homonymic clash can lead to subsequent readjustments, they do not regularly prevent the development that caused it. There was, for instance, no particular reason in the first place for the loss of the intervocalic [b] of UBI or IBI, the development that precipitated the clashes with AUT and ET; [-b-] survives more often than not (e.g. *subir* < SUBIRE, *haba* < FABAM). ET > *y* is a similarly unusual change, since [i] > [e] is commoner than the reverse. The loss of the aspiration in FENUCULUM > *hinojo* > *hinojo* was isolative, for [h] does not exist in Standard Modern Castilian and the word could not therefore survive as such, but strengthening to [f] might have been a way of escape. Vincent has argued, in a brief but brilliant study, that since in such cases the sound changes concerned were not stopped in time to halt the creation of the pathological state, all the traditional examples of homonymic clash are "counter-examples to the view that sound change is itself directly teleological" (1978: 416). The clash is on us before it is foreseen. In another influential study, Andersen concluded that teleology is acceptable as a "teleology of function" rather than a "teleology of purpose" (1973: 789), but the point cannot be hidden; sound changes do not occur because the speakers have a positive desire to arrive at their destination, even if they sometimes occur because speakers have a negative desire to leave their starting-point. If the desire to avoid clash were as strong as it has sometimes been presented, FLAMMAS, for instance, would have followed its phonetic analogues and survived as *flamas* in Spanish, since *llamas* < CLAMAS has become an exact homonym for *llamas* < FLAMMAS.

This is unfortunate for our desire to explain why some words go to the back of the queue for a sound change; an initially promising and traditionally trumpeted cause célèbre turns out to be little more than a damp squib. However, one of the diffusion theorists has considered this question. Although he agrees with Vincent, that "homophony-inducing sound-changes will cause compensatory mechanisms to develop ..." subsequently, Lyovin (1977: 132) also suggests from his own evidence that until such mechanisms are developed the standardization of the form of both the relevant items might be slightly delayed. Given this, the general pattern might be for homonymic clashes that arise, but are thought intolerable, to lead to irregularities of various kinds; and one of these irregularities might, if the old form is still synchronically acceptable, be a subsequent reversal of the change: i.e. not the prevention of a hypothetical change [a] > [b], but its being followed by another change that happens to take the form [b] > [a]. This is observable in the Modern English pronunciation of *guerrilla*; aware of unfortunate consequences of failing to distinguish *guerrilla* from *gorilla*, given that [gə] is the naturally evolved initial syllable of both, the BBC has self-consciously adopted [ge-] for *guerrilla*. As a result this appears to be comparable with a case of strengthening, for surely the [ge] cannot have been delivered so emphatically before this therapeutic reaction. Within the next century, unless terrorism disappears, the BBC is likely to have a similar problem with *gunmen* and *government* [gʌnmən]. I have caught myself doing the same when lecturing on the additions to the 1502 editions of *Celestina*, distinguishing *addition* from *edition* with an emphatic [a-]. Blaylock (1973: 53) rephrased this phenomenon as a decision to choose unevolved variants: "If a tendential loss is to be thwarted, it can only be through the eventual favoring of variants in which the loss never occurred." This recognition of the coexistence, at some time, of both old and new forms in the community as a whole, is a key idea developed in the next section.

One minor group of words might have the traditional theory of homonymic clash available still to explain retardation; those in which the homonym avoided is taboo. The case of the avoidance of [ʃɪt] in the unchanged English forms *shut* and *shuttle* is mentioned by Samuels (1972: 143). Exactly the same mechanism has been thought to explain the non-diphthongization of stressed [e] and the retention of internal atonic [i] in the Spanish town of *Mérida* < EMERITAM, a provincial capital in Roman times; the desire not to be associated with *mierda* < MERDAM. Dialectal explanations are less implausible than usual here, however, judging from what we know of Western Mozárabe. On the other hand there is the delightful case of the citizens of Coyanza complaining to the King about the embarrassing name of their town in c.1208[6]; this problem was solved not by retarding or reevolving the

---

6. I am grateful to Derek Lomax for drawing this to my attention. The petition to Alfonso IX of León is mentioned by one Jimeno de Daroca in Sanchis y Sivera (1921, II: 374). The King changed the name and imposed a fine of 100 *solidi* on anyone who spoke the old name. Coyanza, on the Esla just south of

name to distance it further from *cojones* (< COLEONES, "testicles"),
but by changing it entirely to Valencia de Campos, and eventually to
Valencia de Don Juan.

### b) The Formation of Doublets

The avoidance of the production of homonyms is probably a
reddish herring; but the application of sound changes to already
existing homonyms and polysemic forms can have the effect of appearing to retard phonetically one of a pair of homonyms or part of the
meaning of a polysemic form. In the case of two distinct homonymic
words, it is reasonable to expect under diffusion theory that one will
start to change before the other. In the case of a polysemic word — a
word with more than one meaning — the mechanism for such differentiation is less straightforward but no less real. In each case, the effective
result is the production of what are often known as "doublets".

Sometimes two Romance descendants from the same one
etymon coexist in the same modern language. For example, Latin
PENSO gives both Spanish *pienso* ("I think") and *peso* ("I weigh");
MUNDUM gives both *mundo* ("world") and *mondo* ("clean"); RATIO-
NEM gives *razón* ("reason") and *ración* ("ration"); CATHEDRAM gives
*cadera* ("hip") and *cátedra* ("University Chair"); LITIGARE gives *lidiar*
("fight" — now confined to the bullring) and *litigar* ("litigate");
RADIUM gives *rayo* ("ray"), *radio* ("radius") and *radium* ("radium");
etc. In some of these cases it is clear that the less evolved variant has
been consciously borrowed from the old Latin form at some time later
than the arrival of the twelfth-century Renaissance into Spain. *Radium*,
for example, was recently borrowed, as in English ("radium"). *Radio* was
borrowed ("radius") at an earlier time when the endings of Latinisms
were normally adjusted to the norms of Spanish morpheme structure.
*Cátedra* was a borrowing from educated Latin, probably in the thirteenth century. *Litigare* was a literary transliteration made by e.g. Juan
de Mena in the fifteenth century. In these cases the origin of the less
evolved form is obvious and indisputable; *rayo*, *cadera* and *lidiar*, the
more evolved forms, were in the vernacular all along, but *radio*, *radium*,
*cátedra* and *litigar* were comparatively recent borrowings.

Unfortunately it has become traditional to use these words
as the model for cases in which both forms are already in current use at

León, was an ecclesiastical centre, variously spelt with *i*, *y*, or *gi*, probably representing a [j]. For the Council of Coyanza in 1055, see Chap.V. COLEONES
in Old Leonese would have given both [koʎones] and [kojones], so the connection would indeed be perceptible. For Leonese, see Zamora Vicente (1970:
146-49); for COLEO see Cela (1969).

the time of the earliest texts in reformed Spanish orthography (c.1200). In the same way as *litigar* is demonstrably a borrowing from Latin rather than a word existing in that form in the vernacular throughout, it has been assumed that surviving pairs of descendants from the same etymon are ascribable to comparable causes; that the more evolved form was used in the vernacular and the less evolved form was used by the educated in the "Latin" they were thought to speak. Thus it is that *pensar*, *mundo* and *ración* are said to be "culto" forms used by the educated, and *pesar*, *mondo* and *razón* to be "popular" vernacular words. In this way, doublets were seen as clinching evidence for the two-norm theory.

There is, however, a reasonable linguistic explanation for such doublets that does not depend on the postulation of a hypothetical Latinizing pronunciation; not only that, it has a recognized parallel in the development of English, wherein the same phenomenon is dealt with by philologists in a different manner.

It is generally realized that language change is neither uniform nor sudden. A development takes time to become established, within both the community and the individual. This means that while a change is in progress, both the old and the new form of a word will be encountered, and either form will be functionally sufficient. For example, during the progress of the diffusion of the [ĕs] pronunciation, with nasalized vowel, instead of [ens], MENSA would sometimes have been uttered with and sometimes without a consonantal [n], and either form would have been intelligible to all speakers, regardless of which form they preferred to use themselves. Normally this state of variation tends eventually to resolve itself into the survival of one form (e.g. > Sp. *mesa*); the surviving form will usually be the newer form, since whatever reason it was that led to its original emergence is likely to continue to be valid at the time of the decision to standardize one form at the expense of the other. There are, however, cases in which the retained form is the original form, and we appear to be confronted with a change that reversed direction in mid-flight; a much discussed case is that of Latin NOCTEM > O.Sp. *noche* > *noch* > *noche*; *noch* was apparently a common twelfth-century variant which eventually failed to become the standard form (e.g. Lapesa 1975; Hooper 1974: 126-30).

If, however, for any reason, both the coexisting forms survive, with different meanings, then we have an institutionalized pair of doublets. This will only happen in practice should there be a sensible reason for speakers to prefer the survival of two forms rather than one. In cases of homonymy — two words with the same pronunciation — or of polysemy — one word with more than one meaning — there often is a clear advantage in preserving two forms, in that the previous potential ambiguity can thereby be resolved. This has happened in English, for example, to the word *person*. The change of *-er-* to *-ar-* led to the co-existence in functionally free variation of at least two pronunciations for the affected forms. Most English words eventually chose the evolved form (*clerk*, *carve*), although some chose to remain with the older form (*swerve*, *clergy*), but *person* and *parson* both survived. This survival is almost certainly due to the usefulness of being able to distinguish people in general from vicars in particular, and we need not posit the existence of systematically distinct dialect systems to explain it. (In addition, the fact that *parson* happens to be the more evolved form is enough to demonstrate the falsity of the idea that ecclesiastical terms are *ipso facto* more archaic in phonology than the general vocabulary.) In practice noone has thought of ascribing the older forms of such doublets to a special retarded norm of educated pronunciation in English philology, and if anyone did they would be laughed out of court (Waldron 1967: chap.3).

The idea that doublets are evidence of two systematically distinct pronunciation norms ought to imply that each word of such pairs meant the same thing. Otherwise we will have to postulate that educated and uneducated people talk about systematically distinct subjects; for example, that in early Medieval Spain only the uneducated talked about weighing or sorrow (*pesar*) and only the educated talked about thinking or feeding horses with *pensar* (see below). If we concede that even illiterate people are likely to have used this common word to talk about thinking or feeding horses, we must also concede that in Medieval Spain they used a "literate" form when they did so, since even the earliest attestations regularly include the [n] or the manuscript tilde; and we can hardly avoid conceding that the literate used the *pesar* lexical item, since there it is, abundantly attested in early medieval Spanish literature. This systematic separation of subject matter according to the relative level of education in different groups is unconvincing; the two-norm explanation of doublets raises more awkward questions than it solves, despite its apparently charismatic initial attractions.

Homonymy is common in many languages, and is not usually in practice a cause of great ambiguity or awkwardness. If the chance arises to avoid it, however, it is easy to see why it might be thought sensible to differentiate the items in some way; within a lexical diffusion image of linguistic evolution, such a differentiation can be easily achieved by having one of the items near the front of the queue and the other at the back. Since the meanings are semantically separate in homonymy, no problem arises there. Chen has documented some startling evidence of extensive and pervasive "homonym splits that cannot be accounted for either as phonologically conditioned divergences or as a result of inter-dialect borrowing" in Chinese (1972: 492); if this is an accurate diagnosis, we need not be too chary of proffering comparable evidence in Romance.

For example, Latin MUNDUS was homonymic, with the two meanings of "clean" and of "world". Originally short Latin [u] regu-larly develops to Spanish [o], as in the second syllable of these forms; this has happened in Spanish *mondo*, "clean" (and its cognate verb *mondar*, "to clean"), but the surviving form for "world" is *mundo*. According to the rules engraved in the philological handbooks, there-fore, the [u] of *mundo* is under-evolved, and *mundo* is thus categorized as "culto". Thereby the impression has been given that the uneducated in Spain rarely or never used this form when referring to the world. But such a conclusion can be avoided if we suggest that during the in-evitable period of free variation a gradual decision was taken to factorize out one meaning per form, and thereby permit each form to survive with its own no longer confusable meaning. The phoneme /u/ of *mundo* is not at all strange phonologically in the superseding phono-logy, being the regular development of the originally long /ū/, and the form has no reason to be thought undesirable. There are conditions under which Latin [ŭ] becomes Spanish [u]; e.g. before laterals (e.g. CŬLTELLUM > *cuchillo*, CŬLMINE > *cumbre*, SŬLPHUR > *azufre*) and before a yod (e.g. FŬGIO > *huyo* etc., CŬNEAM > *cuña*, ŬNGULAM > *uña*). Other examples include *cruz*, *culpa*, *duda*, *lucha*, *trucha*, *mucho*, *puña*, *nunca*. Ŭ > *u* is not in itself avoided or considered unacceptable.

A similar case to *mundo* and *mondo* in Modern English concerns *blooming*; at present, given the [u] / [u:] variation in Britain, it usually has the long [u:] when it is used to refer to flourishing vegetation, and the short [u] as an adjectival expression of mild annoyance. Consider, for example, the likely pronunciations represented by:

1) The ivy is blooming in my garden.
2) Get that blooming ivy out of my garden!

When the orthographic revolution comes, the doublets will for the first time be attested in writing. The semantic separation will by then be ancient, but any postulated accompanying separation between educated and illiterate usage will be chimeric. Both the literate and the illiterate can and do get annoyed; both can and do discuss flourishing vegetation.

Cases of polysemy are not likely to resolve themselves like this so simply. Polysemy is normal in language, and not in itself pathological. The fact that many words have more than one meaning, or vagueness of potential reference, is often a pragmatic advantage, since if it was always essential to be precise in speech people would hardly ever talk at all. Even so, polysemy can lead to a word becoming unacceptably vague, ambiguous, or even misleading, and should a sound change begin to affect the form at a time when speakers are subconsciously becoming aware of the existence of an excessive range of semantic possibilities connected with the form, the same separation into two forms with distinguishable meanings can eventually be achieved.

The Spanish adventures of PENSARE are, in fact, of particular interest in this connection. Latin PENSARE meant originally to "weigh"; the Romance languages have words for "weigh" that presumably derive from a Proto-Romance form without the nasal (Sp. *pesar*, Cat. *pesar*, Ptg. *pesar*, It. *pesare*, Fr. *peser*, etc.). A metaphorical extension of this, meaning to "depress, grieve, weigh down with sorrow", seems to have been particularly widespread in Spain; in the nominalized forms, a further distinction arose between *pesar* "sorrow" and *peso* "weight". The verb remained potentially ambiguous between "weigh" and "grieve", although in practice a problem would very rarely arise since "grieve" requires an animate object and "weigh" usually took an inanimate one. The adjective *pesado*, however, is still occasionally ambiguous between "heavy" and "wearisome". As well as this extension of the semantic area covered by PENSO, there existed a particular use confined to the weighing out of animal foodstuffs. PENSO in this meaning developed a separate use in which the object of the verb was not any more the fodder (Sp. *pienso* < PENSUM) but the animal itself. It is possible that a potential semantic confusion between weighing a cow and feeding a cow could have been felt worth avoiding by the eventual decision to specialize the "fodder" meaning into the variants containing the consonantal nasal. In this way, Spanish *pensar las vacas* can only mean to "feed the cows". But this was not all. A further metaphorical extension from "weigh" arose to become, in some areas at least, apparently the statistically commonest use of PENSO; the sense of "mentally weigh up", "consider". This meaning has survived in the Romance languages with a nasal consonant (Sp. *pensar*, Cat. *pensar*, Ptg. *pensar*, It. *pensare*, Fr. *penser*, etc.), which should suggest that the Proto-Romance form had the nasal consonant. (This choice does not lead to Spanish confusion with "to feed", since "to think, intend" does not take a direct object.) This conclusion concerning Proto-Romance has not been the usual analysis, however. The traditional analysis of *penser*, etc., was that at a later date every Romance area decided to borrow this form, exclusive to "Latinate" speakers, into their vernacular language; by coincidence every Romance area seems to have done this at approximately the same time, and by further coincidence they all chose to give it more or less the same meaning; and by a coincidence that verges on the miraculous, they all decided to give it a meaning that it did not regularly have in Imperial Latin. This analysis overlooked the awkward fact that the Spanish forms that preserved the nasal, and were thus declared to belong to the Latinate, were exactly the same forms as the ones that diphthongized the [e] in the vernacular manner; whereas the Spanish forms that lost the nasal, and were thus declared to be vernacular, did not diphthongize.

This latter failure to diphthongize in *peso*, but success in *pienso*, is legitimately surprising. The sequence *-ens* in Old Latin was regularly "long", even in words whose immediate cognates were short − cp. INGĒNS, INGĔNTIS; DĒNS, DĔNTIS, DĔNTIO −, which means that technically PENSO > *peso*, MENSAM > *mesa* are, from the point of view of the vowel, "regular", and PENSO > *pienso*, TENSUM > *tieso* ("stiff") "irregular". Whatever the reason, the Romance evidence shows that after the loss of phonemic length the vowel in PENSO was open enough to qualify for diphthongization in Spanish. The diphthongization of [ĕ] began early (as can be seen from the comments of Pompeius quoted in Chapter 2), and may have been early enough to coincide with the [ns] ∼ [s] variation. The fact that in this possible simultaneity of free variations both affecting PENSO some forms chose the evolved [je] and the old [n], and the other forms chose the old [e] and omitted the [n], suggests that the choice of variants was not made on the criterion of which variant was the older and which was the newer. It is unlikely that many speakers knew whether the [n] forms were older or newer, or whether the [j] forms were older or newer, or considered the information relevant to their own choice of usage if they did. The average Briton neither knows nor cares which is the older of [kʌp] and [kup], etc., and if he has a reason for choosing one rather than the other it is usually connected with neither his relative literacy nor his relative conservatism.

There are so many difficulties arising from the traditional explanation of *pensar* and *pesar* that it is bewildering to find that this word has become the standard oft-repeated example of a "cultismo" in contemporary textbooks. Hall (1974: 107), for example, used it as the paradigm case and even theoreticians of historical linguistics cheerfully repeat this awkward case as the standard example; Anderson (1973: 185), for instance, holds it aloft, despite knowing Spanish reasonably well.

Other doublets can be explained in the same way. The desire to resolve homonymy can be invoked to explain, for example, the medieval pair of *obra* and *huebra* (< OPERA). *Razón* and *ración* (< RATIONEM) is another fairly clear case, although the waters are muddied by the apparently deep-rooted idea that *-ación* and *-ancia* are in some way necessarily "learnèd" forms rather than being, as they are, much the commonest medieval Spanish result of -ATIONEM and -ANTIAM. Sometimes they occur in free variation with the *-azón* and *-anza* forms that were given the accolade of "regularity"; Pattison's evidence (1975: 93) concerning forms with verbal roots has suggested, however, that the *-ción* ending is so much commoner than *-zón* that it can plausibly be regarded as the statistically normal vernacular form. Of 149 derivatives he listed, only 2 are attested with the *-zón* form alone, *cabazon* and *fayçon*, and these are rare words, which were used in literate circles anyway (Berceo and the *Primera Crónica General*)[7]. In Medieval Spanish, *razón* was a very common word with an unboundedly generic meaning — "thing", "words", "affair" — which it has since lost (Lanchetas 1900: 626). Lapesa still apparently thinks that "cultismos" are likely to be generic; here is a case of the supposedly non-"culto" form gaining a bafflingly "generic" use while the supposedly "culto" form has a comparatively precise use. The four attestations of *ración* in the *Poema de Mio Cid*, for example, have recognizably the meaning of "part", "share" (lines 2329, 2467, 2772, 3388).

This concept, of doublets exploiting free variation for semantic convenience, applies equally well to doublets that are not of Latin origin in the first place. The reconstructable Germanic root RAUP-, for example, "pillage", provided a noun (> Sp. *ropa*) and a verb (> Sp. *roba*). It is probable that the word was borrowed at a time when [-p-] and [-b-] were in variation in several parts of Iberia; the preservation of the unvoiced [p] in *ropa* commits no solecism against the phonemic system — cp. the AUP > *op* postulated in SAPUIT > *SAUPIT > *sopo* > *supo*; or *copa*, from the geminate CUPPAM — and in view of the semantic divergence of *ropa* ("booty" > "clothes") and *roba* ("pillage" > "rob") there is no semantic value in maintaining cognate transparency. Here we apparently have a phonetically retarded word which unfortunately happens not to be Latin, so calling it a "cultismo" is impossible.

---

7. If *-ancia* were "culto", how could it combine with a Germanic root in *ganancia*?

The differentiating mechanism envisaged here can even be exploited consciously (like the [ge] in *guerrilla*, above); the current Spanish spelling of *barón* "baron" and *varón* "male", identically pronounced, exploits a free variation in spelling that does not correspond to any phonetic distinction to separate the polysemy that has arisen from the originally Germanic BARO, "noble male". The spelling of English *flour* and *flower* achieves the same result. One of a pair can also change gender for the same purpose; e.g. Sp. *el mañana* ("tomorrow"), *la mañana* ("morning"); German *der Schild* ("shield"), *das Schild* ("sign").

The doublets once seemed to be selfevidently convincing evidence in favour of the two-norm theory. The existence of comparable phenomena in English, and of doublets of Germanic origin in Romance, show that they are not; the fact that the doublet forms can be explained with recourse to established principles of historical linguistics, and without recourse to hypothetical Latinizing speech systems, shows that the two-norm theory cannot use the doublets as a crutch. If the two-norm theory is to survive, it must be for other reasons than that.

### Subsequently Obscured Regularities

It is likely that in some cases a statistically regular conditioned sound-change has had its statistical regularity obscured from the eyes of later scholars because of the accretion of new vocabulary that arrived too late to be affected. For example, it now seems certain from the surviving graffiti that several of the well-known developments from original Latin to Old Romance were already well under way by the time of the eruption at Pompeii (79 A.D.); so it is reasonable to propose that some of the new Christian vocabulary borrowed from Greek in the fourth century and later might in fact have turned up at a time when the conditions for phonetic changes already suffered by analogously spelt words had ceased to have evolutionary consequences. Lapesa was quoted above as exemplifying "cultismo" with *ángel* < ANGELUS < ἄγγελος; the unexpected loss of final [-o] makes this attribution to Latinate speakers implausible anyway, but the reason for the attribution of "cultismo" is the retention of the atonic interconsonantal vowel, which is often lost in comparable words; cp. SINGULOS > *sendos*, QUIN-DECIM > *quince*, etc. This syncopation, however, is likely to have been well under way by the time of the wide Christianization of the Empire, and the [e] of the new Graecisms could well have been phonologically distinguishable from the short [ə] of the forms with which *ángel* is compared at the time [ángelo] (or [ánd3elo]) was first uttered by monolingual Romance Christians. These Church words are as often over-evolved as under-evolved, in fact; the [-o] > ø of *ángel* is glossed over by the "culto" analysis as neatly as is the strange [e] > [o] of *obispo* < EPISCOPUM, which has in fact lost the syncopated inter-consonantal vowel, but is called "culto" because the [i] did not become [e]. Given that the time of borrowing is unclear and the stage reached by any phonetic change at any specified time is also unclear, few such words are likely to be clarified surely in the light of this possibility; on the other hand, we cannot necessarily expect new vocabulary to fall under the scope of conditioned changes that have by the time of the borrowing lost their vigour. It seems that some did and some did not.

I have examined elsewhere (Wright 1976c) a more recent example in which the existence of a conditioned development can be glimpsed in Medieval Spanish, but that development has not normally applied to an untypically large number of comparable words borrowed subsequently; the conclusions alone are presented here. (Malkiel 1980a comes to a contrary conclusion concerning countertonics.) It concerns the fate of the pretonic diphthong [wa], which in Old Castilian is only found after initial velars (e.g. *cuaderno*, *guardar*). In Latin the [w] was part of the /kʷ/ phoneme; /gʷ-/ did not originally exist, but arose in order to accommodate Germanic vocabulary with initial /w/. Pretonic [wa] was the only pretonic rising labial diphthong; before all other vowels the [w] had dropped long before (e.g. QUEM > *quien* [kjen]). Partly as the final fling of that development, partly perhaps in the wake of a contemporary decision to confine [je] to tonic position (e.g. GERMANUM > *iermano* > *hermano*), a change began which lost the [w] in pretonic positions (e.g. *catorce*, *galardón*). The philologists stated that [wa] > [a] was the rule, and thus surviving pretonic [wa] was said to be a sign of "culto" vocabulary confined to educated usage. Hence words such as *cuaderno* and *cuarenta* were said, on this evidence alone, to be "learned" forms. *Cuarenta* has developed considerably from QUADRAGINTA, but that was not thought relevant; *cuarenta*, like *engendrar*, was exceptional.

One word, which had a Latin QUA-, is in Spanish both an undeniable Latin borrowing and a word which has lost the [w]. *Casi* "almost", borrowed from QUASI, apparently c.1400, is a "cultismo" without a [w]. This ought to cast doubt on the wisdom of using the retention of the [w] as a sure symptom of Latinate usage. Two other words make the picture even less certain; the strange case of *guadamecí*, borrowed from an Arabic word in which there was no [w], and the stranger case still of the adjective *cuadril*, formed off the noun *cadera* (< CATHEDRAM: there was never a [w] in this root), in which a pretonic [w] has actually been inserted.

What seems to have been happening is that for several centuries the change of [wa] to [a] was gradually working through the list of morphemes. The words at the front of the queue for this change included all cases in which there was the condition of a following [s] or [z]: literally all, whether tonic or not (*cascar* < ?QUASSICARE, *gastar* < VASTARE, *gascones* < VASCONES); and (with specifiable exceptions mentioned below) all cases in which the syllable was not originally immediately pretonic (ante-pretonic: not necessarily countertonic): QUALITÁTEM > *calidad*, QUANTITÁTEM > *cantidad*, QUATTUÓRDECIM > *catorce*, Germanic *WITHRALAÚN > *galardón*, Germanic WRANJÓNS > *garañón*. *Casi* is a pre-clitic word in which the initial syllable was regularly ante-pretonic, so when borrowed, even though new, it could plausibly have shot straight to the front of the diffusion queue. Words to the back of the queue include all words in which the [a] is followed by a [ð]: *cuaderno*, the Germanisms *guadafiones*, *guadaña*, *guadanyar* (Aragonese), *guadapero*, and the many Arabic-based toponyms such as *Guadalquivir*, *Guadalajara*, *Guadiana*, in some of which the initial syllable might once have had full stress anyway; all words in which [a] is tonic: *guante*, *guay*, *cuadro* and cognates, *cual*, *cuando*, *cuanto*, *cuarto* and cognates, *cuatro* and cognates; and all words with a following [r] (except for ante-pretonic *garañón* mentioned above): *cuarenta*, *cuaresma*, *guardar* and cognates, *guarir* and cognates, *guarnir* and cognates. This is not particularly neat, but it is a possible form for a diffusion queue to have taken. Given that the evidence of indigenous forms shows that both a following [s] and ante-pretonic position encouraged priority for the change, it is understandable that the newly borrowed *casi* should go to the front; given that the evidence of indigenous forms shows a strong preference for [wa] rather than [a] before a [ð], it is at least understandable, even if unpredictable, to find the newly borrowed *guadamecí* acquiring an etymologically inexplicable [w], and the newly formed *cuadril* doing the same. Even now there is only one word with initial [gað-] in the Academy Dictionary: the rare (and Latinate) *gaditano*, "citizen of Cádiz".

If the vocabulary of Castilian in c.1900 had been approximately the same as that of c.1500, this conditioned regularity would probably have been noticed by Romance philologists. During the decades following 1500, however, Castilian took on board a large number of words from various American Indian languages, including a remarkably high number of words with initial [gwa]. There were at least 25 words, both with initial stress and initially atonic, and several of them included a following [s]: e.g. *guano, guacamayo, guacho, guagua, guayaba, guasanga, guasasa, guasca, guaso*. The number of words with [g] or [k] + [wa] had never been high, and the original ones were outnumbered by the newcomers. The regularity that a fifteenth-century Castilian might have been able to intuit dimly as a morpheme structure rule had gone by 1600, and the diffusion of the change stopped where it was. Those at the latter end of the queue never arrived, and almost certainly never will, but those at the front had changed and have never looked back. Modern philologists, lacking the time to hack away the brambles and perceive that a kind of regularity did once exist, peered through the undergrowth, perceived chaos, and cut the knot with the well tried formula, that pretonic [wa] > [a] was the norm and therefore the [wa] forms were exceptional (Menéndez Pidal 1904: paras 39, 68; 1944: 176-77).

There might well have been a number of such cases in which a change is methodically working through the diffusion queue and is then suddenly stopped in its tracks and rendered unforeseeably impotent by the action of such extrinsic forces as the sudden accretion of extra vocabulary. Vocabulary borrowing does not occur at a uniform rate. New vocabulary can either succumb to changes under way, integrating as neatly as *casi* or the [o] > ∅ of EPISCOPUM, or it can disorientate the progress of that change, as in *guaso*, or the [e] (> [o]) and the survival of the [i] of EPISCOPUM. The latter is likely to be the result of the arrival of sudden large chunks of new vocabulary such as the Graecisms in the fourth-century Church, or the Indianisms in sixteenth-century Spain; the former is likely to be the result of the occasional assimilable individual borrowings that occur all the time. In the light of the effects of large-scale vocabulary influences, the attribution of "Latinate" archaizing speech levels either to the new vocabulary, or to old vocabulary undergoing a development whose progress is affected by that new vocabulary, is likely to be unjustified if made simply on the grounds of historical phonetic pecularity.

### Postdating Latinisms

There can be no doubt at all of the coexistence of two pronunciation norms, at least for those with some knowledge of official liturgical practice, after the operation of the Carolingian Reforms (in France after c.800; in Spain, outside Catalonia, after 1080); the only problematic issue is whether or not the distinction between Latin and Romance has any validity before these reforms. Accordingly, any apparently Latinate form whose first use in Romance can be plausibly dated to a time subsequent to the reforms might remain attributable to "Latin"-speakers, as a borrowing from the new spelling-pronunciation institutionalized as the ecclesiastical standard. Such a form is not the property of archaizing conservatives but of innovating progressives, yet meaningfully "Latinate" even so. This can only apply to words that undergo none of the changes that have run their course before 1080 in Spain and 800 in France; the loss of the final syllable of *ángel*, the backing of the first vowel in *obispo*, the reduction of -AGI- to [e] in *cuarenta*, the diphthongization of *pienso*, etc., are sufficient to prevent many of the traditionally "culto" words from retaining their "culto" status by escaping through this loophole. Some of the evidence adduced by Rice for France, however, which led him to his categorical affirmation of the existence of Latinate speech in the seventh century (quoted above), is quite compatible with the idea that the forms concerned did not exist in Romance before the ninth century.

Malkiel (1975b) has offered a very interesting case of a word which had a large number of competing forms in Old Spanish, which were eventually all abandoned for a Latinizing pronunciation instead. Malkiel showed that *dulce*, Latin DULCIS, was in fact an innovation in twelfth-century Spain, a new form introduced to resolve the anarchy, confusion and embarrassment caused by the existence of at least ten attested competing variant pre-existing forms. This evidence, that a twelfth-century "cultismo" can be an innovation rather than an archaic survival, as later borrowings from Latin are, is of greater significance than Malkiel seemed to realize, and the case is worth analysing in greater detail.

Castilian *dulce* is clearly "retarded" for some reason. The preservation of the [l] and of the [e], the retention of [u] rather than opening to [o], might be individually explicable, but collectively they suggest Latin influence of some kind. This influence, however, cannot be certainly ascribed to before the twelfth century. In the twelfth century the traditional orthography taught to scribes was still DULCIS; but there seems to have been a multiplicity of spoken forms, none of them sufficiently authoritative or widespread to be the obviously correct Castilian. Malkiel listed ten different attested written forms: e.g. *dulz*, *doz*, *duz*, *duce*. (Hartman has since argued (1979) that [dultse] could be one of the popular variants as well; in which case the arrival of Latin [dultse] had the effect of favouring an existing variant rather than introducing a new one.)

DULCIS had been in a dilemma considerably worse than that faced by the FL- words discussed above, or even than LIMPIDUM. It was not at all clear which sound changes it was supposed to be due for. The [k] before the front vowel evolved to [ts] without any problem; that was achieved early. (The [ts] seems to have been a regular feature of Hispanic reformed Latin also, whatever the Carolingians had originally decreed about written 'c' leading to spoken [k]: see Chapter 3.) But the -UL- and the -E were not so easy to deal with. If the -UL- was to be regarded as comparable to the -ULT- in e.g. MULTUM > *mucho*, which would be reasonable given the following [ts] in *dulce*, that would lead to an awkward [dujtse] (or even [dutʃse]) in need of further resolution: hence written *duce*, presumably representing [dutse]. If the -U- was to be regarded as a candidate for the normal [u] > [o] change, then *dolce* would be the result. If the -LC- cluster was thought to have a casting vote, DULCEM might have been expected to follow the pattern of FALCEM > *\*foze* > *hoz*, the [l] thereby disappearing and a form *doze* resulting. The [ts] of [lts] would not normally have voiced in the presence of the preceding consonant – cp. LANCEAM > *lança* – but in the versions that lost the [l] the problem would arise of being thought to qualify for the queue for the voicing change [ts] > [dz], as happened in FACERE > O.Sp. *fazer* ([hadzer]). After which, about the eleventh century, there arose the development of the loss of final [e]; this seems to have been dropped quite simply after single alveolar or dental consonants (e.g. RETEM > *rede* > *red*, etc.), but in other words the change seems to have reached a stage of free variation (e.g. *corte/ cort*, *noche/noch*, *dende/dend*) which eventually resolved itself in favour of the original form. Final [ts] and [dz] remained without a subsequent [e] (e.g. *paz*, *juez*, etc.), which is the model followed by *duz, dulz, doz, dolz*; but speakers using the forms in final [-lts] would not have felt easy, since in most words ending in consonantal clusters the [-e] in fact remained; in addition all analogous words seem to have been verbs (e.g. the subjunctive of *alzar* [altse]). In all finite verbs the [-e] was reinstitutionalized whatever the preceding consonant (e.g. *fize* "I did", *viene* "he comes"). Even if speakers who normally pronounced the word without an [l] then lost the [-e] as well, that was not the final problem, because it looks as if there might have been some vacillation over whether [dz] and [ts] at the end of a word – a position which they had never occupied before the loss of [-e] – ought to neutralize their opposition or not, as final [-t] and [-d] had. In the event, the modern view is that the spelling -z often came to represent a [ts] sound in the thirteenth century, long before the unvoicing of [dz]

to [ts] in other positions in sixteenth-century Castilian. The consequence of all this cumulative uncertainty was the simultaneous
presence in twelfth-century Castille of a large number of variant pronunciations for the one word, all of them reasonable on the basis of
analogous words, none of them authoritatively taken to be the ordinary
spoken form. At this point the new Medieval Latin turns up, following
the adoption of the Roman liturgy in 1080, offering yet another
alternative, but in a reassuringly acceptable context. Speakers can
occasionally become conscious of free variations and alternative pronunciations, and when they do, they often become awkward or em-
barrassed when of necessity they have to choose one form rather than
another in speech; if there are a large number of available pronunciations,
it is possible that the arrival of an apparently authoritative alternative
could be used as a lifeline. In any event, [dultse] was taken into the
vernacular and used increasingly in the thirteenth century. This was a
case when "speakers favoured the culturally unmotivated "learned"
form on account of some collateral feature not immediately related to
its erudite status" (Malkiel 1963-64: 162).

The suggestion that the arrival of Medieval Latin in the twelfth
century had a deciding influence in cases of vernacular vacillation can
be applied to phonology as well as to the lexicon. Penny's analysis
(1972) of Medieval Spanish /f/ argues that [f], which was in the tenth
and eleventh centuries either absent or an occasional allophone of /φ/,
become reestablished as /f/, a separate phoneme from /φ/, in approximately the twelfth century. The labiodental [f] of French and other
Romance languages may never have existed previously in Old Castille,
for it has been suggested that a bilabial [φ] corresponded there all
along to the written Latin letter *f*; whether this is true or not, the
Castilian phoneme could have been phonetically, according to Penny's
evidence, some kind of fricative bilabial ([φ], [hφ]) or [h], such as
survives in many rural areas still. This may have been an uneasy and
awkward moment, when the dialect speakers were beginning to wish for
some clearer form. In any event, the twelfth century is the period when
French and French-taught clerics were dominant in educated circles;
among other things they were doing their best to spread the pronunciation of official liturgical Medieval Latin to be used in conjunction
with the Roman liturgy, newly adopted in North-West Spain from
1080. Penny suggested that in urban or educated Castilian of the
twelfth century the [f] sound emerged "under the superstratum influence of French and Provençal speakers", to become a distinct phoneme again "on the introduction of large numbers of learned words"

(1972: 482). The implication of Penny's comments is that the [f] is
due to the pronunciation of French or Occitan. The influence of
French or Occitan phonology in Spanish is not an initially attractive
hypothesis, despite Lapesa's much-reiterated view (1975) that it was
largely French or Occitan pronunciation that led to the [-e] > ø development. (Arabic /f/ was labiodental, and could have helped in such
loans as *alférez*; [f] existed in Aragón, León, and probably *mozárabe*
as well.) Many urban and educated Spaniards were self-consciously
learning the new artificial Medieval Latin as it was taught by Frenchmen, but there is no reason to suppose that many learnt French; it
seems more plausible to suggest that the /f/ arises not from French or
Occitan itself, but from the European pronunciation of Medieval Latin.
If this Latin is indeed new at this time, the (re)emergence of [f] is
interpretable rationally; if there was a "Latin" [f]-preserving layer of
speech in previous centuries, the problem remains.

The influence of French pronunciation of Latin might also have
contributed to the decision to reverse the loss of [-e] in words ending
in other than single alveolar or dental consonants and in verbs (RETEM
> *rede* > *red*, COHORTEM > *corte* > *cort* > *corte*, POTUI > *pude* > *pud*
> *pude*, etc.); this reversal can be partly attributed to the phonetic con-
ditions of syllable structure, and partly to morphological conditions,
but (despite Lapesa 1975) not at all to the French, who apocopated
throughout. The presence of a final syllable in the new Latin, however,
could have been one factor to give the reversal in different forms at the
end of the queue a push.

In twelfth-century Spain, according to the theory outlined later
in this book, the introduction of Medieval Latin was something new. It
was taught largely by Frenchmen. The European pronunciation of
Latin can plausibly be seen to have been a serious factor in cases where
the direction of the vernacular was in the balance at this time. In earlier
centuries it is very doubtful whether a distinct Latin phonology existed,
so it may not be justifiable to use it as a source of enlightenment. In
later centuries, vernacular spelling could be looked to for a similar
casting vote, but that was not in general use yet in the twelfth. For a
brief period, in the twelfth century, it remains plausible to postulate
the influence of Latin pronunciation on vernacular development in the
way that it has traditionally been postulated for previous centuries.
Latin -ATIO might, for example, have then helped decide vacillation in
the vernacular between *-ación* and *-azón*. In later centuries, when at last
Latin and the vernacular were coming to be thought of as fully
separable languages each with its own speech and writing systems, the

influence of Latin on vernacular is noticeable in the growth of the vocabulary, but can only rarely be perceived in the phonology of individual forms. The coining of *cátedra*, *litigar* and other Latinisms, for example, seems to have had no effect on the development of *cadera* and *lidiar*. From the late thirteenth century, Latin would have had the same kind of influence on Spanish as any other non-native language.

## Morphological Archaism

Morphological considerations can also retard or channel a phonetic change (e.g. in Malkiel 1968). The eventual decision mentioned above not to lose [-e] in Medieval Castilian finite verbs, for example, is perhaps attributable to the greater morphological usefulness of [-e] as a marker than -ø, given the syllabic nature of all other Spanish verb endings. A further case concerns the Spanish decision, which remained widely valid till recently, not to lose [-s], which was needed both to distinguish the familiar from the formal second person singular (e.g. tú *cantas* < CANTAS, Vd. *canta* < CANTAT) and to preserve the marking of nominal plurals. Once the Latin accusative form was all that survived in Spain, it became – presumably by accident – normal for [-s] to be the sole distinguishing feature of plural forms (e.g. LUPUM > *lobo*, LUPOS > *lobos*; MENSAM > *mesa*, MENSAS > *mesas*; MONTEM > *monte*, MONTES > *montes*). Whereupon some originally singular forms with an [-s] were reanalysed as plural and acquired a singular without an [-s] (e.g. TEMPUS > *tiempos*; *tiempo*). It is possible that [-s] was beginning to disappear in Spain (as it did in Italy); in Italy the nominative form of nouns was usually the one to survive, and second-person verb forms developed other distinctive marks (e.g. -*i* in *canti*), so [-s] had no such status, but in Spain it became an essential morphological marker, and survived in verbs and nouns where it was needed. We may be entitled to envisage here a period of free variation in Spain between [-s] and either [-h] or ø, which ended in most cases in a victory for the [-s], which was the older form in most but not all relevant words. The [-s] > ø development, however, was merely postponed; in Andalucía and much of América the [-s] has since either aspirated to [-h] or gone entirely. (Felix's analysis (1979) of the nature of this development in the Canary Islands is illuminating on the interaction of the phonetic, morphological and lexical forces.)

We have here a case in which the second-person forms of all verbs and the plural forms of all nouns and adjectives have refrained from undergoing a phonetic change that otherwise, judging from Pan-Romance evidence, might perhaps have been expected to occur (cp. the adverb *fuera* < FORAS). Common sense has prevented scholars from suggesting that only the educated used plurals or second-person verbs; but in any event, morphological forms are not thought to fall under the "cultismos" category in the same way as other sounds.

The dissociation of morphology from phonetics is sensible in synchronic analysis; even so, it might seem reasonable to expect the analysis of morphological evolution to have some features analogous to the analysis of phonetic evolution. In practice, however, the neo-grammarians never expected that regularities of morphological change would "operate without exception" in the same way as they seem to have instinctively expected sound laws to apply. Except for the fact that morphemes have meaning and sounds do not, there is no *a priori* reason why the two should be expected not to operate in comparable ways; in both phonology and inflectional morphology there is an inventory of bound forms, individually combined in different words, with the items on that inventory being considered as the units of change, rather than each separate form in which the item can occur. We say that [-k-] > [-ɣ-], for example, rather than enumerating the catalogue of LACUM > *lago*, PLICANT > *llegan*, AQUAM > *agua*, etc.; we say that the Old Latin futures (-BO, -AM, etc.) were replaced with a compound of the infinitive plus HABEO (-*é*, -*á* etc.), rather than saying that IBIS was replaced with *irás*, LEGET by *leerá*, etc. And yet when cases occur of statistical regularity in morphological change, comparable to the statistically regular sound laws mentioned above, the forms which survive unchanged have never been ascribed to the influence of "Latin"-speakers.

For example, it is a regularity of the development of Latin to Spanish that many of the verbs that originally had strong perfect forms abandon those forms in favour of new analogous ones created in the usual manner by adding the regular past endings to the verbal stem; e.g. CURRERE > *correr*, but CUCURRI > ø, and the formation of *corrí*; CRESCERE > *crecer*, CREVI > ø, *crecí*; RIDERE > *reír*, RISI > ø, *reí*; etc. But several of these verbs have remained irregular in the past tense; e.g. CONDUCERE > *conducir*, CONDUXI > *conduje*; FACERE > *hacer*, FECI > *hice*, etc.

These latter strong perfect forms belong to paradigms that are no longer productive, and yet have managed to avoid entirely the opprobrium that has been cast on such forms as *pensar*, *mundo* and *cuaderno*. However, there seems to have been no consistent phonetic or semantic rationale for the choice of which perfect forms to re-organize. For example, Latin VIXI (from VIVERE, "live") survived into Old Spanish *visque*, but from the fourteenth century a syn-chronically regular form *viví* seems to have been commoner, and *viví* is the only modern survivor. DIXI (from DICERE, "say"), on the other hand, developed with phonetic regularity to *dije*. Both are very common ordinary words. I know of no scholar who has even con-sidered calling *dije* and the other strong perfects "cultismos", despite their being exceptions to the perceptible vernacular regularity. This reluctance is understandable, for nearly all the surviving strong per-fects belong to common verbs that were clearly in vernacular all the time.

It is likely that there is a process of lexical diffusion here too, in which the timelag from head to tail of the queue is abnormally long. Spanish verbs are still in the process of reallocating their pasts; *andar*, for example, is said in the grammars to have the past form *an-duve*, but the form *andé* is often the one used now. English has also been undergoing this development for several centuries; it looks, for instance, as though *dreamed* is currently overtaking *dreamt*. Vincent (1980) has discussed the fascinating (but probably unverifiable) idea that morphological forms which resist changes may be just the ones that occur in those verbs whose irregular forms have to be individually specified in the lexicon rather than being derived by productive in-flexional rules, with the consequence that they can remain stable even when the rule changes; in which case the change in e.g. *creí* is the lexical loss of CREVI (as part of the entry for CRESCERE — *crecer*) rather than a specifically morphological change. The recalcitrant forms could well be those which occur very often precisely because they are encountered early by the child as he learns to speak, and are thus stored lexically "before there is a sufficient range of data to permit the extraction of generalizations"; whether or not Vincent is right, there is no arguing away the fact that the exceptions to morpho-logical developments often belong to words that cannot possibly be said to be exclusive to literate levels of speech. If, even so, we wished to attempt to explain the retention of the irregular *dije* as the result of "Latin" influence, we would be faced with a further awkward fact: that Latin words indubitably borrowed from Latin into Spanish in later centuries when the distinction between the two is indisputable, and borrowed by speakers who are by definition Latinate, are taken without the strong perfect forms they had in the original Latin and are given analogous weak ones instead. Latin PRAESUMERE had a past PRAESUMPSI; when *presumir* was borrowed in the fifteenth century, it was allotted the "regular" past *presumí*. Latin PERSUADERE had a past PERSUASI; the fifteenth-century borrowing *persuadir* has a past *persuadí*. Latin CEDERE had a past CESSI; the sixteenth-century borrowing *ceder* has a past *cedí*. And so on.

The fact that discernibly retarded processes of morphological evolution are analysable along lines quite different from the way in which equivalent processes of phonetic evolution have been traditionally analysed cannot be explained away by the generalization that morphological developments are by their very nature prone not to be all-inclusive. For the generalization is not true. There are no pockets at all in Romance, neither lexical nor geographical, of, for example, the retention of a morphologically distinct paradigm of neuter nouns, of synthetic passives, or of ablative cases. The loss of a complete gender, voice or case might be thought to be a sufficiently radical revision of a linguistic system to encourage recalcitrance among some of the affected vocabulary, but it has not. These laws have indeed "operated without exception", to a greater extent than many sound-laws, which were reputed to be more remorseless.

Morphological developments have not normally been treated with the same puritanical rigour as phonetic developments. The parallel cannot be wholly irrelevant, however. The fact that recourse to hypothetical Latinizing dialects in order to account for retarded or evaded change has, to judge from the evidence, little plausibility within the history of Romance morphology is enough to cast doubt on the wisdom of such a recourse within phonetics. Language is divisible into units for analytical purposes, but even so it would be reasonable to hope that generalities applicable to one variety of change might refrain from being incompatible with those applied to an allied variety.

The fact that in early medieval Romance Europe the educated cannot easily be envisaged as having used archaic morphology in speech, while the uneducated evolved, lies oddly with the treatment of morphology in the grammatical treatises of the same period. The grammars used and compiled before the Carolingian Renaissance have little to say on pronunciation, as will be shown in the next chapter, and could not have been used as a serious teaching aid to reinforce Latinate pronunciation norms. On the other hand they do lay an inordinate amount of stress on morphological forms. The grammatical patterns of Latin verbs and nouns are reproduced in considerable detail; they take up, for example, almost the entire subject matter of Donatus's standard manual, the *Ars Minor* (Keil 1855-80: IV 355-66). There we find neuter nouns, nominal case systems, synthetic passives and synthetic futures, all lovingly elaborated in full technicolor. Accordingly, there can be no doubt that the educated had indeed encountered old-fashioned word-endings. In order to write at all acceptably the aspirant scribe needed to master a whole array of such endings. It is thus initially rational to hypothesize that the old synthetic future and passive forms of verbs might have existed in educated speech, since the educated undoubtedly had to use them in writing. And yet there are *no* surviving synthetic futures at all in Spanish. All Spanish futures come from infinitive plus HABEO. There are *no* surviving synthetic passives in Spanish. All Spanish passive forms come from "to be" plus the past participle. Outside pronouns, there are *no* morphological inflexions at all in Spanish nouns other than the plural-marking [-s]. In short, the whole old-fashioned morphological apparatus that the educated encountered inevitably when learning to read and write seems to have had absolutely no effect whatsoever on the development of the vernacular. This makes it all the more surprising that the old-fashioned phonology, which the educated need not necessarily have ever encountered, should ever have been assumed to have had a serious impact on the development of the vernacular.

It is more plausible to propose that noone, however educated, actively used the old morphology in their speech. The morphological endings preserved on paper (e.g. -ITUR, -ABIS, -IBUS) would have formed a subsection of the passive vocabulary of those who could read and write, as comparable English forms such as *-eth* do now. Sabatini's analysis (1965: 994) of legal documents compiled in Early Romance Europe has shown that outside the formulaic sections of those documents the case system tends to break down, with the cases being used as they were in the local vernacular. That is, Italian scribes use the original nominative form, scribes in Spain use the original accusative form, scribes in France usually use only the nominative and their "oblique" case, whatever the syntax. For more literary genres, more "correct" morphology was required, and apparently taught. The practical question in writing the old morphology may well have involved such matters as when to insert a silent 'bu' into plural nouns such as MENSIBUS (i.e. into Spanish vernacular *meses* < MENSES), comparable to the problem of whether or not to insert a silent 'n' into the same word. Occasional written hypercorrections including an extra 'n' before 's' (e.g. *occansionibus, Herculens, ariens*), or an extra 'bu' into ablatives of nouns from other declensions (e.g. *annibus, dorsibus*), suggest that this was just one more problem encountered in trying to use the old writing system. The problem of what to write in a future tense, when vernacular used HABEO after the infinitive (e.g. *estará* <

STARE HABET) rather than the earlier analytic form (in this case, STABIT), was no less possible to resolve in practice; omitting writing the spoken [ɾ] in [estaɾáβe], STABIT, is no less learnable than the comparable routine needed to ignore the spoken [e] at the start and to insert a "silent" written 't' at the end[8]. It is child's-play compared with the modern French child's needing to learn to write [swet] as *souhaitent*, or the modern English child's needing to learn to write [wenzdɪ] as *Wednesday*. Morphological developments made spelling harder than it had been in earlier centuries, but it did not make it impossible, and those who could write need never necessarily have used the archaic morphology in their speech. Indeed, Politzer (1961) even argued that the more accurately suffixes were transcribed, the less likely they are to have existed in speech.

Archaic morphology is accessible to the literate from written works. Archaic phonology is not similarly accessible; it cannot be taken from books; if it could, historical phonology would be simple. As regards Romance, if the hypothesis of a Latinate speech level were true, morphology might have been expected to play an important part in the influence of that speech level on subsequent vernacular; it plays no part at all. This casts considerable doubt on the existence of such a level, and since within historical linguistic theory there is no great problem in envisaging its absence, we can now be prepared to examine the textual evidence to see if it is compatible with the proposal that Old Romance was the only speech used in Old Romance communities.

### Conclusion

Irregularity is regular in phonetic change; cp. Wang (1969: 21):

> A close scrutiny reveals that even the best phonetic laws are frequently riddled with irregularities.

Samuels (1972: 125) may have been led by Wang's article to remark:

> In view of such possibilities, it would seem that completely regular sound-changes can be expected only as rarities.

Concerning Romance, Malkiel has often pointed this out (e.g. 1963-64: 148):

> Instead of further laboring the infelicitously posed issue of the regularity of sound change one may candidly admit that, within each set of diachronic sound correspondences, some (whatever the reason for this peculiarity) allow a distinctly higher degree of predictability than do others.

---

8. Perhaps popular etymology considered -ABIT and the identically pronounced HABET to be the same in any case.

Those irregular forms thought to have proved the existence of a Latin pronunciation system distinct from Old Romance, before the implementation of the Carolingian reforms into any community, can be explained in a reasonable manner in other ways. Lexical diffusion, as the simple statement that some words change later than others, is widely accepted; reasons for some words being late in this list are not difficult to find; indeed, a common view of non-Romance specialists is that "items . . . of high incidence of use are among the most resistant to regular sound-change" (Collinge 1978: 71), rather than that such resistant items should be attributed to esoteric minorities.

The idea that any group of people could resist phonetic changes that were generally affecting the rest of the community, for a thousand years or more, is difficult to take seriously. It is a view that has never been suggested in any other context, and would probably strike any historical linguist from another field as absurd, even if he or she were well acquainted with the manner in which in Romance Philology interim hypotheses regularly fossilize into accepted wisdom. Nor would historical linguists see much to be said for the traditional Romance assumptions that people who spell well necessarily speak in an archaic way, or that their "pressure" can hold back a sound change. This is supposed to have happened in the Early Middle Ages, with no mass communications and a very small literate community.

Given the sociolinguistic and stylistic variation to be found in any community, "Proto"-Romance was the speech of all; it is unnecessary to postulate anything else. From the point of view of theoretical historical linguistics it is reasonable to suggest that "Latin" as distinct from vernacular did not exist in Romance communities before the Carolingian reforms. After these reforms, "Latin" influence can on occasion be justifiably adduced to explain vernacular developments, but previously existing phenomena can and should be analysed with the usual tools of historical linguistic theory. If the textual evidence analysed in Chapter 2, from grammarians, scholars, lawyers, poets and liturgists, can be seen to be compatible with this view, there can no longer be justification for believing in pre-Carolingian "Latin" speech. It was once thought that the sun revolves round the earth. Pliny asserted that when their tusks fall off, elephants bury them underground (*Natural History*: VIII 4). Western civilization has acquired the telescope, a knowledge of elephants, and a theoretical understanding of linguistic evolution; primitive misconceptions formed in the absence of such modern aids can be discarded.

# 2

## PRONUNCIATION IN PRE-CAROLINGIAN ROMANCE COMMUNITIES: THE TEXTUAL EVIDENCE

Latin and the Romance language of any community are now-adays regarded as separate languages. As we saw in the first chapter, it has been normal for this division to be postulated as existing as far back as the final stage of the Roman Empire. One result of this has been that many specialists in the early Romance languages have felt instinctively that the study of "Late Latin" is outside their brief, and many specialists in Medieval Latin have felt that "Early Romance" is outside theirs; thus the assumption that they are separate fields of study has been reinforced. The existence of two distinguishable languages in the period between the fall of the Roman Empire and the twelfth-century Renaissance is usually taken for granted to the extent that scholars of Romance confidently talk of the influence of Latin on the vernacular, and scholars of Latin can talk of the influence of the vernacular on Latin, as if the existence of two names were a guarantee that there are two separate entities. But, as we have seen in the first chapter, the evidence available to the historical linguist is such that there is no longer any need to assume *a priori* that the two were separate or separable before the arrival of the Carolingian reforms into any community. The reforms themselves will be examined in the next chapter. In this chapter the textual evidence from earlier centuries will be examined to see if it is compatible with the theory that there is no general distinction between two co-existing languages at that time, and that the linguistic state of the Romance communities was approximately that prevailing in Modern France or England: i.e. that there may on occasions be visible stylistic variation in syntax and vocabulary between the usage of those who can write and the usage of those who cannot, but there is no general phonological variation correlated with the ability to write.

There exist further differences of attitude concerning the nature of "Latin" and "Romance" in the Early Middle Ages. Some philologists and most linguists appreciate that in any community vernacular speech evolves long before signs of these changes are reflected in the techniques of writing taught to professional scribes; in this case, that Latin vernacular was always evolving, like every other vernacular, and the majority of the orthographic changes visible in early Romance texts reflect phonetic changes undergone in the distant past. Most of them, however, accept at the same time the theory that "Latin" also existed in some circles for some purposes in the Early Middle Ages as we know it did in the Late Middle Ages, spoken, if only by a tiny minority, more or less as it had been in Classical times.

Latinists, on the other hand, and a few philologists also, have often not realized how early and how widespread the evolution was, and tend to operate as if there was very little change in speech from the first century to the seventh. Muller, for example, believed he had shown that the spoken language of the time was close to the written version. Many medieval historians follow the Latinists, understandably assuming that Latinists know best (e.g. McKitterick 1977: 186-87). These arguments need to be considered before the texts.

### Unity and Evolution

The history of the sixth and seventh centuries shows that people from the separate Romance communities were able to communicate with each other. This has led to the idea that there must necessarily have been some kind of "lingua franca", of a nature at least partly archaic, as a standard available for such communication between members of the different early Romance areas to be possible (e.g. Burger 1943). The assumption that such a common language had necessarily to exist is possible to refute if we consider the state of Modern English. The English vernaculars of Somerset, Stornoway, Pakistan, Jamaica, Vancouver, etc., pronounce words in recognizably different manners, even though schoolmasters in these communities still teach the same spelling norms for most of those words. Given practice, at least, a Scot and a Pakistani, etc., can communicate without difficulty; and even if they could not, their problems would be aggravated rather than alleviated if they attempted to use some pronunciation based on treating traditional orthography as a phonetic script, in the manner of post-Carolingian liturgical Latin. Even if these varieties of English are due to become mutually unintelligible in a millennium's time, as Early Romance has since become Portuguese, Tuscan, etc., such mutual unintelligibility is not the norm now despite the dissimilarity between the phonology of Somerset and Jamaican English. Mutual intelligibility does not of itself imply similarity, nor lack of evolution. St Leander of Seville and Latin speakers from Byzantium may have sounded odd to each other, but they seem to have succeeded in communicating.

### Non-differentiation

A slightly different view has in the past been influential; the hypothesis of the "non-differentiation of the Western κοινή". The proponents of this view agree with the consensus of many medieval Latinists that Western Latin hardly evolved at all until the seventh century, and the dialectal diversification in separate areas was only just beginning in the ninth. This theory arose from Muller's study of written texts of the time (Muller and Taylor 1932; Muller 1945) and came to be endorsed by E. Löfstedt (1959: 2-4) and others. The arguments were originally concerned with morphology and syntax rather than pronunciation, but some scholars have taken Muller to have demonstrated that the pronunciation was probably not evolved much until the eighth century. To a historical linguist such an idea seems absurd, so some have attempted to rephrase these views into something more acceptable. For example, Gaeng (1968: 296) has reinterpreted Muller as follows:

> The question arises in our mind as to whether Muller indeed meant an *absolute* unity of speech throughout the Western Roman world, with practically non-existent dialectal variations, as his critics seem to think. Muller may have had in mind the kind of *relative* unity of speech that has been attributed to American English.

Whatever Muller may have "had in mind", this relative unity is a useful idea; if we accept that varying dialects can be mutually intelligible, we can simultaneously suggest that a Leonese might have understood the Strasbourg Oaths in French (842), particularly if he cottoned on to the apocopation of final vowels, and that neither speaker would have needed to archaize for communication to be possible. Indeed, even in the twelfth and thirteenth centuries, the literature of the time suggests that many people found no great problem in understanding speakers of other Romance languages (e.g. in macaronic verse); the fact that at this later time reformed vernacular spellings were in use can hide from us phonetic similarities, just as much as eighth-century orthographical uniformity can conceal phonetic dissimilarities.

It was not immediately clear whether Muller believed in two coexisting separate pronunciation norms or not, although he does contrast "Vulgar" with "Ecclesiastical" Latin. His main thesis was that until the late eighth century Latin had in general changed so little that "the living language of Christianization, of practical civilization, was probably similar enough everywhere to retard dialectalization" (Muller and Taylor 1932: 24). This undifferentiated κοινή, however, is similar to the kind of Latin envisaged within the two-norm theory discussed in the previous chapter (e.g. by Rice 1909 and Pope 1934); it seems that the one language that Muller was envisaging was not so much the Romance vernacular part of the vernacular/Latin pair as usually envisaged, but the "Latin" part. He refers to seventh- and eighth-century documents being written by people who "wrote the language they spoke and heard" for example (Muller and Taylor 1932: v). The one language that I argue for here is the Romance part of that dichotomy.

The view that "Romance" only evolves after the seventh century has been untenable since the discovery of the Pompeii graffiti (datable to A.D. 79), which attest many of the changes postulated as not existing before then. Analysis of the graffiti, and other recent analyses of informal writing such as Adams' (1977a) discussion of scribal habits in the letters of Claudius Terentianus (early second century), make it clear that several of the important differences between Romance and "Classical" Latin had at least begun by then. No linguist can seriously doubt any more that the vernacular was changing long before 600 A.D. The only debatable point concerns the postulated co-existence alongside that vernacular of an unchanged spoken "Latin".

### Proto-Romance Reconstruction

The theory that dialectal divergence, as well as evolution, began very early, has in the past also been influential. The "substratum" theory held that Latin in each area of the Roman world was profoundly affected by the preexisting languages spoken in that area by the pre-Roman inhabitants, with the result that speech differentiation began with colonization (Mohl 1899; for a sophisticated modern version of the general theory, see Whinnom 1980). Within Romance this theory is no longer held in much regard, since no phonological development of any consequence has ever been shown to have undeniable origins in a substratum language, and most of the linguistic features that were originally candidates for such influence have since been found to occur outside the zone of the language in question. The early chronology remains respectable, however. There are those who have "reconstructed" Proto-Romance by arguing backwards from the evidence of later attested Romance forms. R.A. Hall Jr (1950, 1976), for example, regards deductions based on the evidence of later vernaculars as more likely to reflect the speech of the early times than deductions made on the evidence of pre-Carolingian spelling, and has produced trees of diverging dialects that apparently date back to before Christ. This seems to imply that the speech of the Empire was already in several distinguishable vernacular divisions long before the period of what Muller and many others regard as a fairly uniform speech. In Hall's view Proto-Romance was only uniform for a short while, if at all, and contemporary with the related but largely artificial language called "Classical Latin". This view is sometimes interpreted as suggesting a coexistence of separate spoken systems (Classical and Vulgar Latin) from 200 B.C. onwards (e.g. Maurer 1962, Leonard 1980), but the evidence that is supposed to support this duality is easily compatible with the normal phenomena of social and geographical differentiation to be found in any one language used in a complex society.

Thus it is that in the Proto-Romance "reconstruction" theories the early chronology for dialectalization remains current; an early date for several sound changes is certain, and whether or not we believe distinguishable dialects from such an early period to be identifiable depends essentially on our definition of a dialect. As long as we do not imply any mutual unintelligibility, and we realize that any suggestion of strict geographical delimitations of such dialects would be an anachronism (conditioned by the modern tendency for isoglosses to coincide as a result of the politics of national education), we can accept much of Hall's theory. His views would probably be seen generally as extreme, however; partly because he seems to assume that language change is neat, linear and unidirectional, when it seems from modern evidence that it tends to be haphazard, non-teleological and multi-directional, and it is notoriously difficult to locate early medieval texts on the basis of their "vulgar" phenomena; and partly because he proclaims that recourse to documentary evidence is not only pointless but "unscientific". What is unscientific is to see documentary material as face-value evidence of speech; if we can accept the existence of old Romance vernaculars approximately as the reconstructionists have envisaged them, examination of documents can be a rational and indeed illuminating exercise. Even so, Hall's instinctive mistrust of written texts as evidence for contemporary pronunciation has a sound basis. This mistrust has also been well expressed by Pulgram (1950), who pointed out that nobody writes unless they have taken time and trouble to *learn* to write; that learning to write is a practical discipline, consciously taught in accordance with established norms; and that until the norms are consciously reformed they remain the same. The scribe is likely to reflect linguistic evolution in semantics and syntax, particularly in word order, but is unlikely to reproduce changes in pronunciation. Whoever he is and wherever he is writing, he will not produce simple phonetic script:

> He cannot help it, for he has learned to write in the literary language only, according to certain rules of spelling and grammar. What he produces may not always conform to those rules, but neither will it be a faithful rendering of what he would SAY.
>
> (459)

A comparison with Modern English will help to make this point clear. For example, virtually all written English documents of the twentieth century that include the words *orange* or *knight* have them spelt "correctly". A thirtieth-century Muller might deduce that speakers of the twentieth century must have said [ɔɾangɛ], or [orandʒə], or [oraŋgə], and [knight] or [knɪxt]; but if the evidence of linguistic reconstruction is going to suggest that we probably now say [ɔɾɪndʒ] and [nait], specialists will be right to accept the reconstructed forms in preference to the apparent testimony of the texts. In the same way, later evidence (the written form *sieglo*) suggests that SAECULUM in a written Spanish text of the ninth century is more likely to represent a vernacular [sjeglo] than [sɛkulum]. Noone wrote *sieglo* in the ninth century; noone writes *orindzh* or *nait* nowadays; because noone is taught to write without also being taught how to spell. Phonetic (or phonemic) script does not come automatically to people in the way speech does. Indeed, there is every reason to suppose that this analogy underestimates the extent to which written pre-Carolingian "Latin" falls short of being a phonetic script; any manuscript thought worth preserving would probably have enough care expended on it to approximate to correct old-fashioned orthography, and many were in any event re-copied "correctly" in the Carolingian period (as happened, for example, to the Benedictine Rule: see Mohrmann 1952).

### Phonetic Script and Education

Anyone who has attempted to teach phonetic script will be aware that even the best student does not find it natural, and has to be taught how to do it. Those who have already been taught how to write in the "correct" way, as everyone has who has been taught to write at all, is likely to find the traditional spelling of a word springing more easily to his ballpoint than the phonetic transcription of the same word. Yet discussion of both Medieval "Latin" and early Romance texts tends to assume that writing an unfamiliar phonetic script is as natural to the human being as speech. On the contrary; in its initial stages, the operation of a novel spelling technique is a complex and demanding task. For example, early written French vernacular texts show evidence of diphthongization (e.g. *ciel, buona, bellezour* in the *Cantilène de Sainte Eulalie* of c.880); we can assume that these diphthongs correspond to speech habits of that time; the *Appendix Probi* of the seventh century (Robson 1963) shows no such forms, but this cannot be seen as evidence that diphthongization is a post-*Appendix Probi* evolution. It may have been only allophonic, but it certainly existed.

This situation has analogies in Modern English; Americans write *United States* as the British do, despite it being standard American for the first *t* to represent a spoken [D]. Thus the first *t* and the *d* in this phrase represent similar sounds, which are different from that represented by the two *t*s in *States* [steits]; similarly a ninth-century Leonese would write TOTUM representing a spoken [todo]. Even new vocabulary can be given old spelling. Neologisms in the U.S. ending in *-ator* or *-ating*, etc. (e.g. *deescalating*) are given a written *t* and a spoken [D] on the analogy of all the other comparable cases. The late eighth-century Northern French Glosses of Reichenau include items of "new" vocabulary (such as SPARNIAVIT, i.e. Fr. *épargna*, of Germanic origin), which are given unreformed Latin spelling even though they did not exist in Imperial times when that spelling corresponded more closely to pronunciation (Elcock 1975: 324-29).

Thus those who assume that the survival of old orthography implies the survival of old speech habits are in danger of appearing to underestimate the difference there can be between speech and spelling. What happens in a case such as Early Romance, as the two diverge with time, is that the rules for writing become more and more involved, including not only "silent" letters and syllables but even "silent" morphological forms. This is a reasonable explanation for the enormous stress on noun and verb endings in all early Medieval writing manuals (*Artes Grammaticae*). The same occurs in Modern France, where children can say [ʃɑ̃:t] indiscriminately for four grammatical persons, and are then bewildered at having to learn to write, and distinguish between, *chante, chantes* and *chantent*; for the many French children lacking the [e]/[ɛ] contrast, [ʃɑ̃:te] can be spelt *chanter, chantez, chanté, chantée, chantés, chantées, chantai, chantais, chantait* or *chantaient*. It is hardly surprising that learning to write in the Early Middle Ages took so long; and it is logical to conclude that relative correctness of written Latinity in pre-Reform Europe was as much a question of the effectiveness of education as it was of relatively evolved vernaculars. Scholars have talked of the "purer Latin" of seventh-century documents from Spain as if this were evidence of a greatly retarded process of linguistic evolution in the peninsula, rather than merely being the visible consequence of the higher level of education in Spain than in the rest of the Romance world in the seventh century.

As regards the emergence of new orthographies, general spelling reform can only occur as a positive act with a conscious purpose. It does not happen on its own, as pronunciation change does, and the social instability of the Early Middle Ages would not in practice have been conducive to the success of such a move, as Battisti (1960) has observed. The Carolingian reformers initially saw their linguistic task as that of re-establishing old norms; the subsequent emergence and invention of written Old French may well have been originally unforeseen.

If we are able to regard the emergence of vernacular orthography from the ninth century onwards as a spelling reform that recognizes changes that had long since occurred in everyone's speech, most of the problems that worried Muller resolve themselves; the phenomena attested in earlier texts can be seen not as questions concerning the coexistence of two separate dialects (the two-norm theory) but as questions concerning scribal practices and the nature of education in communities where the writing norms did not correspond closely to anyone's normal speech.

### "Vulgar" Latin

The much-used term "Vulgar Latin" is multivalent and best avoided. Lloyd (1979) has discovered thirteen different meanings for the phrase. In this book, *Romance* is used to refer to the vernacular of any time after the end of the Western Roman Empire; *Imperial Latin* is used to refer to any variety of Latin before that time; *Latin* is used to refer to anything spoken after the end of the Empire which is used by the educated and is systematically and archaically distinct from contemporary Romance. This present book is examining the theory that this Latin is a Carolingian invention, with no previous existence, and no direct continuity with Imperial Latin. The concomitant suggestion of a one-norm Proto-Romance hypothesis is not intended to imply that there was any particular similarity between the norms of different communities.

The phrase *sermo vulgaris*, and assorted cognate expressions, as Díaz y Díaz pointed out long ago (1951-52), seem in pre-Carolingian communities to be applicable to the speech of everybody, not just of the uneducated. The tendency to identify words of the *vulgus* with Proto-Romance, tout court, is untenable. Several of the words qualified as *vulgo* in glossaries have no direct Romance descendants; among others Díaz y Díaz mentions *cacida, caelio, conditum, fiscla, teredo, verbosus, vullus*. In this study Díaz y Díaz also performed the simple but necessary task of clarifying a remark made by Servius in the fifth century which was supposed in the nineteenth century to be a confirmation of the separate existence of a "Vulgar Latin". Commenting on Vergil's *Georgics* 3.147-8 (*... cui nomen asilo/Romanum est, oestrum Grai vertere vocantes*), Servius said "latine asilus, vulgo tabanus vocatur." Servius used *latine* where Vergil used *Romanum*; as Díaz y Díaz pointed out, *latine* here is used by Servius to refer to the local speech of Latium (and thus of Vergil), and *tabanus* is in fact the general word for a horsefly (as in Sp. *tábano*), being used by Varro and Pliny, among others. *Vulgo* refers here to the speech of all, including Servius. In this case the anachronistic class sensitivity of the nineteenth-century German Schuchardt obliterated the geographical knowledge of the early fifth-century North African Servius; Schuchardt largely built the theory of a separate "Vulgärlateins" on such remarks, being among the first to use the phrase and responsible for rigidifying the concept (1866-68). As regards vocabulary, at least, the idea of a "vulgar" level is earlier than Schuchardt (see Coseriu 1977); the examination of the views of Isidore (later in this chapter) suggests that non-imperial vocabulary is all that he means to refer to with the word *vulgus*. Mohrmann (1961a) considered the theory from a Latinist's viewpoint with no hint of a belief in separate varieties of pronunciation. Geographical and social differentiation of vocabulary is normal in any complex language community, and has no implications in itself for pronunciation.

Menéndez Pidal (1926) saw spoken "Vulgar Latin" as still existing in tenth- and eleventh-century León, specifically distinguishable from both Romance and Latin, being the direct descendant of the speech of the late empire and thus opposable to Classical Latin as well as tenth-century Leonese. This view is still standard, but hardly defensible (see below, Chapter 4). Lloyd's conclusion (119) concerning the term "Vulgar Latin" is that "it is, in fact, a carry-over from the pre-scientific view of language, based on a tradition reflecting a lack of comprehension of the nature of linguistic evolution and of the complexity of social and stylistic stratification." He is right. The similar ambiguity of the term "Medieval Latin" may soon seem equally open to criticism, as Díaz y Díaz (1960), Bastardas (1960) and others have hinted. Pre-reform Medieval Latin was a written form of the vernacular, different in kind from post-reform Medieval Latin, which was in theory a separate language. The phrase "Vulgar Latin", however, deserves to be banished at once from serious scholarly use, as have been *phlogiston*, *humours*, and *the music of the spheres*.

### The Evidence of Grammarians before 500

The pronunciation of Imperial Latin has been described by Allen (1970) and Bassols (1976). Allen makes it clear that speech did not correspond particularly closely to spelling, although even he may have underestimated the lack of congruence between post-medieval pronunciations of Latin and that of the Roman Empire. Kramer (1976) has produced a collection of quotations from grammarians concerning pronunciation, in which he apparently subscribes to the view that "Vulgar Latin" was largely immutable from Varro to Alcuin. What the contemporary grammarians say on this subject has not been seriously studied by philologists; the general assumption is that grammarians naturally recommended classical usage and opposed any phonetically evolved forms; although Janson (1979) points out that this is not so, he refrains from further discussion. The assumption is unjustified. A study of the grammarians in Keil's *Grammatici Latini* reveals that they are not much concerned with pronunciation at all. When they mention it their remarks are seldom easy to interpret precisely, mainly because written letters and spoken sounds are not theoretically distinguished, but some of them say enough to make it clear that they and their public use the vernacular of their time and place. If a dichotomy between "Latin" and (Proto-) "Romance" actually existed in these centuries (from the second to the fifth), the grammarians would have done what it has been customary for grammarians of the last thousand years to do, that is, they would have prescribed that "correct" pronunciation of Latin was to be that which corresponds sound for letter to the correct Latin orthography; they would have stigmatized and attacked any "vulgar", vernacular or evolved features. "Correctness", as advocated by these grammarians, would, if the traditional view were well-founded, combine a reverence for archaism with the prescription that the traditional spelling is to be used as the guide for speech.

The grammarians do not take this line. On the contrary, a reverence for archaic usage is no part of their approach. Aulus Gellius, for example, in the second century A.D., says with regard to the *h*: "inserebant eam veteres nostri . . . nulla ratio visa est" (II 3; Kramer 1976: 48). Diomedes, in the fourth century, declared that "quod vulgo obsepio dicimus, veteres obsipio dixerunt" (Keil I 383.10-11; Kramer

1976: 26), allying himself roundly with the *vulgus*, by using the first
person form *dicimus*, rather than with the *veteres*. As regards the "silent"
letters such as *h*, *-m*, and the *n* in *ns*, it is noticeable that although it
was thought advisable to write them if that was the established practice,
there was no recommendation that they should be pronounced.

### a) The Second Century

Velius Longus, in the second century, is particularly clear concerning contemporary lack of congruence between speech and spelling.
His comments on the intervocalic *h*, for example, show that it is to be
written in *vehemens* and *reprehendit* even though "elegantiores et
*vementem* dicant et *reprendit*, ... *prendo* enim dicimus, non *pre-
hendo*" (Keil VII 68.14-17; Kramer 1976: 54); Velius is happy to speak
the evolved form while writing the established orthography. *Elegans* is
a word employed by Velius to praise a usage: e.g. "alimenta quoque per
*i* elegantius scribemus quam alumenta per *u*" (Keil VII 77.8); elegance
is not to be overdone, however — "nimiae rursus elegantiae sectatores
non arbitror imitandos" (Keil VII 79.19) — for normal usage is his
target. The usage of the *antiqui* is not recommended if it clashes with
the normal usage of Velius' day: "*Mium* et *commircium* quoque per *i*
antiquis relinquamus ... nostris iam auribus placet per *e*, ut et *Mer-
curius* et *commercia* dicantur" (Keil VII 77.13-15). As regards *maxumus*
and *maximus*, the former is both *antiquum* and *rusticanum* (Keil VII
49.21), neither of which is a term of approval; the apparent belief of
some philologists that the "rustic" was necessarily more evolved than
the "urban" is unjustified. *Rusticanum* is also used by Velius to criticize
the form *artubus*: "mihi videtur nimis rusticana enuntiatio futura, si per
*u* extulerimus" (Keil VII 68.6-7). For Velius Longus, if people want to
write like the *antiqui* they can, but they are not to talk as they write:
"concedamus talia nomina per *u* scribere iis qui antiquorum voluntates
sequuntur, ne tamen sic enuntient, quo modo scribunt" (Keil VII 50.
4-6). Velius is equally precise as regards word-final *-m*; before a vowel,
at least, it is a silent letter, written not spoken. He makes in this connection the general observation that spelling is *not* exactly a correspondence of the manner in which "we" talk:

> Ingredienti mihi rationem scribendi occurrit statim ita quosdam
> censuisse esse scribendum, ut loquimur et audimus. nam ita sane
> se habet nonnumquam forma enuntiandi, ut litterae in ipsa
> scriptione positae non[1] audiantur enuntiatae. sic enim cum dicitur

---

1. The editors of the Rome edition of 1587 were unable to believe this and
omitted the *non*. Suggested translations of the longer extracts from grammarians are included in an appendix (263-70).

*illum ego* et *omnium optimum, illum* et *omnium* aeque *m* ter-
minat nec tamen in enuntiatione apparet . . . confitendum aliter
scribi, aliter enuntiari . . . (Keil VII 54.1-13; Kramer 1976: 60)
. . . saepe aliud scribamus, aliud enuntiemus . . . (Keil VII 75.15)

Not even Quintilian in the previous century had recommended a
consonantal [-m] in such circumstances: his comment "neque enim
eximitur, sed obscuratur" (9.4.40) suggests that written *-m* represented
to Quintilian a nasalized vowel. No reader or speaker of Latin has
followed Velius' prescription in the last thousand years, since the
practice of giving a sound to every Latin letter has been routine; but
Velius, and second-century vernacular speakers in general, were happy
to write *-m* in some circumstances where they did not pronounce it.
Velius prides himself on not confusing *orthographia* with *orthoepeia*
(Keil VII 71.8-12); his *orthographia* is specifically not intended to prescribe pronunciations, for both he and his public talk their own
language naturally anyway, and writing is the technique that has to be
taught and learnt. "Proprium ὀρϑογραφίας est, quotiens in vocis enuntiatione nihil videmus ambiguum, at in scriptione tota haesitatio posita
est, ut, cum dico *Troia*, per *i* unum an per duo scribere debeam" (Keil
VII 72.2-4). Similarly, concerning the *n* of *ns*, Velius believes it is
*elegantia* to follow Cicero's (spoken) use of *foresia, Megalesia, hortesia*,
without the [n] (Keil VII 78.21–79.5; Kramer 1976: 64). Quintilian
had said that "*consules* exempta *n* littera legimus" (1.7.29), allying
himself in the first person with those who do not pronounce the [n] in
such a word; Quintilian, Velius, and their public, at least, are not to
blame by virtue of their literacy for the [n] in Fr. *penser*, etc. If we still
seriously believe that Proto-Romance was the speech of only the uneducated, it is surely strange to see Quintilian reveal himself as "vulgar"
in such a matter-of-fact tone. The comments examined here are more
compatible with the view that this vernacular pronunciation is in fact
the pronuncation of everyone in the first two centuries A.D.; that the
educated Latin used by scholars ever since the Carolingian Renaissance
was not the same as that used by the literate in the Roman Empire, and
may never have been used at all by anyone before the Carolingian
scholars invented it. Velius Longus has held the stage in this section
because he is untypically explicit, but there is no need to suppose that
his usage was untypical of that of his time.

### b) The Fifth Century

When vernacular loses sounds entirely, such as [h], [-m], and [n]
before [s] in Imperial Latin, their subsistence in the orthography makes
the difference between speech and spelling immediately perceptible.

Grammarians are less likely to be aware of other kinds of change in progress, since allophonic variation is notoriously hard for native speakers to perceive. Imperial Latin developed considerably from the second century to the fifth, however, and by the time of the fifth-century grammarians some such developments are beginning to be noticed. These later writers occasionally mention vowel allophony in a way that makes it clear that the old quantitative vowel system was already superseded in their vernacular by that of "Proto-Romance". In Early Latin, there were distinctions of length of pronunciation between a long and short ā and ă, ē and ĕ, etc., but the evidence of all the later Romance languages suggests that such distinctions were no longer functional in speech by the fifth century. Consentius, for example (from Southern Gaul), noticed that the written letter *i* represents different sounds in the words *ite, habui* (and *tenui*), and *hominem*, and that the distinction is not explicable in terms of old-fashioned quantity alone. His terminology verges on the opaque, but if we consider these words in the light of their Romance descendants — e.g. ITE > Sp. *id*, HABUI > Sp. *hube*, TENUI > Sp. *tuve*, HOMINEM > OSp. *omne* > *hombre* — it seems likely that he is referring to a closed [i̞] in *ite*, an open [i̞] = closed [e̞] in *habui* and *tenui*, and a tendency to a centralized schwa ([ə] — as in the second vowel of English *father*) in *hominem*:

> Romanae linguae in hoc erit moderatio, ut exilis eius sonus sit, ubi ab ea verbum incipit, ut *ite*, aut pinguior, ubi in ea desinit verbum, ut *habui, tenui*; medium quendam sonum inter *e* et *i* habet, ubi in medio sermone est, ut *hominem*. Mihi tamen videtur, quando producta est, plenior vel acutior esse; quando autem brevis est, medium sonum exhibere debet, sicut eadem exempla, quae posita sunt, possunt declarare.

(Keil V 394.16-22; Kramer 1976: 26; Allen 1970: 48)

This final comment shows that his readers will see what he means if they pronounce these words for themselves; his readers too, it seems, are not archaizing unevolved "Latin" speakers either. Consentius is proud of the way he trusts his own observation of contemporary usage rather than merely accepting the authority of long-dead writers: "nos exempla huius modi dabimus quae in usu loquentium animadvertere possumus" (approvingly quoted by Díaz y Díaz 1951-52: 215, n.4).

In the same century, Pompeius has similar advice for his readers. When discussing the remarks made in the second century by Terentianus Maurus about "long" and "short" vowels, which would have been intelligible in that distant age when that distinction was probably still perceptible, Pompeius suggests that you can tell whether an *o* is technically *longa* or *brevis* by the following practical test:

> *O* longa sit an brevis? si longa est, debet sonus ipse intra palatum
> sonare, ut si dicas *orator*, quasi intra sonat, intra palatum. si
> brevis est, debet primis labris sonare, quasi extremis labris, ut
> puta si dicas *obit*. habes istam regulam expressam in Terentiano:
> *quando vis exprimere quia brevis est, primis labris sonat; quando*
> *exprimis longam, intra palatum sonat*
> > (Keil V 102.13-18; Kramer 1976: 22; Allen 1970: 48)

For Pompeius, *longa* and *brevis* are technical terms unconnected with
any distinction between a long and a short vowel. The distinction is
instead based on relative manner of articulation, although neither
*primis labris* nor *intra palatum* is clear to a modern reader; what was
accidental and allophonic to Terentianus seems crucial and criterial
to Pompeius. The [w] of the diphthong developed from [ŏ] is noticeably produced with the lips: this may be the meaning of *primis labris*.

According to reconstructed evidence from later Romance, in
fifth-century Proto-Romance vernacular the originally short [ɛ] and
[ɔ] are diphthongized when stressed, in most geographical areas,
although since this is still simple positional allophony no special orthography is adopted to represent this in writing. Writers of modern
English never write *pat* as *phat*, even though an allophonic aspiration is
present. "Long" [ē] and [ō] do not suffer diphthongization, so a
distinction between words containing the two phonemes is still in
existence: it is no longer made in speech on the basis of length, but the
traditional terminology of *brevis* (or *correptus*) and *longus* (or *pro-*
*ductus*) remains. Grammarians tend to agree that the two letters *e* and *o*
each represent two pronunciations. Modern linguists usually distinguish
these as a more closed [ẹ] and [ọ] opposed to a more open [ɛ] and [ɔ]
which had begun to diphthongize, to [je] and to [wo], [we], or [wə]
respectively. (Closeness and openness refer to the distance between the
tongue and the top of the mouth.) The grammarians of the time are
unaware of the criterial importance of the relative aperture of the vocal
tract, however. Three fifth-century commentators on Donatus, the
North Africans Pompeius, Servius and Sergius, proclaim that the two
pronunciations are distinguishable in that the open *e* or *o* (called *brevis*
or *correptus*) is pronounced as if it were a diphthong:

> vocales sunt quinque. hae non omnes varios habent sonos, sed
> tantum duae, *e* et *o*. nam quando *e* correptum est, sic sonat, quasi
> diphthongus: *equus*; quando productum est, sic sonat, quasi *i*, ut
> *demens*. similiter et *o*, quando longa est, intra palatum sonat:
> *Roma, orator*; quando brevis est, primis labris exprimitur: *opus*,
> *rosa*.
> > (Sergius: Keil IV 520.27-31; Kramer 1976: 22)

vocales sunt quinque, *a, e, i, o, u*. ex his duae, *e* et *o*, aliter sonant
productae, aliter correptae. nam *o* productum quando est, ore
sublato vox sonat, ut *Roma*; quando correptum, de labris vox
exprimitur, ut *rosa*. item *e* quando producitur, vicinum est ad
sonum *i* litterae, ut *meta*; quando autem correptum, vicinum est
ad sonum diphthongi, ut *equus*.

(Servius: Keil IV 421.16-21; Kramer 1976: 22)

Allen (1970: 49) believed the diphthong referred to here as existing in
the *e* of *equus* is the *ae*; but this is surely unlikely. *ae* has long since
stopped representing [ai], as Allen himself shows; the comments of
Pompeius (below) make it clear that he positively wishes to distinguish
*equus* from *aequus*. In view of the development of Spanish *yegua* <
EQUAM there can be little doubt that [je] is the diphthong to which
Servius refers (Spanish is generally taken to be the closest surviving
relative to the lost Romance of North Africa). *Dēmens* and *mēta* involve the closed [ẹ], which in vernacular was indeed "vicinum" to short
[i], as Servius and Sergius say — so much so that in Romance languages
original short [ĭ] and long [ē] develop into the same sound. *Opus*, with
a short [ɔ], became O.Sp. *huebos*, so the labial diphthong with [w] is
likely to be what Sergius is referring to: *rŏsa*, however, has for some
reason not survived into Romance as a diphthongized form.

Pompeius actually offers us a diphthongized spelling. He is
unexpectedly explicit on this subject in another context, that of
"barbarisms". He says that one of the barbarisms people sometimes
commit is to confuse technically *brevis* and *longa* syllables, but the
confusion is exemplified in his study neither by mistaken aperture
height, nor by length, but by the diphthongization of the wrong cases.
Choosing a standard example of closed, originally long, [o], the word
*Roma*, Pompeius spells its mispronunciation with *uo*: *Ruoma*. It is
ironic that the presence of diphthongization at the time, as firmly
postulated by the reconstructors of Proto-Romance vernacular, is
guaranteed by this spelling of a mispronunciation of a word which
normally does not diphthongize:

> Est alter [barbarismus] qui fit in pronuntiatu. plerumque male
> pronuntiamus et facimus vitium, ut brevis syllaba longo tractu
> sonet aut iterum longa breviore sono; siqui velit dicere *Ruoma*,
> aut si velit dicere *aequus* pro eo quod est *equus*, in pronuntiatione
> hoc fit.                                    (Keil V 285.5-9; Kramer 1976: 24)

The point here appears to be that it is *equus* that has the diphthongized
pronunciation in normal vernacular, the barbarism being to give a diphthong to the normally monophthongal *aequus*. The barbarism (which
often happens even, it seems, in the mouth of Pompeius himself: "male

pronuntiamus") is not that of talking some evolved "vulgar" non-Classical Latin, but that of not talking ordinary acceptable fifth-century southern vernacular. That vernacular would diphthongize OPUS and EQUUS but not ROMA nor – probably – AEQUUS. (*Aequus* does not survive now, but the evidence of closure in the cognate Sp. *igual* or It. *uguale* < AEQUALEM suggests that this word was closed in its first syllable to at least as great an extent as *demens* or *meta*, and thereby "strengthened" itself out of diphthongization.) Not surprisingly to a linguist, Pompeius and his readers speak their own vernacular. We have cause to be grateful to Pompeius, for on the next page (in Keil) we find this long discussion concerning how to pronounce words spelt with *ti* or *di* and a following vowel (this section is here reproduced from Kramer 1976: 70, whose edition makes the point clearer):

> sunt aliqua uitia, quae uitare debemus. istas quinque res debes uitare: iotacismos, labdacismos, myotacismos, collisiones, hiatus. iotacismi sunt, qui fiunt per *i* litteram, siqui ita dicat, *Titius* pro eo quod est *Tit<s>ius*, *Auentius* pro eo quod est *Auent<s>ius*, *Amantius* pro eo quod est *Amant<s>ius*. quo modo ergo hoc fit uitium? definiamus illud, et uidebimus postea, quo modo cauere debemus. fit hoc uitium, quotiens post *ti* uel *di* syllabam sequitur uocalis, si non sibilus sit. quotienscumque enim post *ti* uel *di* syllabam sequitur uocalis, illud *ti* uel *di* in sibilum uertendum est. non debemus dicere ita, quem ad modum scribitur *Titius*, sed *Tit<s>ius*: media illa syllaba mutatur in sibilum. ergo si uolueris dicere *ti* uel *di*, noli, quem ad modum scribitur, sic proferre, sed sibilo profer. sed illud scire debes, quia tunc hoc facere debes, si media sit. si autem prima fuerit in prima parte orationis, etiamsi sequatur uocalis, non illam uertit in sibilum. ecce *dies* habet post se uocalem; debemus dicere *d<z>ies*, sed non dicimus. adde illi partem priorem, ut istam mediam facias, et dicis *merid<z>ies*: non possumus dicere *meridies*, ut scias quoniam tunc contigit hoc huic syllabae, quotiens media est, non, quotiens prior est . . .

"Non debemus dicere ita, quem ad modum scribitur . . .;" "noli quem ad modum scribitur sic proferre." No instruction could be clearer; do not pronounce the word exactly as it is written. What is here called a "vitium" is precisely the pronunciation that is advocated as correct by the scholars of Carolingian times and later, viz. pronouncing written *ti* and *di* as [ti] and [di], and failing to palatalize intervocalic [t] to [ts] and [d] to [dz] before the semivowel [j]. The pronunciation advocated by Pompeius is that which still survives in Italian words such as *giustizia*; the pronunciation criticized is that which follows the spelling. The difference mentioned by Pompeius between the palatalizing *meridies*, with a [dz], and *dies*, with just a [d], is presumably due to the fact that there is a stressed [i] in *dies*

(> Sp. *día*) but a semivocalic [j] in *meridies*. The spelling-pronunciation [meridies] without the [z] is something which cannot be said, "non possumus dicere". Pompeius not only *does not* talk in the normal post-Carolingian Latin manner here, he *cannot*. Holtz (1981: 236) comments that in general Pompeius used "African Latin", pointing out that he often used *habere* to form the future tense, in the normal spoken way.

The evidence suggests that the fifth-century grammarians, on the few occasions that they mention pronunciation, discuss, prescribe and use the normal vernacular of their time and place. In previous centuries, Cicero, Quintilian, Caper, Velius Longus and others did the same. They were writing for an audience who already knew how to pronounce and did not need to be taught. The evidence does not support the traditional view that the language of the educated classes had failed to undergo vernacular sound changes; and if the grammarians and their public did not speak such an underdeveloped archaic language, who did? Nor does it offer any comfort to the general view of Medieval Latinists, that the developments from "Classical" Latin to Romance only begin to any extent after 600 A.D. The evidence is not large. Much of it is opaque or ambiguous. But what there is supports the view that the grammarians themselves spoke the vernacular of their time, which had evolved as much, broadly speaking, as the reconstructionist philologists now claim, and more than Latinists and historians tend to believe: in short, that there is only one norm of pronunciation in an area (routine social and stylistic variations included), and that this norm can, if we wish, be called "Proto-Romance".

### The Evidence of Legal Documents

The following three extracts from Italian legal documents were reproduced (among many others) in Sabatini (1965: 983-84):

1) from Colonna (near Grosseto), 762 A.D.:
... *per omnem annum iustitia ipsei case reddere debeam* porco uno valente tremisse uno et uno pullo et quinque ovas et camisia una valente tremisse uno et uno animale in mense magio valente tremisse uno, vinum et labore *secundum consuetudinem ipsei case* ...

2) from Lusciano (near Bolsena), 762 A.D.:
... *per omnem annum de ipsa casa vel res reddere debeam* uno animale annutino in mense magio, porco uno annutino in octummio, sex decimate de vino, grano siligine bono modia quattuor, *angaria quantas utilitas fuerit* ...

3) from Lucca, 765 A.D.:
... *prandium eorum tali sit per omnem septimana*: scaphilo

grano, pane cocto et duo congia vino, et duo congia de pulmentario, faba et panico mixto, bene spisso et condito de uncto aut
de oleo, *et nullus de heredibus nostris* . . .

It is time to turn our attention to the manner in which practical
literate men put to use their instruction in writing, *Grammatica*. One
such group are lawyers, producing workaday documents such as the
above. Sabatini has demonstrated that the language of notarial documents, from at least as early as the sixth century, falls into two categories. In the first place, those parts of the text which are oft-repeated
formulae, copied from a standard version, are generally more "correct".
The existence of these sections is not evidence that the scribe naturally
produced Latinate forms in his own vernacular; he had learnt to copy
such expressions as part of the tools of his trade, as a lawyer might do
today. These sections are often longer than the rest, and can thus give
an impression that the language of the scribe was more archaic than in
fact it was. (These *formulae* are often unclassical; e.g. above, *ipsei case*,
*de ipsa casa, per omnem septimana*.) Sabatini calls these passages the
"parti formulistiche"; they are distinguished from the rest, the "parti
libere". These latter "free" sections deal with specific details of the
individual transaction, which are intrinsically less amenable to prior
formalization, and have in practice to be some kind of representation of
the depositor's vernacular. For this purpose scribes worked with a
"scripta latina rustica", consciously deployed for a practical end (cp.
also Sabatini 1968). The fact that these free sections are not couched in
authentic old-fashioned Imperial Latin is not the result of mere scribal
ignorance, but of the intentional use of a less formal technique of
writing. Under this perspective Merovingian or early Leonese lawyers
can retain some professional self-respect, for this was a sensible and
rational procedure. The once common patronizing approach to such
documents, that "these barbarians couldn't cope", has been slightly
refined – E. Löfstedt (1959: 3), for example, describes the style of such
documents as a "haphazard mixture" – but should be entirely discarded. Lawyers adopted "incorrect" forms for a practical reason.

Modern scholars have at times interpreted the general truth of a
low level of education in much of the early medieval Romance areas
(e.g. seventh- and eighth-century Northern France, ninth- and tenth-
century León) as being a particular truth concerning the intelligence of
individuals. Yet there is no reason to postulate a necessary variation in
the intelligence of individual scribes proportional to the level of literacy
in their community. If a man is writing obviously "incorrect" forms on
purpose, rather than just scattering slips of the pen, it is pointless to

criticize him for inaccuracy. The lawyers are operating in an age when the connection between speech and spelling was becoming tenuous, and such practical adjustments are a reasonable compromise between stultifying pedantry and unacceptable imprecision.

The non-imperial innovations in these sections are of all kinds. They include new vocabulary, for example of Germanic origin, or in Spain of Arabic origin also; there is the limitation to the reduced case systems proper to the Romance of specific areas (for example, only the accusative form of plural nouns in Iberian texts of the tenth and eleventh centuries, where Romance nouns preserve only their accusative form); and they include experiments with occasional new graphic representations, such as the use of *uu* for [w], or of *g* for [j].

In the documents reproduced above, italics represent formulae and the rest is *libera*. Sabatini points out that *octummio* (in no. 2) is a splendid confirmation of the postulated AUTUMNIUS form (> Sp. *otoño*; Italian *autunno* is a later borrowing from Latin). In Italy, -CT-became -*tt*- (OCTO > *otto*, LACTEM > *latte*), with the result that the [ot] pronunciation was sometimes spellable correctly as OCT. Hence the attempt to write it correctly as *octummio*. Unknown to the scribe, [aw] > [o] was also a regular change (e.g. CAUSA > *cosa*), and in this case AU was the correct orthography. This form can only be interpreted as the attempt of a vernacular-speaking scribe to come up with official orthography. In the same passage, *decimate* represents the one case of the contemporary vernacular, which in Italy kept the originally nominative form (-*e* < -AE, in this case) whereas the old grammar would here require the -AS form. The -AS is written in *ovas*, but this is presumably either a misconstrued plural of the neuter plural OVA (> It. *uova*), "eggs", or a variant form for "sheep", *oves*. *Octummio* and *ovas* seem thus to be "mythical" forms, created on paper alone in an attempt to be correct. Other, correctly spelt, forms in the *parti libere* are thus likely to be the result of successful attempts to create official-looking orthography for vernacular forms. Further non-imperial usages visible here include -*o* for -UM (passim), *de pulmentario* for the simple genitive ("two measures of relish", no.3), and the Celtic *camisia* (no.1).

Sabatini is himself a proponent of the two-norm theory, in its diglossic guise, and assumes that scribes knew "Latin" as well as their vernacular; in his view they are consciously vernacularizing their Latin in the *parti libere* to aid subsequent reading aloud. The main thrust of his argument is that the various experiments adopted in the representation of evolved speech formed the practical basis of the subsequent techniques used in the elaboration of new Romance orthographies. But his insight is more valuable than that. His discoveries are fully consistent with the hypothesis that lawyers did not know of "Latin" as a separate norm; that they learnt established formulae, but need not have used themselves the kind of language expressed in those formulae, nor even have known what they literally meant. At times the formulae are incorrectly transcribed in a manner that betrays their nature as set learnt phrases. Since the *parti libere* are the graphic representation of actual speech, and thus presumably simple enough for the lawyer to read back to the original depositor of the document if required, the main problem for a one-norm Proto-Romance theory of early medieval speech communities is not how to explain the existence of the *parti libere*, but how to visualize the *parti formulistiche* being read aloud in the absence of a Latinizing pronunciation norm alongside the vernacular.

This problem is dealt with in detail in Chapter 4 with reference to a document from tenth-century León, but the general answer can be summarized here. Anyone wishing to reproduce aloud sections of archaic language will have no problem in reading words that exist in the vernacular in any case; they will be read aloud as that vernacular word. *Veniunt*, for example, would be in Castille read as [bjénen]. Words that have died out would be given the pronunciation that analogously spelt surviving words had in the contemporary vernacular; e.g. intervocalic -*t*- will be pronounced as [d] in those areas where it voiced in the vernacular (e.g. France and Spain), but as [t] where it remained unvoiced in the vernacular (e.g. Southern Italy). Inflectional morphemes that are no longer current, such as the old passive ending -*itur*, would be treated in exactly the same way; i.e. in Spain [idor], in Italy [itor]. The reader would not have any knowledge of how these words sounded half a millennium or more before; that would not prevent their being read aloud as if they were still in common use. The fact that the Latin syntax of these formulae might make the vernacular pronunciation quite meaningless is irrelevant, since in formulae intelligibility is not the point. Lawyers normally prefer their formulae to be opaque to laymen.

This is simple to illustrate with another analogy from Modern English. When reading aloud the Authorized Bible (of 1611) in church, modern Englishmen give to archaic words and morphemes (such as the -*est* of *thou makest*, or the -*eth* of *doeth*) the pronunciation which they would have had were they not archaisms, without worrying about the early seventeenth-century phonetic realization of what is now the /θ/ phoneme, in exactly the same way as they also give those words and morphemes that are not archaic a normal modern twentieth-century vernacular pronunciation. The -*est* of *makest* will sound exactly like the

*-est* of *greatest*.

The objection could be raised that this hypothesis, of vernacular pronunciation even of the formulaic sections of notarial documents, would still have made the resulting speech sufficiently distinctive for it to count as a separate non-vernacular language, for syntactic and lexical reasons. This argument does not follow unless we always wish to view the lawyers of any community as speaking a literally different language from that of their clients.

Generally there is good reason to see the forms used in legal documents as examples of a separate style or register rather than as a separate language. For example, Crystal and Davy (1969: Chap. 8) have produced an illuminating stylistic study on "The Language of Legal Documents" in English. This is only concerned with modern Britain, but many comments could apply to the documents of early Romance:

> There is a strong motivation for any lawyer to turn to a form of words that he knows he can rely on rather than take a chance on concocting something entirely new ... much legal writing is by no means spontaneous but is copied directly from 'form books', as they are called, in which established formulae are collected ... it is a form of language which is about as far removed as possible from informal spontaneous conversation ...          (194)

> It is especially noticeable that any passage of legal English is usually well studded with archaic words and phrases of a kind that could be used by noone else but lawyers.          (207)

This archaism, mainly in syntax but also in vocabulary and morphology (e.g. *witnesseth*), is a known and provable phenomenon; yet it would be absurd to propose that modern British lawyers normally converse with each other according to a pronunciation system which is centuries older than that of the rest of the community. Indeed, they clearly pronounce archaisms according to the phonological system of their modern vernacular. If that is the case now, there is no reason to propose that lawyers in early medieval Romance communities need have spoken anything other than the phonology of the community they were in. We can regard the lawyers of those centuries as drawing up documents in a traditional and practical manner, but we can hardly expect them to be capable of linguistic feats which border on the impossible, such as successfully imitating the phonology of a far distant era. A professional linguist of our time finds it hard to copy a long-defunct phonology accurately; a working medieval lawyer, in a pre-philological age, would have found it impossible in practice to imitate Imperial Latin even if it could have occurred to him to try. In short, the language of legal documents contains no evidence to point to the coexistence of an archaizing "Latin" pronunciation alongside the vernacular of their region, since it can be naturally explained in other ways. (For the semantics of legal language, see Baldinger 1980: I 4c.)

In a more recent study (1978) Sabatini has discussed a seventh-century papyrus from Ravenna which contains the same Latin text in both the Latin and the Greek alphabets. He mentions that, for example, Latin *huic chartule* is written in the Greek alphabet as the equivalent of *ouiki caretule* (sic), *donationis* as *donazione*, *portionis* as *porezone*, *fundi* as *fondi*. The significance of such transcriptions is not lost on Sabatini; the scribe using the Greek alphabet interpreted the written *-is* as an [e] in speech, the written *u* of *fundi* as a spoken [o], the written *ti* as either [tsj] or [dsj], the *h* of *chartule* as representing no sound at all. Here is a member of the legal profession who spoke the vernacular of seventh-century Ravenna. Sabatini's conclusion (453) is surely right; the first "Romance text" later represented more than anything else an orthographical reform. But despite all the evidence Sabatini has adduced, not even he has yet proposed (in print, at least) the hypothesis of a single early Romance pronunciation system, without a coexisting Latin system, for lawyers in early medieval communities; the hypothesis seems natural to a historical linguist and is quite compatible with the surviving evidence.

### The Evidence of "Rhythmic" Poetry

Another kind of text which might be expected to yield us some information concerning the relationship between speech and writing in the Early Middle Ages is the variety of poetry known as "rhythmic". This evidence is slippery, for several reasons. Firstly, much poetry is consciously written in imitation of earlier models. Secondly, there is no need to assume that even metres ostensibly based on an equal number of syllables per line always require these mathematics to be satisfied exactly. Thirdly, the same line of music can be used for texts of differing numbers of syllables. Fourthly, hymns in particular, but other songs also, often induce performers to pronounce in a manner that would be regarded as strange outside a musical context. And fifthly, modern editions of surviving texts have often at some stage been "emended" in accordance with later scholars' preconceptions concerning what these texts ought to have been. Even so, it is instructive for our present purposes to consider the genre.

The techniques of post-Classical poetry are usually divided into two categories. "Quantitative", or "metrical", verses use the old traditional metres based on distinctions of vowel quantity and syllable length. "Qualitative", or "rhythmic", poetry takes no account of the ancient distinctions of length; instead it imitates the old forms by substituting a vernacular stress pattern for the original length pattern. Stress concerns the greater effort given to the pronunciation of some syllables than is given to others; some monosyllables (e.g. *et*) and a few disyllables (e.g. *quasi*) were usually unstressed, "atonic", but otherwise each word in Proto-Romance seems to have had a predetermined stress, and rhythmic patterns could be created by the arrangement of the stresses of the words within the lines. As Norberg (1958) convincingly showed, much poetry is based in this way on accentuation patterns that we can plausibly envisage as being those of normal vernacular.

The production of metric Latin poetry on the original quantitative basis is a recherché pursuit of the learnèd, an esoteric accomplishment of antiquarians, and has been so ever since the quantitative distinctions ceased to have any counterpart in ordinary speech. The existence of a few early medieval quantitative verses cannot be taken as evidence that phonemic length persisted in the speech of their composers any more than it is evidence of phonemic length in the speech of nineteenth-century scholars who also dabbled in the same pastime; it has to be seen now, as then, as a symptom of a sophisticated education system. For example, seventh-century Spanish poets used classical metres for much of their extant work, and, as Raby observed (1934: I 153), this poetry "derives its form and expression from what remained of the methods and practices of the ancient schools". Visigothic Spain was educationally the most sophisticated of the seventh-century Romance realms, and the quantitative verse there produced is visible evidence of this preeminence. Norberg (1965) suggested that after the length distinctions fell, metric verse was recited with the normal vernacular stresses on the words; otherwise, the only available technique would have involved stressing the long syllables and giving no stress to the short syllables, and in the many cases where the consequentially produced stresses did not correspond to those of the vernacular words involved, that can only have been thought of as a peculiarity of the rules of such sophisticated creations. When the rules of metrics were known, it was because they had been studied in authoritative works, and such a result as odd-sounding lines would thus be thought a sign of erudition rather than eccentricity.

Rhythmic verse, however, usually was destined for oral performance in an intelligible manner; if any evidence concerning pronunciation is to be discovered in poetry of the period, it will be here. What classicists once considered to be the ignorant miscegenations of uncouth barbarians have now been reinterpreted as the results of techniques of composing in a poetic style of the vernacular. If such poems look "Latin" on paper, that is a consequence of their being written before the orthographic innovation consequent upon the Carolingian reforms.

Rhythmic poetry is not, however, the same as popular verse. Popular songs and verses undoubtedly existed then, as they have in all known cultures, but by their very nature have left little trace. Rhythmic poetry was a written genre. Many poems of this type that have survived were shown by Norberg to belong to carefully defined schemata and patterns that needed to be learnt. The number of syllables was the most important criterion for a line of "rhythmic" verse; the academic definition of a syllable was included in *Grammatica*. "Rhythmic poetry" is thus an educated genre with its own standards, rather than a collective label for all verse that fails to conform to quantitative metrics: "A rhythmic poem is one in which the old system has been replaced by a new one, not a poem whose characteristics are the absence of rules and anarchy" (Norberg 1958: 94). It is a simplification, therefore, to call all non-metric verse "rhythmic".

Regularity was based on the number of syllables per line, and in the grammatical tradition syllables were defined on the basis of written vowels. The only features of pronunciation in these poems that might not have accorded with normal vernacular thus concern vowels; in particular the occasional avoidance of syncopation of short vowels and a routine tendency to leave vowels in hiatus. This reluctance to elide is often extended to an apparently deliberate avoidance of having a word-final vowel followed by a word beginning with a vowel at all. These phenomena probably have something to do with the normal style of song performance, which is usually slower than spontaneous speech.

Some rhythmic verses imitate most of the structural aspects of an old form. In these, patterns of stressed and unstressed syllables replace the old patterns of long and short ones, and caesuras are still observed at the mid-points of longer lines. Rhyme and assonance begin to be used regularly in addition, and the formal complexities are often increased by the inclusion of such intellectual games as acrostics and telestichs. In consequence, many of these compositions represent an intellectual achievement, whatever we may think in this Romantic age of their poetic value. They are signs of changes in procedure and in taste, but are nonetheless the conscious products of skilful writers. Other rhythmic verses disregard the strict pattern of stressed and unstressed syllables except before the caesura and at the end of a line; in

these the number of syllables (i.e. of written vowels and Classical diphthongs) per line remains theoretically constant, and the caesura is in the
traditional place, preceded by a paroxytone. These verses are the
intellectual forerunners of the later Romance verse systems, many of
which follow a similar pattern and come to be identified through the
same criteria of rhythmic pattern and regularity of line length (e.g.
the hendecasyllable).

For example, the ninth-century Spanish hymn to St Jerome
(*AH* XXVII 126) begins as follows:

1.  Christus est virtus, patris sapientia,
    Cunctos qui replet spiritali gratia,
    Ut possint probe digerere normulam
    Et proximorum illustrare opaca,
    Ut digne possint fruere caelestia.

2.  Ipsius dono perflatus egregius
    Olim hic vates nomine Ieronymus,
    Omnibus notus doctrinarum fontibus,
    Cunctos irrigans ex almis dogmatibus,
    Ut sol resplendet in ortu ignicomus.

3.  Hic procul cuncta saeculi negotia
    Percalcans pede velut ᵉspurcissima
    Dedecorosa respuitque saecula,
    Alens inopum egenaque viscera,
    Sibi aeterna acquirens stipendia.

(Blume 1897: 180)

The basic pattern here is of 5 syllables plus 7 syllables; by the
ninth century this rhythmic "iambic" line is as traditional as any other.
The caesura is observed throughout the seventeen stanzas. Elision is
conspicuously not required, and the music may have also had the effect
of relengthening into full syllables some vowels that were in the process
of syncopating in normal speech (e.g. the *u* in *saecula*, 3.3). The prothetic *e* that Blume adds before *spurcissima* (3.2) might be unnecessary
in view of the possible emendation of *velut* to *veluti*, but in the
following lines it seems unavoidable:

4.2   Et sese valde (e)stringit ad regulam
5.2   Gentiliumque summo cum (e)studio
6.4   Obsequiorum tantum ut (e)spiritum
14.2  Te criminatur (e)stultorum factio
17.4  Iugiter, semper, per aevi (e)spatio

This is not a regularity, however: the prothesis is not required in other
lines such as 1.2 and 3.5 above, and the metric licence common to
hymn-singing in most languages seems to have been exploited here.

Rhyme is another possible indication of the composer's speech: in this poem, if we can assume that every line in a stanza is meant to rhyme, we can deduce that [-m] is not pronounced from *normulam* in 1.3, which rhymes with four words in *-a*. It also seems that *-u* and *-o* represent the one sound [o], for stanza 6 has the following five rhyme words: *corpusculum, ferculo, vulgarium, spiritum, tumulo. Spiritu* also rhymes with four *-o* words in stanza 7, and with three *-o* words (and *Deus*, in Blume's emendation) in stanza 17; there is no support here for the normal view that the *-u* in Modern Spanish *espíritu* derives from Early Medieval "learnèd" ecclesiastical pronunciation of the word.

Within hymns and comparable performed verse, the preservation of syllables that otherwise might have been disappearing seems to be the only reconstructable feature distinguishing hymns from vernacular. The presence of an internal vowel in *saeculo* in hymns may seem to be attested, but that in performance that vowel was [u], or that the congregation pronounced the word like this in any other context, is an unjustifiable conclusion. English hymns can give the word *heaven* any number of syllables from one to four (or more), but that does not affect our pronunciation of it elsewhere; it is a feature of the style of song-performance. [sjeglo] could similarly be made to cover three notes.

The defining feature of a rhythmic verse form thus, with time, became a regular number of syllables (written vowels) per line. This might appear to have implications for our reconstruction of the number of syllables with which words were pronounced, but because of the common feature of artificial slowness of song-performance, it is not of great help in many cases. The argument does not lead far in communities where most vernacular words of this time seem likely to have still had as many syllables as their Imperial etyma, such as Italy, Visigothic Spain, or even Moslem Spain. It might be relevant to ninth-, tenth- and eleventh-century Northern Spain, although the available material is small and awkward to analyse for other reasons (see Chapter 4); it could well be relevant to pre-Carolingian Northern France, though the reforms arrive here before other areas and the available material is similarly not large. Even so, Norberg has shown convincingly that many features of specifically vernacular speech have to be postulated in his analyses in order to account for apparent syllabic anomalies, even after the traditional assumption of the existence of a "Latin" speech has led to the distorting introduction of palaeographically unmotivated "emendations". The formation of semivocalic glides from what were originally unstressed close vowels, with the consequent formation of monosyllabic diphthongs instead of two adjacent syllabic vowels, is commonly attested: "the oldest example of a rhythmic poem, Saint Augustine's alphabetical psalm, has several examples such as *ecclesîam, gladîum, nescîo, petîit, fîeri, sûum*" (Norberg 1958: 29). The prothetic vowel added in vernacular to initial [s] followed by a consonant (as in the examples quoted above) is required in many lines, particularly from Spain, in order to preserve syllabic regularity (Norberg 1958: 31; Blume 1897: 54). And despite the general effect that song has on the avoidance of syncope, there are also cases of syncope of unstressed close vowels in internal syllables in long words. Many of these poems are composed to be sung to preexisting melodies; they are not necessarily isosyllabically organized, with a syllable per note, as was to happen in the Carolingian church (most notably in the sequence), so there is no reason to suppose that the music would in practice inhibit natural syncopation, epenthesis, or any other development, in subsequent performance, however the author originally expected and envisaged its reproduction (cp. Norberg 1954: 25-29; 1958: 186-87). The surviving texts are not the records of actual performances.

The evidence of rhyme and of vowel assonance also supports the conclusion that this verse was normally performed with the ordinary vernacular sounds of the performer. Norberg points out, for example, (1958: 48), that even an Archbishop, the seventh-century Eugenio de Toledo, assonated *delectatio* with *solacium*, *recogito* with *transeunt*, etc., following the regular vernacular pattern of collapsing the old distinctions between (i) stressed originally short /ŭ/ and originally long /ō/, and between both of these and originally short /ŏ/ in unstressed positions, and (ii) stressed originally short /ĭ/ and originally long /ē/, and between both of these and originally short /ĕ/ in unstressed positions, into one /o/ and one /e/ phoneme respectively. (Stressed /ĕ/ and /ŏ/ were the ones to diphthongize). Consequently the same sound is represented by the *o* of *delectatio* and *recogito* and the *u* of *solacium* and *transeunt*; and the same sound is represented by the *i* of *recogito* and the *e* of *transeunt*. The lines in question are from Eugenio's *Carmen* XIV 25-28:

> Potus cibique nulla delectatio
> Lamenta sola conferunt solacium.
> Haec taediosa mente dum recogito,
> Libet, relictis omnibus quae transeunt.

> (Vollmer 1895: 243)

In France, Venantius Fortunatus assonated *concinit* with *carmine*, *redditum* with *prospero*, etc., in the same way: e.g. *inpleta sunt que concinit | David fideli carmine* (*MGH Auctores Antiquissimi* IV 34;

Norberg 1968: 45). This collapse of atonic /ĭ, ē, ĕ/ and /ŏ, ō, ŭ/ and of tonic /ĭ, ē/ and /ō, ŭ/ is found in assonance patterns of Latin poetry from all Romance-speaking communities, but not in the poetry composed in the British Isles, where there was little native Romance vernacular after the fifth century and the poems were performed according to a largely artificial usage kept alive through spelling-pronunciations. The Anglo-Saxon habits may in this respect have been roughly similar to Muller's envisaged language of the fifth to the early eighth centuries, but they did not coexist with an evolving Romance in the same community (see below, *re* Bede).

The evidence of rhythmic poetry from pre-Carolingian times suggests that it was originally expected to have the normal vernacular sounds of the time and place where it was composed. Neither this, nor the erudite metric verse, can be adduced as evidence in favour of the hypothesis that their authors regularly used an archaic Latinate speech systematically distinct from the coexisting Old Romance.

Some of the surviving Merovingian examples have baffled even Norberg with their apparent lack of organization on recognizable patterns: e.g. King Chilperic's hymn to St Médard, Theofridus of Corbie's hymn XLI, parts of the versified life of St Eligius (Norberg 1954: 32, 52, 70 n.20).

The third of these was examined by Meyer (1936: 234-42), whose study suggests that the author may have thought that metric hexameters are lines containing six word-stresses. By permitting two accents on some long words, and ignoring the atonic words, such lines as the following can become "regular" after a fashion (the accents are Meyer's); e.g. lines 495-500:

> Sátis fecísse me réor          succíncto cármine pléctro;
> plúra nam réferre grávor,      necésse quóque nec opínor.
> Haéc paúca hexámetris         reciprocáre stúdui versículis,
> ádludéntibus dígitis            tánti amóre antéstitis.
> Cúr aútem haec métrica        volúerim immóque perpaúca
> rátióne compónere             non dífferam bréviter explanáre.

It is possible that the poet, probably writing soon after Bishop Eligius' death in 660, was working on a regular proto-Romance oral basis of some kind. For example, the second half of l.497 could become a rhythmic hexameter, with the long/short pattern replaced by a stress/unstressed one, if the *-are* of *reciprocare* could be seen as a single stressed syllable, the *-ui* as a single unstressed syllable, and the *u* of *versiculis* as absent, all of which are quite plausible reconstructions for the Romance of the time. It would in this way be possible to turn much of this into a popular-stress-based poem, although there are too many imponderables for any such conjecture to be convincing in detail. The general point holds, though: whatever these verses are, it seems absurd to suppose that their authors were not, in fact, operating with Merovingian vernacular, which was written down in the only available spelling, the traditional Roman. More successfully elaborated poems, on the other hand, are signs of well-educated poets rather than of bilinguals.

### The Evidence of the Visigothic Liturgy

> Liturgy is a field that the philologist cannot ignore. The hispanic liturgy is fuller and wider than probably any other in the West; through many sources we know that the most notable literary figures of Spain were involved in preparing the texts . . .
>
> (Díaz y Díaz 1976: 50)

Collins (1977: 33) has stated baldly but accurately that most of the current accepted wisdom concerning Visigothic Spanish society is based on "whimsical concatenation of fantasy". A large corpus of texts survives from the period 589-711, however, including the many books of the Visigothic (or "mozarabic") liturgy elaborated by the best group of scholars in Europe at the time, led by Isidore of Seville. If there is to be found anywhere in Romance Europe between 500 and 700 evidence of a "learnèd" pronunciation norm distinct from the vernacular, one would expect it to have existed in the performance of the Visigothic liturgy. The texts are long and provide a full picture of liturgical practice; they are filled with rhetoric and elevated style, such as clausular rhythm and high-sounding vocabulary.

Rhetorical skills, literary style and elevated vocabulary, however, are all teachable and learnable in accordance with the techniques of written composition incorporated in the grammars used in Visigothic Spain. Whether they, or arcane and archaic pronunciations, existed in the spoken vernacular of those who prepared and used the liturgy, is open to doubt. It used to be assumed that any spelling or grammatical errors found in the texts were errors introduced by subsequent copyists; Férotin (1912: xix), for example, commented adversely on "the incorrectness of mozarabic manuscripts and the ignorance of the copyists". As a consequence, the inherited textual versions ran the risk of being tetchily "corrected" by modern editors as if they were schoolboy compositions (see the strongly-worded comments of Gil 1973b). Fortunately the evidence remains; Díaz y Díaz studied the language of the manuscripts and demonstrated that most of the apparently "incorrect" features of these texts are faithful to the original versions rather than ascribable to the negligence of later copyists[2]. Most of these "incorrections" seem in fact to be forms used in seventh-century Spain, as far as can be reconstructed from later evidence. This is even visible in the vocabulary, which the authors were in general keen to keep as "elevated" as possible.

As regards morphology, many reconstructable features of seventh-century Spanish vernacular are perceptible in the texts. For example, we can guess that originally fourth-declension nouns have been by now reallocated to the second (cp. GRADUM, MANUM > Spanish *grado, mano*); this is here attested e.g. by the liturgical form *fluctos* (*Orac.*969), accusative plural, instead of the Imperial *fluctus*. We can guess that originally neuter plural forms in *-a* have by now been reinterpreted as feminine singulars; the forms are thus available for pluralization with an etymologically ridiculous *-s*. This is attested in the liturgy e.g. by the form *erratas* (*Ord.*361.21); the Imperial *errata* was already a plural of the neuter *erratum*. Such reinterpreted forms are also capable in the liturgy of being the subject of verbs in the singular (*nos subsequatur munera pietatis, Orac.*989), whereas Imperial Latin neuter plurals took plural verbs. We can guess that most verbs of the third conjugation, with infinitives in *-ere* with an open [ɛ], have by now been reallocated either to the second conjugation, with infinitives in *-ere* with a closed [ẹ], or to the fourth conjugation, with infinitives in *-ire*; Spanish has no distinct third conjugation, and the verbs in question are now either conjugated as *-er* verbs (e.g. VINCERE > *vencer*, CAPERE > *caber*) or as *-ir* verbs (e.g. FUGERE > *huir*, SCRIBERE > *escribir*). This is attested in the liturgy by e.g. the present-tense form *vinces* (*Orac.* 413), instead of Imperial *vincis*; the form *capuisse* (*Orac.* 686) (which was the past infinitive of -ĒRE verbs: cp. Modern Spanish *cupe* < \*CAPUI, not < CEPI) rather than the Imperial *cepisse*; and the form *fugire* (*Sacr.*288.34) rather than the Imperial *fugere*. We know from the evidence of Spanish that many irregular verbs lost irregular forms in favour of regular forms created by analogy with the normal pattern; in the liturgy we find, for example, present-tense *auferes* and *auferet* (*Ord.*95.26; *Sacr.*50.9) for Imperial *aufers, aufert* (cp. Spanish *sufre* < \*SUFFERET rather than SUFFERT). The loss of the passive caused many deponent verbs to be reallocated to active forms (e.g. MORI > *morir*); this is attested in the liturgy by e.g. *egredere* (*Ord.*46.2)

2. Díaz y Díaz (1965). Printed editions of the texts used in his study are Vives (1946) = *Orac.*; Férotin (1904) = *Ord.* and (1912) = *Sacr.*; Brou and Vives (1959). The subsequent examples all come from Díaz y Díaz's study unless otherwise stated.

rather than Imperial *egredi*. We know that medieval Spanish had a love
of compound prepositions with *de*, such as *depués* < DE POST, *después*
< DE EX POST, *desde* < DE EX DE; in the liturgy we find, as single
words, *depost* (*Ord*.152.24) and *desub* (*Sacr*.128.40). We can see the
latter as evidence for a seventh-century vernacular [dezó], *desó*, even
though *so* eventually survives in preference (as in *so pena de ex-
comunión*) and *deso* is not attested as such. We know that Spanish
nouns normally derive from the accusative form of the original etymon;
that the accusative was probably the only surviving form even as early
as this can be seen by the way that prepositions which once required
other cases take accusatives in the liturgy: e.g. *de insidias* (*Ord*.240.1)
rather than *de insidiis*, the Imperial ablative. These, and other, features
are sufficient to show that the evolved vernacular form in question is
the one used in the morphology of the normal speech of those who
prepared the text; despite the lengthy lists of old morphology found in
all their manuals of "correct" writing, they were not able to avoid their
natural usage on every occasion. In contrast, the relatively insignificant
probable archaisms of morphology that occur in these texts, such as
the synthetic passive forms and imperatives in *-to* that the reconstructionists of Proto-Romance would prefer to think did not exist in
normal vernacular at this time, are simple to account for as being the
result of education rather than symptoms of the writers' own usage.

Similarly, the spelling is sufficiently non-standard to suggest
that the "correct" forms are the result of strict training rather than a
simple phonetic transcription of archaic pronunciation (as English
written *knight* reflects a well-taught speller rather than a producer of
[knɪxt] or [knight]). It seems probable, as we attempt to reconstruct
the vernacular of the time, that between two vowels the original [t],
[k], [f] and [p] – traditionally spelt respectively *t*, *c* (or *qu*), *f* (or *ph*)
and *p* – have become in speech the voiced counterparts of these
sounds: i.e. [t] > [d], [k] > [g], [f] > [v], [p] > [b]. The spelling
taught and learnt has not changed, of course, so the norm is – if the
reconstruction is correct – for sounds in many words pronounced with
a [g], [d], [v], [b] to be written as *c* (or *qu*), *t*, *f*, *p*, respectively. This
produces uncertainty in both directions; words that used traditionally
to be spelt with *c* (or *qu*), *t*, *f* (or *ph*), or *p* can be misspelt with a *g*, *d*,
*v* or *b* because that is how they are now pronounced; conversely, words
that traditionally were spelt with *g*, *d*, *v*, or *b* can be misspelt with a *c*,
*t*, *f* or *p* precisely because so many words are indeed at this time written
with *c*, *t*, *f* or *p* and pronounced with a [k], [d], [v] or [b]. The first
type of misspelling even occurs in Greek borrowings and technical

ecclesiastical terms such as *eglesiae* (e.g. *Orac*.1030: Greek ἐκκλησία >
Latin *ecclesia* > Spanish *iglesia*), *paraglitum* (*Orac*.1036: "paraclete"),
and *psalmograue* (*Orac*.705) – in which the penultimate letter *u* represents what was normally spelt as *ph*, Gk. γραφή: other examples
include *memedipsum* (*Ord*.253: i.e. MEMET IPSUM : > Sp. *mí mismo*,
cp. Italian *medesimo*), *nebbotum* (*Ord*.417: NEPOTUM; in Spanish the
[b] has since disappeared regularly before a syncopated internal vowel
and a dental, > *nieto*), *prevatio* and *provana* (*Ord*.440 and *Sacr*.116.31:
PREFATIO and PROFANA; Sp. *prefacio* and *profano* are fifteenth-
century reborrowings). The similar neutralization of the [t]/[d] distinction at the end of words leads to written forms such as the common
*reliquid* for *reliquit*. The second type of misspelling, in which *c* and *t*
are used to represent a sound which had never been anything other than
[g] and [d], is exemplifiable with *cloriae* (*Orac*.120: for *gloriae*),
*cliscenti* (*Sacr*.609.2: for *gliscenti*), and the common *aliut* (for *aliud*),
*at* (for *ad*). The problems concerning the manner of written representation of final [d] are a perpetual preoccupation of the early medieval
grammarians as they attempt to prescribe when to write *it* or *id*, *quit* or
*quid*, *at* or *ad*, etc.; it is one of the few linguistic features discussed by
St Isidore himself. It does not look as though these scholars spoke a
dialect in which written final -*t* and -*d* represented distinct sounds. (The
old hypothesis that the Spanish of Moslem Spain preserved unvoiced
intervocalic [t], [p], [k], has been by now exploded; see e.g. Corriente
1978, Galmés 1977).

 Other evolutions of the sound system that have occurred by the
seventh century in the vernacular of Spain are also perceptible in its
transcription in the liturgy. The positional instability of the [r] sound
in Iberia (e.g. *quebrar* < CREPARE, *entrego* < INTEGRO, etc.) is visible
in written *prespicuus* (*Orac*.841) and *prescrutator* (*Sacr*.329), for
*perspicuus* and *perscrutator*. The common Spanish metathesis of [r]
and [l] (e.g. *peligro* < PERICULUM) is visible in written *fraglabit* (*Sacr*.
461.23), for *flagrabit*. The intrusion of unexpected [r] after [t] (e.g.
*estrella* < STELLAM) is perceptible in *retrorsere* (*Sacr*.118.7), for *re-*
*torsere*. The prothetic [e-] of words begining with [s] plus a consonant
is not usually transcribed in liturgical manuscripts any more than in
hymns, being an allophonic and predictable variant of /s/, as [we] was
of [ɔ] and [je] was of /ɛ/, but the presence of the extra vowel in
speech is deducible from the common converse misspelling of *ste* (*Sacr*.
276.15, etc.) for original *iste* (by now pronounced [este], as in Sp.
*este*), on the analogy of the correct spelling *sto* for contemporary
[estó] (STO > *estó* > *estoy*). Even the use of clausular rhythms has

been shown to require a basis in the vernacular prothesis; the syllable apparently missing in the clausula *coronandos statuas* (*Orac*.8 and 674), for example, is discoverable in a pronunciation comparable to modern Spanish *estatuas*.

This study by Díaz y Díaz, ignored by Romance philologists, ought to have had the effect of removing one of the last legs on which the two-norm theory can rest. If the liturgy of the most literate area of seventh-century Europe required and implied a contemporary vernacular pronunciation from both its authors and its performers, who is there left in the whole of seventh-century Romania to whom the hypothetical existence of a Latinate norm can apply? The common admission that only a very few men of the time "knew Latin" needs to be revised into a firm recognition that nobody of that time "knew Latin", neither imperial vernacular nor the artificial language used since the twelfth-century Renaissance: Latin as we know it now had not yet been invented. What existed was the vernacular Old Romance of seventh-century Spain; and when that was written, traditional orthography and the prescriptions of the "grammatical" manuals of writing succeeded in making the written version an inexact copy of the spoken. It was only the assumption that the clerics must have spoken "Latin" that prevented modern scholars from perceiving that they could not have spoken "Latin"; and as Collins observed, with his customary lapidary directness, "interpretations based on *a priori* assumptions as to how clerics think and behave must be regarded with some scepticism" (1977: 35).

As regards the Roman liturgy used elsewhere, the extensive researches of Mohrmann (e.g. 1961b) have effectively discounted the possibility that the Roman liturgy of pre-Carolingian times was pronounced differently from the vernacular of the congregation, whatever its stylistic or lexical level. Saint Augustine himself said "melius est reprehendant nos grammatici quam non intelligant populi" as regards grammatical comprehensibility; and although Mohrmann does believe in a kind of bilingualism in the Christian hierarchy, she noticeably refrains from extending this to support for the theory of separate manners of pronunciation. In all her voluminous work there appears no hint that liturgical or Christian Latin involved a non-vernacular phonetic system. We can be sure that she would have noticed if it had.

Early medieval liturgists seem no more to be aware of the modern consensus that they did not speak contemporary Romance than were poets, lawyers, or the fifth-century grammarians; the crucial evidence has effectively been narrowed to the testimony of the grammarians of 500-770 A.D. If they cannot be shown to demonstrate the existence of the two norms at that time, the suggestion that Early Romance alone existed then can surely be resisted no more.

### The Evidence of Grammarians, 500-770

Most grammatical training from 400 to 800 A.D. was based on the works of Aelius Donatus, written in the mid fourth century, and his subsequent commentators (Keil 1864: 353-402; Holtz 1981). Donatus was giving instruction on how to compose acceptable written works to a community for which Imperial Latin was the vernacular, already known, and consequently he hardly mentions pronunciation. These works were the basis of education in the four following centuries and beyond, but can hardly have been of much practical use to anyone wishing to teach old-fashioned pronunciation to Romance-speaking pupils. If the distinction between Latin and Romance speech existed at all between the Roman and Carolingian empires, it would have been likely to be reflected, consciously or unconsciously, in the works composed by grammarians of that period; in particular, in Cassiodorus of Vivarium (Italy), Isidore of Seville, and Julian of Toledo, who, unlike Bede and the insular grammarians, were writing for Romance-speaking clients.

#### Cassiodorus

In 573, apparently at the age of 93, the Italian scholar Cassiodorus (c.480-575) wrote a treatise *De Orthographia* (*PL* LXX 1240-70; Keil VII 143-210. Cp. also Cappuyns 1949; Roger 1905: 175-86; Riché 1962: 204-12). This was intended as a guide to the monks in his scriptorium at Vivarium in the art of manuscript copying, and pays particular attention to the circumstances in which the correction of texts is deemed permissible. It is based on the comments of eight previous authorities, including the first two books of the *Institutiones* of Priscian, which seem to be otherwise unknown in Romance Europe before the late eighth century. *De Orthographia* is an accurate title for this work, since the desire for acceptable spelling is the incentive for producing it, but there are occasional references to pronunciation too.

The pronunciation Cassiodorus implies for himself and his monastic audience seems, so far as we can tell, to be simply that of his time and place. This was not greatly evolved from the imperial vernacular, but there are enough indications to show that he is not prescribing any non-vernacular "literate" pronunciation patterns based on the spelling. For example, in the following case Cassiodorus specifies that the pronunciation and the spelling ought to be different: although *tantus* is, as a matter of ordinary vernacular practice, pronounced with [n], it is, for etymological reasons, to be written *tamtus*:

> *Tamtus* et *quamtus* in medio *m* habere debent, *quam* enim et *tam* est: unde *quamtitas*, *quamtus*, *tamtus*. Nec quosdam moveat, si *n* sonat; jam enim supra docui *n* sonare debere, tametsi in prima scriptura *m* posita sit.          (*PL* 1245C; Keil VII 152.3-5)

Similarly, he explains that although, as another matter of simple vernacular fact, the final written *-m* before a word-initial vowel represents no sound, it is to be written even so:

> igitur si duo verba conjugantur, quorum prius *m* consonantem novissimam habeat, posterius a vocalibus incipiat, *m* consonans perscribitur quidem; caeterum in enuntiando durum et barbarum sonat.          (*PL* 1243B; Keil VII 147.27 – 148.2)

This prescription is reiterated more baldly later (*PL* 1267C; Keil VII 206.17-18): "*M* litteram, ad vocales primo loco in verbis positas si accesserit, non enuntiabimus."

Much of the *De Orthographia* (*PL* 1252D – 1263A; Keil VII 167-199) concerns the prescriptions of Adamantius Martyrius regarding when to write *b* and when to write *v*. The implication of the tone adopted is unmistakably that with some words neither Cassiodorus nor the scribes to whom the instructions are directed can see any phonetic distinction correlated with this orthographic distinction. The problems over when to write *h* are discussed in a similar manner (*PL* 1263A – 1265A; Keil VII 199-202). Where there may be cases of possible alternative pronunciations as well as possible alternative spellings, current practice (*consuetudo*) is the arbiter: concerning *maximus* or *maxumus*,

> melius tamen est, et ad enuntiandum, et ad scribendum, *i* litteram pro *u* ponere, in quod iam consuetudo inclinavit.
>           (*PL* 1244D; Keil VII 150.16-17)

The current normal pronunciation determines the spelling:

> quando autem fiant, quando non, sono internoscemus: *accedo* duo *cc*, *attuli* duo *tt* . . . in his non solum propter lenitatem [levitatem: Keil] consonantes mutantur, sed etiam quod nullo modo sonare *d* littera potest. Ubi sonat, et ibi scribitur [est ubi sonet et ubi scribatur: Keil], cum *f* consonanti adjungitur; ut *adfluo*, *adfui*, *adfectus*; contra *b* non sonat, *offui*, *offero*, *offendo*.
>           (*PL* 1245B; Keil VII 151.13-17)

This is a simple statement that in the speech of his time there is a [d] – or, more probably, an unvoiced [t], in the event – in such *-df-* compounds as *adfui*, but not in *accedo* or *attuli*; nor is there a [b] in *offui*. This is fully compatible with reconstructable evidence of sixth-century Italian Romance, although [df] became [f] or [ff] over the next three centuries. Phonetic factors make it plausible for [bf] (or [pf]), two labials, [dt], two dentals, and [dk], dental plus velar, to simplify earlier than the [df] cluster.

In his preface, Cassiodorus discusses *pronuntiatio*. This does not, however, mean "pronunciation", for which his term is *enuntiatio*, and the verb *enuntio*. *Pronuntiatio* refers to the manner of delivery, as it had done for centuries (e.g. in Cicero, *De Inventione* I vii 9: "pronuntiatio est ex rerum et verborum dignitate vocis et corporis moderatio"). This is the requirement to make a reading aloud intelligible through appropriate intonation, speed and pauses:

> ... ut quae incipis bene discere, ad finem perfectionis inoffensa debeas pronuntiatione perducere. Nam si vobis adsit capiendi desiderium, quae prius per moram quaesistis, protinus inoffensa velocitate transcurretis. Gloriosum profecto studium ... quod loqui debeas, competenter scribere; et quae scripta sunt, sine aliqua erroris ambiguitate proferre.
>
> (*PL* 1241C; Keil VII 145.3-8)

> illud etiam vos magnopere credidi commonendos, ut distinctiones sensuum sollicita mente perquirere ac ponere debeatis, sine quibus neque legere quidquam competenter neque intelligere praevalemus.
>
> (*PL* 1242A; Keil VII 145.28-30)

The following section concerns pauses, *distinctiones, seu posituras*. These remarks on *pronuntiatio* concern the natural good habits to adopt when reading aloud; how to make the texts intelligible, by competent presentation of the ordinary pronunciation, but not how to make it "Latinate" rather than Romance. If the two norms did coexist here, it is strange that Cassiodorus' comments include no reflection of their possible confusion; reinforcement of the "Latin" version would have required considerably more precise specification than Cassiodorus gives it.

There are further indications that Cassiodorus and his audience used their own vernacular in his *Institutiones Divinarum et Saecularium Litterarum* (Mynors 1937; *PL* LXX 1105-50). For example, he mentioned *euphonia* in *Inst. Div. Litt.* xv 9 (*PL* 1129A), but as Cappuyns pointed out (1949: col.1405), "he is not only thinking of particular spellings, grammatical forms or syntactic arrangements, but of whole phrases whose function is merely decorative". This Chapter xv is entitled *Sub qua cautela relegi debeant coelestis auctoritas*, and concerns the appropriateness of emending scriptural or patristic works that appear to have been wrongly copied. For example (xv 9):

> In verbis quae accusativis et ablativis praepositionibus serviunt, situm motumque diligenter observa, quoniam librarii grammaticae

artis expertes ibi maxime probantur errare. Nam si *m* litteram
inconvenienter addas aut demas, dictio tota confusa est.

(*PL* 1128C)

This last remark is not a reference to any prescribed Latinate
pronunciation, but a reference to the morphological confusion that can
be caused by wrongly transcribing or failing to transcribe the final -*m*
that distinguishes in writing between the accusative and the ablative
case of many nouns, with the result that the reader may be unable to
understand the expression (*dictio*) concerned. This seems to confirm
that even the educated no longer naturally use the old case system or
pronounce anything corresponding to the accusative -*m*, and that they
regard the letter *m* at the end of a noun as a written signposting device
to indicate the syntactic relationships of nouns rather than the representation of a live phonetic entity. In general, discrepancies between
speech and spelling can be taken in native speakers' stride. The forms
preferred *respectu euphoniae* or *propter euphoniam* are the respectably
Classical compounds *illuminatio, irrisio, immutabilis, impius, improbus*,
and *quicquam*; orthographic practice is prescribed to suit normal pronunciation, "ne articulatae vocis pulchra modulatio, peregrinis litteris
maculata, absona potius et indecora reddatur" (1129A). The final consonants of *in* and *quid* had a potentially destructive psychological
validity, and an overanxious monk might have caused confusion by
writing *inrisio* when he and his audience naturally said [ir-].

Neither this Chapter xv, nor Chapter xxiv, *Quo studio scriptura
sancta cum expositoribus legenda sit*, nor Chapter xxx, *De antiquariis
et commemoratione orthographiae* (in which he apparently refers to an
earlier, now lost, *De Orthographia* of his own), suggest that Cassiodorus
was aware of the existence of regular phonetic differences between the
speech of his monks and that of their secular neighbours. On the
contrary, it seems that they used the vernacular of their time and place.
Cassiodorus is simply reinforcing the traditional spelling requirements
in a community who might be tempted by their vernacular to cut
corners. If he tells them to be sure to write the -*m* on *solem*, that is
equivalent to telling modern typists not to miss the *k* off *knife*; it does
not imply that anyone pronounced [m] then or pronounces [k] now.

Gaul appears not to have harboured many sixth-century grammarians. Indeed, Caesarius, bishop of Arles from 502 to 542, makes it
clear that it was hard work encouraging literacy at all. His sermon *De
Adsiduitate Legendi* is an attempt to promote the knowledge of reading
and writing in general, including the reading of sacred works, with no
hint that a specialised pronunciation is required to do so. As regards the

reading of lessons from the Old Testament, Caesarius prescribes that the reader should make the points as intelligibly as possible for the assembled congregation (Morin 1953: sermons VIII, I 41-45 and LXXXIX, I 865-69). This would be impractical in sixth-century France if the reading pronunciation were Latinate, as Lot (1931) pointed out. The congregation would not have understood.

In the seventh century, attention turns to Spain.

### *Isidore of Seville*

Modern histories of Medieval Europe tend to regard the sixth and seventh centuries as a dismal low point in European culture. This can only come from a deep-rooted and apparently long-standing instinct on the part of modern historians that Spain is not part of Europe. Latinists seem to feel the same; Mohrmann, for example, is merely one of many modern medieval Latinists to have devoted almost no attention at all to Spain.

The Visigothic Renaissance in Spain of the late sixth and seventh centuries was a constructive revival of Latin culture in a Christian context. Spanish scholars of the age appear as the epitome of cheerfulness in comparison with writers further north-east. The Byzantine Empire touched the Mediterranean edge of the Peninsula until 629, and much of the North African coast until the Moslems came; the cultural contexts this involved may have been of the North African Latin heritage rather than anything particularly Byzantine (see Scudieri 1959). Gothic was almost certainly not spoken by the seventh century, and both Goths and Romans consciously wished to preserve the old Roman culture (Wallace-Hadrill 1967: chap.6).

The most important representative of this Renaissance is Isidore, bishop of Seville and then archbishop of Toledo (c.560-636). In retrospect, his great work, *Etymologiae, sive Origines* (Lindsay 1962), has been cast in the rôle of a hinge between Classical and European Medieval culture; at the time Isidore was naturally unaware of the future use to which his work was to be put, and was concentrating on collecting as much of the knowledge and practice of Classical civilisation as he could for the benefit of his contemporaries. Until Fontaine's book (1959), Isidore's work was not normally seen in context, partly because the context was not easy to assess. It is probable, however, that the school system of the Roman Empire cannot have lasted between the early fifth and the mid sixth century in anything more than a rudimentary form. Díaz y Díaz pointed out (1976a: 23) that in the late sixth century there was nobody in the diocese of Cartagena who met the educational standards for ordination laid down by the Pope, Gregory the Great. Isidore and the other scholars of the age were not, it seems, the last outcrop of the old system, but a new generation positively keen to salvage and restore much of the old culture that was largely unavailable in Spain. This included the study and discussion of available grammarians; as Riché said (1962: 305), "the superiority of Visigothic Latin over Merovingian can only be explained as the result of a serious study of the grammarians". In a general sense, Isidore is the most "Latinate" scholar between the Roman and Carolingian Empires, although, as Rodríguez Pantoja (1974) made clear, Fontaine and Lindsay greatly overestimated the Latinity of his orthography. For present purposes, his work is worth choosing for detailed examination.

*a) The Differentiae*

In Isidore's work there are several different kinds of evidence concerning the nature of his own speech and that of his community. His first remarks of a linguistic nature were in the *Differentiae* (*PL* LXXXIII 9-97), of which the first half, *De differentiis verborum*, is a work in the traditional genre that included, for example, the *Orthographia* of Caper (2nd century) and the brief imitation by Agroecius (5th century) (Keil VII 92-105). This is a list of 610 pairs, or occasionally trios, of words whose meaning needs to be differentiated. Usually the ambiguity is the result of semantic contiguity, e.g.:

313.   Inter *inquirere* et *quaerere*. Inquirimus ea de quibus dubitamus, quaerimus ignota.
426.   Inter *pigritiam* et *torporem*. Torpor dormitantis est, pigritia vigilantis.
594.   Inter *vocem* et *sonum*. Vox est hominis, sonus crepidinis.

Occasionally, however, the ambiguity is the result of phonetic indistinctiveness of two words whose meaning could not be confused, e.g.:

593.   Inter *vae* et *ve*. Ve sine *a* conjunctio conjunctiva est. Vae cum *a*, interjectio dolentis est.
602.   Inter *vivit* et *bibit*. Vivit de vita, bibit de potione.

If Isidore did not himself join in the reconstructable Romance Spanish pronunciations of his time, in which *vae* and *ve*, *vivit* and *bibit* could have represented the same sound sequences, it is hard to see why these distinctions needed to be made. Such examples as these, implying homonymy, are sometimes repeated in his *Origines* I 27.

*b) Origines I*

The first chapter of Isidore's *Origines* is a grammar, based largely on the African commentaries on Donatus. As Fontaine showed

(1959: Part I chaps.2, 6), this is not in arrangement a work of pedagogical intent; Isidore gives the impression that his readers already
know the language under discussion. The most didactic section is the
brief chapter on *orthographia* (I 27), mostly concerned with orthographical distinctions between homonyms, in the manner of the *Differentiae*. The fact that most of his examples are taken from elsewhere
led Fontaine to conclude, sadly, that this work cannot be used as
evidence for dialectal traits of Southern Spanish pronunciation. Even
so, it is clear from the examples he chooses that Isidore pronounces
vernacular homonyms homonymously, regardless of orthographical
distinctions.

> nam sicut ars tractat de partium declinatione, ita orthographia
> de scribendi peritia, utputa *ad*, cum est praepositio, *d* litteram;
> cum est coniunctio, *t* litteram accipit. *Haud*, quando adverbium
> est negandi, *d* littera terminatur et aspiratur in capite; quando
> autem coniunctio disiunctiva est, per *t* litteram sine aspiratione
> scribitur.                                              (I 27.12)

These are old precepts. *At* and *ad* appear in *Differentiae*; Isidore
probably took them from Cassiodorus (*PL* 1246C-D; Keil VII 154.13-
16 and *PL* 1249A; Keil VII 158.20-22; cp. Lehmann 1913), who took
them from Velius Longus (Keil VII 69.20-24) and Papirianus. But the
fact that the examples are taken from elsewhere cannot be taken to
mean that he does not regard them as relevant, for it is his practice to
use his sources constructively rather than merely copy them. His
phrasing here suggests that he sees [ad] and [awd] as one word each; in
the first case, if it means "to" it is spelt with a *d*, if it means "but" it is
spelt with a *t*; in the second, if it means "not" it is spelt with a *d* and
an *h* (*aspiratur* always refers to the letter, not the sound), if it means
"or" it is spelt with a *t* and no *h*. Neither Isidore nor the scribes he is
addressing seem to make a phonetic distinction here. There are five
other similar examples concerning *-t* and *-d*, such as:

> *id* pronomen neutri generis per *d* scribitur, ab eo quod est *is, ea*,
> *id*, quia facit *idem*. Quod si verbum est tertiae personae, per *t*
> notabitur, ab eo quod est *eo, is, it*, quia facit *itur*.     (I 27.12)

Other distinctions that we can most logically assume are orthographic alone include that between *ae* and *e*. *Laetus* (I 27.14), for
example, is said to need the written *a* because of an etymological
connection between *laetitia* and *latitudo*[3]. The original [ai], *ae*, and
"short" [e], *e*, had been indistinguishable in vernacular for several

---

3. Jiménez (1961: 484), shows that the scribe of the León MS spells it *letitia* here
   anyway.

centuries. Concerning -*s*- and -*ns*-, where the [n] had dropped long since in ordinary speech, Isidore regards the *n* as a "silent" letter; *formosus*, he says, "sine *n* scribitur, quia a forma vocatur" (I 27.9), taking the example from Cassiodorus (*PL* 1250A; Keil VII 160.12-15) but adding his own reason. He also takes over Cassiodorus' mention of an *m* in *tamtus*, etc. (see above), but rephrases it into the past tense with *habebant* (I 27.25).

This chapter (I 27) deals with spelling alone. Isidore is not concerned to prescribe pronunciation; his audience can do that naturally in any case, it seems, and Isidore feels no need to reinforce or even mention any distinction such as that postulated by modern scholars between his own supposedly "Latin" speech and the Romance of the majority of the community. For example, Fontaine said (1959: 93) that Isidore was "combating the mistakes of a spoken language in full evolution"; but there is no evidence for this hostility other than Fontaine's assumption that Isidore must have been hostile. Such evidence as there is is to the contrary. For example:

> nam cum *iustitia* sonum *z* littera exprimat, tamen, quia Latinum est, per *t* scribendum est. Sic *militia*, *malitia*, *nequitia*, et cetera similia.     (I 27.28)

*Z* was a Greek written letter, representing [ts] or [dz]; early Romance developed this sound in such words as *malitia* (> Spanish *maleza*), although original Imperial Latin had no such affricates, and the letter *z* was quite often used. Isidore disapproves of that spelling, not because it represents an unacceptable sound — he concedes that it is indeed a 'z' sound — but on the historical grounds that these are not Greek words. The example of *iustitia*, but not this reasoning, probably comes from Q. Papirius (Keil VII 216,8-14). Isidore is later to use the *z* himself in a famous passage (e.g. Fontaine 1959: 92 n.3; Kramer 1976: 72): "solent itali dicere *ozie* pro hodie" (XX 9.4). This is reconstructably simple Proto-Romance; Italian had affricated [-dj-] (e.g. HODIE > Modern *oggi*) and Spanish had not (HODIE > *hoy*), whereas both affricated [-tj-] as in MALITIA. It also seems certain that he used the prothetic [e-] on words beginning with [s] plus a consonant, for he later gives etymologies for *scurra* ("jester" or "parasite") and *scarus* (a kind of sea-fish) based on *esca* ("bait", or simply "food"). The first of these is even catalogued alphabetically under the letter I:

> *iscurra* vocatur quia causa escae quempiam consectatur     (X 152)
> *escarus* dictus eo quod solus escam ruminare perhibetur(XII 6.30)

It would be hard to find clearer indications that Isidore did not himself use a systematically archaic pronunciation norm. He hardly mentions phonetics; Fontaine was right to point out that "unlike an authentic grammarian such as Varro, Isidore hardly bothers with methodical or objective comments on phonetics itself" (1959: 112). This can only be because it is of no great interest to him. It is fair to conjecture that had there been a systematic duality of phonetic norms, his voracious intellectual curiosity would probably have led him to mention it in considerable detail.

In I 32, Isidore discusses *Barbarismus*.

> Barbarismus est verbum corrupta littera vel sono enuntiatum. Littera, ut *floriet*, dum *florebit* dicere oporteat; sono, si pro media syllaba prima producatur, ut *latebrae, tenebrae*. Appellatus autem *barbarismus* a barbaris gentibus, dum latinae orationis integritatem nescirent.                                           (I 32.1)

This is substratum theory. Barbarisms are mistakes committed by non-native Romance speakers when learning to speak *latina oratio*; although it might seem at first sight that Isidore is defending "correct Latin" against Romance, he is not, for *latina* is never opposed to "Romance" in Spain and the features criticized are not Proto-Romance at all. The particular examples of I 32.1 are not particularly illuminating. *Floriet* for *florebit* is, to the eyes of a modern linguist, a morphological rather than a pronunciation "mistake" — using the normal -IRE future form, instead of the -ĒRE, for FLORĒRE. The Modern Italian is *fiorire*; yet the later Spanish is not *florir* but *florecer*, and the Proto-Romance future of the seventh century was in any event formed from the infinitive and HABEO (e.g. DARE HABES > Sp. *darás*), so the castigated form is not likely to have been a native Romance one. The mistaken conjugation of FLOREO is thus the opposite of the contemporary liturgical use of CAPĒRE and FUGIRE mentioned above, which are both acceptable and Old Romance. *Latebrae* and *tenebrae* are examples taken from Donatus. In Imperial Latin these words apparently had alternative pronunciations: *tĕnĕbrae ~ tĕnébrae, lătĕbrae ~ lătébrae*. The source of Spanish *tinieblas* is presumably the non-Classical *TENÉ-BRAE, since the [je] diphthong arises from a stressed "short" [ɛ]. *Producatur* is probably used here to refer to stress; the use of *pro*, "instead of," suggests this, in that words can have only one stress, but any number of long vowels. If so, the barbarism is unacceptable in seventh-century Spanish, but would not have been in Imperial Latin (*tĕnebrae*). If Isidore is referring to length here, [teːn-] would indeed have been a barbarism in any kind of Latin; but Isidore tends to use for "short" and "long" *brevis* and *longus*, as in the following section, which reflects traditional preoccupations:

Pronuntiatione autem fit in temporibus, tonis, aspirationibus et reliquis quae sequuntur. Per tempora quippe fit barbarismus, si pro longa syllaba brevis ponatur, aut pro brevi longa. Per tonos, si accentus in alia syllaba commutetur. Per aspirationem, si adiciatur *h* littera ubi non debet aut detrahatur ubi esse oportet. Per hiatum, quotiens in pronuntiatione scinditur versus antequam conpleatur, sive quotiens vocalis vocalem sequitur, ut *Musae Aonides*. Fit barbarismus et per motacismos, [iotacismos] et labdacismos. Motacismus est, quotiens *m* litteram vocalis sequitur, ut *bonum aurum, iustum amicum*; sed hoc vitium aut suspensione *m* litterae, aut detractione vitamus. Iotacismus est, quotiens in iota littera duplicatur sonus ut *Troia, Maia*; ubi earum litterarum adeo exilis erit pronuntiatio, ut unum iota, non duo sonare videantur. Labdacismus est, si pro una *l* duo pronuntientur, ut Afri faciunt, sicut *colloquium* pro *conloquium*; vel quotiens unam *l* exilius, duo largius proferimus.        (I 32.3-8)

The *barbarismi* include the use of hiatus rather than elision in, e.g. *Musae Aonides* – a "barbarism" apparently committed in contemporary hymns, but, as we know, the hymn-singing style can legitimate avoidance of such surface constraints –, and the pronunciation of [m] in e.g. *bonum aurum*, neither of which can have been normal seventh-century Spanish usage; the reinforcement of the [j] sound in e.g. *Maia* is incorrect old Spanish (but correct Old Tuscan: MAIUM > Sp. *mayo*, MAIUS > Ital. *maggio*), and the pronunciation of a double [ll] in e.g. *conloquium*, "as Africans do," is not correct old Spanish either (CONLOQUIUM > *coloquio*); so the barbarisms castigated are all, in fact, reconstructably unacceptable as attempts at the vernacular. In a later summary (I 34.2) Isidore's example of *barbarismus* is "ut si tertiam syllabam quis producat in *ignoscere*"; this may refer to either stress-shift or vowel-closing or both (IGNÓSCĔRE > IGNOSCĒRE), and is in modern eyes another morphological reanalysis rather than a phonetic change. This might be Proto-Romance; IGNOSCERE does not survive, but this shift is reconstructable for COGNOSCERE (> *conocer*). Apart from this morphological example, Isidore does not castigate Old Romance as the wrong pronunciation. Had there been two norms, surely Isidore of Seville, if anyone, would have used the "Latin" and mentioned evolved *vitia* as to be avoided; but the evidence is that he did not, and that he spoke in vernacular pronunciation. Fontaine is surely wrong to suggest that Isidore was "combating" the vernacular speech of his community.

## c) De Lectoribus

Isidore's *De Ecclesiasticis Officiis* II 11 (*PL* LXXXIII: 791-92), entitled *De lectoribus*, deals with the proper manner of reading aloud the word of God. He mentions in detail the care for proper audibility, accurate intonation, appropriate pauses, as Cassiodorus had before him; there is no hint at all that a special non-vernacular pronunciation is involved here, as it was later in Carolingian times. Nothing phonetic is thought relevant. The chapter is here reproduced in full:

## CAPUT XI
### De lectoribus

1.    Lectorum ordo formam et initium a prophetis accepit. Sunt igitur lectores qui verbum Dei praedicant, quibus dicitur: *Clama, ne cesses, quasi tuba exalta vocem tuam (Isai.* LVIII). Isti quippe, dum ordinantur, primum de eorum conversatione episcopus verbum facit ad populum. Deinde coram plebe tradit eis Codicem apicum divinorum ad Dei verbum annuntiandum.

2.    Qui autem ad hujusmodi provehitur gradum, iste erit doctrina et libris imbutus, sensuumque ac verborum scientia perornatus, ita ut in distinctionibus sententiarum intelligat ubi finiatur junctura, ubi adhuc pendet oratio, ubi sententia extrema claudatur. Sicque expeditus vim pronuntiationis tenebit, ut ad intellectum omnium mentes sensusque promoveat, discernendo genera pronuntiationum, atque exprimendo sententiarum proprius affectus, modo indicantis voce, modo dolentis, modo increpantis, modo exhortantis, sive his similia secundum genera propriae pronuntiationis.

3.    In quo maxime illa ambigua sententiarum adhibenda cognitio est. Multa enim sunt in Scripturis, quae nisi proprio modo pronuntientur, in contrariam recidunt sententiam, sicuti est: *Quis accusabit adversus electos Dei? Deus, qui justificat (Rom.* VIII 33. 34)? Quod si quasi confirmative, non servato genere pronuntiationis suae, dicatur, magna perversitas oritur. Sic ergo pronuntiandum est, ac si diceret: *Deusne qui justificat?* ut subaudiatur *non*.

4.    Necesse est ergo in tantis rebus scientiae ingenium, quo proprie singula, convenienterque pronuntientur. Propterea et accentuum vim oportet scire lectorem, ut noverit, in qua syllaba vox protendatur pronuntiantis. Plerumque enim imperiti lectores in verborum accentibus errant, et solent irridere nos imperitiae hi qui videntur habere notitiam, detrahentes, et jurantes penitus nescire quod dicimus.

5.    Porro vox lectoris simplex erit, et clara, et ad omne pronuntiationis genus accommodata, plena succo virili, agrestem, et subrusticum effugiens sonum, non humilis, nec adeo sublimis, non fracta, vel tenera, nihilque femineum sonans, neque cum motu corporis, sed tantummodo cum gravitatis specie. Auribus enim et cordi consulere debet lector, non oculis, ne potius ex seipso spectatores magis quam auditores faciat. Vetus opinio est lectores pronuntiandi causa praecipuam curam vocis habuisse, ut exaudiri in tumultu possent. Unde et dudum lectores praecones vel proclamatores vocabantur.

Section 4 deals with the need for accurate stress-positioning on unfamiliar vocabulary, but does not discuss the phonetics. (*Subrusticus* is "boorish" or "frivolous".) Neither this chapter, nor Chapter I 10 *De lectionibus*, nor any other chapter of the *De Ecclesiasticis Officiis*, mentions or hints at any need to use an official archaic pronunciation rather than vernacular. Isidore was the most educated scholar of his age, keen to preserve the old culture, but his remarks give little weight to the modern assumption that the church of his time is supposed to have preserved archaic speech.

### d) Isidore's Comments on Linguistic Variety

This reticence on phonetic matters is not the result of linguistic insensitivity on Isidore's part. On the contrary, he has many comments to make in the *Origines* concerning varieties of speech (cp. Sofer 1930). For example, Isidore is sometimes concerned to distinguish present-day usage from that of the past. The relevant word used here is often *veteres*: e.g.

> Erat enim apud veteres hoc signum meretriciae vestis, nunc in
> Hispania honestatis                                     (XIX 25.5)
> Portus . . . hunc veteres a baiolandis mercibus baias vocabant.
>                                                          (XIV 8.40)

*Veteres* take a past tense. So, usually, do *Romani*:

> Ideo autem Romani aquam et ignem interdicebant quibusdam
> damnatis.                                                (V 27.38)

On one occasion, *Romani* take a present tense, but since it is exemplified by a quotation from Horace (*Carmen* III 18.1) this present can only be a historic present (VIII 11.103-04). *Romani* and *veteres* have usages that do not survive. The words *Latini*, *Latine* and *Latina lingua* are usually used with much wider reference, contrasting Latin-Romance to other languages entirely. (Occasionally Isidore takes over another scholar's reference to *Latina* as the speech of Latium: see below.) This was evident in the already quoted comment on the causes of *barbarismus* (see above). The other language to which *Latina* is contrasted is often Greek:

> Phlomos, quam Latini herbam lucernarem vocant    (XVII 9.73)
> Strychnos, quae Latine herba salutaris vocatur    (XVII 9.78)
> Chronica . . . Hieronymus presbyter in Latinam linguam convertit.
> Χρόνος enim Graece, Latine tempus interpretatur.    (V 28.1)

These words continued to have the wide meaning, of the Latin-Romance tongue as opposed to other languages entirely, in Moslem Spain, where *Latinus* is often contrasted specifically to Arabic, and means the vernacular old Spanish (see Chapter 4); Christians in Moslem Spain were educated in the Visigothic tradition, and this meaning for *latinus* is part of it. Thus it is that, within the *Origines*, the *vulgus* can be said to speak *Latine*:

> Framea ... quam vulgo spatam vocant ... alii spatam Latine autumant dictam eo quod spatiosa sit ...     (XVIII 6.3-4)

Within the speech of his own time, Isidore is aware of national differences of vocabulary.

> Toles Gallica lingua dicuntur, quas vulgo per diminutionem tusillas vocant     (XI 1.57)
>
> Tucos, quos Hispani ciculos vocant     (XII 7.67)
>
> Unde et eos Hispani et Galli tautanos vocant.     (XVIII 7.7)

His only apparent comments on contemporary geographical variation in phonetics are the previously mentioned remarks on African *colloquium* (I 32.8) and Italian *ozie* (XX 9.4); otherwise, the examples are of vocabulary alone. Within Spain, he mentions the particular usages of his native province:

> Actus quadratus ... hunc Baetici arapennem dicunt     (XV 15.4)
>
> Actum provinciae Baeticae rustici acnuam vocant.     (XV 15.5)

On other occasions, Isidore discusses variation without being specific about who chooses which words; *multi* say this, *alii* that, *quidam* the other:

> Molochinia ... quam alii molocinam, alii malvellam vocant.
>
>                                        (XIX 22.12)

*Vulgus* is a key term for present purposes. Isidore defines *vulgus*: "vulgus est passim inhabitans multitudo, quasi quisque quo vult" (IX 4.6). This seems clear enough: "everyone and anyone". The usage of the *vulgus* is often adduced; with one exception it is given a present tense. The exception is based on a remark in Pliny's *Natural History* XXXIII 12.40, *viriolae Celtice dicuntur* ("bracelets"), which is by Isidore's time no longer normal: "Armillae ... Unde et quondam vulgo viriolae dicebantur" (XIX 31.16). Such uses with a present synthetic passive are usually taken from a source.

If *vulgus* is the subject, it often takes a plural verb:

> Palumbes ... quas vulgus titos vocant.     (XII 7.62)

Occasionally it takes a singular verb:

> Regiones ... quas vulgus conventus vocat.     (XIV 5.21)

And occasionally *vulgo* appears adverbially with a general third person plural:

> Abactor ... quem vulgo abigeium vocant.     (X 14)

In all grammatical circumstances, *vulgus* is most naturally taken to mean "everyone here and now", referring to the normal usage of Isidore's time and place; it is not used to contrast any "Vulgar Latin" with anything else contemporary. Isidore uses *vulgus* vocabulary himself, without apparent self-consciousness: e.g. the words *lunaticos* and *burgos* are said to be used by the *vulgus*, but are also used by Isidore elsewhere:

Epilemsia . . . hos etiam vulgus lunaticos vocant    (IV 7.5-6)

Caducus a cadendo dictus. Idem et lunaticus, eo quod certo lunae tempore patiatur    (X 61)

Crebra per limites habitacula constituta burgos vulgo vocant
(IX 2.99; also IX 4.28)

Burdigalim appellatam ferunt quod Burgos Gallos primum colonos habuerit.    (XV 1.64)

The following passage is particularly indicative:

Solidum nuncupatum, quia nihil illi deesse videtur; solidum enim veteres integrum dicebant . . . hunc, ut diximus, vulgus aureum solidum vocant.    (XVI 25.14)

In this case, a previous remark without the word *vulgus* ("solidum nuncupatum") is taken up again ("ut diximus, vulgus aureum solidum vocant") in such a way as to imply that the unspecified agent of such a generic passive as *nuncupatum* is understood to be the *vulgus*.

Isidore's use of the first person plural suggests that he too is happy to use terms the *vulgus* use. The following remarks come in successive sections:

Poderis est sacerdotalis linea . . . quam vulgo camisiam vocant
(XIX 21.1)

Camisias vocari quod in his dormimus in camis, id est in stratis nostris.    (XIX 22.29)

There is often no obvious difference in meaning or tone between Isidore's use of *vulgus* and of the first person plural:

Lactuca agrestis est quam serraliam nominamus, quod dorsum eius in modum serrae est    (XVII 10.11)
(SERRALIAM became Spanish *cerraja*, "sow-thistle".)

Viticella herba a Latinis appellata quod . . . adprehendat corymbis, quos anulos appellamus.    (XVII 9.92)

The majority of cases in which the *vulgus* are specified involve a lexical usage not normally attested in the old texts that Isidore has inherited. The number of occasions in which the *vulgus* form is said to have unacceptable pronunciation is very few; on all such occasions the word *vulgus* is accompanied by either the word *imprudens* or the word *corrupte*, and it is simple to see that the undesirable phonetic element is referred to with the *imprudens* or the *corrupte* rather than with the *vulgus*:

Corus . . . quem plerique Argesten dicunt, non ut imprudens vulgus Agrestem    (XIII 11.10)

Rhododendron, quod corrupte vulgo lorandrum vocatur

(XVII 7.54)

(or, according to other manuscripts, *Rodandarum, rodandarus, lorandeum, laurandus, laurandrum*; Sofer 1930: 99)

Citocacia vocata quod ventrem cito depurgat; quam vulgus corrupte citocociam vocant                               (XVII 9.65)

(or, according to other manuscripts, *viticociam, citociam,* or *cito-cacium*; Sofer 1930: 53)

Sagma, quae corrupte vulgo salma dicitur.              (XX 16.5)

Such imprudence and corruption can occur without it being specifically attributed to the *vulgus*:

Gubellum corrupte a globo dictum per diminutionem, quasi globellum.                                              (XIX 29.6)

On two occasions Isidore allies his own usage with the *corrupte* form:

Phaselus est navigium quem nos corrupte baselum dicimus

(XIX 1.17)

Propina Graeco sermo est, quae apud nos corrupte popina dicitur.

(XV 2.42)

On the other hand, there are no occasions on which a *vulgo* usage, without *corrupte* or *imprudens*, is contrasted with a phonetic variant of the same word rather than with a different lexical item. The following is a morphological variant, not a mispronunciation:

Capitulum est quod vulgo capitulare dicunt.            (XIX 31.3)

In general, however, Isidore is only concerned to mention variations in items of vocabulary (cp. Rabanal 1970: 189). Items that are ascribed to the *vulgus* seem to be unashamedly part of his own repertoire, and such ascription in itself is not intended to imply anything at all of a phonetic nature. The words of the *vulgus* are regularly said to be so because they are seventh-century usage, and not authoritatively attested ancient forms (see Sofer 1937); these forms of seventh-century Spanish are thus indeed contrasted to the "Classical Latin", but to the Latin of the distant past rather than to the usage of a contemporary learnèd élite.

In IX 1 Isidore briefly discusses languages. His entire comment on Latin is as follows:

Latinas autem linguas quattuor esse quidam dixerunt, id est Priscam, Latinam, Romanam, Mixtam. Prisca est, quam vetustissimi Italiae sub Iano et Saturno sunt usi, incondita, ut se habent carmina Saliorum. Latina, quam sub Latino et regibus Tusci et ceteri in Latio sunt locuti, ex qua fuerunt duodecim tabulae scriptae. Romana, quae post reges exactos a populo Romano coepta est, qua Naevius, Plautus, Ennius, Vergilius poetae, et ex oratoribus Gracchus et Cato et Cicero vel ceteri effuderunt. Mixta, quae post imperium latius promotum simul cum moribus

et hominibus in Romanam civitatem inrupit, integritatem verbi
per soloecismos et barbarismos corrumpens.          (IX 1.6-7)

There are four divisions of "Latinae linguae", viewed as a temporal progression. *Prisca* is the pre-historical. *Latina*, used in the narrow
sense, is that of Latium. *Romana* comes after the expulsion of the
Kings. Finally, *mixta* dates from the days of the empire, and a more
cosmopolitan speech community. Fortunately, Isidore has just previously defined the word *mixta* for us in the context of Greek, where it
is the translation of κοινή: "κοινή, id est mixta, sive communis quae
omnes utuntur"; a common language used by all, opposed here neither
to high-class language, nor to archaic language, but to the regional
Greek forms, Attic, Doric, Ionic and Aeolic (IX 1.5). As regards Isidore's comments on Latin, this cannot be interpreted to mean that
Isidore was so keen to avoid regional usage that he used a distinct
Latinate κοινή; nor can it be interpreted as Maurer interprets it (1962:
96 n.143), apparently unaware of the previously explained Greek
model, to mean that *mixta* is "Vulgar Latin" coexisting with a conceptually separate "Classical Latin" from imperial times; it is clear that
all regional varieties come under the one general heading of the one
common language in use for at least five centuries, called *Latina mixta*
precisely because it incorporates diversity and variety within it, and
specifically stated to be *later* than the other kinds of Latin, rather than
still coexisting with anything more respectable. Isidore himself certainly
regards himself as speaking the language of the community that he is in:

Cum autem omnium linguarum scientia difficilis sit cuiquam,
nemo tamen tam desidiosus est ut in sua gente positus suae gentis
linguam nesciat.                                   (IX 1.10)

"Noone is so feeble that he cannot speak the language of his own
community." It is surely preferable to conclude that Isidore also speaks
and uses the language of his time and place.

*e) Vulgus and Rustici*

The reconstructionists cannot claim to reconstruct most of the
vocabulary of seventh-century Spanish, on the basis of thirteenth-
century Spanish, as accurately as they claim to be able to reconstruct
the phonology in its essential features. Vocabulary comes and goes.
Often, the words said to belong to the *vulgus* in the *Origines* can be
postulated as probably existing in the Romance of seventh-century
Spain, on the basis of the later developed form's existence: e.g.

| | | |
|---|---|---|
| COLOMELLOS | > Sp. *colmillos* | (XI 1.52, "tusks") |
| IRICIUM | > Sp. *erizo* | (XII 6.57, "hedgehog") |
| FURCA | > Sp. *horca* | (V 27.34, "gallows") |

| SARNAM | > Sp. *sarna* | (IV 8.6, "impetigo") |
| SUILLOS | > Sp. *sollos* | (XII 6.12, "sturgeon") |

But other words said to belong to the *vulgus* seem subsequently to have died out, as vocabulary often does. The following have no Romance descendants (according to Meyer-Lübke 1935, at least): RASILIS (XIX 22.23), REPTOS (XIX 23.4), SCOTICA (V 27.15), STINCUM (XVII 9.43), etc. But in addition, as Sofer stressed, there are many non-Classical words used by Isidore himself, without being specifically attributed to the *vulgus*, which a reconstructionist would like to postulate as existing in the ordinary vernacular of his time. This causes neither surprise nor problems if we can admit that Isidore is writing his own seventh-century vernacular anyway. For example, the following words are the etyma for subsequent Spanish developments:

| CATENATUM | > Sp. *candado* | (XX 13.4, "lock") |
| INCINCTA | > Sp. *encinta* | (X 151, "pregnant") |
| MERENDA | > Sp. *merienda* | (XX 1.12, "afternoon snack") |
| PROSTRARE | > Sp. *postrar* (XVIII 42.2, XVIII 56, "prostrate") |
| TIUS | > Sp. *tío* | (IX 6.15, "uncle") |

There are several conclusions to be drawn from this. One concerns the practice of etymological dictionaries. If Isidore and the other Visigothic scholars are writing their own language, and that is the language of the *vulgus*, then the earliest attestation of a word in vernacular can be attributed to these writers. Corominas' etymological dictionary (1954-57) occasionally mentions Isidore (e.g. in his article on *tío*), but eventually it can be the only sensible course to admit that words consistently used in the vernacular were consistently used in the vernacular, rather than pretending that they suddenly spring to life at exactly the same time as the spelling reforms that make them intelligible, or at least recognizable, to a modern Spaniard. (Some studies, such as that on *jerigonza* by Moralejo 1978, have in fact recently used Visigothic evidence.) A second conclusion might be a mild caveat against trusting the reconstructionist techniques too implicitly; they are at best partial. It can be seen that some of the vocabulary attributed by Isidore to the *vulgus* did not survive until the thirteenth century; therefore it looks as if that section of the vocabulary which can be reconstructed for seventh-century vernacular, on the basis of its earlier imperial origin and of its existence in an evolved form in the thirteenth century, is only a part of the whole. It may thus be that the reconstructed very old Spanish phonology as envisaged by R.A. Hall, and others, is only partial; phonetic features can arise and then disappear, changes can begin and then reverse without trace, never to be reflected on paper. The reconstructed phonology is too neat and tidy to be realistic: it is at best skeletal.

*Rustici* in Isidore means "country people": "Rusticus dictus quod rus operetur, id est terram", X 239. Isidore mentions "rustic" nomenclature for wine terms (XVII 5.7 and 9), sticks (XX 13.2 and V 27.16), trees (XVII 7.66) and plants (XVII 11.9). The word regularly has a non-linguistic application, as in the titles of book XVII, *De rebus rusticis* (On Agriculture), section XV.12, *De aedificiis rusticis*, and section XX 14, *De instrumentis rusticis*. *Rustica* seems to have become a semi-technical linguistic term for "uneducated speech" (as contrasted with the new Church Latin) two centuries later and several hundred miles to the north-east, in the Carolingian scholarly circle, but this fact is no more relevant to the study of Isidore than is the specialized use of a word by Goethe to the study of a word with the same etymological root in Shakespeare. (*Hortulani* are similarly invoked for the terminology of irrigation in XX 15.3.) The post-Carolingian use of *rusticus* to mean "non-Latinate" unreformed natural vernacular can be seen, for example, in the famous mention of *rustica romana lingua* in 813 (see Chapter 3). The semantic ground is prepared for this development by such previous comments as those of Gregory of Tours (*MGH Scriptorum* I 1.31.14):

Philosophantem rhetorem intellegunt pauci, loquentem rusticum multi

(in his preface to the *Historia Francorum* — referring to his own style); in this the *rusticum* is still literally a countryman, but his talk is the object of interest; or the comment in Marculf's preface to his formulary (*MGH Legum* V 37.15):

Iuxta simplicitate et rusticitate meae naturae . . . ita scripsi

which refers to writing. Here the usage is metaphorical, "unpolishedness", as in Quintilian's contrast of *rusticitas* with *urbanitas* (*Inst. Or.* VII 3.17), for a real *rusticus* would not write at all. With *rusticus*, a change of meaning in time and place can be seen, from "rustic-boorish" to "Romance", and it is over-simple to talk of the meaning of *rusticus* in Medieval Latin, tout court.

*Vulgus*, on the other hand, means "everyone at the time and place concerned". It is all the more worth avoiding the pejorative and contrastive implications of the term "Vulgar Latin" when the word *vulgus* itself had no such implications.

*Julian of Toledo*

Isidore died in 636. During the rest of the century the educational systems and habits that he had helped to spread became
institutionalized, and the educational level of at least the ecclesiastical
élite remained high. There is a considerable corpus of linguistically
competent metric verse, church councils, liturgical texts and historical
material that survives. It used to be thought, on no evidence (see Collins
1977), that the intellectual level of the community was already in considerable decline at the time of the Moslem invasion of 711; political
instability can be accompanied by intellectual advance, however, and
the atmosphere of knowledge and intellectual life established in the
early seventh century continues with sufficient impetus and vigour for
Toledo, Córdoba, Catalonia, the Rioja and the Asturian court to carry
forward a recognizably Visigothic cultural tradition in the decades
following the Moslem invasion. In addition, Visigothic texts and
scholars are of considerable influence in the eighth-century cultural
expansion of both the British Isles and France.

Of Isidore's Spanish successors, only Julian of Toledo seems to
have been involved in the composition of an *Ars Grammatica* (c.685;
Maestre Yenes 1973; not in Hillgarth 1976). Beeson stated that "in
writing a school book on grammar, metric and rhetoric, Julian is simply
following in the footsteps of the compiler of the *Origines*" (1924: 50).
This is inaccurate. In the first place, it seems likely that the written
compilation was made from lecture-notes by a pupil or pupils of Julian,
although Maestre Yenes graciously permits us to call it Julian's *Ars* even
so (1973: XVIII n.23); more importantly, this work is quite unlike the
*Origines*. It is in the catechetical question-and-answer mode of the
traditional teaching manual, lacking the philosophical and cultural air
adopted by Isidore; although Julian takes material from Isidore, its
form is based on Donatus' *Ars Minor* and on his African commentators.
They are operating in different contexts. Isidore was working, initially
at least, in an age when schools were not common. Either he, or
possibly his contemporary Juan de Bíclaro, trained Braulio de Zaragoza,
whom Díaz y Díaz called "the best informed man in Visigothic Spain"
(1976a: 32). Braulio in turn was able to impart sufficient knowledge
of quantitative metrics to Eugenio de Toledo, the archbishop whose
poems are the most technically competent of the time; and Eugenio
taught Julian. Julian was thus learning and then teaching within a semi-
institutionalized atmosphere that had established a continuity over
several decades. By his time there were several educational centres
functioning in the peninsula, usually in the form of an eminent scholar

accompanied by several students. Isidore's *Origines* would not have been at all wieldy as a practical textbook for linguistic instruction. Fontaine (1959: 192-94) suggested that Pompeius' commentary on Donatus was the one Isidore himself learnt from, but even if that is so, there seems to have been a lack of a practical textbook felt by Julian in his own language classes at Toledo's episcopal school. For example, Maestre's study of his chapter on punctuation (1973: LII-LV) led her to see it as the result of Julian's concern for "live and direct teaching."

Julian's technique seems to have been normally to take the text of Donatus, with commentaries, and the remarks of Isidore if applicable, and then add something of his own, such as examples from Christian poetry (Beeson 1924: 53-55). The only sections not based on Donatus are the metrical chapters at the end, based largely on Mallius Theodorus, and the immediately preceding sections concerning the length of final syllables, which may descend from Marius Victorinus (Maestre 1973: XXXII) and are designed to aid the proper organization of the metric verse. At the least this shows that people could not be expected to know the length difference without being told. The rationale of the distinction is not presented in phonetic terms at all: e.g.

> Verbum quod *a* terminatur, longum est, aut breve? In omnibus modis, numeris, personis, temporibus, coniugationibus, si *a* fuerit terminatus longus est, ut *ama*                    (II V 1)

In the main body of the grammar, Julian shows no interest in instilling a "correct" pronunciation into the pupils at the Toledo school; he makes even less mention of phonetics than Pompeius did. Here, for example, are the opening comments on vowels:

> Quot sunt litterae vocales? quinque.
> Quae? *a, e, i, o, u.*
> Semper vocales sunt? *a, e* et *o* semper vocales sunt, *i* et *u* varias habent conexiones.
> Quomodo? quia modo vocales sunt, modo transeunt in consonantium potestatem, modo inter se geminantur, modo cum aliis vocalibus iunguntur, modo mediae sunt, modo *u* inter *q* et aliquam vocalem posita nec vocalis, nec consonans habetur, modo *u* per digammon adscribitur quando sibi ipsa praeponitur, modo *i* inter duas vocales posita in unam partem orationis pro duabus consonantibus accipitur.                    (Maestre 1973: II I 6)
> (Cp. Donatus, Keil IV 367.12-20; Sergius, Keil IV 520.31 – 522. 12; Pompeius, Keil V 102.19 – 103.6.)

This is a description of the uses of the written letters *i* and *u*. *Geminantur*, for example, refers not to phonetic gemination but to such consonant plus vowel sequences as *deiicit, revulsum*. The sections that follow also prescribe traditional orthographic practice. There is, in short, no evidence that Julian is concerned to train people to utter "Latin" rather than vernacular pronunciation, nor that he did that himself.

Julian is well educated. Other scholars of his age are also well educated. Valerio del Bierzo, for example, is a competent and prolific scholar; Aherne (1949: 34) made it clear that the stylistic achievements of his work are "evidence of no little skill in their author, and argue a rather elaborate education" (cp. the discussion of Visigothic prose style in Garvin 1946). Valerio shares with his contemporaries a delight in prose rhyme and rhythmic cursus. Julian regarded rhythmic verse as undignified: "rithmis uti, quod plebegis est solitum ex toto refugiat" (see Bischoff 1959); in his grammar, Julian declared: "Quid est rhythmus? Verborum modulata compositio, non metrica ratione sed in numero ad iudicium aurium examinata, utputa velut sunt cantica vulgarium poetarum ... rhythmus modulatio sine ratione" (II XX 4-5; further discussed in chapter 4; Bischoff 1959: 254). The written skills in poetry and prose were taught and learnt, as we can see from the surviving grammars and commentaries. But the grammars and commentaries used in Visigothic Spain have nothing to say about learnèd and erudite pronunciation. There is no support here for any belief that the Visigothic scholars used a Latinate non-vernacular pronunciation, and good reason to presume that they did not.

### Bede and the Insular Tradition

Julian's grammar has not survived in any Spanish manuscript. It is still thought probable that Aldhelm used Julian in a letter to the King of Northumbria (c.700); this is plausible, since there is evidence that Aldhelm was aware of Visigothic scholarship (Winterbottom 1977). Bede (673-735) uses Julian as a source in his *De Schematibus et Tropis* (Beeson 1924: 56; Maestre Yenes 1973: C); both Isidore and Julian seem to have been taken on board in the British Isles, and of both authors the earliest manuscripts are in an insular hand. In general, Visigothic scholarship was part of the intellectual equipment of the Insular scholars (Hillgarth 1958, 1962).

The Irish and Anglo-Saxon monks wanted and needed works that could help them learn and teach the use of the normal working language of their church. They were working in quite a different context from that of Donatus, his commentators, Cassiodorus, Isidore or Julian; these latter could assume that their audience were native speakers of some variety of Late Latin/Early Romance, but Aldhelm, Bede, Boniface and Tatwine (etc.) were hoping to train native speakers of some variety of Germanic. Latin-Romance did not last into the sixth century in the islands as a spoken language, and subsequently everything had to be taught from scratch.

There are Irish Latin texts that pre-date the Gothic connection, but they strike Latinists as being very peculiar (e.g. Riché 1962: 357-59; Löfstedt 1965). The glee with which the Irish scholars fell on grammatical works can be explained by the previously precarious domination that they had had of this language that was so very different from their own. Hillgarth established that the route from Spain to Northumbria proceeded via Ireland, as early as the seventh century (1962: 174), carrying Biblical commentaries, liturgical books and grammatical works.

As Blair pointed out (1970: 244), "When Bede made his first approach to Latin, he did so as to a wholly foreign language, unlike his contemporaries in the schools of the more southerly countries where Latin still remained the living spoken tongue, and perhaps it was this distinction which led not only Bede himself, when he came to be the teacher, but also other English scholars, to compile their own grammatical treatises" (cp. Riché 1962: 436-37; Roger 1905: chaps. 8-11). No existing textbook had been elaborated with non-native speakers in mind. Pronunciation was not given an important rôle in the Anglo-Saxon treatises either, however; Tatwine's *Ars* helps the foreigner with its practical inclusion of much vocabulary, but has nothing on pronunciation (De Marco 1968). Even so, there can be no doubt that the learning of Latin in eighth-century England did involve reading it aloud, or reciting from memory, even if it did not involve spontaneous conversations in the language. The Bible and the works of the Holy Fathers were read aloud regularly in monastic communities. Ceolfrith, Bede's teacher, recited the Psalter twice every day (Blair 1970: 255).

Ceolfrith had been to Rome. Benedict Biscop went to Rome between 671 and 684, returning with some manuscripts, including a Vulgate. There was an English community in Rome in the eighth century, and at least one Italian came to England to teach church music. This seems to have involved the *cantor* singing from a text and the others learning it by heart. The evidence is so thin that we cannot tell whether the pronunciation of the sung words was simple eighth-century Roman Italian or not, but in church song, as we have seen, the music had (and has) a distorting effect on phonetics. In general, though, it could be that the pronunciation taught to at least some of the Saxons was of an Italianate tinge. This cannot be taken to be the norm, however. Alcuin was happy, for example, to continue the native insular tradition of composing alliterative verse involving alliteration of *ca-* and *ce-* (e.g. *care* and *certo*; Norberg 1958: 52). Bede alliterated *celsa* with *caritas*. There is the alliterative Irish chant which includes the phrase *et clara caeli celsi culmina*. The Irish never assonated written Latin *i* and *e*, nor *o* and *u*, as was normal practice in Romance areas. Norberg also mentions the insular ability to alliterate *f* and *v* (1958: 51), as in *flamine* and *versus*, *verba* and *fudit*; no Romance speech has ever merged these two sounds in initial position. This confusion is a feature of German Latin for some time, and has one echo in Alcuin's *De Orthographia*:

> *Vel* si coniunctio est, per *v*; si humorem significat, per *f*; si idolum,
> per *b* scribendum est                                    (*PL* CI 918C)

If there was some Italianate influence in Anglo-Saxon Latin pronunciation, it did not get very ingrained. In general it seems that in order to teach Latin pronunciation to Anglo-Saxon students, a rule of thumb was based, faute de mieux, on some kind of correspondence between written letters and subsequent spoken sounds. No native language is ever learnt in this manner; in the Romance communities everyone learnt automatically to speak their local vernacular when young, and then learnt to spell the old-fashioned "correct" way several years later, if at all. The reverse applied in England, where the pronounced form was taught as a function of the already learnt traditional spelling, regardless of the habits of faraway native speakers. (Occasionally people learn English in this manner nowadays, pronouncing *would* as [would], *your* as [jour], etc. They are quite unintelligible, even if fluent.) As a consequence, although Isidore pronounced *haud* and *aut*, *at* and *ad*, etc., as homonyms, Bede probably did not.

The only text on pronunciation which circulated in Britain in the eighth century was the following passage from Martianus Capella (III 261; Dick 1969: 95.14 – 96.16), which was copied and recopied independently of the *De Nuptiis* itself, and attributed to various authors (Law 1982):

> Namque A sub hiatu oris congruo solo spiritu memoramus.
> B labris per spiritus impetum reclusis edicimus.
> C molaribus super linguae extrema appulsis exprimitur.
> D appulsu linguae circa superiores dentes innascitur.
> E spiritus facit lingua paululum pressiore.
> F dentes labrum inferius deprimentes.
> G spiritus cum palato.
> H contractis paululum faucibus ventus exhalat.
> I spiritus prope dentibus pressis.
> K faucibus palatoque formatur.
> L lingua palatoque dulcescit.

M labris imprimitur.
N lingua dentibus appulsa collidit.
O rotundi oris spiritu comparatur.
P labris spiritus erumpit.
Q appulsu palati ore restricto.
R spiritum lingua crispante corraditur.
S sibilum facit dentibus verberatis.
T appulsu linguae dentibusque impulsis excutitur.
V ore constricto labrisque prominulis exhibetur.
X quicquid C atque S formavit exsibilat.
Y appressis labris spirituque procedit.
Z vero idcirco Appius Claudius detestatur, quod dentes
  mortui, dum exprimitur, imitatur.

This list could have been used as a teaching aid for novice Latinists; something similar probably underlies Alcuin's instincts as eventually propounded for Carolingian students. Without accompanying demonstrations these prescriptions would have been insufficient to specify the exact sound.

Bede's own *De Orthographia* (Jones and King 1975: 7-57), unlike earlier works of the same name, deals with much more than spelling. It used to be regarded as a very early work (e.g. by Blair 1970: 248-50), but as its most recent editor points out (Jones 1975: X-XI) it is in form a random collection of pedagogical notes filed under the letters of the alphabet, derived from very many sources, and almost certainly, in its surviving form, the fruit of many years' practical experience. Some of the specifications are indeed orthographical; e.g.

Aeger animo, aegrotus corpore; utrumque per *ae* diphthongon
scribendum                                                    (9.45-46)

Grammatical comments are more numerous; e.g.

Psallo perfectum facit psallui                                (45.936)

There are many semantic distinctions made on the lines of Isidore's *Differentiae* (which is one of the sources):

Caerulus naturae color est, caeruleus fingitur; ita alterum est,
alterum fit                                                   (16.229-30)

The comment in Isidore's *Differentiae* I 154 (*PL* LXXXIII 26):

Inter *deportare*, *comportare* et *exportare*. Deportare est aliquid
afferre, comportare in unum locum conferre, exportare tollere,

is rephrased as

Adportare est aliquid adferre; conportare in unum locum conferre; deportare, deponere; exportare, tollere.              (12.126-27)

As these examples show, Bede is not merely the passive compiler of other people's aperçus. He includes and rephrases anything that experience suggests might be useful in Latin classes, being prepared to

rephrase, and in particular abbreviate, when he sees fit. Even so, pronunciation does not seem to appear to Bede to be a matter of much
significance. The discussions of Romance homonyms such as *ad* and *at*,
carefully distinguished in both the *Differentiae* and the *Origines*, leave
Bede cold; *ad* is mentioned only in the context of a semantic distinction from *in* (10.74-78). *Origines* I 27 has little interest for Bede,
despite being entitled *De orthographia*: only one comment seems to be
taken verbatim, from I 27.19:

> Pene, quod est coniunctio, per *e*; poena, quod est supplicium, per
> *oe*                                                         (44.912-13)

*Recte dicere* is not applied to the manner of pronunciation:

> Alvus virorum recte dicitur; uterus mulierum; venter in utroque
> sexo                                                        (12.136-37)

Indeed *dicere* can specifically mean "write":

> Caseus masculini generis est, sed Pomponius neutraliter dixit,
> *caseum molle*                                             (15.200-01)

Sometimes, however, *dicere* does mean "say":

> Sollemne cum dicis sive scribis, *m* sequenti syllabae conectis.
> Somnium similiter.                                         (49.1056-57)

Jones notes no source for this: perhaps it came from the Italian connection, since church usage may have been the only context in which
syllable division was relevant. Similarly:

> Maiestas, cum scribis aut dicis, *s* secundae syllabae complicari
> debet. Sic in similibus                                    (35.685-86)

The source is: "Si maiestas scribis, *stas* in diductione vocis esse debet,
non *tas*" (Caper; Keil VII 96.11). Latin was read and recited, almost
certainly on a rough basis of one sound per already written letter, but
phonetic detail does not worry Bede.

Bede also composed a *De Arte Metrica* (Jones and King 1975:
81-141). King said of this (74) that "only now are we beginning to
realize how skilfully and intelligently Bede shaped the exhausted
heritage of the past to meet the new requirements of the early medieval
monastic community." The implication that the earlier Spanish writers
were not meeting the needs of their own community is extraordinary,
but the recognition of Bede's practicality is refreshing. Palmer (1959)
commented that the *De Arte Metrica* is a practical classroom tool, a
critical synthesis. This down-to-earth approach made his a standard
course book all over Europe, becoming, for example, the normal
metrical manual at Ripoll in Catalonia (Nicolau 1920: 3). Bede's *De
Orthographia* is, similarly, practically pedagogical; and the language
taught was not in this case any variety of the contemporary vernacular
of the recipient community, but an artifical text-based construction.

Bede taught Egbert of York, who taught Aelbert, who taught Alcuin. A tradition of education became established in eighth-century Britain, and unlike that of the seventh-century Spaniards, hampered by the Moslem invasions, the Anglo-Saxon tradition expanded and grew into the foundation of much of later educational practice. Alcuin of York was taught an Anglo-Saxon tradition of Latin pronunciation, divorced from any Romance community, but regarded as normal and acceptable in York. In the late eighth century Alcuin seems to have succeeded in conversing in Italy, where the vernacular was not hopelessly unlike his own usage, but it is quite understandable that the pronunciation he met in Northern France should have taken him aback. The French of Northern France had evolved considerably more; Alcuin's practice, based on a unit of sound for each unit of spelling, was quite unlike the vernacular of the Romance-speakers in the Carolingian realms. Here for the first time, the artificial and, in fact, archaic pronunciation of the Anglo-Saxons did coexist with vernacular in the same place.

Alcuin had grown up in a community in which this artificial "Latin" and the vernacular were self-evidently different languages. Anglo-Saxon was obviously not the written Church language of Latin. In previous Romance communities, however, the modern postulation of a similar distinction can only be a mirage and an anachronism. There is no need to postulate that both existed in Romance areas before Alcuin's arrival at the Carolingian court; since the evidence is consistent with the absence of such a distinction, it seems rational to regard the postulation of a "Latin" coexisting with Romance in Romance communities as a simple misconception of now outdated scholarship. With Alcuin's arrival in France, the stage is set for the imposition of the Anglo-Saxon style of reading aloud on the European ecclesiastical education systems; in short, for the invention of "Medieval Latin."

Mohrmann nearly realized this: "Thus for the first time, among the Irish and Anglo-Saxons, that symbiosis is found of Latin as the language of the Church, of education and of higher culture, with the vernacular as the language of everyday life . . . this Irish-Anglo-Saxon culture, which was the first to assign to Latin a place alongside the vernacular . . ." (1961c: 166). If she had only followed this remark up in the context of pre-Carolingian philology, or if only Romance philologists took more interest in the nature of their primary document sources (Late Latin), much misconceived argument could have been avoided. But now we can at last admit that in earlier centuries the grammarians, scholars, lawyers, poets and bishops spoke their own vernacular. As one would expect.

# 3
## CAROLINGIAN FRANCE:
## THE INVENTION OF MEDIEVAL LATIN

A great deal has been written about the Carolingian "Renaissance". Much of this scholarship has concentrated on the revival of interest in Classical culture, but this was merely one by-product of a wider reconstruction; in McKitterick's words (1977: xx), "Carolingian rule meant a consolidation, a reform, and a positive attempt at the re-shaping of society within a Christian framework ... the whole of society was to be taught and a Christian society created." This did not imply universal education, but it did necessitate a regenerated educational system for members of the Church. In the end, the re-shaping of European society was to take a few more centuries, but part of the foundation for the intellectual life of the later Middle Ages rests on the establishment of professional education for clerics in the early 800s; and that education rested on the international standard language we now know as "Medieval Latin", learnt for and used in official contexts by the Carolingian Church.

### Standard Delivery of the Liturgy
Liturgical standardization seemed a necessity. By the eighth century there had arisen considerable variety in liturgical practice throughout Europe. In Merovingian Gaul, where Christianity had in any event a weak hold, there were the "Gallican" rites. When Pepin began the attempt to revive the intellectual life of his realms, he introduced features of the Roman rites, intended in time to become the normal usage. The extension of Papal practice into Gaul became a part of Charlemagne's policy for the reorganization of his church in the late eighth century, and in 787 the Roman rite was decreed to be the standard (McKitterick 1977: chap.4). The introduction of Roman

elements had in the event led to less uniformity, as bishops in different areas chose to mix Gallican and Roman features in different ways, so a need for a standard usage seemed as pressing as ever. The problem was not immediately solved by the decree of 787, mainly because the *Hadrianum*, the supposedly authoritative book sent to Charlemagne by the Pope in 781, was deficient in a number of ways. The task of producing acceptable liturgical texts, which could become the official versions, was entrusted to Alcuin; the English church had a good reputation for preserving well the Roman traditions, so Anglo-Saxon scholars seemed suitable for this purpose (Bullough 1973b).

The whole Bible needed a standard edition. This need was particularly pressing for the Gospels and the Psalms, much used in liturgy (Ganshof 1947). This in turn required correct spelling; so at the same time as Alcuin was preparing his Vulgate, he compiled a *De Ortho-graphia*. In the performance of the liturgy, the standard text, however well spelt, would not produce the required uniformity of excellence over all the Empire without some kind of decreed method for the manner of reading the texts aloud. The decreed method for reading aloud was not based on any Old French vernacular, but on the method Alcuin had learnt himself; each letter on the page had to be given a sound, and that sound was specified (as in lists such as that from Martianus Capella, printed above pp.100-01). This was how Alcuin had learnt to recite Latin, on the basis of the written forms, and this was how his clergy had to read aloud in Church. In the absence of a phonetic script the standard pronunciation could not be unambiguously described on paper, but it is possible to reconstruct most of the details of the original instructions as follows. When reading aloud in Church it is probable that the written letters listed in the left-hand column were to be read aloud as the sounds listed in the right-hand column:

| Written letter | | Sound |
|---|---|---|
| *a* | to be read aloud as | [a] |
| *ae* | | [e] |
| *b* | | [b] |
| *c* | | [k] |
| *d* | | [d] |
| *e* | | [e] |
| *f* | | [f] |
| *g* | | [q] |
| *i* | | [i] in some specified circumstances |
| | | [j] in other specified circumstances |
| *k* | | [k] when found |
| *l* | | [l] |
| *m* | | [m] |

Written letter                          Sound
    *n*    to be read aloud as  [n]
    *o*                        [o]
    *p*                        [p]
    *q*                        [k]
    *r*                        [ɾ]
    *s*                        [s]
    *t*                        [t]
    *u*                        [u] in some specified circumstances
                                       [v] in other specified circumstances
                                     [w] after *a* or *q*

*x* was presumably [ks] (as in Martianus Capella III 261), although Alcuin's *De Orthographia* does not mention it. The above prescriptions were easy enough for Alcuin to prescribe, but the letter *h* was awkward; it looks as if *h-* might have been prescribed [h], and *th*, *rh*, *ph* and *ch* might even have been [th], [ɾh], [ph], [kh] "ut plurimum sonent". This list did not solve every problem that arose — in particular, concerning which syllable in polysyllabic words ought to receive the stress — but it has provided a solid basis for the pronunciation of Latin for the last 1200 years (as well as for phonetic script, as can be seen from the symbols above).

Norberg detailed some of the linguistic consequences of this reform, most pithily in his *Manuel* (1968: 50-53). For example, the prescription that all words spelt with *i* are now pronounced with [i], and all words spelt with *e* are now pronounced with [e], means that rhyme of these written vowels no longer occurs in verse; previously such syllables often could rhyme, as originally short [ĭ] and long [ē] had merged into the one vernacular sound. Similarly, words written with *u* and *o* cease to be found rhyming. Conversely, no distinction is now made in the new Latin between those words spelt with an *e* which was originally short and those with an *e* which was originally long; all have in the new Latin [e], so all could rhyme in later Latin, whereas in previous years vernacular had distinguished the two. Similarly, all words in *o* can now rhyme. These prescriptions also established a distinction between plosive *b* [b] and fricative *v* [v] that was often not there in the vernacular. These particular reforms seem to have been acceptable in recitation, since [i], [e], [o], [u], [v] and [b] existed anyway in the Romance inventory. Words borrowed later from this innovating pronunciation into French testify to the success of the reform; e.g. the [i] in *digne* from DIGNUS, the [u] in *étude* from STUDIUM, the [-b-] in *habile* from HABILIS. The practice of the Anglo-Saxon scholars was successful in these respects, and indeed in the general prescription that every written letter (or digraph such as *ph*) should be given some sound (cp. Allen 1970: 106; Beaulieux 1927). This requirement inspired many long-silent letters into new productive life.

In other respects, the strict prescriptions seem not to have been generally followed. [k] may have been required by Alcuin before [e] and [i] — or it may not, since [tʃ] before a front vowel could well have been an allophone of Anglo-Saxon /k/ as it was of Italian — but a palatalized [tse], [tsi] or [tʃe], [tʃi] seems to have become usual for written *ce, ci*; the same may well have applied to *-ti-* before a vowel (e.g. *rationem* [ɾatsionem]) and to *ɡɜ* and *gi* ([dʒ] rather than [g]). The prescriptions concerning *h* were in any event odd, and the aspirate seems often to have been ignored. (Hence the common spellings of *nichil* and *michi* with *ch* to specify the presence of [h].) Nor was it clear to all how to produce geminate consonants. But on the whole, the introduction of the new reading pronunciation stuck, and ever since then the Latin pronunciation of a word has been a function of its traditional spelling (cp. Lüdtke 1978: 441).

It is worth pausing here to stress how different this prescribed method of production was from contemporary French. For example, VIRIDIARIUM now had six syllables; in Old French *vergier* it had two. FERIT, DIRECTUM, COGNITUM, IACET, etc., became in the new system unrecognizable as vernacular *fiert, dreit, cointe, gist*, etc. At a stroke, much of the vocabulary had become unintelligible to the uninitiated. Were such a reform to be introduced into Modern England or France, words generally pronounced as [ɔɾɪndʒ], [nait], [wɪmɪn], [steiʃən], [pɛ] and [swet] would be unrecognizable in the new system as [orange], [knɪght] or [knɪxt], [women], [station], [paiks] or [paix], and [souhaitent]. There has turned up suddenly the strict distinction between Latin and vernacular pronunciation that scholars have liked to think existed throughout the Middle Ages.

Charlemagne's court was probably bilingual, being more or less on the Romance-Germanic border, although many of its most powerful members came from further east. Some of the German Christians would have met Insular missionaries, and many had already been taught the Anglo-Saxon pronunciation of Latin before encountering vernacular French. The difference between this Latin and that French would have been as noticeable to them as it was to Alcuin, and Alcuin's prescriptions probably coincided in most respects with what native German-speakers tended to do anyway. Nor was Alcuin the only scholar involved in the educational reforms; some of the works once attributed to Alcuin have recently been reallocated to St Benedict of Aniane and Theodulf of Orléans, who were scholars in the Visigothic

Spanish tradition. It is undoubtedly true that the Carolingian Renaissance owed a great deal to the Spanish Renaissance of the 600s, and indeed also to the Italian pair Peter the Deacon (of Pisa) and Paul the Deacon (of Monte Cassino); Peter was for many years the Court authority on grammar, and Peter and Paul each wrote an *Ars Grammatica* in the Donatus tradition. It is almost certain that Peter introduced Priscian's *Institutionum Grammaticarum Libri XVIII* to the Court from Italy; Priscian taught Latin in Constantinople in the sixth century, and his work was known in Italy at least at Vivarium, Monte Cassino and Benevento. Eventually, Priscian became the standard advanced textbook as Donatus continued to be the beginners'; Alcuin studied Priscian avidly in France[1] (mainly, it seems, for information about Greek) (O'Donnell 1976). Yet despite the activities of other scholars of the time, it does seem that Alcuin was the *primum mobile* of the newly decreed pronunciation of Latin, particularly during his time at Tours after leaving the Court in 796; and in this respect a key work, for all that it has been neglected since c.830, is Alcuin's *De Orthographia* (*PL* CI 901-20; Keil VII 295-312; Marsili 1952).

Much of Alcuin's *De Orthographia* is derived from Bede's work of that name; other details are taken from Cassiodorus, Isidore and Priscian (books 1, 5, 7, 8 and 14). This debt to Priscian helps confirm the date of 796-800 usually given to the *De Orthographia*, for Alcuin is known to have been studying Priscian at that time and there is no reason to suppose that he had read the *Institutiones* in detail earlier. Assuming this rough dating to be correct, it thus coincides with the time when Alcuin was based at St Martin of Tours, working on his Vulgate (Ganshof 1947; Fischer 1957); it also coincides with the circular Alcuin drew up for Charlemagne under the heading of *De Litteris Colendis* ("On the necessity of studying *litterae*"). It is thus reasonable to see all these works as manifestations of a desire for linguistic correctness in church.

Alcuin's *De Orthographia* may have been given that title as a result of the general later impression that it was merely a summary of Bede's work of the same name. Jones, for example, said it was "little more than a digest of Bede's" (Jones and King 1975: 2). As I have shown exhaustively elsewhere (Wright 1981), this is not true; there are many entries not in Alcuin that are in Bede, but also vice versa. For example, under the letter A, Bede lists c.68 words and Alcuin c.71, but

---

1. There is no reason to suppose that the "Priscian" mentioned in Alcuin's poem on York was the complete *Institutiones*.

only 20 of the entries coincide, and the statistics are similar throughout. Those chosen from Bede are usually the comments that are relevant to spelling and pronunciation, and even then they are not often transcribed verbatim. This is the key to the constructive use Alcuin made of Bede and of his other scholarly sources; he was particularly concerned with authoritative comments made by established scholars on matters of spelling and pronunciation, and not particularly concerned with anything else. So although Alcuin does not seem to have given the title *De Orthographia* to his work himself, it is at least more accurate than it is as applied to Bede's work. Unfortunately (with the honourable exception of Roger 1905: 343-49) modern scholars have been led by this title not to notice that it also deals with pronunciation. Originally, instead of such a pithy title, Alcuin headed his work with an elegiac couplet:

Me legat antiquas vult qui proferre loquelas
me qui non sequitur vult sene lege loqui.

(Vienna Nationalbibliothek 795; printed by Migne, with *sene* corrected to *sine*, *PL* CI 902D.) The use of *legat, proferre, loquelas* and *loqui* makes it unambiguously clear that at least one of the aims of the work is to have its clients reading aloud in the correct old manner. This heading caught on, being often used in later manuscripts of Priscian[2].

Alcuin's concern for pronunciation in his *De Orthographia* formed the subject of Wright (1981), which will not be recapitulated here. The evidence includes: the fact that Alcuin chooses many remarks from his sources relevant to pronunciation, and most of those not selected are not relevant; the fact that he adds information relevant to pronunciation to many of those chosen remarks; a concern for *euphonia* in a narrowly phonetic sense; prescriptions as to whether written vowel pairs are or are not diphthongs; the implication that the pronunciation is determined by the spelling; the implication that variation in spelling implies a variation in pronunciation; the use of *dicere* to refer specifically to phonetic matters; the similar use of *proferre*, and *legitur*; the assumption that the letter *h* has some consequential effect on the sound, even though Alcuin is not sure what. These interests are new. They are not the concerns of Cassiodorus, Isidore, Bede, or any other earlier grammarian. Alcuin was having to prescribe the "correct" manner of speaking for a clientele already used to reading aloud the same words in a vernacular manner; this was something new, that had to be taught and learnt.

---

2. Marsili (1952) printed a variant: *Me legat antiquas cupiat qui scire loquelas/me spernens loquitur mox sine lege patrum.*

Vienna 795 is an intriguing manuscript, probably compiled in 799, and recently published in a facsimile edition (Unterkircher 1969). Of its 205 folios, folios 21r-150v concern Biblical exegesis, folios 184r-191v concern the geography of Rome, and folios 1v-4v, 150v-183v, 192r-197v contain 20 letters of Alcuin's (including eight to Arno of Salzburg). The folios from 5r to 20v form two separate *quaterniones*, which may have had originally a separate existence before the collation of the MS. Folios 5r-18v contain the *De Orthographia*, headed by the couplet quoted above; folio 19 contains the Greek alphabet, 20r the Runic alphabet and 20v the Gothic. The Greek alphabet is headed by the phrase "FORMAE LITTERARUM SECUNDUM GRECOS"; it is written mostly but not exclusively in capitals, with the equivalent Latin letter on the left (except for O, presumably omitted by mistake), the name of the Greek letter above, the number it represents in Greek mathematics and the equivalent Roman numeral to the right. In addition, there are three number symbols (for 6, 90 and 900) with no alphabetical use, inserted in arithmetical position. It is interesting to note that Latin *e* is said to be the equivalent of both epsilon and eta (spelt *hita*); that *z* is the equivalent of zeta; that theta, spelt *thita*, is said to correspond to *t et h*; that kappa, spelt *cappa*, is said to correspond to *c et q*; that xi causes graphical confusion, but is unhesitatingly for *x*; that tau is spelt *thau*; that upsilon, called *eu vel ui*, is for *y*; that phi, spelt *fi*, is for *f*, even though alpha is spelt *alpha*; that chi, spelt *hi*, is for *h*. This might be taken to help fix what Alcuin and his associates understood by *h* in various positions, although the state of 19r does not inspire total confidence in the competence of the scribe.

19v is even more fascinating. The left hand column contains all the Greek consonants except rho and chi, each with a line to itself in which it is followed successively by $\alpha\iota$, $\epsilon\iota$, $o\iota$ and $oy$ (sic). Above each syllabic group is a Latin alphabetical equivalent, successively with *e, i, y, u*[3]. Thus, for example, l.9 runs as follows:

$$\begin{array}{cccc} ne & ni & ny & nu \\ N\alpha\iota & N\epsilon\iota & No\iota & Noy \end{array}$$

This is presumably interpretable as being the instructions for the correct pronunciation of Greek vowel pairs. At the top right corner of this left hand half of 19v appears this list: ay au, ey eu, ai e, H i·, ei i·, oy u, oi y, $\omega$ o; which is also likely to be prescribing the pronunciation (on the right) of the Greek letters (on the left), even though the left entries are in Latin writing (other than H and $\omega$). What *y* represents in speech

---

3. The one exception (*fe* instead of *fi*, over $\varphi\epsilon\iota$) is presumably a scribal error.

is not at all clear; the *eu vel ui* comment suggests that it could be the front rounded high vowel [y] (as in French *tu*); it is not mentioned in the *De Orthographia*. But the general point, that folio 19 is in part designed for the correct oral reproduction of Greek script, fits the suggestion that these folios are collectively a manual for reading aloud as well as for writing. (The right hand column of 19v deals with compound Greek numbers.) The entries for the Runic and Gothic alphabets (on folio 20) have similar Latin equivalents added above them; the thorn (þ), spelt *ðorn*, is said to represent *ð*, the *wyn* to represent *u u*, for example. The experimental interest shown here in letter-sound correspondences, allied to the contemporary spread of written Germanic (one of the six marginal glosses in the *De Orthographia* is Germanic: *uuonenli*, for *perpes*, 11v), could have proved a useful first step for the elaboration later in the century of a new orthography designed to represent Old French pronunciation.

The novelty of Alcuin's concerns at this time may be referred to (with the words *novas* and *incipiamus*) in a letter Alcuin wrote to Charlemagne in March 798:

> ... quid faciemus de litteris syllabis etiam et verbis, quibus uti nobis necesse est cotidie, nisi novas grammaticae artis regulas excogitare incipiamus?

Alcuin definitely wished the Court to participate in the reform; in a later letter to Charlemagne (799), he comments:

> Ego itaque licet parum proficiens cum Turonica cotidie pugno rusticitate. Vestra vero auctoritas palatinos erudiat pueros, ut elegantissime proferant quicquid vestri sensus lucidissima dictaverit eloquentia.

The "rusticity" of Tours suggests that before Alcuin came they used French rather than the Anglo-Saxon reformed Latin even in this respected cultural centre; the use of *proferant* suggests that pronunciation is uppermost in his mind at this time. The word *rusticitas* is here in the middle of its semantic change from "lack of culture" to "non-Latinity", having both meanings at once. The letter which Alcuin wrote to Arno in 798, when Arno was bishop of Salzburg, starts its final paragraph as follows:

> Nunc velim te properare in patriam et ordinare puerorum lectiones, quis grammaticum discat, quis epistolas et parvos libellos legat, quis sanctam scripturam (*sic*) sobria mente haurire dignus sit. Tu vero, sancte pater, evangelicis maxime studeas lectionibus et canonicis sanctorum scripturarum inservire eruditionibus ...

This letter is included immediately prior to the *De Orthographia* in Vienna 795, and may have been what inspired the composition of the manuscript in 799. Several letters from these years show Alcuin's continual concern with the reform (the word *cotidie* turns up often)[4].

Quintilian declared that grammar was the *recte loquendi scientia*. Isidore agreed: "Grammatica est scientia recte loquendi, et origo et fundamentum liberalium litterarum" (I 5.1). Neither of them seem to have been thinking of pronunciation; the precepts are aimed at the written mode. Alcuin picked up this traditional phrase but, as often, altered it significantly to suit his own context: "Grammatica est litteralis scientia, et est custos recte loquendi et scribendi" (Alcuin's *Grammatica*: *PL* CI 857D). The old phrase used *loquendi* for language in general; Alcuin adds *scribendi*, apparently with the specific intention of distinguishing correct talk from correct writing. The two together, intimately connected in Alcuin's mind, form a single science of *litterae*; the *litteralis scientia*, "knowledge of how to read and write properly", becomes from this time on a fundamental requirement of all educated men, and is based on *litterae* in its simple meaning of "written letters and the sounds with which to read them aloud".[5]

### Standard Education

Alcuin was a serious scholar with a demanding project to carry out from 796 to 800. He would not have wasted time in a mere copying exercise, as is suggested in the usual dismissive approach to his *De Orthographia*; it is, instead, part of his interest in the propagation of correct Latin literacy, *Litterae*. This concern is also attested in the circular known as *De Litteris Colendis*.

In 789 there had been issued an edict known as the *Admonitio Generalis*, concerning the need for education (*MGH Legum* II i 52-62). At some date in the late 790s this was given a supplementary section entitled *De Litteris Colendis*, "On the need to learn *litterae*" (Wallach 1959: 202-04). Wallach showed that Alcuin had an important hand in this; it is roughly contemporary to the *De Orthographia*, and stresses a requirement that had not been spelled out in the same detail in 789 but was much in Alcuin's mind after 796. It begins as follows:

... nos una cum fidelibus nostris consideravimus utile esse ut episcopia et monasteria, nobis Christo propitio ad gubernandum commissa, praeter regularis vitae ordinem atque sanctae religionis

---

4. Alcuin's letters are printed in *MGH Epistolae* IV and in *PL* C. These are *MGH* 145.232.33 – 233.2; 172.285.21-23; 161.260.13-16.
5. In verses ascribed to Theodulf of Orléans and put in the mouth of *Grammatica*, Grammar is seen as a medicine for incorrect *loquelas, oris vitia*: "Pulchra medela fio balbis dum reddo loquelas/Oris enim vitiis sum medicina potens" (*PL* CV 334D).

conversationem etiam in litterarum meditationibus eis qui, do-
nante Domino, discere possunt, secundum unuscuiusque capaci-
tatem docendi studium debeant impendere, qualiter, sicut regularis
norma honestatem morum, ita quoque docendi et discendi in-
stantia ordinet et ornet seriem verborum ut, qui Deo placere
appetunt recte vivendo, ei etiam placere non neglegant recte
loquendo . . .

"We, in company with our *fideles*, have thought it desirable that
bishoprics and monasteries, entrusted to us to be governed by the
Grace of Christ, should emphasize, in addition to the observance
of monastic discipline and the practice of holy religion, the study
of *litterae* for those who by God's grace are able to learn, according to their ability to teach them; for as observance of the
monastic rule preserves purity of behaviour, so in the same way
this perseverance in teaching and learning should direct and embellish the series of words, in order that those who aim to please
God by living correctly should in addition not fail to please him
by speaking correctly . . ."

(translation based on Laistner 1957: 196-97)

The training in the correct life had formed the subject of the
original *Admonitio Generalis*; the concern for *litterae*, "to embellish
the series of words" already written, is the new prescription here. The
intention is to have the clerics, in the traditional phrase, *recte loquendo*
(later: *quamobrem hortamur vos litterarum studia . . . non neglegere*).
In practice, the main requirement of the system advocated, and ex-
tensively put into effect over the following decades, was that the priesthood should be able to read aloud the corrected texts entrusted to
them by the specialist scribes. This is normally a desire for reading
aloud only (see Riché 1973: IV chap.2); the acquisition of the ability
to write is an achievement of a higher order to which the average cleric
would not need to aspire. Reading aloud included chanting; hence the
common connection in texts of succeeding centuries between *legere*
and *cantare*, with masters of both teaching in schools of both reading
and singing. (Later in the *De Litteris Colendis* there are mentioned
*scolasticos bene loquendo . . . in legendo seu cantando*.) The performance of the Church service involved the oral reproduction of
authorized texts. Even the sermons were specified in advance; priests
were not expected to make up their own. So, at first, the practical
requirement involved in the learning of *litterae* was merely the ability
to read texts aloud *in situ* by correctly allotting a sound to every single
previously written letter (or digraph) in accordance with the system
promulgated by Alcuin and his colleagues.

What Alcuin understood by the word *littera* is partly based on

Donatus and Priscian. They had explicitly associated individual *litterae* with particular noises; Alcuin repeats, "litterae est pars minima vocis articulatae" (*PL* CI 855A) ". . . syllabas in litteras dividimus". The etymology Alcuin gives to the word, however, is adapted from that offered by Isidore: "Littera est quasi legitera, quia legentibus iter praebent" (ibid.). "Letters are so called because they show the way to the readers", as indeed they do in the Carolingian system (used ever since). This is not quite what Isidore meant, however:

> usus litterarum repertus est propter memoriam rerum. nam ne oblivione fugiant, litteris alligantur. in tanta enim rerum varietate nec disci audiendo poterant omnia, nec memoria contineri. litterae autem dictae quasi legiterae, quod iter legentibus praestent, vel quod in legendo iterentur.         (*Origines* I 3.2-3)

Isidore's phrasing here is based on Sergius; for them the value of letters (apparently as a collective noun: i.e. = "writing" in general) is as an aid to remembering what might otherwise be forgotten. Alcuin has either misunderstood Isidore, or, more probably, consciously adapted Isidore's words for his own purposes, since he seems to mean that individual letters help the reader to read correctly. As usual, the fact that an eminent scholar used words previously used by another is no indication at all that the two meant the same thing by those words; often, a scholar with something new to say tried to disguise the novelty and pretend to respectability by using authoritative turns of speech to his own ends.

The use of such *litterae* depends closely on both the legibility and the consistency of the written texts to be read. Not only should the words be spelt correctly, but each individual letter had to be immediately recognizable in order to aid the reader. Pre-Carolingian scripts were of at least a dozen varieties; several were cursive, and not all were easy to read even at the time (see Lesne 1938: 379-89; Reynolds and Wilson 1968: 80-82). In addition, manuscript punctuation was eccentric when it existed at all, with words sometimes not divided from each other, or split arbitrarily. Any cursive script would have been awkward for a reader who had to see the separate letters clearly in order to *recte loqui*; it is probably for this reason that the so-called Caroline Minuscule script was adopted, at least for the elaboration of important manuscripts designed to be read in church. In this script each letter was quite small, but separately written as an independent unit, with only a few, well-known, contractions. This script was, it appears, used first in a developed form at Corbie in the 770s; at that time it was one among many. Alcuin seems to have been instrumental in having it widely adopted as a standard practice. His scriptorium at Tours became an important centre for both scribal training and the minuscule script, and the Bible that Alcuin had presented to Charlemagne at his imperial coronation (Christmas, 800) is also an important landmark in the establishment of the Tours script as the official model. By the middle of the ninth century, this script was in general use, for important texts, over all the empire. There was no necessity to use it for other contexts. Bischoff has, for example (according to Bullough 1973b: 585), identified Alcuin's hand in some marginalia in insular style dated to Tours, 797-8. Multiple copies could be made, once the system was established; a *lector* could read letters sound-perfect to several scribes at once, who could then reconvert to letters with professional accuracy (Riché 1973: 246-49). Punctuation begins to be more systematically introduced, both as a semantic aid to reduce possible ambiguity, and as a sophisticated series of phonetic hints for the performers (Parkes 1978; Hubert 1972); Alcuin mentioned the desirability of punctuation in a letter to Charlemagne of 799 (*MGH* 172.285.16-20). Further evidence of a desire for linguistic correctness at this time can be seen, for example, in the rewriting of the Benedictine Rule (Mohrmann 1952), or in the avoidance of non-Classical elements in the official *Annales Regni Francorum* after 796, and the elimination in c.814 of non-Classical vocabulary from the annals for 741-95, originally "written by someone untouched by the Carolingian revival" (Adams 1977b: 258). These dates of 796-800, when Alcuin was at Tours, keep recurring as a time of concern for linguistic accuracy.

The evidence of the *De Litteris Colendis* implies that the new system of *litterae* was intended to be established in centres outside Alcuin's own personal influence as well as at Tours; the extent to which other institutions took notice of the prescriptions is indeterminable. Perhaps it was only Alcuin's immediate circle who took it seriously at first. One of that circle was Bishop Theodulf of Orléans (see McKitterick 1977: 52-57). Theodulf carried out the prescriptions of the *Admonitio Generalis* energetically. In his *Capitula ad Presbyteros Parochiae Suae* (Canon 20) he instructed his clergy to teach *litterae* free of charge to the children of the faithful (*PL* CV 196), "ut scholas ipsi habeant in quibus fidelium parvulos gratis erudiant". Theodulf declared that *grammatica* is the root of all education, as in a picture of a tree where "huius grammatica ingens in radice sedebat" (*PL* CV 333B; *Carmina* IV ii 3). This archdiocese, at least, was doing its duty.

One of Alcuin's pupils was Rabanus Maurus. Rabanus wrote *De Clericorum Institutione* — it is not clear when — of which Book III

Chapter 18 begins as follows:

De arte grammatica, et speciebus eius.

Prima ergo liberalium artium est grammatica, secunda rhetorica, tertia dialectica, quarta arithmetica, quinta geometria, sexta musica, septima astronomia; grammatica enim a litteris nomen accepit, sicut vocabuli illius derivatus sonus ostendit. Diffinitio autem eius talis est: Grammatica est scientia interpretandi poetas atque historicos, et recte scribendi loquendique ratio. Haec et origo et fundamentum est artium liberalium. Hanc itaque scholam Dominicam legere convenit, quia scientia recte loquendi et scribendi ratio in ipsa consistit. Quomodo quis vim vocis articulatae seu litterarum et syllabarum potestatem cognoscit, si non prius per eam id didicit? Aut quomodo pedum, accentuum et positurarum discretionem scit, si non per hanc disciplinam eius scientiam ante percepit? Aut quomodo partium orationis jura, schematum decorem, troporum virtutem, etymologiarum rationem, et orthographiae rectitudinem novit, si non grammaticam artem ante sibi notam fecit? Inculpabiliter enim, imo laudabiliter hanc artem discit, quisquis in ea non inanem pugnam verborum facere diligit, sed rectae locutionis scientiam et scribendi peritiam habere appetit.          (*PL* CVII 395)

"Grammar is the discipline of interpreting poets and historians, and also the rationale of correct writing and speaking; the means of correct speaking and writing. Who would know the value of speech sounds or letters and syllables if they had not first learnt it in *grammatica*?" (After this Rabanus moves on to *tropi*.) Speaking *recte* might in Rabanus' mind have become a technical term, with the meaning it had in Alcuin's *Grammatica* and the *De Litteris Colendis*; Rabanus declares that those who have not studied this kind of *grammatica* are unable to talk correctly[6].

Institutionally, there can be no doubt that schools were eventually established in the Alcuinian tradition. In a few centres, at least, the Carolingian reforms left a lasting mark. The basic ability to read Latin letters as the reformers wished continues. "The educational machine which Charlemagne and Alcuin had set in motion, working through the monastic and Cathedral schools, had sufficient momentum to keep going until a new age could take over ..." (Reynolds and Wilson 1968: 91; cp. Gibson 1975; Bullough 1970). Over the next three centuries, some monastic and episcopal schools suffered depradations from Moslems, Vikings, Magyars or organizational apathy, but Émile

---

6. Rabanus declared in a letter of 814 giving advice on how to read aloud, that "H non littera, sed nota aspirationis esse" (*MGH Epistolae* V 383.33); under any modern definition, *h* was a letter, but *litterae* here are specifically those letters from which sounds are proffered.

Lesne's enormous volume (1940) on *Les écoles de la fin du VIII$^e$ siècle à la fin du XII$^e$* is sufficient to reassure us that "la tradition des institutions scolaires ecclésiastiques a survécu par sa force propre" (443). Lesne also confirms here that all schools in these centuries were dependent on the church (414ff.); that there is an inherent connection between the teaching of *grammatica* and *scholae cantorum* (e.g. 415, 469, 574); and that *grammatica* continued to be the basis of all other disciplines (e.g. 587-93). Grundmann (1958) showed at length how *litteratus* continued to mean "Latinate" rather than "literate" throughout the Middle Ages. There can, in short, be little doubt that the reformed *litterae* remained the ideal; that in at least a few intellectual centres the coexistence of vernacular Romance and Latinate pronunciation is an established fact after the ninth century.

Riché (1973: 254-61) has described what actually occurred in these schools (also Lesne 1940: 572-77; Boussard 1972). The alphabet was an early lesson. It was taught so that the pupils could read aloud; not so that they could write, nor so that they could understand a text, but so that they could recite. "Savoir lire, c'est savoir le latin" (Riché 1973: 257). The initial grammatical primer was Donatus's *Ars Minor*. The teaching was almost all oral in nature, either by recitation of passages or mnemonics or through established question and answer routines; for trainee priests or monks this included the techniques of church recitation. The official standard was thus inevitably encountered by any literate person. Writing was usually only learnt by specialist scribes at a later stage. There were thus many who had learnt to read only, or had taken a short cut by learning by heart selected passages for recitation parrot-fashion, with no ability to write, nor compose speech independently in the artificial non-vernacular manner. (There had survived a comparable tradition of reciting Greek without knowing what it meant.)

Education was mainly, but not exclusively, for members of the church. If laymen wished to learn, they could do so, but only in the clerical schools. Nithard, for example, aristocrat, warrior and grandson of Charlemagne, learnt enough to compose his history on behalf of Charles the Bald. But he was exceptional; the training of priests, monks and choirs had been the initial point of the reform, and so it was to continue. The teaching of "Latin" pronunciation was essentially confined to the church schools; in Norberg's words, "L'histoire du latin médiéval est, en d'autres termes, l'histoire de l'école médiévale" (1977: 63). The teaching of correct written Latin was essentially intended to ensure accuracy in the oral reproduction of the written texts of the gospel, psalter and missal:

> Et ut scolae legentium puerorum fiant. Psalmos, notas, cantus, compotum, grammaticam, per singula monasteria vel episcopia et libros catholicos bene emendate; quia saepe, dum bene aliqui Deum rogare cupiunt, sed per inemendatos libros male rogant. Et pueros vestros non sinite eos vel legendo vel scribendo corrumpere; et si opus est evangelium, psalterium et missale scribere, perfectae aetatis homines scribant cum omni diligentia.
>
> (*Admonitio Generalis* Canon 72)

If there is a risk of God not understanding the supplications made to him, correct spelling and recitation of the texts becomes essential[7].


### Sermons

Once the reformed pronunciation was introduced, the services stopped being intelligible to the congregation. They were no longer the collective celebrations of all the community; the congregation were uncomprehending spectators. The texts to be used were fixed. Their manner of performance was fixed. At first, this may have seemed admirable; when Alcuin died in 804 he may not have realized a worrying practical consequence of the new celebration. This correct but uncomprehended performance was incapable of achieving another of the essential aims of the church: the requirement to preach. Every church instruction of this time stresses how important it was for the clergy to preach. The clergy of the late eighth century, however, could not be trusted to make up their own sermons; if it was essential to preach, it seemed even more essential that the contents of their preaching should be certified in advance. Specific previously written texts were allotted to particular occasions, and priests were forbidden from using their own words:

> ... ut presbyteros quos mittitis per parrochias vestras ad regendum et ad praedicandum per ecclesias populum Deo servientem, ut recte et honeste praedicent: et non sinatis nova vel non canonica aliquos ex suo sensu et non secundum scripturas sacras fingere et praedicare populo.    (*Admonitio Generalis* Canon 82)

The set texts were the homilies of the *patres*, the Fathers of the Church; Saints Gregory, Augustine, Ambrose, Jerome and soon Caesarius of Arles. Of these the most important collection was the *40 Homilies on the Gospel* of Gregory. While at Tours, Alcuin had collected together

---

7. Hohler (1957: 225) grasps this point, but has apparently not heard of the Romance languages; he says that before the reform the texts were "gibberish". In fact it would be the new recitation that sounded incomprehensible to the congregation.

authorized homilies into two large manuscript volumes (Lesne 1938: 147-48). Rabanus Maurus collected many of his own (*PL* CX 13-468; McKitterick 1977: 97-104). One of the headings found in manuscripts of Alcuin's *De Orthographia* points out that those who pronounce in the prescribed manner will talk like the *Patres*, who had written these homilies. Accordingly, at Tours at least, the homilies must at first have been given the "Latin" treatment; they were the last and longest of the group of set passages fixed for recitation during the service. The purpose of the homilies was to improve those who heard them, but that could hardly be achieved if the congregation did not understand them. The reforms had created a problem. At this early time, when it may well only have been the diocese of Tours that was wholeheartedly carrying out Alcuin's prescriptions, it may similarly have been only a problem at Tours.

In 813 the Church held five regional councils, at Arles, Chalon, Mainz, Rheims and Tours, designed to assess the state of the Church at the time and set guidelines for the future establishment of a Christian community (for a full account, see McKitterick 1977: chap.1). The bishoprics based on these five towns cover most of the Empire. Charlemagne did not attend any of them, but he gave them his blessing. The five councils had similar long agendas; they each produced many recommendations (*Canones*), and a composite list of their resolutions was produced (printed in *MGH Legum* III ii 1). Many practical questions were raised, discussed and decided, in a markedly business-like spirit. The fourteenth item in the composite list of decrees concerns the general need to make preaching more intelligible, under the heading of *De officio praedicationis, ut iuxta quod intellegere vulgus possit assiduae* (sic) *fiat*. This wording seems to have been taken from the 25th Canon of the Council of Mainz, . . . *qui verbum Dei praedicet iuxta quod intellegere vulgus possit*. Here, perhaps for the first time, is at last attested the use of *vulgus* to mean "laymen" in specific contrast to the Latinate; a distinction which, as we have seen, was not made before. At Rheims, the same idea was expressed with *omnes*, in Canon 15: *Ut episcopi sermones et omelias sanctorum patrum, prout omnes intellegere possent, secundum proprietatem linguae praedicare studeant*. These requirements are most easily understood to refer to the manner of pronunciation, since the words are fixed and invariant; it is likely that in practice some substitution of vocabulary, or even glossing, could have taken place, but this does not seem to be the intention of these decrees.

The Council of Tours, however, went into this question in more detail. Alcuin was no longer alive, but active followers of his such as

Theodulf were there. Canon 2 of the Council suggests that bishops should learn to recite by heart the gospels, the epistles of St Paul, the works of the *Patres* as far as possible, and *caeteri libri canonici*. Canon 4 suggests that they have a duty both to preach and to set a good example. (Theodulf elaborates this theme in the instructions to his own clerics of c.814: *PL* CV 191-224.) The next 12 and last 34 Canons are on other topics, but Canon 17 returns to the question. This Canon begins with an emphatic introduction stressing that the council members are unanimous; this introduction appears in no other Canon, and its inclusion seems to suggest that the matter in question had been the subject of considerable argument previously in the church at large:

> Visum est unanimitati nostrae, ut quilibet episcopus habeat omelias continentes necessarias ammonitiones, quibus subiecti erudiantur, id est de fide catholica, prout capere possint, de perpetua retributione bonorum et aeterna damnatione malorum, de resurrectione quoque futura et ultimo iudicio et quibus operibus possit promereri beata quibusve excludi. et ut easdem omelias quisque aperte transferre studeat in rusticam Romanam linguam aut Thiotiscam, quo facilius cuncti possint intellegere quae dicuntur.

This canon specifies not only the content and purpose of the essential homilies, but the manner in which they are delivered; the preacher should be sure to switch into *rustica Romana lingua* or German (*Thiotiscam*), so that the congregation can follow. Here the word *rustica* appears in specific contrast to the Latinity of the rest of the Church services[8]. There can be no doubt that this instruction was aimed at exactly the same people who were simultaneously being nagged to use the new "Latin" elsewhere; the novelty of this problem explains why no council in preceding centuries had even mentioned the subject (Riché 1962: 537). It was a new problem, possibly confined to Tours.

I have argued at length (Wright 1981: 355-58) that *transferre* in the usage of the time does not mean "translate" but "transfer"; in linguistic contexts it means "to use metaphorically", as in St Augustine's *translato verbo* and in Donatus himself. Rabanus uses it in the same way in his *De Clericorum Institutione*, chapters VIII, X and XIII. Caelius Sedulius, in the second preface to his combined verse and prose work (*Carmen* and *Opus Paschale*: *PL* XIX 547A-B) in the late fourth

---

8. This use of *rustica* may have been Tours' practice already. There is a famous gloss by Berno of Tours, of the early ninth century; *rates rustice dicitur reth*, which suggests a) that *rustice* refers to non-Latin pronunciation, and b) that *th* indeed represented a fricative [θ] (or possibly [ð]). It was made famous by Savage (1928).

century, said that he composed the verse *Carmen* first and then trans-
ferred it to prose (*in rhetoricum me transferre sermonem*), the later
operation being called *translatio* (*dicentque nonnulli fidem translationis
esse corruptam*). This is unambiguously not a transfer from one
language to another, but from one style to another within the same
language. There is, in short, no justification for assuming that *transferre*
in this 17th Canon necessarily means "translate". Since it appears that
the wording of the text of the authorized homilies was not supposed to
be altered, "translation" is probably the wrong interpretation in
Romance communities such as the Tours bishopric. In Germanic
communities, translation would be necessary, so transferring to *Thio-
tisca* would indeed involve different words and grammar; in Romance
communities, the old method, used anyway before 796, of reading
texts aloud in vernacular pronunciation, was here being reestablished.
The distinction may not be being made here between two separate
languages, Latin and Romance, but between two methods of reading
aloud written texts, the *litteralis* and the *rustica*.

Unfortunately, this picture has been confused by modern philologists. The last part of Canon 17 has been reprinted many times in
their handbooks, often without any explanation at all of the context. It
has been claimed to be conclusive proof of the theory that Latin and
Romance had coexisted as separate distinct spoken norms for centuries;
that the natural speech of the educated had hardly changed for five
hundred years or more, and was thus so far removed from popular
Romance that translation was now necessary (e.g. Hall 1974: 105;
Rickard 1974: 27; etc.). Some of the philological comments seem to
imply that the vernacular was something new, or "emergent". This is
impossible to take seriously. Every community has its own vernacular,
by definition. There is no possible doubt that vernacular existed
through the preceding centuries; what does seem to be new in the early
ninth century is the Latinizing alternative. There is no reason to
suppose that Latin and Romance were thought of as completely
different languages for at least another two centuries. The decision of
philologists to interpret *transferre* as "translate" is merely a consequence of their inbuilt assumptions, and can no longer seriously be
used to support them.

Tours was the only centre to decree the switch in reading styles
in 813. By the middle of the century, most of Alcuin's precepts had become standard practice; the Roman liturgy and Caroline minuscule were
normal usage, Priscian and Donatus were mainstays of an ambitious
educational system firmly based on *litterae*, and the existence in many

areas of Latinizing pronunciation alongside the Romance was accepted. The Council of Mainz in 847 reproduced the 17th Canon of the Council of Tours whole in its second Canon, saying that although the old Canons ought to be prescribed reading for all priests anyway, the Council specifically thought it essential to repeat this one. In total, this Canon runs as follows:

> De dogmate ecclesiastico. cum igitur omnia concilia canonum, qui recipiuntur, sint a sacerdotibus legenda et intellegenda et per ea sit eis vivendum et predicandum, necessarium duximus ut ea, quae ad fidem pertinent et ubi de extirpandis vitiis et plantandis virtutibus scribitur, hoc ab eis crebro legatur et bene intellegatur et in populo praedicetur. et quilibet episcopus habeat omelias continentes necessarias ammonitiones, quibus subiecti erudiantur, id est de fide catholica, prout capere possint, de perpetua retributione bonorum et aeterna damnatione malorum, de resurrectione quoque futura et ultimo iudicio et quibus operibus possit promereri beata quibusve excludi. et ut easdem omelias quisque aperte transferre studeat in rusticam Romanam linguam aut in Thiotiscam quo facilius cuncti possint intellegere quae dicuntur.

Rabanus Maurus was bishop of Mainz at this time and keenly interested in effective preaching; the prescription of the Council of Tours seems by 847 to be accepted practice.

### The Invention of "Romance" Writing

#### a) Oaths

By 847, however, we have already passed the most famous linguistic event of the century; the "Strasbourg Oaths" of 842. These were oaths taken by the Romance-speaking Charles the Bald and the German-speaking Louis the German to cement their agreement against their brother Lothair. They were included by Nithard in his *De Dissensionibus Filiorum Ludovici Pii*, and in recent years have been discussed in minute detail. Ewert (1935) put them into their context in a classic study. He concluded that although the two French and the two German sections are not translations of any surviving Latin passage, they are probably produced from a first draft in Latin; in Elcock's words, "It seems almost to be a Latin consciously vulgarized by adaptation to the most common features in the vernacular of the day, features which were widespread over Northern France" (1975: 351). Elcock may have included the word "almost" in order to prevent the need for the logical next step, that of wondering why the language was "vulgarized" at all, when Latin transcriptions of ordinary speech in historical works were normal practice. In fact, as Elcock points out, Nithard, cousin to the

Princes and chronicler of these events, may well have helped to draft the oaths himself. In any event, the written forms of the oaths were certainly prepared before the oaths were taken rather than being an earwitness account of how they actually sounded. Such oaths would be very carefully scrutinized in detail in advance; in this case, that these texts had to be fixed in advance for subsequent reading aloud becomes clear when we see the strange linguistic character of the sequence of events.

By 842 the official "Latinate" pronunciation of reading aloud was known to the literate. German-speakers of that time could easily have been much more fluent in reading aloud in Latin than they were in French vernacular. It is possible that Louis the German might not have known how to read aloud an oath in French vernacular pronunciation, had he held in his hand a version in traditional Latin orthography. In this situation, where it was essential that the Romance-speakers at Strasbourg should hear and understand exactly what Louis was saying, it is understandable that Nithard, or someone else in the Chancery of Charles the Bald, should have taken the peculiar step of attempting to transcribe what Louis was to say according to the sound-letter correspondences that had become current in the reformed Latin system, but with the sounds to which the written letters corresponded being the sounds of vernacular French rather than those of reformed Latin. Louis must have been able to read, or else the Romance text would be no more help than any other. The text of the Oaths could have been enough to prompt him into a passable rendition of contemporary French, if he produced the sounds he had already learnt to use for written letters.

In short, whereas the Romance Strasbourg Oaths are usually thought to be produced for the benefit of French-speakers inexpert in Latin, I suggest that the evidence points to their being produced for the benefit of a Germanic-speaker who had learnt to read Latin but was not fluent in French.

The scene is solemn. Louis the German-speaker and Charles the Romance-speaker (the first native Romance-speaker in the dynasty) assembled with their respectively German-speaking and Romance-speaking troops. The Princes addressed their own troops in their own language, and the gist of what they said is presented by Nithard in ordinary Latin (transcriptions from Elcock 1975: 346-48)[9]:

9. Most early Romance texts have recently been collected together in Sampson (1980); the Oaths are no.50.

Ergo xvi kal. marcii Lodhuvicus et Karolus in civitate que olim Argentaria vocabatur, nunc autem Strazburg vulgo dicitur, convenerunt et sacramenta que subter notata sunt, Lodhuvicus romana, Karolus vero teudisca lingua, juraverunt. Ac sic, ante sacramentum circumfusam plebem, alter teudisca, alter romana lingua, alloquuti sunt. Lodhuvicus autem, quia major natu, prior exorsus sic coepit:

'Quotiens Lodharius me et hunc fratrem meum, post obitum patris nostri, insectando usque ad internecionem delere conatus sit nostis. Cum autem nec fraternitas nec christianitas nec quodlibet ingenium, salva justicia, ut pax inter nos esset, adjuvare posset, tandem coacti rem ad juditium omnipotentis Dei detulimus, ut suo nutu quid cuique deberetur contenti essemus . . .'

Cumque Karolus haec eadem verba romana lingua perorasset . . .

It is worth noting that *vulgo* at the start here applies to German; Strasbourg is in the Germanic area.

The exact wording of these initial addresses is not of legal or other significance, so there is no need for Nithard to transcribe these verbatim in German and Romance, even if he could. Louis speaks in German, then Charles says *haec eadem verba* in Romance, which refers to the content of the words rather than the words themselves.

In the following oaths of alliance, Louis the German spoke the Romance oath and Charles spoke the German one. Both were thus using the tongue that was not their normal native language, and in Louis' case, at least, a tongue he may not have known well. The German oath was concocted according to what was becoming common practice in Eastern scriptoria. The Romance oath was more unusual, but it had precedents in all those pre-Carolingian legal documents designed to be in substance intelligible when read back to their depositors (cp. Chapter 2), and the usage of Merovingian notaries has been detected in it. (That this old notarial tradition was known in Carolingian scriptoria can be seen from the *Lex Salica*, a sixth-century code that only survives to us in Carolingian script, with the original quasi-vernacular passages left uncorrected, presumably on purpose, to preserve intelligibility; Elcock 1975: 320-22.) Nithard's text presents them as follows (continuing the previous extract):

. . . Lodhuvicus, quoniam major natu erat, prior haec deinde se servaturum testatus est:

'Pro Deo amur et pro christian poblo et nostro commun salvament, d'ist di in avant, in quant Deus savir et podir me dunat, si salvarai eo cist meon fradre Karlo et in ajudha et in cadhuna cosa, si cum om per dreit son fradra salvar dift, in o quid il mi altresi fazet, et ab Ludher nul plaid nunquam prindrai, qui,

meon vol, cist meon fradre Karle in damno sit.'
    Quod cum Lodhuvicus explesset, Karolus teudisca lingua
sic hec eadem verba testatus est:
    'In Godes minna ind in thes christianes folches ind unser
    bedhero . . .

The only surviving manuscript is of the late tenth century, so may not
reproduce Nithard's version precisely. There are, for example, the
following contractions in the manuscript (Paris BN, *FL* 9768) which
may well have been spelt out fully in the original: *dõ* for *deo*, *p* for *pro*,
*xr̄ian* for *christian*, *nrõ* for *nostro*, *cõmun* for *commun*, *dš* for *deus*,
*sicũ* for *sicum*, *p* for *per*, *nũquã* for *nunquam*. There is also a punctuation point (·), probably designed to indicate proper pausing, after
*salvament, avant, dunat, eo, Karlo, adiudha, cosa, dist, fazet* and at the
end. To this extent the standard reproduction as in Elcock may be
mildly confusing.

    After that, the followers of each side (*utrorumque populus*)
pronounced an oath in their own language, which Nithard also reproduces in the two vernaculars:

    Sacramentum autem quod utrorumque populus, quique propria
    lingua, testatus est, romana lingua sic se habet:
    'Si Lodhuuigs sagrament que son fradre Karlo jurat con-
    servat et Karlus, meos sendra, de suo part lo fraint, si io returnar
    non l'int pois, ne io ne neuls cui eo returnar int pois, in nulla
    ajudha contra Lodhuuuig nun li iv er.'
    Teudisca autem lingua:
    'Oba Karl then eid then er sinemo bruodher Ludhuuuige
    gesuor . . .

It is not clear why this second Romance oath was written in this way;
not many of Charles' *populus* could have been likely to be able to read
at all, let alone from a baffling orthography that they had not met
before. The answer may simply be that once Nithard, or whoever it
was, had worked out the first oath for Louis to read, they felt they
were sufficiently pleased with what they had achieved to carry on in
the same vein for the other Romance oath, even if strictly it was going
to be of less use as Charles' *populus* knew French anyway.

    The nature of the connection between these Oaths and contem-
porary Romance has given rise to a huge bibliography that will not be
recapitulated here. Copious references appear in Ewert (1935) and in
Sabatini (1968). Sabatini points to the close descent from Merovingian
legal practice; he does not argue that this is in fact Merovingian Latin
making a comeback (as Nelson 1966 does), nor that it is a "precocious"
phonetic script representing in accurate detail some actual localizable
Romance dialect, as most early philologists assumed (Castellani 1978

also does, but his approach has been uprooted by Hilty 1978), but the compromise view that although this is indeed an attempt to represent vernacular speech on paper, it is not based on an improbable synchronic phonemic or phonetic analysis so much as on a development of the previously used analogous techniques. Clearly, whoever drafted Louis' oath would prefer to help him rather than hinder him; something in a recognizable tradition might help more than a new system of phonemic transcription. Hilty's conclusion (1978: 141) is that there is not an exact correspondence here of vernacular sounds to letters; he exemplifies this anisomorphism with final [ə] (as in English *paper*), a sound not existing in the prescribed Latin sounds of the Carolingian system, which is represented with different letters in different words in the written version of the French oath.

These Oaths show that by 842 the idea has arisen that on some occasions — for example, when some text has to be fixed in writing but nevertheless its reproduction has to be intelligible — there might be an advantage in a reformed spelling in which the vernacular sounds were the points of reference for fixing the orthography. This is not yet evidence of a general split into two languages; priests continued to read sermons written in the old way with vernacular phonetics, as was demanded five years later in the second Canon of the Council of Mainz. Yet there were others around who could read traditional spelling in Latin pronunciation, but not with the French that every Romance-speaker had used automatically in France before the reform. These would include, in particular, Germanic speakers. The origins here of vernacular spelling seem then to lie not in an attempt to record what the writer has heard others say, but to record what the writer wants others to say. We have entered now the strange stage in Romance culture where most works were written in uniform "Latin", but just a few others, designed for oral reproduction in an unreformed manner (e.g. oaths, songs, sermon notes), were written in a newer more experimental semiphonetic manner that could vary from place to place. The whole is still thought of as one language, but with two possible reading pronunciations and two possible methods of manuscript transcription. This is comparable to the coexistence in modern Britain of traditional orthography and phonetic script in the technical works of some linguists; or to the coexistence of the Initial Teaching Alphabet with traditional orthography in some British primary schools of the 1970s. The additional complicating factor in the Frankish domains was the reformed Latin pronunciation, which had produced as an eventual consequence a need for the adoption of a reformed way of writing vernacular.

*b) The Sequence*

One other invention of the early ninth century seems intimately linked to the reformed "Latin", in which each letter gave rise to a sound; the Sequence (see Ryle 1976; early sequences are printed in *AH* VII). The "classic" sequence that originated then took the form of words composed to fit preexisting melodic lines, specifically allotting one Latin syllable to each note of the music. Nearly all the early sequences were antiphonal, and the parallel isosyllabic structure of most of the surviving sequences appears to guarantee that this practice was normally followed even in the many cases where the precise music is not known to us. To begin with, other considerations such as stress or rhyme were non-existent, or at most secondary, and the melodies used were often the extended melismas on the Alleluia (to which the word *sequentia* was applied first). It may be that their original purpose was merely as a practical mnemonic aid to remembering the contours of these phrases. Since sequences were performed in church, the Latin reading pronunciation would have been the only one ever required. It is only this equivalence of one Latin syllable to each note that seems to be the innovation of the classic Carolingian sequence; antiphonal form predates it. Dronke (1965) has unfortunately confused the two issues in proposing that sequences existed long before 800. He has two arguments for this. Firstly, he decides that some of the early sequences are so sophisticated that the genre cannot have been of recent origin: "the prevalent view that 'postulates the beginnings of sequence composition around 830 at the earliest' is, even on purely stylistic grounds, impossible" (47). By "stylistic" Dronke seems to mean "guesswork" here. Dronke could well be right in his controversial view (50) that Alcuin did indeed compose a sequence attributed to him in an eleventh-century manuscript; even so, a date of c.800 for its invention should be early enough for such a simple concept to have been skilfully elaborated by 830. Dronke's second argument concerns the antiphonal form, which he declares to be reminiscent of the earlier Spanish *preces* of the Visigothic liturgy (as in Férotin 1912: XXXIX-XL). His argument is not convincing (as Szövérffy 1971: 69-70 shows), but even if he is right he is not postulating that the Carolingian equivalence of notes to Latin syllables existed in Spain. The *preces* are verses of a stress-patterned nature and possibly antiphonal in performance. Parallelism of literary structure is constantly present in Iberia from at least the third century until the twelfth and later (Rico 1975). The syllabic equivalence found in the Carolingian sequence, however, seems to have been invented at the same time as the official pronunciation of Latin, being another aspect of the requirement that in church one written vowel implies one oral syllable. There is no reason to suppose that these sequences were ever sung in anything other than strict Latin pronunciation, or before Alcuin's reforms.

One of the main centres of scholarship in the late ninth century was the abbey of St Amand, near Valenciennes in North-Eastern France (Platelle 1962). It had been eminent in pre-Carolingian times (Charles Martel's son was educated there), and it continued to be. Arno was abbot from 782 till 785, when he became bishop of Salzburg, and he seems to have returned at times afterwards. Manuscript Vienna 795 was compiled for Arno, and as well as Alcuin's *De Orthographia* it contains many letters to Arno from Alcuin. Alcuin himself visited St Amand in 798 and 799, apparently leaving behind fifteen metrical inscriptions for churches and altars (*MGH Poetae* I 305-08). It is inconceivable that the active school at St Amand could have been run in the ninth century on any lines other than those laid down by the reformers. In 860, the scriptorium had such renown that Charles the Bald commissioned a sacramentary to be written there. Two of his children were educated at St Amand. Charles' son Carloman became abbot from c.867-70; his successor, Gozlin (870-84 or 86) had been imperial chancellor from 867. Gozlin's successor, Robert (until 922 or 23), was the brother of King Eudes (888-98). Milo, the chief scholar at St Amand (d.872), had been a pupil of Alcuin; Milo and his successor Hucbald (840-930) were two of the most respected scholars of the late ninth and early tenth centuries. Milo's poetry includes a verse life of St Amand which in itself is evidence of expert reformed Latinity (*MGH Poetae* III 557-676).

In 882 the Vikings ransacked the monastery; but the monks had already taken their valuables to St Germain des Prés, of which Gozlin was also abbot. They returned by 886 at the latest, and little serious disruption seems to have been felt. Their library was one of the largest of the age, containing educational and church manuscripts of all kinds, including at least seven ninth-century manuscripts of grammatical works, in particular Priscian and Alcuin's epitome of Priscian. Lesne (1938: 246) declared that St Amand inherited the aura held earlier in the century by St Martin de Tours; cp. also Platelle (1962: 67-69); O'Donnell (1976); Boutemy (1946-47); McKitterick (1977: 27, 134). It is, in short, certain that in the late ninth century it was the base of an enterprising, well-informed, linguistically sophisticated group of Latinate scholars and teachers. It is from here that the next example of written Old French comes.

There is a manuscript from St Amand, probably but not necessarily written there, now at Valenciennes (MS 143), which contains the Romance Sequence of Saint Eulalia. Eulalia of Mérida (Spain) was "a rather unpleasant young virago who had sought and easily obtained martyrdom at the age of thirteen" (Collins 1980: 196). Book III of Prudentius' *Peristephanon* had spread her fame. Relics said to be hers were brought to Hasnon, near St Amand, in 878 (Tagliavini 1972: 486). The manuscript contains a Latin treatise of St Gregory of Nazianzus; at the end there is a Latin sequence on Eulalia, an Old French sequence on Eulalia, the German *Ludwigslied* on the battle between Louis III and the Vikings, and another Latin poem of fifteen couplets (see De Poerck 1963: 4). Writing in German was by this time established practice, nearly always for texts designed to be read aloud or sung in Church to German speakers (see McKitterick 1977: chap.6; by "vernacular" she means "German").

There is a general truth worth remembering at this point; it is easier to write using a system that one has learned than it is to write in a system that one has not learned, even if the latter is closer to one's vernacular habits. Germanic speakers found writing in German considerably harder than the writing in Latin that they had learnt first (until a later time when German was the first form of writing taught to Germans). There are native Catalan-speakers who can only write letters in Spanish. Specialist English phoneticians find ordinary English spelling easier than phonetic script, even after lengthy practice; reflexes need to be deschooled and the ear trained in a novel technique.

The Romance Eulalia sequence must have been written by someone who could also write Latin. Noone could write at all if he had not learnt to write Latin. The invention of the Romance orthography represents an awkward task; that it should have been achieved is a sign of an inventive nature and exceptional linguistic sophistication. It is a virtuoso achievement comparable to the invention of shorthand, or George Bernard Shaw's new alphabet. There is, accordingly, nothing incongruous whatsoever in finding the earliest piece of Romance "literature" in a centre of expert Latinity.

Unlike the Strasbourg Oaths, which are based partly on preceding notarial practices, the techniques used for transcribing the Eulalia sequence seem to have been worked out from scratch. A sequence had (probably) never been sung in anything other than reformed Latin before, with a note per vowel; whoever had invented the Romance words to set to this particular music had presumably done so on the basis of a vowel per note. It seems reasonable to assume that the sound-letter correspondences of the reformed Latin were the starting-point for the new orthography; that the system outlined above for Latin pronunciation could be applied in reverse for the creation of a Romance orthography. The Sequence is thus as good as evidence of Latin pronunciation as it is of Romance. For example, the fact that the [ts] of, e.g. *ciel* (6, 25), is spelt *c*, suggests that in Latin *ci* was pronounced [tsi] here now, whatever Alcuin had done; the fact that the [k] of, e.g. *chi* (6, 12), is spelt *ch*, suggests that in Latin *ch* was pronounced [k] here now, whether or not others elsewhere used [x] or [h]. It is hard to see why these spellings were chosen if this were not the case. For the first time we find diphthongization represented with consistency and even sophistication (e.g. *buona*, 1; *veintre*, 3; etc.); this is because, for the first time, the writer of a new written text specifically wants to have reproduced in performance the [w] in *buona* and the [j] in *veintre*. Outside church, this might have happened all the time, but in church *bona* would be read or sung as [bona]. Porter (1960) has shown the skill and care that has been expended on writing the words in such a way that their phonetic representation could not be in any doubt. *ci* then at St Amand must have been unambiguously [tsi], and *chi* [ki]; *ch* had a precedent in the spelling of words taken from Greek, but the use of *cz* for [ts] before *o* is adventurous (e.g. *czo*, 21). ([ts] is similarly *cz* in the *Ludwigslied*, so the German practice may have come first; the two texts are not, however, in the same hand. See Fought 1979; Penzl 1973.) There is some redundancy in the reverse direction, such as *ko* (as well as *co*) for [ko], e.g. in *eskoltet* (5), but that presents no practical problem to performers. There is an attempt here to specify vernacular reproduction in performance; presumably it is designed to be read by skilled professionals used to reading Latin, or else they could not have read at all; probably it is designed for a choir at least some of whose members were German-speakers and thus uncertain or ignorant of French. Otherwise there seems little point in the exercise, since Latin spelling and Romance pronunciation are still prescribed for the homilies and the same could have been indicated here. (Perhaps some of the choir spoke different forms of Romance; any hesitation or inconsistency would stultify the effect, for a unison performance is required for every word.) As with the Strasbourg Oaths, the St Amand Sequence (from near the linguistic frontier) seems to be specifying Romance sounds for at least some Germanic-speakers. It is quite likely that the written version was concocted while the community of St Amand was at St Germain des Prés in or after 882; if so, we can speculate that one of the communities was transcribing its own invention, a Romance sequence, for the benefit of intrigued parties in the other.

Romance spelling is only needed because of the earlier reform of Latin pronunciation. For those trained in reading Latin correctly, a vernacular French oral performance cannot be unambiguously prescribed except by adapting the standard written letters to the non-Latinate phonetics of French words. Sequences had not previously been performed in anything other than Latin; the novel idea of a Romance sequence necessitated a spelling reform. The phonetics, grammar, morphology, syntax and vocabulary had been current in speech for ages. Only the spelling is new here. That the ninth-century scholars had the technical ability to create a new system for this purpose is attested by the strange fascination some of them felt for alphabets, as in the Vienna manuscript of Alcuin's *De Orthographia*. They were used for "short transliterations" (Bullough 1973a: 117). Germanic writing in Roman letters was developed by them, although, as Bischoff (1961: 213-14) pointed out, they had probably found previous examples of Gothic script in Ravenna. Even so, the fact that this method of Romance writing does not seem to have been widely used suggests that many of the choir were bemused enough by it not to perform the sequence with great fluency.

The transcription designed for this sequence, then, is specifically intended to prompt a desired oral performance. It is not a phonetic transcription of what was actually sung, any more than the Strasbourg Oaths indicate what was actually said. It is, accordingly, a mistake to assume that the text is an infallible guide to north-eastern French. It could well be in a formal style. Perceptible Latinisms such as the *i* in *pulcella* (1), or the words *element* (15), *Christus* (27), *clementia* (29), may indicate that these are Latin borrowings, or ecclesiastical vernacular, or scribal confusion, or all three. The fact that some forms may not represent the contemporary French is no bar to the postulation that that was what they were aiming at; not everyone using an unfamiliar variety of phonetic script always gets everything right.

The Latin sequence (transcribed from von Winterfeld 1901: 135) is similar to the French one (transcribed from Ewert 1933: 353-54):

| | |
|---|---|
| 1a | Cantica virginis Eulaliae |
| 1b | Concine suavisona cithara, |
| | |
| 2a | Est operae quoniam pretium |
| 2b | Clangere carmine martyrium: |
| | |
| 3a | Tuam ego voce sequar melodiam |
| 3b | Atque laudem imitabor Ambrosiam. |

| | |
|---|---|
| 4a | Fidibus cane melos eximium; |
| 4b | Vocibus ministrabo suffragium: |
| 5a | Sic pietatem, sic humanum ingenium |
| 5b | Fudisse fletum compellamus ingenitum. |
| 6a | Hanc puellam nam iuventae sub tempore |
| 6b | Nondum thoris maritalibus habilem |
| 7a | Hostis aequi flammis ignis inplicuit, |
| 7b | Mox columbae evolatu obstipuit; |
| 8a | Spiritus hic erat Eulaliae |
| 8b | Lacteolus celer innocuus. |
| 9a | Nullis actis regi regum displicuit |
| 9b | Ac idcirco stellis caeli se miscuit. |
| 10a | Famulos flagitemus ut protegat, |
| 10b | Qui sibi laeti pangunt armoniam; |
| 11a | Devoto corde modos demus innocuos, |
| 11b | Ut nobis pia deum nostrum conciliet |
| 12a | Eius nobis ac adquirat auxilium, |
| 12b | Cuius sol et luna tremunt imperium, |
| 13a | Nos quoque mundet a criminibus |
| 13b | Inserat et bona sideribus |
| 14 | Stemate luminis aureoli    deo famulantibus. |

Buona pulcella fut Eulalia
Bel auret corps, bellezour anima.
Voldrent la veintre li Deo inimi,
Voldrent la faire diaule servir.
5   Elle no'nt eskoltet les mals conselliers,
Qu'elle Deo raneiet, chi maent sus en ciel,
Ne por or ned argent ne paramenz,
Por manatce regiel ne preiement;
Niule cose non la pouret omque pleier
10   La polle sempre non amast lo Deo menestier.
E por o fut presentede Maximiien,
Chi rex eret a cels dis soure pagiens.
Il li enortet, dont lei nonque chielt,
Qued elle fuiet lo nom christiien.
15   Ell'ent aduret lo suon element;    (Ewert, *adunet*)
Melz sostendreiet les empedementz
Qu'elle perdesse sa virginitét;
Por os furet morte a grand honestét.
Enz enl fou lo getterent com arde tost;
20   Elle colpes non auret, por o nos coist.
A czo nos voldret concreidre li rex pagiens;
Ad une spede li roveret tolir lo chieef.

> La domnizelle celle kose non contredist:
> Volt lo seule lazsier, si ruovet Krist;
> 25 In figure de colomb volat a ciel.
> Tuit oram que por nos degnet preier
> Qued auuisset de nos Christus mercit
> Post la mort et a lui nos laist venir
> Par souue clementia.

Von Winterfeld suggested that the Latin sequence, as printed by him, should be emended by adding an additional line 14a, *Aetheris in globo caerulei*, leaving *Deo famulantibus* as line 15. Given this emendation, the two sequences have the same number of lines (29), with fourteen couplets and a finale; the same liking for assonance, which is at times full rhyme, within each couplet; more or less the same number of syllables in each line of a couplet in both poems, although a little emendation is required if we wish this to be exact; and indeed the same subject matter, although the one is not a simple translation of the other. It is a plausible hypothesis that they might have been intended for the same music, the one version in official language and the other intelligible. (Purczinsky 1965 postulated a Germanic model for the French sequence, but he seems to have been unaware of the Latin genre.)

This analysis implies the presence at St Amand of at least one virtuoso linguist. Was there such a person there at the time (882-900) that the manuscript poems were written? Yes[10]. This was an age of virtuoso poets, skilled in the esoteric arts of acrostic, telestich, alphabetical verse and similar tours-de-force, but one of the most striking pieces of the age was Hucbald's *Ecloga de Calvis*, a poem of 146 hexameters in praise of baldness in which every word begins with the letter C. (*MGH Poetae* IV 267-71. It is the length that startles; the idea had occurred before, e.g. to Valerio del Bierzo; Díaz y Díaz 1958.) As an example of intellectual joie-de-vivre, this is comparable to the extraordinary idea of writing down a musical piece in a phonetic script of one's own devising. And even if the system used in the Eulalia sequence was not Hucbald's idea, one of his associates must have worked hard at it. These things do not "emerge" unbidden in the way some phonetic changes can. (Boutemy 1949 offered a similar argument from virtuosity concerning illuminations.) The *Ecloga de Calvis* begins as follows:

> Carmina convitii cerritus, carpere calvos
> Conatus, cecinit: celebrentur carmine calvi

---

10. The *Ludwigslied* was probably composed in 881, but not written into this manuscript until after Louis' death on 5th August 882. The sequence might be from any time between 878 and 900.

> Conspicuo clari; carmen cognoscite cuncti.
>     Carmina, clarisonae, calvis cantate, Camenae:
> Comere condigno conabor carmine calvos,
> Contra cirrosi crines confundere colli.
> Cantica concelebrent callentes clara Camenae;
> Collaudent calvos, concludant crimine cluras
> Carpere conantes calvos crispante cachinno.
> Conscendat caeli calvorum cause cacumen.
> Conticeant cuncti concreto crine comati
> Cerrito calvos calventes carmine cunctos.
> Consona coniunctim cantentur cantica calvis.

It has been suggested before that Hucbald composed the Eulalia sequence (e.g. Contini 1966; Harvey 1945). He was a musician and a choirmaster; his musical treatise *Harmonica Institutio* advocated a number of practical innvoations, and his biographer stated directly that he composed *cantilenae*. His hagiographic writing also shows an un-typically enquiring approach (see Van der Vyver 1947: 61-62). It has also been suggested that he wrote the *Ludwigslied*; or all three. Harvey (1945: 19-20) dismisses the idea, but it is not implausible; they are all works in search of a skilful author, and must have been composed by someone. Even if they were the inventions of colleagues, it is incon-ceivable that Hucbald would not have known about the outlandish experiment in the Romance sequence. Hucbald was the most admired intellectual and teacher of the time, being invited, for example, to reorganize education at Rheims from 896 to 900 (Van der Vyver 1947: 69; Platelle 1962: 66; Lesne 1940: 276-81). Attributions of authorship have been made on far less evidence than this.

The foregoing observations are neither adventurous nor novel. Unfortunately, philologists have often been as unaware of the back-ground to the Eulalia sequence as of that to the Council of Tours or the Strasbourg Oaths. Barnett, for example, decided (1961: 19, as regards Latin) that "it is hard to imagine that the oral tradition had yet, as it was to do in later centuries, given way to the re-established 'classical' spellings as the guide to pronunciation". Even the most cursory glance at its context shows that it is impossible to imagine anything else; yet Barnett claims to be examining the Latin background. In fact, Barnett's conclusion (and that of Lorenz 1963) supports the view that the Romance sequence must have been composed by someone skilled in the Latin sequence tradition: "the story it tells has its equivalent, point for point, in many Latin 'passions'. A striking number of the words used, when not part of the basic vocabulary, have common Latin equivalents in religious, and more particularly hagiographic, literature . . . it is clear that in content, structure and language, the French *Eulalia* stands very close to the Latin tradition" (Barnett 1961: 24-25). This is not surprising. Porter (1960: 588), however, apparently believed that before such experiments occurred Romance vernaculars did not exist: "I should hesitate to pretend to impose on his language, considering its then nascent state, the dialectal divisions which came into existence only in later centuries." Fought (1979: 846) pointed out, commenting on this remark, that "the vernacular itself was doubtless no more nascent than any other language"; vernaculars exist, by definition, whatever the quirks required for writing them. Porter's comment illustrates how linguists can be as naive about language as any historian, whereas historians tend not to be naive in addition about history.

### The Survival of Latin Speech and Romance Writing past 1000 A.D.

Hucbald died in 930, at the age of 90. The idea of recording words intended subsequently to be spoken in vernacular survived him. By chance there has survived part of a so-called "bilingual" sermon on Jonah, used in the binding of Valenciennes MS 521 (from St Amand), and dated by De Poerck (1956, 1963) to between 937 and 952. Rather than bilingual, it is in appearance a monolingual text with varying orthography. If the whole was to be read aloud on the normal pattern of a sound per letter, the result would have been Latin pronunciation for the text (*Jonah* 4) and French for the commentary. Part of it runs as follows (transcribed from Sampson 1980: no.52):

> Et egressus est Ionas de ciuitate et sedit contra orientem ciuitatis donec uideret quid accideret ciuitati. dunc co dicit cum Ionas propheta cel populum habuit pretiet e convers. et en cele ciuitate . . . habuit demoret. si escit foers de la ciuitate. e si sist contra orientem ciuitatis. e si auardevet cum Deus parfereiet sa promesse. se Ninive destruite astreiet u ne fereiet. Et preparauit Dominus ederam super caput Ione ut faceret ei umbram. laborauerat enim dunc Ionas propheta habebat mult laboret e mult penet a cel populum co dicit. e faciebat grant jholt. et eret mult las et preparauit Dominus en edre sore sen cheve qet umbre li fesist. e repauser si podist. Et letatus est Ionas super edera letitia magna. dunc fut Jonas mult letus co dicit. por qe Deus cel edre li donat a sun souev. et a sun repausement. Et precepit Dominus uermi ut percuteret ederam et exaruit. et parauit Deus uentum calidum super caput Ione et dixit: 'melius est mihi mori quam uiuere.' . . . surrede dunc co dicit si rogat Deus ad un verme. qe percussist cel edre sost qe cil sedebat ec . . . cilge edre fu seche si vint grancesmes jholt la super caput Ione et dixit: 'melius est mihi mori quam uiuere.'

This piece of paper was ephemeral, and would not normally have been preserved for the next thousand years. Anything worth keeping would be written properly. Thanks to its chance survival we know both that the idea of recording vernacular sounds in a quasi-phonetic script did not die out in tenth-century St Amand, and that the prescription of the Councils of Tours and Mainz concerning vernacular speech for sermons was still, sometimes at least, observed. This sermon is not one of the authorized homilies, having been apparently composed for the occasion of a Viking attack, and the French shows syntactic divergence from the Latin as well; the giver of the sermon has no authorized text to follow other than the scriptural passage and feels free to elaborate on this theme (of deliverance from adversity). The discovery by Gysseling (1949: 210) of linguistically comparable marginalia in an eleventh-century manuscript from Douai suggests that these techniques were taught and used during all the period between Hucbald and the first extended texts in French vernacular; a developing tradition exists, hidden from us because such works were not intended for the eyes of posterity.

The continuation of the reformed Latinity in the tenth century can be exemplified in the life of Abbo, abbot of Fleury (c.940-1004: Cousin 1954; Lesne 1938: 549-58; 1940: 191-95). Fleury, on the Loire, had had Theodulf of Orléans as abbot, and had been an active centre of the new culture in the ninth century. After a period of decline, it was reestablished under Odo of Cluny from 931 till his death in 942. Abbo seems to have been entrusted to Fleury in the late 940s at the age of seven, been a star pupil and then a teacher; as his biographer Haimo (Aimoin) puts it, with endearing clumsiness:

> Abbo ... in Floriacensi monasterio scholae clericorum ecclesiae Sancti Petri obsequentium traditur litteris imbuendus, divina pro certo, ut credimus, id praeordinante providentia, ut inde primordia sumeret litterarum, ubi postmodum, plenissime fluenta doctrinae mentibus erat propinaturus sapientiam sitientium, redderetque illis, seu eorum posteris ...
>
> ... iam vero litterariae artis profunda tanta adhuc puerulus rimabatur instantia, ut a didascalis semel audita firmiter intra cordis conderet arcana ...
>
> (*PL* CXXXIX 389A, D)

As usual, when he taught the others, reading and singing were the joint subject:

> ... imbuendis praeficitur scolasticis; quos ille, per aliquot annorum curricula, lectione simul et cantilena cum tanta erudivit cura ...                                                      (390B)

*Litterae*, *doctrina*, *litteraria ars*, *lectio* and *cantilena* were taught and learnt at Fleury in a manner admired by others; Abbo himself was obsessively expert at the *litterarum exercitium* and *studium lectionis* (390A). It is of interest, then, to look at his own comments on grammar as expressed in his *Quaestiones Grammaticales*, compiled for the benefit of English colleagues at Ramsey that he taught from 980 to 982[11].

The problems of where to put the stress, and of what was long and short for metric purposes, were perennial questions not catered for in the simple letter-sound correspondences of elementary *litterae*; these questions occupy sections 2-8. In section 9 the question arises of syllable-final plosives ($p, c, t, b, g, d$); and Abbo apparently embarks on neutralization theory, suggesting that the distinction lapses in "*actus* pro *agtus*, *scriptus* pro *scribtus*, et *attinet* pro *adtinet*" (528A). In section 10, the pronunciation of *c* and *g* is dealt with. When *a*, *o* or *u* follow, the consonants are velar ("sonant in faucibus"). With a following *e* or *i*, however, life is more complicated:

Cum vero *c* litteram sequuntur in eadem syllaba *e* vel *i*, trifariam solet pronuntiari, et nunc quidem ut fere videatur sonare *g*, maxime *s* praecedente, ut *suscipio*, *suscepi*, *suscepit*: nunc autem cum quodam sibilo, ac si *s* illi haereat, ut *civis*, *cepit*: quod magis solet fieri ubi *t* profertur sono *z* in principio syllabae, ut *laetitia*, *justitia*. Denique qui tertium modum addunt sono *quae* vel *qui*, easdem syllabas pronuntiari decernunt, et *susquipio* pro *suscipio*, et *susquepit* pro *suscepit*, et *quivis* pro *civis*; quod quam frivolum constet, omnibus vera sapientibus liquet.

The "strengthened" [g] attributed to *sce*, *sci* is surprising. The sibilant sound elsewhere is almost certainly [ts], here compared to the *z* in *laetitia*. The absurdity of the slip into [kw] is explained at some length, and in the course of this tirade Abbo mentions that a morpheme boundary is no bar to the velar + back vowel // sibilant + front vowel pattern, even in a verbal paradigm: "siquidem *vinco*, *vinci*, *vince*, *vincam*, mutato cum vocalibus sono dicimus, quemadmodum et *lego*, *legi*, *lege*, *legam*." It is certain, therefore, that *ce*, *ci* were read [tse], [tsi], and *ge*, *gi* as [dʒe], [dʒi], in even the best centres of tenth-century Latinity. The scholars of Ramsey might well have raised the question of [k] and [g] here, as Alcuin had before; but the wheel has come full circle. Alcuin had the authority to tell Frenchmen to say [ke], but even

---

11. The edition in *PL* CXXXIX 521-34 is seriously misleading; it is essential to consult Bradley (1921-23) who, unlike Migne, was able to consult the sole MS (Vatican 596). The text reproduced here is as corrected by Bradley. A new edition is currently being prepared in Paris by Anita Guerreau-Jalabert.

if they took notice then, they do not in Abbo's time, and now Abbo has the authority to tell Englishmen to say [tse].

The next problem (section 11) concerns *h*. "Semper absque ullo sono vocalibus praeponimus"; at the start of a word, or between two vowels, it has no sound. After *c, t, p* it is reserved for Graecisms (nearly all of which the manuscript misspells but Migne prints in corrected form). The Greek letters χ, ϑ, φ have attached to them in the manuscript the names *chi, teta* (sic), *fi*, which Migne's printed text ignores. In general, "illas proferimus Graecarum litterarum sonis". *Fi* for φ is as in Vienna MS 795, and causes no problem: *ph* means [f]. The other two are less simple. χ is *hi* in Vienna 795; χ is sometimes thought, says Abbo, to be *x* [ks], but (if the manuscript is correct) should be [k], "Quapropter cum Graece scribitur Χηρηα, ita profertur ac si scriberetur *s. kerea*". Bradley suggests this is a bad copy of *cherea*. The *ch* digraph is only used before *e* and *i*, so there is need of clarity in representation of [ke], [ki]; the fact that the Eulalia Sequence has *chi* for [ki] suggests that [x] or [h] are not the standard reproduction of *ch*, and perhaps the manuscript *k* should be respected despite the general requirement to reproduce the Greek sounds. What the *s* is remains an enigma; short for *sono* perhaps. The immediately following comment is " . . . et παροιχὶα quasi parraechia" (sic, in *PL*), which, if Abbo really wrote it like that, adds to the confusion. As Abbo said earlier, the only doubt about *h* arises "quando inter *c* et *e* vel *i* interponitur nota aspirationis, ut *Chereas* et *parrochia*"; unfortunately the scribe seems to have either transcribed a (hypothetical) (*c*)*herea* as *s. kerea* or a (hypothetical) *parrokia* as *parraechia*, and the confusion persists as to what Abbo originally meant. The best bet could be that Alcuin may have proposed [x] or [h] on the basis of his knowledge of Greek (and his English [h]), but that in France, where [x] and [h] were absent from vernacular, [k] became a common and understandable (if unauthorized) pattern, once *ce* abandoned [ke] for [tse].

ϑ is called *thita* in Vienna 795. In section 12 (which is gibberish in *PL* CXXXIX 529), as Bradley points out, Abbo says to his English audience "sed aspirationes bene vos angli pervidere potestis, qui pro ϑ frequentius þ scribitis" (*effertis* is added here in the margin). The English are better than the French at [θ], having the *thorn* (þ) and its accompanying sound. This seems to confirm that Abbo is aware that ϑ ought to be [θ], but the spelling *teta* — if it is not a copyist's error — may indicate that not everyone could achieve it, [θ] not existing in Old French.

The next problem, in section 13, concerns the need in both speech and writing not to move the final consonant of one word onto the initial syllable of the next: "tandem dicendum est quod vitando cavenda est collisio quae solet fieri vel pronuntiato vel scripto, ut *veni trex* pro eo quod est *venit rex*, et *par sest* pro *pars est*, et *feli xes* pro *felix es*."[12]

This concluded the phonetic section. The nature of reduplicating perfects, second conjugation verbs, the length of *i* in verb-endings, Greek words in *-on*, the plural forms of *bos*, zeugmas, the case used with comparisons, and the implications of negation in a non-complementary predication in the Athanasian Creed, fill the remaining sections.

Given that the pronunciation problems raised by Abbo's English colleagues are (apart from questions of metric length and stress) confined to how to read *c, g, h*, the implication is that there was no great difference between the English pronunciation of Latin and that which Abbo taught at Fleury. Alcuin's reform of Continental Latin, on the English model, has largely stuck. And Fleury is the home of the manuscripts of three of the earliest Romance compositions, as we shall see below; this can no longer be thought to be a coincidence.

The other outstanding intellectual figure of these times is Gerbert of Rheims, who was slightly younger than Abbo and in touch with Fleury. Hucbald of St Amand and Remigius of Auxerre had in the late ninth century reestablished scholarly traditions at Rheims. Southern (1953: 13) dated the intellectual revival of the Central Middle Ages to Gerbert's arrival at Rheims in 972, but the tradition was there before him; Gerbert's real achievement lay in his large number of active students, who began to expand the number of those studying in the fashion set by Alcuin two centuries before.

The two surviving extended works written in French before 1000 come from Clermont-Ferrand MS 240 (formerly 189: De Poerck 1963, 1964). The main text of the manuscript is a large *Liber Glossarum*, wrongly attributed to the Visigoth Ansileubus, written in the ninth or tenth century. On some blank spaces, hands of the late tenth century recorded nine pieces of verse, the sixth and the ninth of which are in Romance; a *Passion* and the *Vie de Saint Léger*. Together these have 756 lines of verse. Until De Poerck attacked it angrily as a "hypothèse nefaste" (1963: 19-20), the dominant view was that these were the work of an unreliable Southern copyist transcribing Northern poems, and thus not evidence of any particular vernacular (Linskill

---

12. The *to vel* of *pronuntiato vel* and the *ni* of *venit* are supplied by Bradley to supplement a hole in the page.

1937; accepted by Sampson 1980: nos. 53-54). Lines 157-172 of the *Passion* are here reproduced from Sampson:

> Sanct Pedre sols venjiar lo vol:
> estrais lo fer que al laz og,
> si consegued u serv fellon,
> la destre aurelia li excos.
> Jesus li bons ben red per mal,
> l'aurelia ad serv semper saned.
> lisade(n)s mans, cume ladron,
> si l'ent menen a passiun.
> Dunc lo en gurpissen sei fedel,
> cum el desanz diz lor aveia;
> sanz Pedre sols seuguen lo vai,
> quae sua fin veder voldrat.
> Anna nomnavent le Judeu
> a cui Jesus furet menez;
> donc s'adunovent li felon,
> veder annovent pres Jesum.

The suggestion that this is a Southern adaptation of a Northern text implies a greater degree of dialectal self-awareness than may be thought plausible; it may merely be that the spelling system used was based closely but not exactly on models from further north. This is quite possible. Hucbald himself travelled widely, and it is quite likely that the experiment at St Amand was known in other centres. St Amand's scriptorium also sent books to many other places (Platelle 1962: 68-69); Hucbald was an associate of the scholars of Auxerre, and Gibson (1975: 8-9) has pointed out that their work established many of the texts available in the tenth century. "On the linguistic side of the curriculum, the school of Auxerre made a contribution that was clearly useful, and may prove to have been fundamental." Monasteries of central and southern France with contacts further north must at the least have been aware of the idea, and probably also of the technique, of recording vernacular in new orthography for vernacular reading; the Clermont poems have a sufficiently confident air to suggest that both their composer and scribe could even have been trained in the art of using vernacular script for notes or poetry. That users of the manuscript had linguistic interests can be seen in the fact that it is a glossary. The third of the Latin poems in the manuscript is a lament for the assassination of William Longsword, the second Duke of Normandy, in 942; as Robson (1955: 132) observed, "only a rich monastery with a strong literary tradition would have undertaken the transcription of this great folio copy of the glossary, and the added Latin and French poems show a considerable range of interests and contacts". De Poerck (1963) argued that the *Saint Léger*, at least, might have come originally from Ébreuil, slightly north of Clermont, and more or less on the dividing line between Occitan and French; his view is that the language used could well represent the usage of some such transitional area. Robson shows that "standard written French existed therefore, in terms of flexion, vocabulary, and consonant-systems, from the tenth century" (1955: 165), implying that instead of representing any usage exactly, the system used here is "inter-regional", although scribes of different vernaculars felt at liberty to adapt if they thought it necessary[13]. It is not logically impossible for unconnected attempts at vernacular writing to arise independently, but Rickard's conclusion (1974: 42) is more probable: "behind the vagaries of southern scribes we can discern important features which confirm and are confirmed by those early texts which were *not* copied by southern scribes, and even more by later texts"; Robson concluded that "the few literary texts copied mainly in monastic centres owed their fixity and lack of local quality to a monastic discipline established in the great age of Cluniac reform" (1955: 135).

If there really is a standard written French even in the tenth century, as seems likely, the Cluniacs could easily be the standardizers. This would mean that the main centres of spoken liturgical Latin were also the main centres of written vernacular, which is a predictable consequence of the theory that the invention of Medieval Latin speech was the precipitating stimulus for the invention of Romance writing. The reformed Benedictines of Cluny were established in Burgundy in the early tenth century under Odo, its first abbot. Odo had probably been taught by Remigius of Auxerre, associate at Rheims of Hucbald of St Amand; it is unlikely that Odo was unaware of the practice of vernacular writing at St Amand (although, as Robson 1955 showed, the "standard" did not adopt the same conventions for representing vowels). The Cluniac order was obsessed with both liturgy and literacy (for their library, see Lesne 1938: 524-33). *Illiterati* were only given manual work. Spoken Latin was essential there; this could explain why a (semi-)standardized written vernacular was also taught there, if indeed it was.

Elcock (1961: 16-18) noticed that the idea of writing in a way other than the traditional Latin was suggested by the model of writing in German (or Anglo-Saxon) to the Carolingian scholars, and spread out geographically from there. This is broadly true. The Norman *Vie*

---

13. This essay is essentially a warning against the belief that spoken Old French was standardized.

*de Saint Alexis* is usually said to date from 1040-50 (but could well be later). The earliest surviving distinguishably Occitan texts probably postdate the Clermont poems slightly. The *Boecis*, 257 decasyllables on Boethius, is written by a scribe of the eleventh century, in an Orleans manuscript that originally came from Fleury in the tenth century (Lavaud and Machicot 1950); the *Chanson de Sainte Foi d'Agen* (593 octosyllables) is probably from the area around Narbonne, although the manuscript is from Fleury. The first stanza of the *Chanson* mentions Latin, and the second stanza apparently mentions French; the third stanza states that the author heard the tale in Latin from *clerczons* and *gramadis* (transcribed from Elcock 1975: 389-90):

I  Legir audi sotz eiss un pin
   Del vell temps un libre Latin;
   Tot l'escoltei tro a la fin.
   Hanc non fo senz q'el nonl declin;
   Parled del pair' al rei Licin
   E del linnadg' al Maximin.
   Cel meirols saintz en tal traïn
   Con fal venairels cervs matin:
   A clusals menan et a fin;
   Mortz los laissavan en sopin.
   Jazon els camps cuma fradin;
   Nolz sebelliron lur vizin.
   Czo fo prob del temps Constantin.

II Canczon audi q'es bella 'n tresca,
   Que fo de razo Espanesca;
   Non fo de paraulla Grezesca
   Ne de lengua Serrazinesca.
   Dolz' e suaus es plus que bresca
   E plus qe nulz pimentz q'om mesca;
   Qui ben la diz a lei Francesca,
   Cuig me qe sos granz pros l'en cresca
   E q'en est segle l'en paresca.

III Tota Basconn' et Aragons
    E l'encontrada delz Gascons
    Sabon quals es aquist canczons
    E ss' es ben vera 'sta razons.
    Eu l'audi legir a clerczons
    Et a gramadis, a molt bons,
    Si qon o monstral passions
    En que om lig estas leiczons
    E si vos plaz est nostre sons,
    Aisi conl guidal primers tons,
    Eu la vos cantarei en dons.

Elcock (1961: 16) suggested, attractively, that *a lei Francesca*, "in the French manner", means "in the vernacular, rather than in

Latin"; not a distinction between vernaculars, but between all vernaculars and Latin. Zaal (1962), however, interpreted *Francesca* as "French" in the sense of "a French genre" rather than anything linguistic. The poem is the second of four in the manuscript, of which the other three are Latin; as usual, early Romance writing is found in the company of expert Latinity.

Arguing from the word *grezesca*, Burger has recently (1978) dated the *Chanson* to 1060-80. The date of the *Boecis* is indeterminable, so it is quite possible that the earliest surviving Occitan poem is the two-line refrain of a Latin *alba* in another manuscript from Fleury, which may be as early as 1000 (and thus contemporary with Abbo's abbacy), and is now in the Vatican (1462). Tagliavini (1972: 495-96) prints the text as follows:

> Phebi claro nondum orto iubare,
> Fert aurora lumen terris tenue:
> Spiculator pigris clamat: "surgite".
> *Lalba par(t) umet mar atra sol*
> *Poy pas abigil miraclar tenebras.*
> En incautos ostium insidie
> Torpentesque gliscunt intercipere,
> Quos suadet preco, clamat surgere
> *Lalba part umet mar atra sol*
> *Poy pas abigil miraclar tenebras.*
> Ab Arcturo disgregatur Aquilo,
> Poli suos condunt astra radios,
> Orienti tendit(ur) Septemtrio,
> *Lalba part umet mar atra sol*
> *Poy pas abigil . . .*

The manuscript includes the music[14]. Every Latin line is a hendecasyllable in the usual Latin pattern (given the emendation to *tenditur*), with a caesura after four syllables, and homoteleutic rhyme, apart from the -*s* of *radios*. The Occitan refrain, of 9 and 11 syllables, represents a conscious attempt to specify vernacular performance. The result is a song with the verse unintelligible to laymen but the chorus not. If this is indeed the earliest surviving Occitan composition, we have here too the origins of the tradition in a combination of "Latin" and "Romance" in the same manuscript (as in the Oaths, the Eulalia sequence and the Jonah sermon).

The Occitan impulse to vernacular poetry in Italy and Catalonia is well known. In Catalonia, Provençal culture and Carolingian education

---

14. Tagliavini summarizes a variety of possible interpretations. Dronke fantasized another (1968: 170-72).

were already well established by the eleventh century. By 1100 or so, in France, the idea is spreading that writing in Romance might be an activity autonomous from writing in Latin. Spain, however, has been quite different. The advent of a distinction between Romance and Latin in Spain (outside Catalonia) does not seem to start until c.1100, or be accepted till the thirteenth century; the complicated history of Romance and Latin in Spain from 700 to 1250 forms the subject matter of the two remaining chapters.

Italy falls outside the brief of this study, but a few initial points can be made. In the first place, it tends to be thought that Northern Italy had many lay schools in the ninth and tenth centuries, with the result that education is not so intimately tied to the requirements of the church; that view was exploded by Bullough (1964), whose arguments have never been rejected. Bullough's study emphasises that *litterae*, reading and singing are all part of the same process in Northern Italy as they were elsewhere in the Carolingian area. In the tenth century, for example, Bullough has found no priest unable to write his name in documents from Novara and Parma, several references to the ecclesiastical establishment of *magistri grammaticae et cantorum*, and no evidence at all of lay schools. Norberg summarizes evidence for the perception of a difference between Latin and Italian vernacular in the tenth century (1968: 34); the coronation of Berenguer I in 915 is said to have been marked by speeches *patrio ore* and *nativa voce*. Gunzo of Novara distinguishes them in his *Epistola ad Augienses* of 965: "Falso putavit sancti Galli monachus me remotum a scientia grammaticae artis, licet aliquando retarder usu nostre vulgaris lingue, que Latinitati vicina est" (Manitius 1958: 27); Pope Gregory V's epitaph (999) mentions his ability to speak *francisca, vulgari et voce Latina*, presumably French, Italian and Latin. Apart from the so-called Veronese "riddle" of c.800, which is notoriously hard to interpret[15], the earliest surviving intentionally vernacular Italian appears in four legal documents of the early 960s, where they are new versions of traditional sentences written elsewhere in normal Latin. Presumably the lawyers were experimenting to see if the reformed orthography aided vernacular reading back to, or by, the depositor (Sampson 1980: no.77). This experiment apparently failed, being dropped after 964. The evidence, in brief, suggests that Carolingian-influenced Northern Italy was in a similar position to France: the invention of Latin speech had led to experimentation in Romance writing.

---

15. *Se pareba boves, alba pratalia araba/Albo versorio teneba, negro semen seminaba* (Sampson 1980: no.76).

# 4

## SPAIN (711-1050)

*(Map drawn by A.G. Hodgkiss)*

The Iberian peninsula is heterogeneous. In the central Middle Ages it was even more heterogeneous than usual. The Moslem invasion of the Visigothic Kingdom began in 711, and until the mid-eleventh century Moslem rulers controlled the central and southern areas. The

North-Western corner, however, was never occupied, and the Kingdom of Asturias (after 914 called León) covered about a fifth of the peninsula. In the tenth century Moslem Spain (Al-Andalus) was a cohesive and powerful unit, but during the eleventh it disintegrated politically, until in c.1050 there were about thirty separate states in the peninsula. (For the history of the period see Sánchez Albornoz 1980; Suárez Fernández 1970; Lomax 1978: chaps.1 and 2).

The North-Eastern corner, now known as Catalonia, had a different history and culture from the other communities. For practical purposes it can be regarded as a part of the Frankish and European area (D'Abadal 1969-70; Lewis 1965).

### Catalonia

The Moslem occupation of parts of Catalonia was comparatively brief, and the area was reinvaded by Carolingian forces in the late eighth century. Girona was taken in 785 and Barcelona in 801. Christian foundations in the area had been strong, and they revived in the ninth century with support from Southern France (Salrach 1978: chap.2). These communities were thus brought into the Benedictine ambit. The Eastern section of Catalonia was under the jurisdiction of the metropolitan see of Narbonne; both the Roman liturgy and the Caroline minuscule script seem to have been introduced there early in the century. In Western Catalonia the Hispanic traditions were more persistent, but by the tenth century Carolingian practice was common there too. There is thus a mixture of traditions. Pujol (1917) concluded that the act of consecration of Urgell Cathedral was written in a script containing both Gothic and Carolingian elements; Serdá (1955) showed that in the ninth century some churches kept the Visigothic rites, others used the Roman, and others were prepared to use either. The Franks themselves, however, felt some distaste for the supposedly heretical Visigothic liturgy, and Catalonia had become a Roman liturgical area by 1000 at the latest.

The abbey of Cuixà had Cluniac connections from 940 to 998, but in general Cluny had no great influence in Catalonia at this time (Cowdrey 1970: 215). The Papacy had an active interest in the area, and in the tenth century the Catalan church seems to have been as alive as anywhere else in Europe; there are several foundations then, and Ripoll (founded in 879-80) became a flourishing cultural centre. Gerbert of Rheims was there in 967-71.

Ripoll's manuscripts were catalogued by Beer (1907-08), and its Latin poetry was printed by Nicolau (1920). Nicolau showed that the basic metric manual used was Bede's *De Arte Metrica*, of which two tenth-century manuscripts survive. Poetic texts known to be present include both Roman and Visigothic hymnals, Classical, Christian, Carolingian and post-Carolingian authors, of which Nicolau demonstrated the most important aids to composition were Vergil and Sedulius (Vergil as the ideal, Sedulius as a practical model). The subject matter of the poetry often included items of local interest, such as in Abbot Oliva's Poem in praise of Ripoll, c.1040 (García Villada 1914). These poems also included the intellectual games of patterned poetry and complicated acrostics, such as the ninth- or tenth-century tour-de-force *Metra suit certa si visat rectius artem* (Nicolau 1920: no.40, p.57), where that palindromic sentence is the first line, last line, acrostic, telestich and double diagonal reading, and the middle line, the palindromic *Ut citius repsit ne ventis persuit ictu*, is also readable downwards through the centre of each line. There can accordingly be no doubt that reformed Latin and linguistic sophistication were present at Ripoll.

One of the best-known poems from Ripoll was not studied by Nicolau: the *Carmen Campi Doctoris* (Menéndez Pidal 1947: 880-84; Wright 1979). This poem in rhythmic sapphics deals with episodes in the early life of Ruy Díaz (El Cid), and is broken off in the manuscript during the description of a skirmish of 1082. It was probably composed soon after that event. The skill in its composition is manifest. Every final line of a stanza, for example, has five written vowels as in the sapphic metre, but in addition the poet has managed to create a near-constant adonic stress pattern of / .. / . which corresponds to the classical sapphic pattern of long and short (−∪∪−∪). This rhythm often recurs in the first half of the hendecasyllables, all of which end paroxytonically (/ .) with homoteleutic rhyme. There can be no doubt that this poem deserves the name of "rhythmic" verse, which is often loosely given to less skilled compositions from other parts of Spain in which the syllable count of written vowels may be constant but the idea of a concomitant rhythm has been lost.

In the fourth stanza, the author says that he learnt this technique as part of his education:

> Verum et ego parum de doctrina
> quamquam aurissem e pluribus pauca
> rihtmice (*sic*) tamen dabo ventis vela
> pavidus nauta.

There is no reason to doubt the literal truth of this; he had once been taught to write *rihtmice*, which as exemplified in his own composition was a sophisticated form using reformed European Latin.

This knowledge and teaching of Latin continues through the twelfth century, at the end of which appear the verses of the 'Anònim Enamorat' (Nicolau 1920: nos.20-39; most recently studied by Dronke 1979), and into the thirteenth. By this time, Catalans have begun writing in vernacular; particularly troubadours, who when writing were following the linguistic norms of written practice already established by then in Occitan. Catalan troubadours continued to make a significant contribution to the corpus of Occitan lyric until c.1280 (see Terry 1972: 4-12); Ramón Llull (1233-1316) wrote Occitan poems and Catalan prose.

Catalan prose had been written before verse. A notarial tradition existed here, as elsewhere, of writing documents in vernacular with a light Latin veneer. (For Catalan philology, see Badía Margarit 1951; Bastardas 1977.) The earliest surviving writing in Catalan comes from the late eleventh and twelfth century; it includes the six sermons known as the *Homílies d'Organyà* (Coromines 1976-77: I 127-53), which usually present a section of Latin text followed by translation and commentary in Romance. It thus seems to be at a more advanced stage of the continuing Carolingian sermon tradition than the Jonah fragment. The sermons are similar to the twenty-two approximately contemporary Piedmontese sermons that are probably among the earliest examples of North Italian prose (Sampson 1980: no.78). There is a late eleventh-century oath among the surviving texts which is almost entirely in Catalan, presumably (as at Strasbourg) designed to aid performance (reproduced from Russell-Gebbett 1965: no.12):

> Juro ego Guille*l*m Ponç, fil d*e* Bonadonna fem*i*na, a ti B*e*rtran,
> fil de Guila fem*i*na, che eu d*e* ista ora in antea fidels te serei sen
> frau e mal engien e ses neguna deceptio, cho<n> om deu esser a
> son senior chui manub*us* se comanda. Juro ego Guille*l*m Ponç, fil
> d*e* Bonadonna fem*i*na, a ti B*e*rtran, fil d*e* Guila fem*i*na, che d*e* ista
> ora in antea no·t prendrei ni no·t reterei ni no·t oucidrei ni no·t
> tolrei ta vita ne ta mem*b*ra q*ui* a ton corps se ten*e*t, ni d*e* achelas
> <alods et de la> onor que odie abes ne che ena[n]t ab meu consel
> acaptarás no la·t tolrei ni no te·n tolrei. E si es om o fem*i*na chi
> la·t tola ni te·n tola, aitori te·n serei p*er* d*i*recta*m* (?) fez sen
> engan, e totes celes veds che me·n comonrás p*er* ti o p*er* tos
> missaticos comoniment no me·n devedarei e del aitori no·t
> engannarei. Sic*ut* sup*er*i*us* es escrit sí t'o tenrei e sí t'o atendrei
> p*er* dreta fez sen engan.

There is also a surviving fragment of a twelfth-century Catalan translation of the *Forum Judicum* (the Visigothic law code; Russell-Gebbett 1965: no.16).

Organyà, where the sermon manuscript was discovered, is in the diocese of Urgell in Western Catalonia (in the modern province of Lleida). There are sufficient Catalan features in the language for this to qualify unequivocally as Catalan, but there are nevertheless signs that the writer had previously received his training in vernacular writing in Occitan. This is hardly surprising; someone who could write in the established vernacular tradition is more likely to have been given the task of writing these sermons than someone who could not. The orthographical practice as used in the eleventh-century *Chanson de Sainte Foi d'Agen* (known to Catalanists as *Cançó de Santa Fe*) from the Narbonne area is likely to have been in essentials the standard taught and used in Catalonia, and whoever adapted it into the system of the *Homílies* must have had considerable linguistic insight to notice those elements that might need to be written differently south of the Pyrenees (although the opposite view, that this is "provençalised Catalan", is found in Russell-Gebbett 1973: 247). So although the fluency of the homilies attests an author practised in writing vernacular, that fluency could have been acquired in what Tagliavini (1972: 499) called the "literary *Koinè* of Provençal". Elcock (1975: 453) pointed out "a multitude of points of resemblance between the language of the *Homílies d'Organyà* and that of the *Chanson de Sainte Foi d'Agen*", although in a more recent study Gökçen (1977) has decided that "the Provençal element in it is minimal". The fifth homily starts as follows (Coromines 1976-77: 143):

### Dominica inicio XLagesima

*In illo tempore, ductus est Jhesus in deserto in spiritu ut tem-
taretur a Diabolo. Et cum jejunaset* .XIª. *diebus et* .XIª.
n<octibus>, *postea esurit.* S<einors>, audir e entendre devem lo Sent Evangèlii per qué aizò vol dir e mostrar que·l N<ostre> S<éiner> grans penas e grans trebals e grans dolors soferí per nós: per aizò qar él nos volg salvar e trer de poder de Diable. Qar enaixí trobam que él dejunà .XLª. dies <e> .XLª. nuitz, que anc no beg ne mengà, e enaprés sí ag fam. S<einors>, él no dejunà gens per zo que él agés peccad feit, per qué él degés fer penitència ni degés dejunar, mas per exemple o fét de nós e per zo que nós dejunàsem per los nostres peccads. E per aizò qar él dejunà .XLª. dies e .XLª. nuits, mostrà que él ere ver Déus; et aizò que él ag fam mostrà <que> ere ver om: e per aizò devem cretre que él fo ver Déus e ver om. Et enaprés sí dix l'Evangeli que can N<ostre> S<éiner> ac fam, sí veng lo Diable a él e volg-lo temtar e dix; *Si filius Dei es, dic ut lapides isti panes fiant.* —Si tu és fil de Déu, di a les pedres que·s tornen pa e manga·n.

Many of the Latin words are abbreviated to the initial letter alone;

probably the preacher would have the Missal open anyway, and such shorthand would save time. The appearance of such "bilingual" material in the Carolingian areas is one of many features to show that Catalonia is a part of "European" culture in these years, sharing the contemporary Latin-Romance distinction.

Catalan writing is unlike French in that it springs into existence fully armed. The monks at Ripoll felt no apparent need to experiment with vernacular writing approximating Catalan, because there was no market and the vernacular pattern was established in Occitan. The twelfth-century poet known as the Anonymous Lover was aware of Provençal literary traditions, and for all we know may have used them in Occitan poems of his own. Catalan writing seems to have lacked the "experimental" phase attested elsewhere, although some eleventh- and twelfth-century documents have the same kind of Latinate camouflage put onto a vernacular base that is common in the rest of Spain (see Chapter 5).

After the fourth Lateran Council (1215) and the Council of Lleida (1229: see the next chapter), attempts were made to increase the level of Latinity among the priesthood. At the Council of Tarragona in 1233, the following order appeared in second place (Tejada 1849-62: III 363):

> Item, statuitur ne aliquis libros veteris vel novi testamenti in Romancio habeat. Et si aliquis habeat, infra octo dies post publicationem hujusmodi constitutionis a tempore sententiae, tradat eos loci episcopo comburendos. quod nisi fecerit, sive clericus fuerit, sive laicus, tamquam suspectus de haeresi, quousque se purgaverit, habeatur.

Jaume I repeated this in 1234. This has been taken to imply the existence of Catalan Biblical translations, although *Romancio* could as easily be Occitan (or French). The decree concerning vernacular scriptures reiterates one made in 1229, against the Cathars, at the Council of Toulouse, so there may not have been any in Catalan at all. (None of the church councils of the previous century in Catalonia even mention this problem, not even that of Girona, convened in 1197 to combat the Waldensians.) Jaume I was in the event the patron of the establishment of Catalan prose as the official language of the Crown of Aragon, and by the end of his reign lengthy Catalan works of many kinds had appeared.

Catalonia is thus a special case of the Carolingian development of Medieval Latin and written Romance. Further west, the relationship is more complicated.

**Moslem Spain**

Moslems dominated three-quarters of the peninsula until the late eleventh century. At times Christian communities prospered in Moslem Spain; these Christians are now usually called *mozárabes*, although the term was not in use at the time (Hitchcock 1978). Toledo remained the archbishopric, in theory with authority over the north as well. Archbishop Elipando of Toledo became an international figure as the proponent of "adoptionism", a view which was condemned in Regensburg in 792 and then with greater force at the Council of Frankfurt in 794 (*MGH Conc.* II i 110-71). He corresponded with Charlemagne, and at greater length with Alcuin, quoting from the Visigothic liturgy in support of his views (the letters are in Gil 1973a: I 93-111; cp. also Rivera 1940). As a result, a slight taint of heresy remained attached to the Spanish church in European eyes. The church was untouched by the Carolingian revival until well into the eleventh century[1].

Ninth-century Córdoba saw considerable literary activity among the Christians, in particular from Albaro (Paulus Alvarus) and Eulogio (Simonet 1903: 338-502; Gil 1973a: I 143-361, II 363-503; Sage 1943). Eulogio was eventually canonized after his martyrdom on 11th March 859. Albaro wrote his life (Gil 1973a: I 330-43; translated in Sage 1943: 190-214). According to Albaro, Eulogio made a visit to some of the Pyrenean monasteries of Navarra and Aragón in 848 (Lambert 1953; López 1961). It may have been from Leyre that Eulogio brought back the following books:

> librum Civitatis beatissimi Agustini et Eneidos Vergilii sive
> Iubenalis metricos itidem libros atque Flacci saturata poemata seu
> Porfirii depincta opuscula vel Adhelelmi epigramatum opera nec-
> non et Abieni Fabule metrice et Ymnorum catholicorum fulgida
> carmina . . .                                         (chap.9; Gil 1973a: 335-36)[2]

collectively described as *multa volumina librorum . . . abstrusa*.

The poetry in particular seems not to have been previously known in Córdoba. Eulogio recovered the secrets of metric verse and taught them to his associates from the time of his imprisonment in 851; *ibi metricos quos adhuc nesciebant sapientes Hispanie pedes perfectissime docuit nobisque post egressionem suam hostendit*[3]. No metrical

1. The supposed papal authorization of the Visigothic rites in 924 (printed in Tejada 1849-62: III 217) is now thought to be an eleventh-century invention: see Hitchcock (1973: 21).
2. The *Porfirii depincta opuscula* must have been the "shaped" poetry of the fourth-century Publilius Optatianus Porfirius, which was often given rubrics in coloured ink; it was a genre fashionable among the Carolingians and imitated in the Rioja and in Catalonia.
3. The Latin says unambiguously *docuit* (Gil 1973a: 333, ll.15-16), but Sage declares this to be a mistake for *didicit* (1943: 195, n.18).

work of Eulogio's survives, but several hexameters and elegiacs composed by Albaro do (Gil 1973a: 344-61). Pérez de Urbel (1926: 9) said unkindly that if Eulogio had taught Albaro metrics, then the latter's poems show that Eulogio's efforts were in vain: Sage asserted that "of his writings, only the poems are of negligible value" (1943: 216). In fact, given that he thought it permissible to lengthen a final syllable, particularly before the caesura, his poems are not unacceptable. For example, his *Versi in Biblioteca Leobegildi Eiusdem Albari* start as follows:

> Sunt hic plura sacra, sunt vero docmate clara,
> Que Deitatis ope fulgent per cardina mundi,
> Hic noba cum uetera pariter sunt clare decora,
> Aurea dicta Dei, summi prudentia Patris,
> Que totus celebrat quadrato uertice mundus.
> Principium libri Genesis primordia pandit
> Mundi, qui rerum naturas certe reuelat.
> Exodus Egypto populum per bracio ducit.
> Tertjus Leuiticus ornat insigne camillas.
> > (Gil 1973a: 350)

Albaro sometimes points out that his poem is indeed written *metrice*; his *Lamentum metricum* declares "Albarus . . . metrice set ecce revoat" (i.e. *reboat*; 1.4: Gil 1973a: 349). Other scholars to benefit from the rediscovery of metrics (while disregarding the strict rules of elision) were Cyprian (Gil 1973a: 685-88) and the abbot Samson, whose acrostic epitaph for abbot Offilo runs as follows:

> Offilo hic tenui uersus in puluere dormit,
> Fallentem mundum olim qui mente subegit
> Fraglantesque dapes tempsit et pocula fulua,
> Infestum uirgo mallens uitare celidrum.
> Laudetur talis multorum lingua sacerdos,
> > Obtetur illi et celi portio dari.
> > (Gil 1973a: 665)

There is no way of knowing how these were read.

Rhythmic poetry, however, was known before Eulogio's voyage. This erudite genre was taught, within the general grammatical instruction based on Donatus. The traditional hymns were available as models, and the technical definition of a syllable (as a written vowel) was still there in grammars to be used as the basic unit of the rhythmic genre. According to Albaro (Gil 1973a: 332, ll.1-2), he and Eulogio were taught this skill by the abbot Speraindeo, and wrote poems to each other: "rithmicis versibus nos laudibus mulcebamus; et hoc erat exercitium nobis melle suabior, fabis iucundior."[4] Rhythmic poetry was still

4. Sage points out (1943: 193) that this wording comes from Ps. 18,11 (= 19,10).

meant to be sung, and Eulogio was apparently expert at that too: "ubi versi quorum ille ignoraret canora?" (Gil 1973a: 335, l.11). None of these early productions seem to be among the surviving texts. One which Simonet (1903: 342 n.5) by implication dates to the 830s is Vincent's *Carmen Poenitentiale*, described by Simonet as "preciosa muestra del romance octosílabo, usado ya por San Agustín, perfeccionado por los mozárabes" (1903: 343); "a precious example of the octosyllabic ballad form, as used by St Augustine and perfected by the mozarabs". This poem knows no elision and is structured on an octosyllabic hemistich, usually with rhyme:

> Deus miserere mei, D*eus* miserere mei,
> Miserere, miserere, parce in peccatis meis.
> Alme Rector et Redemtor cernuo uultu precamur,
> Qui uenisti liberare sauciumq*ue* telis grauem.
> Tu me libera de penis, pone finem malis meis,
> Ablue que tanta gessi nec sinas baratro mergi.
> Dignum quid minime egi, sed sem*per* in preceps rui,
> Men<te> et corpore deliqui, desiderans malum fui,
> Peccatorum mole pressus erigi post lapsus mallens,
> Manu porrige iacenti et a sorde terge clemens.
> Inmensum malum insectans, nequiter funeste uibens,
> <Sum> lacrimans eiulanter cum merore obsecranti:
> Solue uinculum delicti, excipe precem poscenti<s>,
> Confitenti iam reatu depende quod supplicatur.
> Edidi os uersus idem tristis et amarus quidem:
> Zabulo diu consensi Uincent*jus* ego ipse,
> Miscerique s*anctis* tuis non confido bonis meis.
> Nactus ueniam conmisi<s>, propit*jus* esto mici.
> Gloria tibi creator, gloria, inmense nate:
> Uaiulans crucem suplicii omnem mundum redemisti.

(Gil 1973a: 688)

Julian of Toledo had repeated in his Grammar (II xx 2-4) the old view that rhythmic verse, unlike metric verse, was meant to appeal to the ear. After a list of eight principal metres he added:

> Siquid praeter haec, quod non ad certam pedum legem, sed ad temporum rationem modumque referatur, vel scribit quispiam, vel ab alio scriptum legerit, id non metrum sed rhythmon esse sciat[5].
> ... rhythmus ... numero syllabarum ad iudicium aurium examinata, ut puta veluti sunt cantica vulgarium poetarum. Da eius

---

5. That sentence is taken from Mallius Theodorus (Keil VI 588,23-25), and seems to imply that metric verse was sometimes read aloud in "rhythmic" fashion, i.e. with normal stress. The phrase *cantica vulgarium poetarum* (below) comes from the fourth-century African Marius Victorinus, but the example does not (Keil VI 206).

exemplum: "Lupus dum ambularet viam incontravit asinum"[6].
Potest esse metrum sine rhythmo, aut rhythmus sine metro?
Metrum sine rhythmo esse non potest, rhythmus sine metro esse
potest. Quare? quia metrum est ratio cum modulatione, rhythmus
modulatio sine ratione.

Metric verse is *ratio* — an artificial mathematical calculation — and
*modulatio* — speech pattern, rhythm; rhythmic verse is rhythm without
the calculations. At the time when the Carolingians are elaborating their
own techniques, in Córdoba the "rhythmic poets" seem to be broadly
continuing the tradition as taught by Julian 150 years earlier. Germán
Prado (1928: 56) pointed out that this *Carmen Poenitentiale* was like
the *preces* or *miserationes* of the mozarabic liturgy; that liturgy was
daily performed by such as Vincent and the pattern was familiar to the
ear of any Christian.

Some of the rhymes in this *Carmen* will have "pleased their
ears" by not following the post-Alcuinian precepts of giving the same
pronunciation to a letter on every occasion. E.g. it seems probable that
rhyme is intended in line 3 between *redemtor* and *precamur*; rhyme is
there if we concede contemporary pronunciation even of vanished
morphology (i.e. [preqamor] for *precamur*), but not in post-Carolingian
medieval Latin, where *ur* and *or* require distinct vowels. The same recourse to vernacular can apply to *liberare/gravem* (4), *consensi/ipse*
(16) and *nate/redemisti* (19-20).

Presumably this is modelled on earlier hymns and exploits the
traditional licence to lengthen or preserve syllables unnaturally in performance for the purposes of the musical form. Elision, present in
colloquial speech but not in formal song styles, is absent where it might
be expected in lines 2, 7, 10, 11, 12, 13, 16, 19 and 20. Gil's emendation to *mente* in l.8, however, would require elision with *et*. Romance
palatalizations are similarly avoided in *saucium* (4), *diu* (16), *Vincentius*
himself (16), *propitius* (18), but not in *supplicii* (20), since in the
grammars *ii* is regularly said to be one vowel, not two. This poem is
carefully arranged, but, as Simonet cannily observed, octosyllables
please the natural Spanish ear (as in the ballads) rather than the educated classicist, who does not think in isosyllabic terms, and this

---

6. This line is tantalizing. If it is indeed from a popular song, subsequent Spanish
developments suggest the stresses are on *Lúp-, -ár-, ví-, -tráu-, ás-* (cp. *lobo,
andare, vía, encontró, asno*), which form no clear pattern. Julian says it is
based on the number of syllables; in strict rhythmic technique this, like Vincent's *Carmen*, has sixteen written syllables but without a caesura (as does the
manuscript variant *lupus dum ambulabat viam obviavit asynum*; Bischoff 1959
n.27). The odds are, then, that this is not a popular song; all that "rhythmic"
and popular verse share is a disregard of quantity.

*Carmen* is interpretable as high-style but vernacular Spanish of the ninth century.

There are perhaps thirty to forty mozarabic hymns surviving from Moslem Spain. *Analecta Hymnica* XXVII is the mozarabic volume, but makes no systematic attempt to distinguish those composed in Moslem Spain from those composed further north. Some have been attributed to Albaro and Eulogio. Thorsberg (1962) ascribes *AH* XXVII no.113 to Eulogio because of the acrostic, and suggests nos.111 and 167 are also his; she also suggests that nos.126 and 207 could be Albaro's. Szövérffy (1971: 55) also ascribes no.118 to Albaro, which celebrates Eulogio himself and has the acrostic *Albarus te rogat saves* (?=*salves*). (Messenger (1946) discusses these hymns as if the composers knew of Frankish customs, which is doubtful.) Hymns are intrinsically intended for oral reproduction, and are thus rhythmic rather than metric. Norberg (1968: 135-46) has devoted an extended study to Albaro's *Christus est virtus* (no.126), pointing out that *-o*, *-u* and *-um* rhyme, that *cui* is disyllabic, only two cases of syncopation (*deifica*, *idoneus*) and "exemples d'une prosodie extrêmement bizarre" such as the stressed [e] in *fuero* (IX 5, as in O. Sp. *fuere*).

Szövérffy said of the Spanish hymns that "in some cases the exact rhythmical principles determining the verse forms are not yet clear" (1971: 201). Editors have long been prepared to allow for the prothetic *e-* before words beginning with *s* and another consonant; e.g. *AH* XXVII no.207, Stanza 4, 1.2: *Deceptis oculis cernunt (e)squalida*. If Thorsbaro is right to attribute this hymn to Albaro, then he must be assumed to have used such a prothetic syllable himself. This hymn has assonance with final *-a*; if we postulate vernacular pronunciation, with *-m* and *-t* as "silent" letters, the whole hymn rhymes in [-a] with the exception of stanza 9. (In stanza 9 the rhyme words are *nuptias, serviant, referant, maneant*.) Some of the regularity Szövérffy seeks is to be found in vernacular phonetics.

Most of Albaro's work was in carefully worked prose, with an elaborate literary style, including prose rhyme and the rhythmic clausulae to be found in Augustine and Jerome (Sage 1943: III 4). The manuscript of his prose works, now MS 123 in the archive of Córdoba cathedral (García y García et al 1976) is said by Díaz y Díaz (1979: 167 n.6) to be a tenth-century Northern copy, but there is no reason not to assume that it is a faithful copy; and Díaz y Díaz previously pointed out (1957: 381) what a number of confusions there are here between voiced and unvoiced consonants (e.g. *reveratur* for *referatur*). Eulogio's prose works only survive in the transcription made in 1574 by Ambrosio de Morales of Alcalá, whose version was reprinted by Migne (*PL* CXV 703-966). Morales said (918B) that the Latin of his text was too bad to be reproduced verbatim. He edited it, reluctantly ("nos religione quadam reverenter tacti, nihil emendare voluimus"), but printed a selection of solecisms to show that within it there were "genera confusa, casus perversi, numeri in nominibus et verbis neglecti: et tota inde Latini sermonis structura dissipata, describentium; non auctoris fuisse vitia, est manifestum. Idcirco nos omnia eiusmodi emendavimus . . .". It seemed obvious (*manifestum*) to Morales that the non-Classical nature of the text could not be ascribed to Eulogio himself, but that seems less likely now. Simonet (1888: CXXXVI-VII) pointed out that the same abundance of "solecisms" is to be found in virtually all mozarabic documents, including the works of Elipando of Toledo, Albaro, Samson, and the Acts of the Council of Córdoba in 839. In particular he showed the breakdown of the original case system, with such examples as *vestro scripto accepi, cum complices, ad nullo misterio, per toto orbe*, etc., where singular forms end in vowels and the plural adds *s*; Gil (1971: 201) concluded that "the collapse of the case system could hardly be more complete" in Albaro's works. Miles (1950: 113) mentions bilingual gold coins, dated to 716-17, of which the non-Arabic inscription reads FERITOSSOLIINSPANANXCVII (SOLI for *solidos*, as Amador 1862: II 582 suggests; unless FERITOS is a mistake for FERITUS, as Miles proposes).

The Early Romance of Moslem Spain was known to its users as *latinus*. This word can lead to modern confusion; the Visigothic scholars used it to contrast with Greek or Hebrew, and Simonet (1888: XXIII-IV, XXXV-VII) established that in Moslem Spain it was used to refer to the non-Arabic vernacular (as was Arabic *Al-Lathiní*). It is not contrasted with any other variety of Latin-Romance speech, and no hint appears of the existence of two spoken layers. There are indications, however, that the writing of this *latinus* in the correct manner was hard.

There is a famous but obscure passage at the end of Albaro's *Indiculus Luminosus*, an anti-Moslem tract, in which Albaro seems to be complaining that many Christians do not know their own language. What he seems to mean is that they can read and write Arabic but cannot read and write their native *latinus*:

Sic et dum illor*um* sacramenta inquirim*us* et filosoforu*m*, immo filocomporu*m* sectas scire non pro ipsor*um* con*u*inciendos herrores, set pro elegantjam leporis et locutjonem luculenter dissertam neglectis *sanct*is lectjonib*us* congregamus, nicil aliut quam numerum nom*i*nis ei*us* in cuuiculo nostro qvasi idola conlocamus. Quis, rogo, odie sollers in nostris fidelib*us* laycis inuenit*u*r,

qui scripturis *sanct*is intentus uolumina quor*um*quu*m*que doctor*um* Latine conscripta respiciat? Quis euangelico, q*uis* profetico,
quis ap*osto*lico ustus tenetur amore? Nonne hom*n*es iubenes
X͞piani uultu decori, lingue disserti, habitu gestuq*ue* co*n*spicui,
gentilici<a> erudit*j*oni preclari, Harabico eloquio sublimati
uolumina Caldeor*um* hauidissime tractant, intentissime leg*un*t,
ardentissime disserunt et ingenti studio congregantes lata con-
strinctaq*ue* lingua laudando diuulgant, eclesiastica*m* pulcritu-
dinem ignorantes et eclesiae flumina de paradiso manant*j*a quasi
uilissima contemnentes? Heu pro dolor, legem sua*m* nesciunt
X͞piani et linguam propria*m* non aduertunt Latini, ita ut omni
X͞pi collegio uix inueniatur unus in milleno hominum numero qui
salutatorias f*ratr*i possit rat*j*onauiliter dirigere litteras, et repperitur
absque numero multiplices turbas qui erudite Caldaicas uerbor*um*
explicet pompas, ita ut metrice erudit*j*ori ab ipsis gentib*us*
carmine et sublimiori pulcritudine finales clausulas unius littere
coartat*j*one decorent, et iuxta quod lingue ipsius requirit idioma,
q*ue* om*n*es uocales apices co*m*mata claudit et cola, rithmice,
immo ut ipsis conpetit, metrice uniuersi alfabeti littere p*er* uarias
dict*j*ones plurimas uariantes uno fine constringuntur u*el* simili
apice. Multa et alia erant que *nostr*e huic exposit*j*oni exiberent
firmitatem, immo q*ue* ipsam patule in lucem producer*et*.

(Gil 1973a: 314-15)

The section from *Quis, rogo, . . .* onwards has been bravely
translated by Colbert (1962: 301) as follows:

What trained person, I ask, can be found today among our laity
who with a knowledge of Holy Scripture looks into the Latin
volumes of any of the doctors? Who is there on fire with evan-
gelical love, with love like that of the prophets, like that of the
apostles? Do not all the Christian youths, handsome in appearance, fluent of tongue, conspicuous in their dress and action,
distinguished for their knowledge of Gentile lore, highly regarded
for their ability to speak Arabic, do they not all eagerly use the
volumes of the Chaldeans, read them with the greatest interest,
discuss them ardently, and, collecting them with great trouble,
make them known with every praise of their tongue, the while
they are ignorant of the beauty of the Church and look with
disgust upon the Church's rivers of paradise as something vile.
Alas! Christians do not know their own law, and Latins do not
use their own tongue, so that in all the college of Christ there will
hardly be found one man in a thousand who can send correct
letters of greeting to a brother. And a manifold crowd without
number will be found who give out learnedly long sentences of
Chaldean rhetoric. So that from the more sophisticated song of
those people they embellish their final clauses metrically and in
more polished beauty with the bond of a single letter, according
to the demands of that tongue, which closes all phrases and
clauses with riming vowels and even, as is possible for them, the

various expressions containing the letters of the whole alphabet are all metrically reduced to one ending or to a similar letter. There are many other things which would have shown the reliability of this explanation of ours; that is, which would have brought out into the light the things we are exposing.

The text is too obscure for a translation of some of the details to be established with certainty, but a few conclusions can be drawn. *Litterae* here are letters of the alphabet or epistolary, but not the *litterae* which have become standard in the contemporary Carolingian civilization as the method for reading aloud. The word *latini* is used to refer to people of Hispano-Roman-Gothic descent, as if it is a near-synonym of *cristiani*; works *latine conscripta* are contrasted to works in Arabic. This meaning of *latinus* is that of the surviving vernacular word *latinado*, as used in the *Poem of the Cid* 1.2667: there the *moro latinado* is so called specifically because he speaks and understands vernacular Spanish (Michael 1976):

> "Ya pues que a dexar avemos      fijas del Campeador,
> "si pudiéssemos matar      el moro Avengalvón.
> "quanta rriquiza tiene      aver la iemos nós.
> "Tan en salvo lo abremos      commo lo de Carrión,
> "nunqua avrié derecho de nós      el Cid Campeador."
> Quando esta falsedad      dizién los de Carrión,
> un moro latinado      bien ge lo entendió;
> non tiene poridad,      dixolo [a] Avengalvón:
> "Acayaz, cúriate d'éstos,      ca eres mío señor,
> "tu muert oí cosseiar      a los ifantes de Carrión."

(2661-70)

The word *ladino* (<LATINUM) survived with the specific linguistic meaning of "Spanish written by Jews", and with the meaning of "cunning", particularly for romance-speaking *moros*; *latinado* was rendered as *ladino* in a Chronicle prosification of the epic (Menéndez Pidal 1944: 729). The word *latín*, which specifically does refer to a non-Romance Latin, is a borrowing from the French, taken in c.1100; its French provenance is made almost certain by the absence of the original final syllable. (The distinction between *latín* and Spanish seems to be adopted then too.) The use of *latinus* to mean Latin-Romance, as opposed to Arabic, is also found north of the religious border; the foundation charter of the Navarrese monastery of San Martín de Albelda (8-1-924) mentions "qui locus vocatur illorum incredulorum chaldea lingua Albelda, nos quoque latino sermone nuncupamus Alba"; Arabic *albaida* and Latin *alba* both mean "white" (Vicuña Ruiz 1971: 219). The much-quoted Toledo document which distinguishes *latinum circa romançum* from *latinum obscurum* is a red herring, for it is dated

1290; Latin and Romance are obviously distinguished by then, and applying this distinction to earlier times is anachronistic[7]. The final section of Albaro's complaint is intriguing. He seems there to be describing a practice whereby Christians take over Arabic verses and add bits of their own to the end. The text is almost unintelligible, but it is tempting to suggest that they might conceivably be using the *muwashshaha* form, the endings of some of which contain the supposedly Romance *kharjas*.

The most interesting comments on Christian language in Moslem Spain, however, come from the Abbot Samson. He seems to have been employed to translate letters from Arabic into *latinum eloquium* in the year 863:

> Et ut mea oratio retrogradet paululum, dum epistole regis Hispanie ad regem Francorum essent sub era DCCCIa dirigende, appellatvs ex regio decreto ego ipse, quatenus, ut pridem facere consue-ueram, ex Caldeo sermone in Latinum eloquium ipsas epistolas deberem transferre, adfui et feci.          (Gil 1973a: 554)

Colbert (1962: 363-64) points out that these letters were sent with a delegation to Charles the Bald (which returned in 865). Samson is proud of his erudition. In his *Apologeticus*, written to defend himself from charges of heresy, he takes the time to attack the language used by his opponent Hostegesis (*Apol.* II 7; Gil 1973a: 569-72; translation, Colbert 1962: 371-78). Samson complains that Hostegesis misspelt *contenti* as *contempti*, and follows it with a nominative rather than the dative, in *contempti essemus simplicitas Xpiana* (I 22); although (as Hagerty 1978: 234 points out) it should in fact take the ablative. Hostegesis mistakes the gender of *pestis* (IV 5-9), and calls Samson an *idoiatrix*, a word never before said nor heard (V 15-20). Such matters are collectively regarded as a lack of *latinitas*. In Hostegesis' written condemnation of Samson, "si latinitatem quis querat, difficile poterit invenire" (I 9-10); he is, by general consent, "magis barbarum quam oratorem latine facundie" (I 19); this ridicule is shared by "omnes latinitatis gnari" (II 1); he is called a "nove latinitatis inventor" (III 12),

---

7. Quoted by Menéndez Pidal 1926: para.95: "Ille est vituperandus qui loquitur latinum circa romançum, maxime coram laicis, ita quod ipso met intelligunt totum; et ille est laudandus qui semper loquitur latinum obscure, ita quod nullus intelligat eum nisi clerici; et ita debent omnes clerici loqui latinum suum obscure in quantum possunt et non circa romançum." This is in any event a translation of an apocryphal remark in Arabic. For its modern misuse as a comment on pre-reform language, see e.g. Avalle (1965) and the excellent review by Harris (1967). *Latinum* is in fact the same noun phrase in both sentences meaning "Latin"; the contrast is between the adverbial phrases *circa romançum* and *obscure*.

even an "auctor lingue nobelle" (V 5-6). As regards *idolatrix*:

> Si latinus sermo ... hoc recipere non recusaret, si Romana facundia caperet, si urbanum labium fari posse monstraret, *idolator vir* et *idolatrix mulier* dicere quispiam posset ...
>
> (V 10-12)

The *barbarus* is criticized for *rusticitas*, and if he gets something right it is only by accident, "furtuitu casu recta conscribere", since he is incapable of consciously achieving "nitorem Romani sermonis" (V 33-36). This latter comment shows that here *latinitas* involves the written skill of emulating the long-dead Romans. Hostegesis's failings are specifically in the art of writing; a failure to use correctly the morphology, orthography and vocabulary taught in the best schools on the basis of venerated ancient texts. Had there been a Latin-Romance distinction, it is hard to believe that Samson could not have found something phonetic to criticize in his opponent's usage; yet the *contenti/contempti* distinction, for example, is discussed in orthographical terms ("per n scribitur, non per m, ut tu, indocte doctor, temptasti scribere"). *Latinitas* here is a skill that can be exercised well or clumsily (*barbare*; *rustice*) according to the ability to write respectably; it has no implications for speech.

This nugget of pedantic invective begins as follows:

> Ait nempe idem hostis Ihesu crudelis[8]: 'In nomine sancte et uenerande Trinitatis nos omnes pusilli famuli X̄p̄i presidentes in concilio Cordobensi minimi sacerdotes, quum in nostro conuentu eclesiastica discernerentur negotia et diuinitus dispensata contempti essemus simplicitas X̄p̄iana, ex improuisu quidam corrupta pestis, Samson nomine, sponte prosiliens, multas impietates in Deum multasque sententias contra regulam predicauit, in tantum ut immo idolatrix quam X̄p̄ianus assertor esse uideretur'. Hec sunt uerba uersi primi ab inpurissimo ore sub nomine dictata concilii. Ubi si Latinitatem quis querat, difficile poterit inuenire, si ortografie disciplinam, nullam sentiet esse, si sensum discutiat, insani capitis uerba mox poterit censere. Quis non dicam grammaticus, non retoricus uel dialecticus, non filosofus aut ortografus, sed, ut ita dicam, communium tantummodo litterarum utcumque imbutus non illum risui dignum poterit definire, non a pueris subsannandum peribere, quem confidentem in stul<ti>tia sua et mentem cutvrno fuco inflatam conspicans habere, adhuc ordinem sillabarum ignarum nec tempora uerborum doctum, tam rancidola orsa inflatis bucis sub nomine episcoporum aniliter audit dictare, quum constet eum magis barbarum quam oratorem Latine facundie esse?
>
> (Gil 1973a: 569 ll.1-19)

---

8. *Hostis Ihesu* is Samson's little joke (i.e. *Hostegesis*).

The Córdoba scholars of this period are, then, capable of written sophistication at a variety of levels; the stylistic distinctiveness of the written from the spoken genres was considerable. We are not justified, however, in seeing a separate "Latin" in existence alongside old *mozárabe* Romance. *Latinus* meant "Romance" and was distinguished from Arabic alone. Eulogio, Albaro, Samson and the others spoke their own language, albeit with an unusually large vocabulary. There is no reflection here of contemporary Carolingian scholarship. Albaro's Christian writings are as determinedly polished as Samson's, but Sage's studies have established that they are within the continuous tradition of the Visigothic scholars' analysis of patristic works; his style is "fundamentally scriptural" (1943: 182). Their culture looked back, not north; their approved linguistic standards are those of the past, not those of a contemporary erudite alternative.

Moslem Spain has acquired philological interest for a further reason: the *kharjas*. These are apparently bilingual (Arabic-Romance) or macaronic final stanzas of some verses in the Hispano-Arabic *muwashshaha* form discovered in some Arabic and Hebrew manuscripts (for bibliography, see Hitchcock 1977; Hitchcock 1980 decides that the Romance element may be minimal). Analyses of these have been hampered in the past by the belief that we know too little about *mozárabe* Romance to discuss the "Romance" element on a sound philological basis; but this is not entirely true. The 700 pages of Gil's *Corpus*, and the mozarabic hymns, can – if used with care – give us evidence of mozarabic vocabulary and even phonetics. The work of Díaz y Díaz on Visigothic and mozarabic "Latin" is largely about the vernacular. The detailed investigations by Galmés de Fuentes (e.g. 1977, 1980) on later documents and toponyms have established the main features of *mozárabe* phonology, and many features of its morphology, on a considerably surer basis than the informed guesswork of Menéndez Pidal and his followers. The conclusion seems to be that *mozárabe* Romance is not particularly different from that of other parts of Iberia. The idea that the "mozarabic" texts represent Latin and therefore not vernacular has hidden from view their use for the *kharja* controversies; the fact that the reconstructable Romance elements of the *kharjas* are colloquial need not mean that their originators were at all ignorant or rustic or uneducated. In practice, they seem more likely to be cultured than popular verse. If so, it is no surprise to find that they are in Romance rather than "Medieval Latin". Medieval Latin did not exist in Moslem Spain before the fall of Toledo (1085), and probably never existed there at all.

### Toledo

Toledo had been the Visigothic capital and its archbishop remained the nominal head of the Spanish Church; after its recapture by
the Christians in 1085 it became again a flourishing cultural centre. It
has thus seemed reasonable to suppose that it was an important centre
of Christian Romance culture throughout the Moslem period. Yet not
many Toledan manuscripts can be dated with certainty to between 711
and 1085 (Díaz y Díaz 1975: 142-52). Simonet listed several (1888:
XXVII-IX), but Simonet shared the general belief that all manuscripts
written in Visigothic script necessarily pre-dated 1085, which is now
known not to be the case. Nor were all manuscripts found in Toledo
necessarily written there. For example, one from Toledo which is specifically dated is Madrid BN 10007, a *Vitae Patrum* including the works
of Valerio del Bierzo, signed "Armentarius" and dated 902; this manuscript contains Persian dress in an illuminated initial (f.176; Guilmain
1976: 186); Díaz y Díaz (1979: 136 n.11), however, declares it to be
*leonés* rather than from Toledo (and Gil 1973b: 192 dates it to the end
of the century from the script). Many of the Toledo manuscripts have
recently been reassigned dates in the twelfth century. One of these
is the Latin-Arabic glossary now at Leiden, which Van Koningsveld
(1977) has redated to a milieu of Arabic-speaking (not necessarily
monolingual) Christians in reconquered Toledo, whereas Menéndez
Pidal (1926), for example, assumed it came from Moslem Spain. Van
Koningsveld, whose expertise is in Arabic palaeography, studied all the
26 surviving manuscripts in Visigothic script with Arabic glosses, and
dated all the glosses to the twelfth century, and most of the codices
also. The European sources found in these manuscripts thus cease to be
usable as evidence for European culture in Moslem Spain[9]. The most
interesting of these manuscripts has been Toledo Cathedral MS 99.30, a
grammatical treatise with Arabic and Latin glosses. Codoñer (1966) had
formerly dated this to the tenth century, and the Latin glosses to a later
date. The sources include Donatus, Priscian and Julian; the Priscian
material has roots further north, and Díaz y Díaz (1976b: 153) concluded that the manuscript was copied in Toledo from material that
came from France, perhaps via Catalonia. This is the manuscript that
contains, inserted onto an originally empty folio (26r), the list of
animals and their noises mentioned in Chapter 1, which Díaz y Díaz
connects with another European tradition as exemplified in a similar

9. Cixila took many manuscripts from Toledo to Abellar, in León, in 927 (see
   e.g. Díaz y Díaz 1975: 161), but these were probably of Visigothic date,
   rather than recent copies.

list in Aldhelm's Metrics. Mundó (1965: 15, and plate 17) first suggested the later date for this, now supported by Van Koningsveld, and the individuality of the codex has thus disappeared.

The same has happened to Madrid BN 10001. Amador declared it to be pre-Reconquest (1862: I 471); Mundó put it to the central eleventh century (1965: 20); and Díaz y Díaz (1976a: 243-45) has proclaimed it to be a twelfth-century copy of a Northern manuscript. Doubts therefore accrue to the early dating given by Brou (1951: 33-35) to the sequence *Alme virginis festum* found in it. The same doubts apply to Brou's two other supposedly "mozarabic" sequences found in a Córdoba manuscript fragment dated, it now seems misguidedly, by Millares Carlo to the tenth century: *Alma sollemnitas* and *Orbis conditor regressus est* (28-30, 35-37). Brou realizes that the dating is crucial: the presence of sequences in Spain at this time is no longer attested in the light of the revised dating of the manuscript, and indeed it can no longer be stated as a certainty that Southern Christians used hymns composed after 711 north of the religious frontier, nor even that Christians in Moslem Toledo were active scholars.

The conclusions of Díaz y Díaz, Mundó and Van Koningsveld, working independently, are that after 1085 the Christian communities of Toledo acquired large numbers of manuscripts from the North, and copied them. The time of the most avid copying of Visigothic liturgy thus coincides understandably with the unpopular proclamation of its abandonment for the Roman. This does not remove the interest from the manuscripts; but it does put them in the quite different context of post-Reconquest Toledo, thereby postponing further discussion to the next chapter.

### Asturias

Events in Moslem Spain were followed with interest in the unconquered areas of the North-Western mountains. There was a steady trickle of exiles, which at times — with official encouragement — became a stream. In 882 Alfonso III of Asturias managed to have the remains of Eulogio and his protégée martyr Leocritia brought to his capital, Oviedo. Tenth-century northern hymnals include hymns almost certainly composed in the south. Much of the written material from the North-West in these centuries was written by, or under the guidance of, immigrants from the south.

This area was strongly Visigothic and Christian in sentiment. They jealously preserved their Visigothic inheritance insofar as they knew what it was. Much of the old Visigothic culture had come there at the time of, and after, the Moslem invasion, from Toledo and elsewhere (Díaz y Díaz 1969: 391; Mahn 1949). In the late eighth century there were schisms in the Asturian church (admirably summarized in Díaz y Díaz 1976a: 247-51), partly connected with fluctuations in policy towards Islam, mainly concerned with the views of their nominal superior Elipando of Toledo. He declared that Christ "was adopted by God in respect of his human nature, but not in respect of his divine nature" (Livermore 1971: 349); the Northern scholars Beato of Liébana and Heterio of Osma rejected this idea. Eventually Felix, Bishop of Urgell, brought this to the attention of the Carolingian Court and of Pope Hadrian I, who also rejected it. The effect was to distance the Asturian church from Toledo, but not to lead to close contacts with the Carolingians. The Asturians kept the Visigothic liturgy, and the Carolingians continued to believe it to be heretical.

Einhard, biographer of Charlemagne, is sometimes thought to have implied that Alfonso II of Asturias declared allegiance to Charlemagne (Garrod and Mowat 1915: chap.16). This is improbable, and in practice meaningless even if true. Leonese chronicles of the twelfth and thirteenth centuries elaborated and expanded this link with imaginative creativity, but (as Défourneaux 1949 pointed out) no Spanish history before 1100 even mentions Charlemagne. (Sholod 1966 also said that Alfonso II had close links, but Sholod is not reliable on Leonese matters.) There are a few pilgrims to Santiago – ninth-century Carolingian coins have been found under Santiago cathedral (Sánchez Albornoz 1980: 96); Alfonso III received a letter from the inhabitants of Tours after the Viking attack on Tours in 903, to which his reply (of 906) survives (Floriano 1951: II 339-42); but contact was unsystematic. Carolingian scholarship, at least, had no great influence.

Whatever links there were with the Carolingians and their successors, we can be sure that liturgical reform was not involved until well into the eleventh century. Tradition weighed stronger than Papal disapproval; the Visigothic rites survived. There seems no reason to suppose that the vigorous advocacy of "correct" liturgical pronunciation as promulgated further East was emulated in Asturias. The Visigothic script remains until the late eleventh century and beyond. It is possible that a very few Iberian monasteries were run on the exclusively Benedictine lines that accompanied the educational standardization in the Carolingian culture; Linage (1973a: 1002-05) believes that some were, other scholars (e.g. Floriano 1951) do not. Generally, individual monasteries tended to choose their own organization eclectically, usually on the basis of the Hispanic rules of Isidore or Fructuoso of Braga, and it is agreed that none used the Roman liturgy. There was also a variety which Bishko (1951) has called "Pactual" monasticism, most common in Galicia, where the community was run democratically according to a charter of rights drawn up between abbot and monks. This kind of monastery spread East to Castille and Southern Navarre from the late ninth century. Although Benedictine influence is not unknown in León no completely Benedictine monastery may have been established before the accession of Alfonso VI in 1072; the simultaneous obsession with liturgy and literacy that characterizes the propagation of the Carolingian reforms on their home territory is not present in (non-Catalan) Spanish monasticism. If the theory outlined in previous chapters is valid, it is impossible to visualize the general arrival of Medieval Latin into Spain outside Catalonia before the increasing cultural contacts of the eleventh century and adoption of the Roman Liturgy after 1080.

### "Leonese Vulgar Latin"

Some people learnt to write. If the theory under examination holds, until the advent of reformed Latin, the documents produced in Asturias-León were written by speakers of Old Leonese. The techniques of official writing were not updated; as time went by the skill needed to make written language appear suitably archaic became increasingly hard to acquire; the vernacular grew ever more dissimilar to the straitjacket decreed in Grammars, while the general educational level continued well below that of the seventh century. It is not surprising that exiles from the south who could write were often asked to do so.

The documents from Asturias (or León, as the kingdom was called after 914) are, therefore, not in very good "Latin". Later copies refurbish the spelling so as to disguise this, but the surviving originals in Floriano's diplomatic collection (1951) look now like a kind of hybrid between Latin and vernacular. This is explicable as the outcome of trying to write in a system devised to suit the purposes of the language of a millennium earlier. The same might occur if we tried to write English with Anglo-Saxon spelling, morphology and vocabulary. Menéndez Pidal (1926: para.95), however, believed that, in addition to the coexistence of Latin and Romance, these documents attested the existence in the same community of yet a third language intermediate between the other two, which he christened *latín vulgar leonés*. Menéndez Pidal's *Orígenes* first appeared in 1926. In context it was an outstanding work, temporarily putting Spain in the vanguard of Romance philology, and it is still indispensable. However, such is his

prestige that his views are still repeated with respect (e.g. Lapesa 1980)
even in cases such as this where they are hard to justify. The idea that
an unsophisticated rural community could produce such a tripartite
system, and also produce documents in a phonetic script designed to
reflect accurately the hybrid Latin-vernacular habits of their originators,
is not only implausible but unnecessary.

We have no direct access to the nature of tenth-century Old
Leonese speech. There are not even any contemporary Grammarians.
Every theory involves speculation. Surviving texts tell us little about
speech, but might tell us something about reading aloud. Reading aloud
is a different question from spontaneous speech in that it can lead the
reader to produce syntax and vocabulary which he would not otherwise
utter; there is absolutely no reason, however, why reading aloud should
make any more difference to phonology than in altering the statistical
incidence of contemporary "variable" sounds. Sociolinguistic theory
has established that – in every community so far studied – careful
speech can have a few features that distinguish it from spontaneous
speech; this does not *per se* involve the systematic retention of archaic
phonetic features, however, since the variability is between a few contemporary alternatives rather than between stages on an evolutionary
scale (e.g. Chambers and Trudgill 1980: chap.4.6). The variation
concerned is slight enough for it to make little difference to the study
of the distant past. Unless we have other extrinsic reasons for thinking
otherwise, we can assume that the reading aloud of a tenth-century
document was in a sociolinguistic and stylistic variety of tenth-century
vernacular phonetics.

The document below concerns a sale of land near León on May
11th 908 A.D. (from Floriano 1951: II 361-62; with a photocopy of
the original):

In Dej nom*i*ne. Ego Splendonius tiui Fredesinde In Dom*i*no
salutem. Id*e*o placuit mici atq*u*e conuenit, nunlljusq*u*e cogentis
Inperio neq*u*e suadentjs artjculo set probria mici acesi uoluntas
ut uinderem tjui Iam dicte Fredesinde terra In uilla Uiasco
suber Illa senrra domniga lloco predicto Agro rrodundo. Ipsa   5
terra atpretiata In duos m*o*di*o*s et duas quartas, et dedistj mici
pro Id*e*m In pretjo sicera et zeuaria cod mici bene conplacuit,
et d*e* Ipso pretjo abut te nicill remansi, aueas, adeas, uindices ac
defendas et quidquid exinde agere facere uel Iudigare uuolue-
ris lljueram In D*e*i nom*i*ne abeas potestatem. Et si quis tamen, cod  10
f*i*eri minime non credo, aljquis tjui contra anc uindicionem
mea at Inr*u*mpendum uenerit u*e*l uenire conauero Imfram u*e*l
Imferat pars m*e*a partjq*u*e tue ipsa terra dubplata. Facta uindi-
cio U. Idus magji era DCCCC X^v VI^a.

Splendonius In anc uindicione ac me facta man*um* mea *(Signum)*.
  a) + Armantarius pres*b*iter test*is (Signum)*. − + Ermegjldus test*is (Signum)*. + Florencjus test*is (Signum)*.
  b) Presencius test*is (Signum)*. − Nebridius test*is (Signum)*.

We can presume that lawyers wrote in this strange way as a result of their professional training; the consequence is a text which contains both legal terminology and Romance elements, and is the kind of text that led to the postulation of "Leonese Vulgar Latin". It could, however, easily have been read aloud by the notary in vernacular Leonese more or less as follows:

[endíenwémne. íoesplendóɲo tíefɾedzínde endwéɲosalúde. ɟjoplógomíe ekombíne núʎjoskekodʒjéntesempéɾjoniswaðjéntesaɾtéʎo sepɾóbɾjamíeatsézevoluntáde ovendjéɾetíejaðíjtafɾedzínde tjéraenvíllavjásko sobɾelaséɾnaðoɲíga ʎwégopɾeðíjto áɣɾorodóndo. ésatjéra apɾetsjádaendózmójoseðúaskwáɾtas eðístemíepoɾíðe empɾétsjo sídzɾaetseβejɾa kemíeβjénekomplógo, eðésepɾétsjoabotíní:lɾemáze áβjas ájas véndzes eðefjéndas, ekékeʃénde adʒéɾe fadzéɾe velʒulgáɾevoljéɾes ʎíβɾa endíenwémne áβjaspodestáde. esekítamne, kefjéɾeménmenokɾéo, alkítíe kwéntɾaŋkvendzónemía aenrompjéndovinjéɾe velveníɾekonáɾo, énfra velénfɾapáɾtemía páɾteketúe, ésatjéraðobláda. féjtavendzóne tsíɲkoíðozmáʒe éɾanovetsjéntoskwaɾéntasjésta. esplendóɲoenánkvendzóne amiféjtamánomía aɾmantéjɾopɾéstɾetjéste eɾmedʒíldotjéste floréntsjotjéste pɾezéntsjotjéste neβɾíjotjéste]

The details of this transcription are not intended to be taken as definitive; the point being made is that reading aloud could have used Old Leonese phonetics even for such apparently Latinate material as a legal document, in the same way as readers of Modern English documents can read legal language aloud with their own phonetic habits. Dutton (1980) has established that legal documents regularly were read aloud to interested parties in a manner they could understand. Those words that still exist in the vernacular as lexical units would be given the pronunciation that they normally had in León in 908[10]. We are legitimately

---

10. The document includes the Visigothic sign for 40 and is ostensibly dated 946; Spanish documents prior to the reign of Juan I (in the 1380s) were dated by the "era hispánica" which started in 38 B.C. For an explanation see Torres Rodríguez (1976). Some details of the transcription are there as the result of my need to make a decision, when transcribing, in doubtful cases. For practical purposes I have omitted the [-s] in the nominative singular but kept it in the genitives of the formulaic sections; added the extra syllable to the imparisyllabic nominatives; omitted [-t] and [-d]; fricativized initial *d-* and *b-* if preceded by a vowel within the breathgroup − e.g. *micibene* (1.7), [mieβjene] − but not voiced any word-initial unvoiced consonants; assumed that *-u* is [-o], even though parts of León preserve [-u] (this does not materially affect the argument); and included the [l] of Leonese *julgar* < IUDICARE. It is likely that many details are wrong, but that does not upset the general point.

entitled to be hazy about what that was in many cases, however much
we trust reconstructions, but some details seem firm enough. For
example, the diphthongization of stressed short [ɛ] will have happened
by then; thus when read aloud, *terra* (1.4) would be [tjéɾa], *cogentis*
(1.2) [kodʒjéntes], etc. The diphthongization of stressed short [ɔ]
would similarly lead to the reading of *loco* (1.5) with [we]. The intervocalic plosives would have voiced; thus *loco* also has [g], *salutem* (1.2)
is [salúde], and *abut* (1.8) – i.e. *apud* – [abo]. Such words would cause
no more difficulty than reading *sovereign* as [sóvɹɪn], or *thoroughly* as
[θʌɹəlɪ], *heureux* as [œʀø] or *travaillent* as [tʀavaj]; the problem
would arise if people felt they had to say [sóvereign], [thórouxlɪ],
[heuʀéux], [tʀaváillent], [térra], [lóco], [salútem], etc. The practical
purpose of writing words on a page is to indicate the right lexical item
to the reader; originally semi-phonetic spellings can achieve this even if
they have in time become distant from evolved phonetics, precisely
because the reader has been taught to recognize them and takes the
discrepancies in his stride.

Vocabulary that has fallen out of vernacular use presents a
different problem to the reader. The archaic words in legal formulae
that make up a large proportion of most documents could be pronounced according to the normal rules of tenth-century Leonese sound-
letter equivalence. For example, *agere* (1.9) would be read as [adʒére]
rather than [ágere], since at that time all infinitives had come to be
stressed on the thematic vowel (cp. FÁCERE > *fazér* > *hacer*) and the
letter *g* before *e* normally represented [dʒ] or even [ʒ] as in *cogentis*
(1.2). *Exinde* (1.9) would be read as [eʃénde] rather than [eksínde] since *x*
normally represented a [ʃ] sound (e.g. O. Sp. *exir*, from EXIRE, pronounced with [ʃ] as in Italian *uscire*) and the *inde* in *deinde* corresponded to O. Sp. *dende*. For us to expect the reader to have attempted
to reproduce the phonology of the previous millennium is less reasonable
than expecting Shakespearean speeches to be delivered now in the
phonology of 1600; not only would it be very difficult, even for a
specialist, it would be quite unnecessary. These principles of reading
aloud are not hard for us to recreate. Where difficulties are more likely
to arise, both for us and for the tenth-century Leonese, is in outdated
morphology. Outdated word order is of no consequence; the words
could be read in the order written, and if this led to problems of comprehension no lawyer is likely to have minded about that. Word-
endings, however, might have worried people. In nominal morphology
there would be little difficulty in cases such as the ablative singular,
where the lack of an ablative function in syntax was of no significance

because the forms were usually indistinguishable in the vernacular from that derived regularly from the accusative. *Rrodundo*, for example (1.5), could be read [rodóndo] – or [redóndo], if the dissimilatory initial vowel change had already happened: it is modern Sp. *redondo* – and no problem would arise since the accusative -UM forms were also pronounced [-o]. Genitive singulars might appear to be a stylistic peculiarity of the legal genre, but would cause no phonetic problem: the transcriptions of *Dej* as [díe], *cogentis* as [kodʒjéntes], in the formulaic parts, are only guesswork on my part, but it would hardly have mattered if they sounded a bit strange (like *-e*, *-en* as now pronounced in texts of Chaucer). The nominative singular provides us – and perhaps them also – with a problem; since the accusative-derived forms were the normal forms of the vernacular, the final [-s] was becoming a marker for the plural, and it could be that a singular written *-s* was regarded as a "silent" *s*. If so, *Splendonius* (1.1) was read as normal vernacular [espléndoɲo], and the witnesses as [eɾmedʒíldo], etc. This seems probable; what may be less justifiable is the transcription here of *voluntas* (1.3) as [voluntáde] (<VOLUNTATEM). This could have been one of the cases of sociolinguistic and stylistic variability beloved of the theoreticians. A reasonable hypothesis is that [voluntáde] would appear when the reader is adopting an informal style, but that [voluntás] (or even [voluntá]) might conceivably have appeared if he was feeling professionally pompous. This is a problem caused not so much by morphology as by imparisyllabicity. There is no problem in [podestáde] (1.10) or [vendzóne] (1.11, 13), here presented in oblique cases; the need to write with *-s* rather than *-te* in some syntactic circumstances was a quirk of the rules of writing and may not have affected even reading aloud. There is absolutely no reason to suppose that lawyers (or anyone else) would say [voluntás] in any other circumstances than reading aloud.

Disyllabic nominal suffixes – i.e. *-arum*, *-orum*, *-ibus* – could have been seen as an esoteric subsection of archaic vocabulary and read in the same manner, i.e. *mensarum* as [mezaɾo] and *luporum* as [loboɾo], since *-um* corresponded to spoken [-o]. *-ibus* is interesting; it might have been read aloud as [-iβos] or [-eβos] – there is no problem with having *-s* here since these forms are indeed plural – but it could also have been read aloud as [-es] with the *bu* seen as a "silent" *bu*. Since the ablative usually follows a preposition, the result is often intelligible. This cannot be dismissed out of hand; it is no less remarkable to find a silent *gh* in *knight*, and surely more remarkable to find a silent *ent* in *chantent*, than a *bu* in *regibus*. No modern English lawyer under any conceivable circumstances would pronounce a [gh] or even a [x] in *knight*, nor a Frenchman an [ent] in *chantent*; *mensibus* could be read as [mezes]. The occasional insertion of written *-ibus* onto second declension stems in texts of this time is evidence in favour of the "silent *bu*" theory (e.g. *annibus*, *dorsibus*, *membribus*; Löfstedt 1976: 123).

This problem with morphology is accentuated in verbs. E.g., the synthetic passive forms have no counterpart in Old Spanish vernacular, so how, for example, did they read *cingitur*? The many verbal suffixes can also be categorized as a subsection of the vocabulary, to be read aloud according to the normal contingent sound-letter correspondences of that community; i.e. since vernacular [vida] is spelt *vita*, etc., and as a result a *t* between two vowels is normally read as [d]; and since a written *u* in the final syllable is always a vernacular [o]; therefore it was reasonable for them to read this word as [tseɲédoɾ] (CINGERE > *ceñir*), AUDIETUR as [ojédoɾ], etc. In Vincent's *Carmen Poenitentiale* discussed above, *precamur* probably rhymes with *redemtor*. In passives there is no impulse to having "silent" letters; omitting *-bu-* in e.g. *montibus* provides the vernacular [montes], but no amount of omission leads from *cingitur* to the vernacular equivalent [estseɲído], *es ceñido*.

Many verb forms in fact offer no problem; e.g. reading *-auit* as [o] provides no great difficulty for those who read *au* as [o] anyway (e.g. *causa* [koza]). A silent *i* is common (cp. the many cases of internal syncopation such as *veritatem* [verdade]). There is no real problem in *placuit* [ploɣo]. The future of first conjugation verbs provides an interesting case; in Chapter 1 it was suggested that e.g. original STARE HABET, pronounced [estaɾáβe] and written *stabit*, might have led some or most or even all writers to see the [aβe] as the equivalent of written *-abit* by false but intelligent etymology. If by the tenth century the [βe] is no longer there in speech — it may well not have been — a "silent *-bi-*" in *stabit* is no problem. The problem is the insertion of a non-silent but unwritten [-aɾ-] into the middle. Here could be another candidate for style variability; informal reading aloud might have included an [aɾ], formal reading aloud might not ([estaβe]). But the difficulty for us lies only in our uncertainty as to the psychological nature of the future tense in tenth-century León, and there is no need to postulate a reading form [stabit]. Futures are rare in documents in any event; futurity there tends to be hypothetical, in the future perfect or perfect subjunctive (as in *venerit*, 1.12), and the Old Spanish future subjunctive that derives from this is a live and easy form, *viniere* ([vinjéɾe]).

Since Old Leonese, like all other vernaculars, is bound to have had geographical, stylistic and sociolinguistic variation, it is inevitable that there were perceptible variables distinguishing formal written styles from informal spoken styles; and reading aloud the written style could lead to features not present in spontaneous speech. This is normal in every community and does not require us to postulate the existence of a whole separate language used by newsreaders, clergymen reading sermons, lawyers reading documents, academics reading learnèd papers, etc. Different people, reading this Leonese document with varying degrees of self-consciousness, would not all have been consistent in detail; no linguistic theory suggests that they should. The point is that, apart from word order and occasional lexical archaisms, including some inflexions, there is no reason to suppose that this reading would not have sounded like the vernacular: a legal style, recognizably, but a style of Old Leonese rather than a separate language used by the educated (or "semi"-educated) in their spontaneous speech. Reading aloud was not a particularly common activity in general, but did not require the learning of any language. Other works, when read, recited or even sung from a written text, could as equally have involved vernacular sounds. The liturgy, for example, could easily have been read aloud in a similar way; renderings would have been subject to inevitable individual inconsistencies of self-consciousness, speed and style, but in essence there is no reason to suppose that they were not vernacular. An ecclesiastical style would be perceptible, but it was and is a style. The Archbishop of Canterbury speaks English.

Menéndez Pidal declared that the spoken *latín vulgar leonés* which he claimed was attested in such texts as this was a survival of the "Vulgar Latin" supposedly common throughout the Romance area from the fifth or sixth centuries, apparently distinguishable even then from Early Romance; in his view this kind of Latin was spoken as well as written, and survived in León precisely because there was no Latinizing movement there as there was in the Carolingian area. His linguistic argument runs as follows (condensed from *Orígenes*, 1926: para.95). Written texts from tenth- and eleventh-century León include many cases in which archaic vocabulary or morphology is given apparently evolved phonetics; e.g. *accebi* (for ACCEPI), *pieatis* (for PIGE-ATIS), *preses* (for PRESENS), *ribolo* (for RIVULO), *orias* (for AUREAS) and the converse hyper-correction *audie* (for HODIE), *amobus* (for AMBOBUS), *lugea* (for LUGEAT), *cingidur* (for CINGITUR), *avidura* (for HABITURA), *abostoli* (for APOSTOLI), etc., etc. Menéndez Pidal is undoubtedly right to mention the commonness of such forms, but he takes the step of assuming that these are the phonetic transcriptions of current spoken forms. They are to him evidence of a "voluntary abandonment to a straightforward current language, halfway between school Latin and the Romance of the people"; the old vocabulary and morphology was preserved in this layer, but "transformed" by popular pronunciation. The argument as presented there thus suggests that the "Leonese vulgar Latin" had old grammar in modern phonetics. This is, in the event, very similar to what I have been proposing as the characteristic nature of the formal style of reading aloud; the difference is that where Menéndez Pidal saw a whole linguistic system reflected faithfully in a skilled phonetic transcription, my hypothesis sees *ad hoc* necessities applied only in reading aloud the already written. The fact that the forms prescribed by the writing manuals – e.g. passives in *-itur* – are sometimes misspelt in accordance with the vernacular pronunciation normally employed by those who had sometimes to read them aloud – e.g. *cingidur* – is not in the least surprising. Archaic vocabulary (including morphemes) is not *per se* immune from misspelling. The presence of the archaic morphology is evidence that the writer had been taught to write, which we can assume anyway, and of nothing at all concerning his speech; the misspelling according to evolved phonetics is consistent with the view that the texts were read aloud, if at all, in ordinary vernacular.

Menéndez Pidal saw three coexisting norms in León: Latin, Vulgar Latin and Romance, of which the last was the speech of *indoctos* (para.109). And although this schema is hard to defend, and the evidence is compatible with the reasonable hypothesis of ill-trained scribes who spoke their own vernacular, it has not been seriously attacked, and has thus not led to the production of any further evidence in its defence. Menéndez Pidal's tone was reasonable and not dogmatic; but his suggestions were seen by others as established fact. Muller, for example, said that "a Vulgar Latin, different both from the vulgar speech and from Medieval Latin, persisted several centuries in Spain . . ." (Muller and Taylor 1932: 256), even though Muller is in fact discussing the Glosses of San Millán, which come not from León but from La Rioja, an area specifically excluded from the hypothesis in *Orígenes* para.95. Valdeavellano's generally valuable history declares that "it seems that at least in the realm of Asturias-León the *semidoctos* used a vulgar Latin that adapted Latin forms to Romance phonetics" (1952: 481, repeated 695). Bustos Tovar's study of *cultismo* is not centrally concerned with the period before 1140, but the discussion of the derivatively-named "época de orígenes" (1974: 67) takes the three-fold distinction for granted as existing from the seventh century.

The misconceptions have multiplied. Menéndez Pidal originally saw this semilearnèd Latin as using largely vernacular pronunciation for largely archaic words, but it has become in the event allied to the different theory of "semicultismo", the idea that semilearnèd people used vernacular words with archaic pronunciation – which is the exact opposite. Yet there is among Menéndez Pidal's texts one which he perhaps might have used, but did not use, to support the hypothesis of yet a fourth level of language on exactly those lines; it is time for us to consider the cheeses.

## The Cheeses

Documents that survive have usually been carefully preserved; transitory material such as shopping lists, ephemeral accounts, sermon notes, messages, etc., usually were not preserved. So there was no incentive to write such material in the officialese of the Grammars. Unlike legal documents, it was not intended to be kept.

Menéndez Pidal found a list of cheeses from the larder of the monastic community of San Justo y Pastor, at Ardón on the Esla, not far from León, which has survived through being written on the back of a document of donation dated 959. This list is undated but palaeographically attributable to the same century; if we knew when the King went to Rozuela (north of Ardón) a closer dating might be possible than Menéndez Pidal's guess of 980. This is it (Menéndez Pidal 1926: 24-25):

> Nodicia de kesos que espisit fr*ater* Semeno jn labore de fr*atres*: jnilo bacelare de cirka S*ancte* Juste, kesos .u .; jnilo alio de apate, .ıı. kesos; en que puseron organo, kesos .ıııı.; jnilo de Kastrelo, .ı.; jnila uinia majore, .ıı.; que lebaron enfosado, .ıı. adila tore; que[le]baron aCegia, .ıı. quando la taliaron; ila mesa, .ıı.; que lebaron aLejone .ı. ... n a... re... que... ... ga uane ece; alio ke leba de soprino de Gomi de do... a...; .ıııı. quespiseron quando jlo rege uenit ad Rocola; .ı. qua salbatore jbi uenit.

This list shows that, even in a monastery, for humdrum purposes written correctness was of no particular concern. If scholars wished, they could claim that this was the first sign of an unofficial norm of writing. If "Latin" of any kind really were the normal means of communication in monasteries, there would have been no need to write in any other way than the traditional. The interesting thing about this list is not so much its spelling as its morphology, syntax and vocabulary. There is no apparent case system; all nouns appear in a form evolved from the original accusative, whatever their function. *Rege*, for example, is used as the subject of the sentence, representing contemporary [reje] < REGEM (REX > ø). *Ila*, *la*, *ilo* are used as articles with no obvious further semantic import (ILLAM > *ila* > *la*). *De kesos*, "of cheeses", is the simple vernacular equivalent of the Latin genitive (*caseorum*). "To León" is *aLejone*, "to Rozuela" is *aRocola*, "to the tower" is *adila tore*; the need stressed in the grammars for a written *-m* is never observed here at all. The third person past of the first conjugation is not *-averunt* but *-aron*; *taliaron* (= Sp. *tallaron*), *lebaron* (= Sp. *llevaron*). The relative conjunction is *que* whatever the syntax, as in Modern Spanish (assuming *qua* at the end to be short for *quando*). In short, the Leonese morphology and syntax usually used for talking about cheese rations is here transcribed more or less neat, disregarding the lexical and morphological refinements that would have been thought necessary were this a document of some legal or institutional importance.

The spelling, however, is not revolutionary. This is not phonetic script of vernacular. The *p* in *soprino*, for example, must represent a [b] or [β] whatever language we think this is: *sobrino* < SOBRINUM; but in *puseron* it must represent a [p]: *pusieron* < POSUERUNT. The *qu* of *que* represents the same [k] as the *k* in *ke*, whereas the *qu* in *quando* must represent [kw] (*cuando* < QUANDO). *Jn* and *en* are presumably the same word. There is no reason to suppose that the quartermaster is even aware of diphthongization: [je] is always *e* – *leba*, *puseron*, *espiseron* – and [we] *o* – *Rocola*; the only non-Latinate spellings other than in suffixes involve the (Greek) letter *k* or simple correspondences such as the *e* in *kesos* [kezos]: Mod. Sp. *quesos* < CASEOS. This looks, then, like vernacular grammar written in generally unevolved spelling.

If the cheeses were to be interpreted as ingenuously as the other documents of the period – i.e. on the assumption that it faithfully reflects its writer's speech – the document seems to offer us a monk using vernacular vocabulary, morphology and syntax with partly *culto* pronunciation. (In my view it indeed shows that monks used vernacular vocabulary, morphology and syntax, and had also been taught how to spell.) If so, this would be a fourth category to be added to Menéndez Pidal's other three. That he did not do so is strange, if only because that would have given some apparent documentary justification to the category of *semicultismo*, of words found in the vernacular with phonetic features recalcitrant to the "rules" of sound change that the philologists wanted to postulate.

The evidence does not support any of these intermediate theories. If we apply Occam's razor at last, we see one vernacular written by scribes of varying sophistication. That is what we would in any event expect; there is in tenth-century León a scattered community of no great education and no mass communication. It is unlikely to have both maintained a sophisticated tripartite (or quadripartite) linguistic division and used a sophisticated phonetic script. We do not have to share Fletcher's uncharitable view (1978: passim) of the Leonese to believe that its inhabitants were incapable of doing so; even Menéndez Pidal liked to call these times "primitive". Lindley Cintra has recently (1978) been the first, to my knowledge, even to have reservations about this theory:

> It seems very unlikely to me that this language should be anything other than an artificial written one. In my view, this manner of writing simply reflects, within certain limitations, the Romance of the Visigothic times as developed into mozarabic Romance. In so saying I dissent from the view ... of Menéndez Pidal, who suggested that these documents reproduced fairly closely a language spoken in the tenth and eleventh centuries 'by laymen who had a higher culture but lacked any systematic study of grammar'. (464)

I have argued previously (Wright 1976a: 14-15) that:

> there is a basic misconception here: that of supposing social registers to lie neatly on a descending scale of Latinity in the early Middle Ages ... this misconception about the spoken language has probably arisen by false analogy with the written language.

In fact, as we shall see below, not only the hybrid Latin of these documents, but also the more respectable "Latin" of hymns, histories and poems, are explicable in a theory of only one spoken level rather than three or two. Given the stylistic and sociolinguistic variation expected of all communities by modern linguistic theory, the kind of language we find in tenth-century León is interpretable on the available evidence as the kind we would expect to find: a single vernacular, with a complex manner of writing attached, used with varying skill by different writers.

### Verse

*a) Rhythmic*

Old-fashioned metric verse was not composed in Asturias-León; anything called a *metrum* was either rhythmic or from elsewhere. Hymns continue to be composed in the "rhythmic" genre, often directly modelled on earlier hymns by Prudentius or the Visigothic writers. They are usually impossible to date, although Szövérffy (1971: chaps.3 and 4) has had a good try. Several do seem to come from the eighth to the eleventh centuries, north of the religious frontier. We are fortunate in that one of the most important is precisely datable: the hymn to St James *O Dei verbum, patris ore proditum* (*AH* XXVII no. 130) is dedicated in its acrostic to King Mauregato. There was only one

King Mauregato, who reigned from 783-88. Díaz y Díaz has edited the hymn (1976a: 239-42) and dated it more precisely to late 784 or 785. There are two early manuscript records: London, BM Add.30851, f.124 and Madrid, BN 10001, f.18. The hymn follows the normal pattern for "rhythmic" iambic trimeters: i.e. there are twelve written vowels (or classical diphthongs) in each line. The syllable thus continues in this tradition to be defined by the original spelling. Apart from *Spaniam* and *Spanie* (ll.25 and 47), required to be quadrisyllabic – and thus presumably *Hispaniam* and *Hispanie* in the original, since this is not a case of prothesis – four lines appear not to have exactly twelve written syllables; Díaz y Díaz prints these as follows:

1.10    Zmaracdus, iaspis, ligurius crisolitus
1.19    Vartolomeus Licaon Iudas Edisse
1.20    Mathias Iudee et Filippus Gallie
1.58    Eterna cuius laus et clementia.

(Blume amended the first three into twelve-syllabled variants.) The caesura comes regularly after the first five technical syllables; this seems to suggest that *ligurĩus*, *Licãon* and either *Mathĩas* or *Iudẽe* are required to become diphthongs. Problems are caused by sources: lines 19-20 derive from Isidore's *De ortu et obitu patrum* 81; l.10 from *AH* XXVII 190, stanza 5. The caesura suggests that in 1.58 *laus* may be meant as a disyllable, rather than *cuius* a trisyllable (as is occasionally found elsewhere). Lorenzana's 1775 edition inserted *est* after *laus*.

Díaz y Díaz established that much of the wording of this hymn comes directly from hymns composed much earlier. The author of this is more skilled at adapting the sources than in producing words of his own. Indeed, he concludes that the author has extreme difficulty in producing any words of his own at all, under the pressure of the rhythmic scheme adopted and of his chosen (and misspelt) acrostic. Given vernacular presentation, rhyme is also visible in e.g. *tonitrui/inclite* (ll.21-22), *pignera/gloriam* (ll.29-30), *copiam/gloriam* (ll.44-45); vernacular stress seems to Díaz y Díaz to be required in e.g. *lápides* (l.6), *duódecim* (l.11: Sp. *doce*), *superpósiti* (l.14: Sp. *sobrepuestos*), which he describes as revealing both clumsiness and ignorance (271). We can refrain from such a pejorative evaluation by observing that the author is feeling that he has to push his vernacular into patterns established by a different age; writing a hymn to order in the techniques of a past tradition, established at a time of more intense education, could not have been easy. As Díaz y Díaz observed, Pérez de Urbel had proposed that the author was Beato de Liébana, on the grounds that the hymn is so successful, but it seems more rational to propose that he was not, partly on the grounds that the original parts of the hymn are so awkward; it is strange to find Sánchez Albornoz supporting Pérez de Urbel in this in his recent *Historia* (1980: 617-19). Apparently archaic features are due to imitation. If the man chosen to dedicate a church to the Kingdom's patron saint and simultaneously praise the King is so ill at ease in this traditional genre, it is unlikely that many others would have been less so; the Visigothic expertise survives, but only just.

Rhythmic verse, in the academic genre based on counting written vowels, continues to be written and sung. We can never be sure whether it was performed with the same number of syllables it appears to have on paper; as argued above (Chapter 2), there seems no particular reason why it should have been. We shall look at further examples, from La Rioja, later in this chapter, but for the minute it is worth considering what other kinds of verse existed in these centuries before the advent of the Carolingian reforms to Spain.

### b) Popular Verse?

Every community has verse in its own vernacular. No community has been discovered that does not. We can assume that early medieval León had verses of some kind in early medieval Leonese. Is there any evidence that can tell us what these were like?

It has been assumed that nothing can be said about the vernacular literature of these centuries because we have no texts written then in Leonese, Castilian, Galician, etc.; yet some of the surviving texts could well be the written representation of the vernaculars, at a time when the only method of writing was in unreformed spelling. If popular poetry did get written down, it certainly would not have been in phonetic script. In addition, some of the surviving "rhythmic" verse — i.e. based on counting syllables — might well show evidence of influence from popular patterns. In particular, it has often been suggested that such natural patterns were indeed rhythmic, unlike "rhythmic" verse, in that they were based on the number of spoken stresses per line rather than the number of written vowels. Norberg (1952: 89), for example, suggested that this might be true of the epitaph of one Oppila (who died at the hands of the Basques), found on a tomb at Villafranca (Córdoba province) and dated to 642 A.D., which Vives (1969: 90, no. 287) printed as follows:

+haec caua saxa Oppilani continet membra,
g[lorios]o ort[u] natalium, gestu abituq. co[nspi]c[u]um.
opibus quippe pollens et artuum uiribus cluens
iacula uehi precipitur predoq. Bacceis destinatur.
in procinctum belli necatur opitulatione sodaliu desolatus

> nauiter cede perculsum clintes rapiunt peremtum.
> exanimis domu reducitur, suis a uernulis humatur.
> lugit coniux cum liberis, fletibus familia prestrepit.
> decies ut ternos ad quater quaternos uixit per annos,
> pridie Septemb(r)ium idus morte a Vasconibus multatus
> era sescentensima et octagensima id gestum memento.
> sepultus sub d. quiescit VI id. Octubres.

Norberg dismissed the idea that these could be rhythmic hexameters, and instead analysed each line as containing two hemistichs, usually in rhyme, with three main word stresses per hemistich, atonic words and secondary stresses being ignored. Thus the first line is balanced:

> haéc cáva sáxa // Oppiláni contínet mémbra.

The first hemistich has five written syllables and the second has nine, but that does not matter; each has three main word-stresses. The epitaph itself contains non-vernacular grammatical elements (such as the passive of *precipitur*), but its structural pattern — if Norberg is right — is not at all academic or "Latinate", and could be based on the patterns of native verse.

There are two peculiar compositions found in one of the manuscripts of the so-called *Historia Albeldense*[11]. The first version of this chronicle was completed in 881. It was subsequently expanded to reach 883, and in between the two sections the San Millán manuscript (*Academia de la Historia* MS *Em.* 39) has the separate items printed by Gómez Moreno (1932: 605-06) as follows:

> Item noticia episcopurum cum sedibus suis.

> Regiamque sedem Hermenegildus tenet
> Flaianus Bracarae Luco episcopus arce
> Rudesindus Dumio Mendunieto degens
> Sisnandus Iriae Sancto Jacobo pollens
> Naustique tenens Conimbriae sedem
> Brandericus quoque locum Lamencensem
> Sebastianus quidem sedis Auriensem
> Justusque similiter in Portucalense
> Aluarus Velegiae Felemirus Oximae
> Maurus Legione necnon Ranulfus Astoricae

> Prefati quoque presules in ecclesiae plebe ex regis prudentia emicant clare.

> Rex quoque clarus omni mundo factus
> jam suprafatus Adefonsus uocatus
> regni culmine datus belli titulo abtus

---

11. Sánchez Albornoz prefers to follow Mommsen and call the chronicle the *Epítome Ovetense* (1980: 651); the text certainly has more in common with Oviedo than Albelda (which is where the other old manuscript was copied by Vigila). Both these MSs are tenth-century copies.

clarus in Astures fortis in Uascones
ulciscens Arabes et protegens ciues
cui principi sacra sit uictoria data
Xpisto duce juuatus semper clarificatus
polleat uictor seculo fulgeat ipse celo
deditus hic triumpho preditus ibi regno
Amen.

Gómez, however, was working at a time when these folios of MS 39 had been lost — they reappeared in 1953 — on the basis of later versions. The manuscript folio (274r), written two columns to a page, looks more like this:

IT̃ NOTITIA EPC̃RŬ · CŨ SEÐbˢ SᵘiS ·

Regiamc̃ sedem· ermenegildus tenet·
Flajarˢ bracare. luco epc̃ps· arce·       new column (same page)
rudesind͛ dumio· mendunieto degens·
Sisnand͛ hJrie· sc̃olacobo polens·
Naustiç̃ˢ tenens conimbrie sedem·
Brandericus quoc̃ˢ locum lamencense·
Sabastiarˢ quidem sedis auriense·
Justusc̃ˢ similiter Inportucalense·
Albarus· uẹl egiẹ· Felemirus
   uxomẹ· Maurus legione. necnon
Ranulfus astorice· Prefatiç̃ˢ presules
   In ecte pleue· Ex regis prudentja
   emicant clare. Rex quoc̃ˢ clarus
   om̃e mundo factus· Jam supra
   fatus· Adefonsus uocatus·
Regni culmine datus. bellititulo
   abtus· Clarus Inastures. fortis
   Inuascones· Ulciscens arabes·
   et protegens ciues· Cui principi
   sacra. sit uictoria data·
Xpo duce Iubatus· sempclarificatus.
Polleat uictor scto· fulgeat Ipse cẹlo·
Deditus hoc triumfho· predictus Ibi
   regno· am̃ · finit·

The right hand edge of each line is close to the edge of the folio. It seems that the copyist realized these were lines of verse, for each verse line begins with a large, usually capital, letter; once *uxome* spilled over a line he preferred to save space and preserve legibility by continuing from there, only recovering synchronization in the last three lines. This cheerful attitude to scribal enjambement continues in the succeeding chapter heading:

INCIPIT ORDOROMA
NORUM⸬⁓

so we can probably accept that this composition is in verse. In practice all critics have agreed that it is verse of some kind. David (1947: 130) repositioned the first line after *Maurus* ... on the grounds that a first line cannot start with *-que*, and printed the two central lines as verse:

> Praefati praesules in ecclesiae plebe
> Ex regis prudentia emicant clare.

If it is verse, what sort of verse is it? It is clearly not metrical. It is not technically "rhythmical"; the written vowels (given resolution of MS abbreviations) range from 11 to 15 per line.

If we attempt to visualize a vernacular reading or recitation, on the lines of Esplondonio's deed of sale above, the result of the list of bishops in the first ten lines could be as follows. This transcription again omits the written *-s* of the nominative singular and of *sedis*, suggesting that its residual presence, perhaps as an aspiration, prevents elision (e.g. in *Ranulfus Astoricae*); but it refrains from lengthening the imparisyllabic present participle. It also includes secondary stresses on long words.

> [rédʒakeséðe    érmedʒíldotjéne
> flajánoβráqe    lúqobíspoártse
> rudzíndoðúmjo    móndoɲédoðédʒe
> siznándoírje    sántiáqopólle
> náwsteketjéne    koním brjeséðe
> brandríqokwóke    lwéqolámedʒéze
> séβastjáno    kéðe    séðeorénse
> dʒústokeseméldre    empwértoqaléze
> álbaroβelédʒje    felmíroózme
> móroleóne    ninóranúlfoastórqe]

This inevitably begs many questions. Apart from anything else, the poem only survives in a copy made the following century, and *quoque, quidem* and in particular *necnon* could easily be later additions, or amplifications of *&*. Yet an advantage of this version, however specious, is that — allowing secondary stress in long proper names — we can envisage this being recited on a rough stress pattern of a hemistich of two stresses followed by a hemistich of three stresses. The lengths of line become, in spoken syllables rather than written, 11, 11, 11, 11, 11, 11, 11, 12, 11, 13; and if we wished to, we could suggest hendecasyllabic versions for lines 8 and 10 by omitting [ke] and [ninó] as possible interpolations. There is no need to do this, for regularity of spoken stress rhythm does not require exact syllabic equivalence, yet if we want to do so, we can, given a spot of *metri gratia*, which is not in itself implausible (we need not suppose that this composition is any good). The main advantage of this transcription, however, is that the rhyme is now visible. Apart from *Dumio* (1.3) and probably *Sabastianus* (1.6) —although *quidem* might precede the caesura — all twenty hemistichs end in [e]. The poem is not itself in origin a vernacular verse, as can be seen from the noun morphology (e.g. with genitives rather than *de*), but it does seem to be written with the intention of having a stress pattern when reproduced in vernacular phonetics. Stress is natural in language; the syllable is an academic construct. Even if David is right to see the next two lines as verse — he does not discuss this at all — they are unlikely to have been originally part of either composition; they look like the scribal linking of two previously composed passages. Even so, *plebe* and *clare* continue the rhyme[12].

The second composition, beginning *Rex quoque* . . ., is more connected and educated in syntax, morphology and vocabulary; yet if it is an attempt at a learnèd "rhythmic" poem it is an exceptionally incompetent one, for the number of written vowels per line ranges from eleven to fifteen. The attempt to visualize a possible vernacular rendering has, in the event, the effect of both increasing syllabic regularity and accentuating a spoken rhythm as of a trochaic trimeter (/./././. /././.). Let us consider the first word, for example, *rex*; the list of cheeses has *rege* as a sentence subject, we know that the vernacular was disyllabic [réje] (or perhaps still [réʒe]; > O. Sp. *reye*, Mod. Sp. *rey*), and [reje] creates a trochee that suits the metre well. "Rhythmic" compositions of twelve-syllabled lines were a traditional guise with available music, so this could even have been put to an existing tune. Other vernacular renderings that support the possibility that this was performed with an intentionally trochaic pattern are: *cumne* for *culmine* (> Sp. *cumbre*), *tildo* (or *-e*) for *titulus*, *sieglo* for *seculo* (> O. Sp. *sieglo*, Sp. *siglo*), *y* for *ibi* (> O. Sp. *y*), perhaps *Alfonso* for *Adefonsus*, the presence of a semivocalic [j] in *victoria*, and the likely loss of the first [i] in *clarificatus*, a word that does not survive in the vernacular, but of a type in which an unstressed [i] would have been lost. *Iam suprafatus* has three stresses, but vernacular fails to supply the extra syllable needed if we want strict syllabic equivalence; *Xpisto duce iuvatus* has three stresses, but *duce* seems to require elision to [dodz] if we want it to become a six-syllable line in speech. ([-e] was

12. The bishops themselves are attested and discussed by David (1947), Sánchez Albornoz (1980) and Floriano (1951: II 658-76). Velegia is on the road from Pamplona to Burgos; Velegia and Osma, 1.9, are the only Castilian sees included. Santiago was in the Iria Flavia diocese at this time. The "royal" see is Oviedo. The purpose of the list is more probably as a kind of roll of honour for an assembly than as a mnemonic. I am very grateful to the Librarian of the History Academy in Madrid for providing me with a photocopy of this folio.

lost in later centuries, but that is perhaps too precocious to envisage here.) Lines 4 and 5 seem to have two-stress hemistichs; the three-stress hemistichs are not all trochaic in this version, but there is a greater regularity than appears in any other. The hemistich assonance pattern visible in both the written and spoken versions remains the same.

> [réjekwókekláɾo    wémnemúndoféjto
> jásóbɾefádo    alfónsoβoɡádo
> réɲekúmneðádo    bélletíldwáwto
> kláɾoenastúɾes    fwéɾteeŋqwaskónes
> ujtsítseáɾaβes    epɾotédʒetsíves
> kújpɾíntsebesáqɾa    séβijtóɾjaðáda
> kɾístoðódzjuvádo    sjémpɾekláɾveɡádo
> póʎaβíjtoɾsjéɡlo    fúldʒaésetsjélo
> déddoítɾiúnfo    pɾeðíjtoíréjno]

As usual, there are many doubtful details in this transcription, and as usual these are doubts about ninth-century Leonese vernacular. What we can be fairly certain of is that the established features of that vernacular, such as [dáda], [tsjélo], [en], [ése], etc., for written *data*, *celo*, *in*, *ipse*, were not read out in any Latinate way. In St Amand, at almost exactly the same time, they wrote *ciel* in the Eulalia Sequence for their vernacular, because otherwise in church *celo* was read with no diphthong and an [o]; there, [data], [in], [ipse] were read in the liturgy; Oviedo and León did not have that choice, and there was no need to change the usual spelling. These poems are explicable if we see them as read in vernacular phonetics, and not if not[13].

Rhythmic recitation seems to have been normal in the Visigothic liturgy. The seventh-century Visigothic scholars loved rhythmic prose. It often seems as if they preferred rhythm to intelligibility. The technique was already traditional and revered, having been used, for example, by Saints Jerome and Augustine. The reason for its cultivation in liturgy may have specifically been to adorn the recitation with aesthetic attraction. Its appeal was not lost on Albaro of Córdoba. It continued to be enjoyed in the twelfth century and beyond. Its presence in the liturgy led to its being heard all the time; since most scholars were active in the church, they were reciting it all the time as well. A feeling for rhythm, for the deliberate patterning of the stresses inherent in words, was thus inevitably likely to exist in any educated person of the time. A bishop, for example, creating a jingle containing his colleagues' names, would almost inevitably tend to some kind of

13. The presumption that any explanation is better than none is one that Norberg severely criticizes Strecker for holding (1954: passim), but they are discussing verse with prose sources.

stress-patterning, whether consciously or not. There is, as a consequence, absolutely no reason to suppose that stress-patterning is somehow an "uneducated" type of language.

The liturgy is usually written down as prose. But at times the rhythmic effect is so pervasive and constant that the distinction between rhythmic prose and accentual verse begins to seem at best porous and at worst artificial. Devoto (1980), for example, has suggested that there was no natural distinction consciously felt between the two; the distinction comes from the subsequent application of artificial literary convention. That the period from 711-1080 continued to see no clear boundary is attested by the way in which one passage in particular has been variously seen by modern scholars: the second of the four prologues to the manuscript of the *Antiphonary* of León. This manuscript is eleventh-century (probably 1069); the prologues have been ascribed to a variety of centuries, but Díaz y Díaz (1954) plausibly ascribed at least the last three to the reign of Fernando I (1035-65), a time when the Leonese were vigorously recovering their Visigothic past. (Vives 1955 disagrees, however, preferring a much earlier date.) The third and fourth of these, called *metro* in the titles, are attempts at rhythmic elegiacs; the second, printed by Férotin and Díaz y Díaz as prose — Férotin (1912: 917) called it "étrange prose" — has such an insistent rhythmic pattern that Meyer (1936: 205) was inspired to print it as verse, adding in his own accent marks to indicate the stresses in question. The version printed here is slightly altered in small details, on the basis of Díaz y Díaz's manuscript research, but otherwise it is Meyer's:

> Item alius prologus eiusdem.

> Tradíctio Toletána institútioque sáncta
> melodíae cántus mirífice promsérunt [oracula].
> Concéntos dúlces, sonóras cónpares
> résonant in chóro diversórum módulis.
> Cámeras fulgéntes nínguide splendéntes
> aúribus demúlcent pre suavitáte sónum.
> Spléndida doctrína et púlcra canóra
> dulcífluas vóces rútilant in chóro.
> In súmis adtóllunt precinéndo laúdes
> iúbilum cármen mirífice proméntes. 10
> Adínstar caeléstium milítiae angelórum
> órdines párant in conspéctu seniórum.
> Bíni aut térni responsúria cánunt,
> vespertínos et laúdes, simíliter et psálmos.
> Ad déxtra lévaque córos consístunt,
> antiphóne módos reciprocátos cánunt:

Úni incipiéntes    et álii subpsalmántes,
tértio post Glóriam    páriter cantántes.
Órdinem angélicum    ténent institútum,
niténtes consístunt    páriter in chóro.    20
Benígnos compónunt    melodíae cántos
in laúde divínaque promulgántes.
Ílares próperant    in sáncta sanctórum,
offícium divínum    súmunt gaudéntes.
Núlla ventilántes    otiósa vérba,
sed sáltim divína    elóquia canéntes,
Lectiónes sánctas    páriter aubscultánt(es).
strépitum vúlgi    nulló modo ibi sónat.

*Promulgantes* (1.22) and *oracula* (1.2) remain the only barriers to accepting this as accentual verse based on two stresses per hemistich. If we wish, line 2 can be emended by omitting *mirifice* as a pre-echo of 1.10, and 1.22 by emending *que* to *quoque*. The prologue implies that it is itself an excellent example of the liturgical language of the *Traditio toletana*, whose musical performance soothes the ears (1.6) and where there are no inappropriate words (*otiosa verba*). The *Antiphonary* itself has music printed above the words; the notation is not easy to interpret but does not suggest any strict equivalence of musical note and sung vowel. Whether this prologue was recited at all is unclear, but Meyer's version shows that at the least a rhythmic patterning would be obvious in the performance. This structural requirement could continue to be satisfied despite the vagaries of phonetic evolution, for none of these words gained nor lost a tonic stress when evolving, so the pattern suits the vernacular of the eleventh century as well as that of the seventh.

It has often been suggested that the presumed unattested popular verse of these centuries was patterned on stress. This patterning has been ascribed to the influence of Germanic (e.g. by Leonard 1931; Hall 1965-66). Unfortunately, Hall presented this view in tandem with a debatable theory of "superstratum" influence and the almost certainly mistaken suggestion that Gothic speech and literature continued after the Moslem invasion; since these latter ideas are easy to argue against – Collins (1977: 40), for example, doubts if the Visigoths spoke Germanic after the fifth century – they have cast disrepute on the Germanic stress connection (e.g. in Martínez 1975: 73). Yet the theory survives. In the first place, rhythmic patterns are logically independent of Germanic origins: noone claims that St Augustine was a Visigoth. In the second place, patterns of sentence stress in verse and recitation could easily survive long after the community lost its Germanic language, as those of Welsh are observable in monolingual

English-speaking Welshmen. Since there seems to be no doubt that stress-patterns existed in the liturgy, which was recited all the time, it seems *a priori* reasonable to expect to find it in other works — epitaphs, lists of bishops, encomia of Kings, prologues to liturgical manuscripts; it also seems reasonable to hypothesize its existence in popular lyric, ballad, epic, or whatever else we wish to envisage.

As regards the versification of early Spanish lyric, Rico, editing the earliest known extant indubitably Castilian lyric, offered the lapidary view that "the metric norm of early traditional lyric is to lack any norm" (1975: 545). This verse is attested (written in prose) as follows: "Cantan de Roldán, cantan de Olivero, e non de Çorraquín Sancho, que fue buen cavallero. Cantan de Olivero, cantan de Roldán, e non de Çorraquín Sancho, que fue buen barragán" (542). It comes in the *Crónica de la población de Avila* (1255), but refers to events of c.1158 (see Mackay 1977: 54-55), and is datable to the mid-twelfth century. These verses are endowed with a variety of emendations by Rico, but can be spared that if we envisage a tune in which *Çorraquín* can be sung quickly: *e nón de Çorraquín Sáncho*[14]. The norm is that of the Antiphonary prologue and the Bishops' list, two stresses per half-line. Similarly, discussion of the *kharjas* will not progress until scholars accept that popular Romance metrics need not have been isosyllabic (unlike e.g. Jones 1980: 41). Non-lyrical genres need have been no more isosyllabic; as regards ballads, although all the surviving texts are much later, some of the venerable old ones (and, indeed, many recently-collected versions) were not as rigidly octosyllabic as the metric manuals tell us. Devoto (1979), for example, points out that one of the most famous lines of all has in fact nine syllables (Smith 1964: 97): "Villanos te maten, Alonso . . .".

The whole of this argument, however, has been skewed in perspective by the existence of the *Poema de Mio Cid* and the surviving fragment of a *Cantar de Roncesvalles* (see Magnotta 1976: chap.7). The metre of these epics is based largely on hemistichs with two or three main stresses; both epics have 39% of their hemistichs heptasyllabic and about a quarter octosyllabic, but this is a consequence of the stress pattern rather than being a pattern in its own right. Some of the *Poema*'s hemistichs have one stress, or four, and no scholar yet knows what to do about that. Yet the liturgy, and such other evidence as survives of recitation patterns before the overwhelming influence of

---

14. A simple conga rhythm, in fact, due no doubt to the Brazilian substratum in Avila.

French syllable-based metres in the early thirteenth century, strongly suggests that stress-patterning came naturally to the community, whereas syllable-counting came awkwardly and only to antiquarians. Smith (1979) has revived the theory of rhythmic patterning in the *Poema*, but suggested that the author of the *Poema* "invented" it. There is no need to suggest that. The fact that a spelling reform operates in about 1200 means that at first sight the Bishops' List and the Antiphonary Prologue seem to be in a different language from the *Poema*, but a spelling reform is a minor thing. Major cultural patterns carry on regardless of spelling reforms. Smith sees the surviving *Poema* as a first draft, "una fase primitiva métricamente imperfecta", of an attempt to imitate the French, but it is surely no less reasonable to see it as one of the last works in the common stress-based anisosyllabic nature of pre-1220s Spanish recitations[15] (although its length probably is unprecedented). There is no need to suppose that "popular" reciters, untrained in the definition of the syllable found in the Grammars by the old-fashioned "rhythmic" poets, even knew what a syllable was.

The preference for rhythm over counting syllables in performed verse survives after the thirteenth-century francophile deluge. In the early fourteenth century, Juan Ruiz humanizes the *mester de clereçía*, and unless we use Corominas' edition (1967) of his *Libro de Buen Amor* we can see that the rhythmic patterns often override the strict syllable count. The only native Spanish metre of the later Middle Ages, the *arte mayor*, is one that contains eight to twelve syllables per line, in two hemistichs with two stresses per hemistich, usually (.) / .. / (.) (Balaguer 1974).

There has been considerable argument over whether the native literature of Spain before the twelfth century was in Latin or in Romance. The theory offered here solves that problem by removing the distinction. What existed was Romance; if written it looks "Latin" to us, but that is only because we have projected an anachronism needlessly back. Monroe (1975; 1979: 114-16) has been arguing that Romance lyric and ballad traditions go back to Roman times; cp. also Menéndez Pidal (1951). Martínez's book (1975) has made a step forward in that he uses early "Latin" popular songs as evidence in his discussion of the genesis of Spanish epic, accepting a continuity between vernacular Latin and Romance. Indeed there is a continuity. Late Latin *is* Early Romance and the true novelty of twelfth-century

---

15. The 1220s see the definitive attempt to train priests in Latin, and the spread of the fashion for French-style syllabic verse: see Chapter 5.

Spain is the arrival of Medieval Latin as a distinct concept. Martínez also, however, uses works of an undoubtedly Medieval Latin nature, such as the *Carmen Campi Doctoris* (397), in this argument, which is surely mistaken. But no less mistaken appears to be the instinctive view of Smith that no vernacular verse existed then at all — "el hecho es que no nos queda ningún testimonio directo o textual acerca de lo que las estructuras métricas castellanas pudieran haber sido (de haber existido) antes de 1207" (1979: 30); "The editors of the [sc. *Historia*] *Silense*, discussing a lively account in the chronicle of the defeat by Ordoño II of the Moslems at San Esteban de Gormaz, hint at the existence of a poem (they do not specify the language) as a source; but there are grave difficulties in postulating this for Ordoño's days in the early tenth century" (1971: 4 = 1977a: 92-93). There are no such difficulties. It would have been in tenth-century vernacular. Had it been written, it would have used the ordinary quaint old writing methods used in the *Historia* itself, but there does not seem to have been any need or point to writing it. Most verses in the world have never been written down. The theory expounded here, that Medieval Latin did not exist till it was invented, solves these arguments and should prevent such knots being tied in future.

### Historiography

Asturians show an interest in their national heritage through the ninth century. In the early 880s there is a flurry of activity. Dulcidio came from Toledo in 880, and the body of San Eulogio from Córdoba in 882; an inventory of books at Oviedo dated 882 (Gil 1973a: II 707-08) may be of those that came with Eulogio. In 881 the first version of the *Historia Albeldense* was written, in 883 the second. This chronicle refers to the Leonese as Goths; after the section called *Ordo gentis gotorum* (as in Isidore), the section on Asturias is labelled *Ordo Gotorum Obetensium Regum* (Gómez Moreno 1932: 601). This new self-consciously Visigothic pride is taken up in the chronicle that bears the name of Alfonso III (Bonnaz 1977; Cotarelo 1933; on historiography in general, Sánchez Alonso 1941). Although it is by the 880s conceivable that Carolingian scholarship might have had an influence, the Visigothic orientation of Asturian culture makes that improbable, and the nature of the texts makes it more so. Of Alfonso III's history, Cotarelo (1933: 583) declared that "being written at a time of total literary decadence, its style is very limited and wearisome"; Gómez Moreno, on the *Albeldense*, stated that "it shows how low Latin sank, even among scholars, in the last third of the ninth century. Its vocabulary is very small; its sentences rarely attain any elegance; the use of particlés is quite *bárbaro*; the inflexions are often nonsense, and so on" (1932: 566). Sánchez Albornoz simply said that Gómez's comments on the language "could not be bettered" (1980: 664). All these remarks miss the simple point: these histories are in vernacular, but awkwardly imitating an ancient genre. The tenth-century *Sampiro* chronicle is in "better" Latin, but this is only known to us in twelfth-century versions that are not usable as testimony to its original language (Pérez de Urbel 1952).

In the tenth century, Visigothic (rather than Frankish) culture continues. Sánchez Albornoz (1944; 1980: 643-50) drew up a list of all the books mentioned in monastic documents in the tenth-century kingdom of León. (He also found a document of 796 that established the cost of a liturgical text at about three times that of a cow.) García Alvarez (1965) prepared a similar list for Galicia. It is clear from these that traditional liturgical texts of all kinds were quite common, much respected, and continually on the move. The largest single collection is that given by Cixila of Toledo on November 5th 927 to the monastery of Saints Cosme and Damian at Abellar (León), described in the only document to mention any Classical work (Díaz Jiménez 1892). The monastery of San Rosendo at Celanova in Galicia was given (by the saint) many books in 942 (Díaz y Díaz 1975: 161; García Alvarez 1965: 310). In León, much of the border resettlement was entrusted to emigrants from the south, some of whom were literate.

In León, it is often not easy, as García Gallo demonstrated (1950: 373-93), to distinguish between a monastery and a church, since both tend to have priests and living quarters. Fletcher (1978: 163) was unsure how to translate *monasteria* in a document as late as 1122. Further east, however, monasteries are more recognizable, and the important centres of tenth-century Spanish Christian culture (outside Catalonia) are those in *La Rioja*.

### The Rioja
The Rioja is approximately that part of Navarre near the Ebro. If Carolingian culture impinged on non-Catalan Spain at all before the eleventh century — if the Latin-Romance contrast existed anywhere — it would have been here. Díaz y Díaz's superb recent book (1979) on the culture of tenth-century Rioja has made much earlier discussion seem jejune (e.g. Vicuña Ruiz 1971; Pérez de Urbel 1950; García de Cortázar 1977); in particular, it has dated and located manuscripts with authority. Among other things, it demonstrates a slight but real

connection with contemporary culture from North of the Pyrenees.

The Rioja was well placed to receive visitors from all directions; from the West (Castille, León), the South (Moslem Spain; Díaz y Díaz 1979: 253-59)[16], the East (Catalonia), the North East (the Navarrese Pyrenees, where Eulogio of Córdoba found his manuscripts in 848) and the North (France). In the 920s the area − long fought over − was resettled by the Navarrese, in particular with the monasteries of San Martín de Albelda and San Millán de la Cogolla. Six others, at least, were active in that century. San Martín and San Millán were culturally akin (García de Cortazár 1969: 26; Cantera Orive 1950-63). San Martín − probably named after Martin of Tours rather than Martin of Braga − was said at its foundation (5 January 924) to be organized "secundum Benedicti regulam vel id quod a sanctis patribus didicisti" (Bishko 1948: 563; Ubieto 1960: 13 calls the surviving document a falsification). The Benedictine rule is also mentioned in three documents from ninth-century Castille (probably referring to Smaragdus' commentary), but in practice most monasteries chose their rules eclectically; in the Rioja the cosmopolitan origins included aspects of both Benedictinism and native Hispanic rules (Linage 1973a; 1976). The most interesting case of this concerns a nuns' rule. Salvo, abbot of Albelda from 951/3-962, is said, according to Vigila's brief biography of him, to have composed hymns, liturgical texts, and a nuns' rule, which may or may not be the *Libellus a regula sancti Benedicti subtractus* found in San Millán MS 62 (which probably came from Nájera: Díaz y Díaz 1979: 30-32), and studied by Bishko (1948) and Linage (1973b). Bishko is sure Salvo wrote it, Linage ascribes it to the scribe Enneco (who dates it 976), and Díaz y Díaz (1979) rejects the latter because Enneco's colophon to the MS is so clumsy. It is an adaptation of Smaragdus for use by nuns. Not only is the content mostly Carolingian, initials and abbreviations are convincingly used by Linage (1973b: 87-93, 101-10) to show that the source manuscript was itself of French origin. The saints to whom the convent is dedicated were Nunilo and Alodia, martyrs in Córdoba in 851, whose bodies were at Leyre in the Pyrenees. This combination of inspirations is typical of the area's ability to fuse together whatever ideas they liked[17].

---

16. Moslem Spain includes Zaragoza, which is close to the Rioja. The common culture of Visigoth, *mozárabe*, *asturiano* and *riojano* is demonstrated at length by G. Menéndez Pidal (1954).

17. Another tenth-century MS (no.53) includes St Leander's Spanish nuns' rule followed by adapted extracts from Smaragdus (Díaz y Díaz 1979: 177-78).

For the present purpose of assessing the nature of the "Latinity" used in the Rioja, the immediate question concerning Benedictinism is whether the Roman liturgy was used at all. It is, in the event, noticeable that all reference in the source to the Roman liturgy is omitted from this *Libellus*, which is designed for a Benedictine community using the Hispanic rites. Linage is, uncharacteristically, at a loss as to how to explain the omission. It is not mere conservatism; profounder changes than ritual are accepted gladly. Linage points out as a contrast that in modern times liturgical change has appeared more acceptable than fundamental reorganization and comments that we can see from this how modern man has lost a sense of ritual: "something providing good material for the history of human mentalities" (1973b: 139). In fact it is practical common sense; establishing a convent on the border zone was awkward enough without requiring the nuns to learn a different method of speaking and run a new kind of education system. The pointedness of the omission might suggest, however, that the Riojans were aware of the Latinity used in Northern rites and consciously preferred to avoid it.

Frankish influence is attested in the Rioja. For example, there is a list of *Reges Francorum* in MS San Millán 78, f.194v, which ends in a first person plural: "Et fuimus sine rege ā vii, postea regnavit Leodevicus ā xvii. Et postea regnat Leutharius filius eius." The present tense of *regnat* dates the list to 954-86 (Menéndez Pidal 1958: 11; Lacarra 1948, however, ascribed the manuscript to Catalonia). Contact would have been increased by the pilgrimage to Santiago; the main route ran further north until the eleventh century, but some pilgrims did come on the southern route through the Rioja. The foundation of Albelda (924) decrees "ut pretereuntes itidem habeant tugurium hospitandi" (Cantera Orive 1950-63: VII 296; V 319). A document of 933 which concedes the village of Uñón to Albelda seems to accept the presence of pilgrims as a fact of life (Ubieto 1960: 31): "Postremo namque liberam in Dei nomine habeatis potestatem in cultura peregrinorum adque in alimonia monachorum, eamdem possidere et sepe ampliare." The most distinguished pilgrim from France was Bishop Gotescalc of Le Puy, Count of Velay and Brioude, who stopped at Albelda in 950, commissioned a copy of San Ildefonso's *De Virginitate Beatae Mariae* from the scribe Gomesano, and then returned to pick it up in 951[18]. Le Puy le Velay,

---

18. Now Paris BN Latin MS 2855. On the visit see Cantera Orive (1948-49); Díaz y Díaz (1979: 55-62 and (Gomesano's additions to the MS) 279-81). Gomesano also copied here two earlier rhythmic poems awkwardly imitative of Eugenio of Toledo, 293-96.

not very far from Clermont-Ferrand, was a centre of Carolingian culture; the Cathedral library, for example, has an edition of Theodulf's Bible that Rand (1931: 337) called "sumptuous". Gomesano's MS was later copied at Cluny (Cantera Orive 1950-63: XVII 202). The excellent state of his manuscript is an encouraging indication of professional competence at Albelda.

The Rioja is also the home of several "rhythmic" compositions. Abbot Salvo of Albelda was described by Vigila as follows (Díaz y Díaz 1979: 282):

> Saluus abba Albaildensis monasterii uir lingua nitidus et scientia eruditus, elegans sententiis, ornatus in uerbis, scripsit sacris uirginibus regularem libellum et eloquio nitidum et rei ueritate prespicuum.

> Cuius oratio, nempe in hymnis, orationibus, uersibus ac missis quas inlustri ipse sermone composuit plurimam cordis compunctionem et magnam suauiloquentiam legentibus audientibusque tribuet.

Díaz y Díaz (1979: 23-24) explains that the vocabulary here is taken from the *De Viris Illustribus* of Ildefonsus and Isidore, to insert Salvo into the glorious Visigothic tradition.

Szövérffy (1971) ascribes two hymns to Salvo: *AH* XXVII no. 153, to St Martin, which is not ascribed to Salvo by Díaz y Díaz (1979: 63), and *AH* XXVII no.160, to Nunilo and Alodia, for whose convent near Nájera the *Libellus* was composed. This latter hymn has thirteen six-line stanzas of alternate 8 and 7 syllable lines, in a traditional pattern. The earliest rhythmic poem from a San Millán manuscript is that of 82 rhythmic verses (printed by Díaz y Díaz 1979: 289-92) appended as a colophon to MS AHN 1007B, the earliest surviving datable San Millán MS (932). The scribe, Jimeno, is thought by Díaz y Díaz to have been trained in León by immigrants from the south (1979: 117), and by Shailor (1979) to have been trained at Cardeña in Castille. Each stanza has three lines of 8 + 7 syllables, thus effectively having the same form as the Nunilo-Alodia hymn; the number of written vowels is accurate and consistent, at least in all the lines that are legible, except for the need for a vernacular diphthong in *apologia* (1.11) and *veniente* (1.34), and the lack of a syllable in the attempted octosyllable *Sic met ipse credensque* (1.76). That the arithmetic is indeed based on written vowels rather than anything else is attested in startling fashion by the following lines:

> Exitus futuri secli Iuliani presagus     (1.26)
>
> Orant Xristo solioque in eterno seculo     (1.45)

*Secli* is necessarily disyllabic in 1.26, and *seculo* trisyllabic in 1.45; the normal vernacular pronunciation at this time was presumably *sieglo*, but variant spellings could be exploited *metri gratia*, since these "rhythmic" forms depended on spelling alone.

The form of Jimeno's colophon is a precedent for that of Salvo's hymn; Szövérffy also offers two earlier models of uncertain provenance in *AH* XXVII nos.119 and 173. The most interesting author of the time, however, is the scribe, and later abbot, Vigila (Díaz y Díaz 1981a and 1981b). In particular, the interest lies in manuscript comments on, and attempts at, scansion.

One of his compositions is a hymn of ten five-line stanzas in imitation of the Santiago hymn mentioned above (p.175), without rhyme; it has the same first line, an acrostic (*O rex genite initium finisque Criste ingeniti patris lumen*) and a telestich (*Martini Sanctissimi atrium tuere ac salva monacorum acmen*)[19]. Given again that *laus* is thought to be disyllabic (as in 1.58 of the model), the equal number of written vowels per line is accurately attained. The text is in capitals; later someone (perhaps Vigila) added in cursive the full acrostic and telestich in the margin, and this comment at the top: "Metrū Iambicū exametrū recipit pedes hos. loco I spondiū. In ultimo pirricium. reliquis iambicum", with a second line in even smaller writing: "huI^S exemplum. Ībis lĭbūrnŭs Īntĕr altă nabĭŭm ita Ō magnĕ rerŭm xrē rector ŏbtĭmĕ et cetera." The first of these is a standard example from Horace *Epodes* 1.1, and the second from Braulio of Zaragoza's hymn to San Millán, incorporated in the Visigothic liturgy. Scansion is added to the text, probably at the time of this later addition, since alternate lines of text are in paler ink but all the scansion is in the darker ink of the other lines and the metric comments. The scanner adds $-\,-\,\cup\,-\,\cup\,-\,\cup\,-\,\cup$ $-\,\cup\,\cup$ over every line, a symbol per written vowel. E.g., 1.46 (with *laus*) runs: LAŪS SĬT PĀTRĬ HŌNŌR ĀTQ⌣ GLŌRĬĂ, which is neither classical nor rhythmical nor stress-based nor vernacular nor anything more than fitting fifteen symbols to fifteen written vowels (including the *que* of *atque*; as in the *xrē* of the heading and elsewhere, abbreviations are resolvable). There is no consistency in words: *Sēcŭlă* is in 1.19 and *SCLA* in 1.50; *xre* is $-\,\cup$ three times but $-\,-$ once; *cŭiŭs mūndĭ* (1.2), *quĭŭs prĕcatu* (1.23); *Dēĭ* (ll.1, 16, 20), *Dēī* (1.13); *sĭc sempĕr* (1.29), *sĭc rēgĭ* (1.36), and *sīc ĭn* (1.44), *sīc lŭmĭnē* (1.18); *florēăt* (1.18), *florĕăt* (1.25); *sempĕr* (1.29), *sĕmpĕr (sĕmp̄)* (1.47). Neither Vigila nor

---

19. Escorial MS *d*.I.2 ("Codex Vigilanus") folio 429r; Díaz y Díaz (1979: 365-66) does not print the scansion. I am very grateful to the Escorial Librarian for letting me have photocopies of several folios of this MS.

the scanner, if it is indeed someone else, seems to have any idea what — or ◡ mean. As Norberg (1958: 129-30) said, it is architectural; lines have 5 + 7 written syllables and no other structure. For example, there are in Norberg's calculations 45 paroxytone and 42 proparoxytone endings. There seems no sign of the cultured "rhythmic" practice of accommodating word-stress to the classical long vowels. Yet there is one surprising piece of evidence to show French influence in this composition; stanza nine includes the date:

> Actus est liber era labens enim hiC
> Ter terna ducta centena in calculO
> Rite decies septem anni pariteR
> Iuncti collectim seni sic in transitU
> Solutum ubi reuolutum circuluM.

As the marginal note in the MS, and Serrano (1925: 173), point out, this means 976 A.D.[20]. Elsewhere Vigila dates the codex (Escorial *d*.I.2) as *era* 1014, in the normal Spanish fashion; someone had also told Vigila the Northern version of fixing the dates by Anno Domini.

This poem is comparable to his other compositions in the same manuscript. Folio 1 contains a poem of fourteen lines, with the acrostic *Dei patris unice* and the telestich *O Criste initium*, in capital letters, with the text in two colours and added scansion in one, and a marginal note that "Metrum trocaicum quod ex troceo nomen accepit locis omnibus ponitur et in septimo cum catalecton huius exemplum: psallăt āltĭtudŏ celĭ sallănt ōmnĕs āngĕlĭ". As usual, Díaz y Díaz (1979: 352) omits the scansion[21]. This example is from Prudentius *Cathemerinon* 9.22 (where — corresponds to word-stress rather than length), which was in the liturgy, and every line is given this written pattern (which is probably what the scanner thinks *metrum trocaicum* means, to judge from his use of *ponitur*). The first line is sufficient to show the absurdity of this: DĪVĬNĀ VĬRTŪS CRĪSTĒ LŬX LŪMĬNĪS FĀBĒ TŬÓ.

The other lengthy composition in the manuscript (428v) has been beautifully reproduced in colour by Sánchez Albornoz (1980: 298; Díaz y Díaz 1979: 364). These are 28 lines supposedly in the lesser Asclepiad (− − − ◡ ◡ / − ◡ ◡ − ◡ ◡ repeated); the marginal note offers "metrum dactilum asclipiadeum pentametrum habet primo spondium secundo dactilum tertio catalecton deinceps duos dactilos huius exemplum",

---

20. The note in the margin runs: "Idt era dcccc lxxvia ab incarnatione dn̄i usq̃ presentē annum Intrinsecus esse Inpressā scito en era" (cp. also Antolín 1910: 403).
21. Unusually, Díaz y Díaz's text is slightly wrong. In l.6 the second word should be DIGERES (not EDIGERES), which makes the number of syllables right; in l.12 INPRIMENS and UNIUSVE (not IMPRIMENS, UNIUSQUE).

without the example. The suspicion that the scansion is a later addition is strengthened by the manner of scansion of line 6: APŌSTŌLŌRŬ CLĂRĪS ŌRNĂTĂ DŌCTRĬNĬS SĂCRĪS LŌTĂ LĬMFĬS RŪTĬLĂT CĒU SŎL; here the omission of the first vowel is made up by marking CĒU SŎL. There is one mistake: in SĪMŪLQ for SĪMŬLQ (1.11). As elsewhere, there is no verbal consistency: 1.23 includes both DĒCĪES and DĒCĬĔS, for example (it is *dĕcĭĕs* in the hymn above, 1.43). As elsewhere the colour of the scanning pen and marginal note is not that of half of the text. In this case, however, both 1.23 and the telestich (*Era millesima sive quarta decima*) have the Spanish era date of 1014 rather than the A.D. date 976. The Q of the telestich is HIQ; Alcuin would not have approved.

One other "rhythmic" piece can be ascribed to Vigila. In 980 he sent a manuscript of some of the Visigothic church councils to the otherwise unknown abbot Montano, with a dedicatory letter of similar ingenious clumsiness (Díaz y Díaz 1979: 368-70, and plate 3). It contains 29 three-line stanzas. The acrostic is *Membrana missa a Vigilane Montano*. Each line of a stanza ends in the same letter. At the top of the first folio (74v) the comment begins: "metrŭ trocaycum decapenta sillaba et trimetrŭ habet locis omnib[S] ponitur ulti...", which runs illegibly onto 75r, returning as "..lecton". This comment is at the top of the page in smaller writing than the text; again it seems to be a later addition. The scansion was given up after four syllables, however: the first line runs *Mōntăno dĕi electo cristi namque famulo*.

Each three lines of verse are given as two lines of prose in the MS, which might have been what led the scanner to give up, but in addition the inappropriateness of the $- \cup$ formula might even have struck the scribe here as it apparently did not in the *Codex Vigilanus*. The fifteen syllables per line are achieved exactly throughout; the last stanza is dated to the Spanish era 1018, i.e. A.D. 980.

Vigila's other compositions are "figurative" jigsaws (Díaz y Díaz 1979: 353-63, 367) in which the letter, rather than the written vowel, is the mathematical unit; lines are of equal number of letters, and patterns are created from that. The language of Vigila's poetry is throughout written and artificial; other than the hymn, set to previous music, there is no need to suppose they were performed aloud at all, but if they were a "Latinate" pronunciation would not have seemed more appropriate than a vernacular one. Pérez de Urbel (1926: 9-10) thought that Vigila "saw nothing in verse other than rhythm"; Díaz y Díaz omitted the scansion from his edition, but had he included it it would be obvious that he certainly saw no rhythm. Díaz y Díaz himself is surely wrong to praise these verses so highly; he claims that they are evidence of detailed metrical knowledge (1979: 73-74; 1981b), but they are not. They are evidence of metrical and rhythmical ignorance, combined with a skill in counting written vowels.

There is one other notable composition from tenth-century Navarre; the *versi domna Leodegundia Regina*, an epithalamion (MS 78, f.232; Díaz y Díaz 1979: 315-18, who discounts the supposed Galician connections; also edited by Lacarra 1948: 272-75, who filled in the many lacunae with his own work). The acrostic, formed by the initial letters of each three-line stanza, reads *Leodegundia pulcra Ordonii filia*. Ordoños I-IV reigned (in León) in 850-66, 914-24, 951-56 and 958-60, so the princess is probably of the tenth century. The Navarrese ascription rests on a reference to celebrations in Pamplona (l.26) and the fact that the manuscript comes from the Nájera area. Leodegundia herself has five syllables in the poem rather than the six written vowels of her name, but otherwise this composition is competently arranged on a 6+6, 7+7, 8+7 pattern (although Díaz y Díaz resorts to three minor emendations *metri causa*).

The Riojan scholars thus continued the techniques of "rhythmic" poetry with fixed numbers of written vowels per line; the evidence suggests that they also had some slight contact with French culture of the time, but were not much influenced by it. There is no reason to suppose they knew much about the Roman liturgy and its "Latinate" performance; Vigila's own *Codex Vigilanus* is a superb collection of the *Hispana* Visigothic canons. That, and the *Emilianense* of 992 (Escorial *d*.I.1), are the best manuscripts of Visigothic church texts we have. But they probably had heard of Frankish Medieval "Latin", as they had heard of the A.D. era, Frankish kings, and bishops of Le Puy; there is therefore a chance that they might have heard of the vernacular spellings being used in the tenth century near, for example, Clermont-Ferrand. If so, that may be part of the explanation of their celebrated Glosses.

### Glosses

There was a party at San Millán in November 1977 to celebrate the thousandth anniversary of the birth of the Spanish language. The mathematics were based on the marginal glosses discovered in what is now the History Academy MS *Emilianense* 60. The manuscript itself is probably of the late ninth century, from somewhere in the South-Western Pyrenees. Its contents have been described by Franquesa (1959) and Díaz y Díaz (1979: 235-41, 249, 266); a version of St Pascasio of Dumio's *Verba Seniorum*; *Passio*, *Missa* and *Orationes* of the blessed martyrs Cosme and Damian; two unidentified *lectiones*; several sermons attributed wrongly to Augustine, taken from the Visigothic *Homiliario de Silos* and most in fact by Caesarius of Arles. The final folios of the *Verba Seniorum* (26 to 28), the second *lectio*, "Interrogatio de nobissimo" (64-67), the first three sermons (67-75) and the sixth (87-91), were later given a number of glosses in a finer nib, several of which are in a consciously reformed spelling we can reasonably call "Romance".

These were added later, but it is not clear when. November 977 was known to be a guess, based on Ramón Menéndez Pidal's (1926: 3-9) edition of these glosses, which dated them to the late tenth century. Díaz y Díaz (1978: 27-30) has recently ascribed them to early or even mid eleventh century, possibly not even added in San Millán but further west, in Castille. Gonzalo Menéndez Pidal (1958) has added further dating problems by confidently visualizing tenth-century palaeographic habits being used by an ancient San Millán scribe in 1060. If they are indeed of the eleventh century, they may be later than the original of another manuscript, BM Add. MS 30853 (Whitehill 1976: 286), which has neatly copied whole comparable glosses from the original text. This eleventh-century MS, from Santo Domingo de Silos (in Eastern Castille), contains sermons – including those glossed in the San Millán MS – under the heading *Homiliae Toletanae*, and letters, and its final section (folios 309r to 324v), which contains the glosses, is a penitential, related to that included in Vigila's *codex*, and, like Vigila's, based on material from North of the Pyrenees (McNeill and Gamer 1938; Le Bras 1931). Silos was refounded from San Millán in the early eleventh century, so it is likely that the original of the Silos copy came from San Millán.

By the early eleventh century at the latest, then, someone has got into the habit of annotating some texts in words of a deliberately "incorrect" spelling. The annotation of sermons, probably so as to facilitate intelligible oral delivery, is precedented north of the Pyrenees; that of a penitential is understandable if not so apparently necessary[22]. No serious study has been given to these 513 glosses since 1926.

Concerning the glosses themselves, only one general comment can be made with some certainty: that most of what has been written about their function and nature is wrong. The 1977 facsimile of the San Millán folios (Olarte 1977) has an introductory panegyric (7-9) which

22. The minimum knowledge of Carolingian priests included "familiarity with the *canones* – which perhaps means the articles in penitentials", according to Ganshof (1971: 217). The main Hispanic departure from Smaragdus in the Riojan *Libellus* is a separate penitential chapter (Chapter XXX).

neatly encapsulates two traditional misconceptions: that "así, vacilante y tímida, nació la lengua que hoy hablamos" – as if nobody talked before 977; and that the glosses are a sign of ignorance, "apuntes para disimular unos conocimientos inseguros, vacilantes, como prendidos con alfileres, de la vieja cultura monacal" (7), when their writer was clearly a man of vision and enterprise. These views are, however, more justifiable than Peña's apparent assumption (1972: 60) that the monks invented the language itself.

Olarte's supposedly "academic" introduction to the facsimile in fact blandly assumes Menéndez Pidal had all the answers. Olarte follows his line in declaring that the glosser was using some kind of glossary as an aid to his task. Latin-Latin glossaries undoubtedly existed, but Latin-Spanish Romance glossaries have not been found from before the late fourteenth century (Castro 1936), and there are serious problems in postulating them for Navarre in c.1000. Even so, Menéndez Pidal's suggestion to this effect has convinced such excellent scholars as Elcock (1975: 421) and Díaz y Díaz (1978) himself. Many of the Latin-Latin glossaries were collections of pre-existing glosses; Vigila may have used glossaries as a kind of thesaurus to aid the composition of his verses and colophons (Díaz y Díaz 1979: 72), but there is no real evidence that scribes usually used glossaries to provide them with further glosses to write on other manuscripts, even in unreformed spelling.

It is worth looking first at how manuscripts were given glosses in Latin. A useful example is BM Add. MS 25600, from San Pedro de Cardeña in Castille – whose monks had helped found San Martín de Albelda –, a tenth-century liturgical manuscript with many glosses[23]. The glosses are not always correctly spelt, but are clearly intended to be the correct form, and to clarify words whose meaning, as used by the seventh-century scholars, was not immediately accessible to the tenth-century reader. The glosser may well have seen glossaries, but his glosses correspond in general to no known glossary. For example (with references to folio and column) *amens* is glossed as "stolidus vel sine mente" (241c) or "turbatus, sine mens" (26d); *amentia* "stultitia" (194b), *amentiam* "sine mente" (33d); the Silos glossaries (García de Diego 1933) offer *amens* "demens, turbatus" and *amens* "sensu carens, sine mente", but not *amentia*. *Demens* is glossed in the Cardeña MS as

---

23. See Cantera (1950-63: XVII 330); and, for Cardeña, Moreta (1971), although he avoids the topic of the monastery's intellectual life. Shailor (1979: 472) doubts if this MS was written at Cardeña itself. The glosses are listed in Fábrega Grau (1951-52); cp. Díaz y Díaz (1978: 23-24). I am grateful to the British Museum for making me a photocopy of this manuscript.

"turbatus, sine mens" (30b), "sine mente" (251b), and *dementem* as "sine mentem" (24a); the glossaries include *demens* "idem que amens vel sine mente vel quod diminutionem habet mentis". There are echoes, but it is unlikely that the glosser is actually copying a glossary. *Sine* takes *mente* in extant glossaries, but *mens*, *mentem* and *mente* in the glosses. *Mens* and *mentem* seem improbable emendations for the glosser to make if the glossary is in fact open in front of him; they look more like the unpredictable case usage we find in contemporary legal documents. *Sine* is used in many glosses as an all-purpose word to gloss the negative prefix *in-*: e.g. *inconsulta* "sine parsimonia" (109c), *innocua* "sine culpa" (94b), *inermem* "sine arma" (*sic*: 260b), *infamie* "sine honore" (58c), *ingrati* "sine gratia" (57d), etc.; and this tendency recurs in the Silos Romance glosses, e.g. *Sil.*136 *inlecebrosum* "sine mundo", *Sil.*18 *in monstruoso tempore* "sine mundo"[24], *Sil.*194 *incontinentie* "de la sine tenienca", as well as more obvious uses as "without" in *Sil.*107 *sine* .. *testibus* "o sen tiestes/testimonio", *Sil.* 256 *absque benedictione* "sine mandatione". In the Silos glosses, the *sen* spelling has the old orthodox meaning, and the new "negative-prefix" meaning has the old spelling *sine*, so there seems to be no clear Latin-Romance distinction in the glosser's mind there; both glossers, however they spell, seem to be inserting glosses of their own similar *ad hoc* invention.

Other indications that the Cardeña glosser is not directly using a glossary can be seen in the glosses on *occulo*: *occuluit* "obcultavit, co-operuit" (235a), *occulendo* "occultandum" (42a), *occulitur* "absconditur" (260a) (cp. e.g. the Silos glossary, now Paris 1298, *occulit* "pro occuluit et clausit"); or on *officio* as "ministerio" (43b), "servitio" (131d), "servicio" (145c); or on *exigimus* "compellimus vel cogimus" (134c), *exigam* "petam" (39a), *exigitur* "evocatur" (177d); and many other cases of wide alternatives of words and spellings that do not suggest a single source. There are unstandardized encyclopaedic glosses, not found elsewhere, such as:

*eculeo* "similis cruce sed tamen non cruce, id est unum lignum" (7c)
*eculeo* "genus tormenti in quo stans homo extenditur in ligno"(47a)
*eculeos* "cruces"                                                                                  (59c)

Such glosses are evidence of thinking on one's feet. That he was not tempted to reform spelling is shown by his comments on *Boreas* and *foro*. *Foro* (88b) "quod vulgo dicitur mercato"; the *-to* represents

24. Meaning "menstrual", although the MS is clearly *mon-*. The numbering follows Menéndez Pidal (1926), not Priebsch (1895).

Romance morphology (*mercado*), since *mercatus* was originally fourth declension and *-o* was no part of its paradigm, but not directly the Romance [d], since *t* for [d] was normal in Cardeña as now in the USA (*potato* [pǝDéjDǝ]). *Vulgo*, as usual, means "by everyone now". *Boreas* "boreas ventus Circius quod dat nomen vulgo"; the north wind is known in the region south of the Pyrenees as *cierzo* (< CERCIUS, presumably a variant of CIRCIUS) and at Cardeña the normal pronunciation would probably have been [tsjérdzo]. *Circius* is thus the traditional spelling given to a modern word; the Cardeña glosser is in this respect acting more like the cheese-lister of Ardón than the phonetician of San Millán, and as far as we can tell, this manuscript has not been glossed directly from a glossary.

Five long glossaries of the tenth- and early eleventh-century Rioja and South-East Castille area have survived. From Silos, Paris MSS 1296 and 1297 were published by García de Diego (1933); Paris MS 1298 by Goetz (1894: V 104-58); that in San Millán MS 46 folios 1v-168 has not been published, but is very similar to Paris 1296 and 1297; San Millán MS 31 has not been published and is, in Goetz's phrase (1923: I 186), *sui generis*[25]. This latter glossary urgently needs further study than can be given to it here. For a start, the leaves are bound in the wrong order (as Díaz y Díaz 1979: plate 32 shows), so that although it is universally said to run from *adspernatus* to *stipulator* (e.g. Díaz y Díaz 1979: 186-87), the alphabetically earliest glosses are in fact on folio 2r, beginning *Acanto*. Collectively, then, at San Millán and Silos there seems to be no doubt that glossaries existed and were actively thought useful.

Glossaries were often compiled by collecting glosses already written on a manuscript, and thus tended to be of most use when reading the particular text that gave rise to them[26]. They could, therefore, be used as source material for adding glosses to unglossed manuscripts of the same text. But otherwise there is no obvious justification

25. I am grateful to the Librarian of the Academia de la Historia for making photocopies for me of the San Millán glossaries and of the glossed folios in MS 60, and to the British Museum for copies of the glossed folios in Add. MS 30853. The similarity of the unpublished *Em.* 46 to the Silos glossaries 1296, and especially 1297, is indisputable. Most of the glosses are the same, allowing occasionally for copying variations such as *h-*, word divisions, and a few reorderings. The subsequent folios 168-71 of *Em.* 46 have French sources, including an incompetent attempt at a Greek alphabet (Díaz y Díaz 1978: 13; 1979: 143-47, comments). *Em.* 31 deserves complete publication, although it may not originate in San Millán (Díaz y Díaz 1978: 15). A few other lists and fragments are mentioned in Díaz y Díaz (1978: 11-19).
26. This also applies to the Leiden Latin-Arabic Glossary which, as Van Koningsveld (1977) established, is a later collection of known glosses rather than their source.

for the belief that glossaries were regularly used as sources for adding glosses to other texts. To begin with, as anyone who has used these manuscripts can testify, the alphabeticization is sufficiently arbitrary to annoy, the equivalences often depend on a different context, and at times the available alternatives add to the confusion; a scribe could often find an alternative more quickly from his own resources, although the memory of glossaries would indeed be a part of those resources. Díaz y Díaz, however, unfortunately gives the impression that glossaries of the type of the Silos ones now in Paris and *Em.* 46 were used by the "Romance" glosser (1978: 30-34). He mentions twelve glosses as a sample from those of San Millán that correspond to the Latin-Latin glossaries, and twenty-two from Silos that have "indudable fuente latina". Further investigation shows that this is misleading. There are approximately 20,000 entries in the Silos glossaries published by García de Diego; there are 368 glosses in the glossed manuscript also from Silos. Although several are very similar, not a single gloss coincides exactly with a glossary entry. (A very few do with items in Goetz's Europe-wide glossary corpus.[27]) Two of the 145 San Millán glosses coincide: *Em.*17, *pudor* "verecundia" and *Em.*118, *iter* "via", are both to be found in these lists, which is not in the least surprising. For only two of 513 glosses to coincide with 20,000 entries is less than one might expect by chance. Only one gloss coincides with an entry in MS 1298 (Goetz): *strages* "occisiones" (*Sil.*52), although *Sil.* adds "matatas". MS *Em.* 31 provides no more evidence of having been consulted. Díaz y Díaz reached his conclusions by ignoring formal variations and sticking to lexical roots alone. E.g. the glossary entry *pudor* "verecundia" (above) is said to be the source for *Sil.*171 *pudoris* "de la vergoina". *Em.*4 *bellum* "pugna" is said to correspond to glossary *bellum* "pugnam"[28]. Díaz y Díaz quotes *Em.*33 *devotos* "promissiones" as being based on the Silos glossary's *devoto*: "deslinata, determinata, dedicata, promissa" and Goetz's *Affatim* glossary's *devotus* "promisus, dedicatus" or *devota* "debita exsolvens et non promissa". *Em.*11 *indica* "amuestra" is said to be based on Goetz IV 94,24, *indicat* "ostendit"; there is no case at all here, and the Silos glossaries offer *indicat* "investigat". Díaz y Díaz's case is weak. The glossaries offer vast choices that are ignored on many occasions, and differently spelt on others; such similarities as there are tend to be obvious and not requiring any source at all.

27. One very minor variant is: *Sil.*106, *reus* "culpaviles"; glossary *reus* "culpavilis".
28. *Bellum* "pugna" is in St Gall MS 912 glossary (Goetz 1889: IV 211,8).

That choices available in the glossaries are not taken can be exemplified by *quousque* and *demum*. *Sil.*240 reads *quousque reconciliet* "ata ke pacifiket". The Silos glossaries offer a wide variety for *quousque*, including "quamdiu", "quatenus", "usque eo vel usque quo", "tandem", "usque ad finem", and "ab utero cantilena patientia nostre quam diu tamen ab initio sermonis mansuetudinis nostre". These comments, intelligible in the original context from which they come into the glossary, are all ignored by the glosser, who prefers an Arabic borrowing (*ata*) here, recently used in two previous glosses (*Sil.*210, 226). *Sil.*22 *De munque* "de puisca" is adduced by Díaz y Díaz: the Silos glossaries offer *demum* "tandem, novissimum, maxime vel postremum, igitur; postea, deinde; consequenter vel iterum vel post modum", but not the DE POSTQUAM from which *de puisca* comes, nor even POSTQUAM[29]; *Sil.*98 *Demum* "de Inde" (two words and capital I) and *Sil.*151 *demunque* "postea" are closer (there is no *-que* in the glossary entry), but there is still no reason here to postulate that the glosser has the glossary in front of him.

The presence of these glossaries is thus a red herring for our understanding of the "Romance" glosses, whose outstanding characteristic is their originality rather than their traditionality. Díaz y Díaz concluded that "por las peculiaridades de estas glosas resulta casi imposible no aceptar que se utilizaba como base un glosario latino; más aún, parece probable que uno de los empleados haya sido el Silense..." (1978: 34); it seems, on the contrary, impossible to accept that the scribes used such glossaries as the base for their own glosses. It is easier to conclude that they had probably met them before but nevertheless made up their own glosses to fit the case.

Díaz y Díaz's view is, however, more plausible than that of Menéndez Pidal and Elcock, who believed that the glossers used existing Latin-Romance glossaries, now lost. Arguing on the basis of the Reichenau glossary, Elcock said that "the practice of using such lexical compilations had already begun in Gaul in the eighth century, and two centuries later they were probably in general circulation in all the monastic schools of the West" (1975: 422). This begs the following questions: whether the Reichenau glossary can be called "Latin-Romance" when the "Romance" half is spelt in the Latin way; whether the Reichenau glossary is one of many such – part of a "practice"; whether they were "used" to insert later glosses; and whether the Rioja

29. Priebsch (1895: 17) suggested POSTEA >*puisca*, but this is unlikely; cp. NUNQUAM>*nunca*.

had a Carolingian-style "monastic school". The answer to all these
questions seems to be no. In addition, since glossaries are usually made
by compiling existing glosses, the existence of a Latin-Riojan glossary
would imply the existence of many earlier manuscripts with Romance
glosses, now lost, whose own origins would be just as debatable as those
that have survived. Indeed, the questions raised by the existence of such
a glossary would far outweigh those answered by it. Even so, it is worth
looking at the internal evidence of the glosses to see if they suggest the
existence of a glossary as the source.

There are many cases of the same Latin word having different
glosses in different places. *Sil.* 1 *aut deponatur* "aut desse poncat", *Sil.*
76 *deponatur* "tolito siegam" (*sic*: the MS is clearly *-m*); *Sil.* 35 *consenserit* "castigatore fueret, consiliu dederit", *Sil.* 46 *consenserit* "casti-
garet et consilio malo dederit", *Sil.* 354 *consenserit* "qui quisieret", and
*Sil.* 125 *consentit* "sientet scuita placet"; *Sil.* 104 *cui reus fuerit* "quale
factu fueret, que gerranza fueret", and in the next line *Sil.* 106 *reus*
"culpaviles"; successive glosses *Sil.* 264 *exercent* "faciunt" and *Sil.* 265
*exercuerit* "escieret" (which slightly mistranslates the text); *Em.* 15
*abicinabunt se* "aluenge seferan", *Em.* 23 *abicinabunt se* "alongarsan";
etc., etc. In most cases the gloss chosen suits the context, even if it does
not seem to be an extrinsic lexical equivalent. The most obvious
example of this concerns *esse*: *Sil.* 72 and 238 *esse* "sedere" (SEDERE >
Sp. *ser*, "to be"), *Sil.* 272 *esse* "ke jet" and *Sil.* 273 "ke son" (after *dicit*
and *credit*, to explain the accusative and infinitive construction). Many
individual glosses are thus inaccurate out of context: e.g. *Sil.* 163 *matri-
monio* "prima junctatione", *Sil.* 321 *coitu* "semen" (discussed in Ariza
1979: 13), *Em.* 59 *occupare* "parare uel aplecare", *Em.* 82 *offero*
"dico", etc. There are also apparent cases of misunderstanding: *Em.* 116
*Denuo* "altra" probably means "again" in context, as the glossaries
suggest (MS 31 "iterato", Silos "iterato, rursus"); and perhaps *Em.* 33
*devotos* "promissiones", which in the text is an adjective but seems to
be understood by the glosser as two words, *de votos*. This misunderstanding is used by Menéndez Pidal and Elcock as proof of the use of
a glossary, but readers do not need the help of a glossary to misread.
There are cases where the glosser provides clarification rather than
synonymy: e.g. *Em.* 131 *dicit etiam* "Esajas" (i.e. Isaiah), which would
be a remarkable coincidence if it came from a glossary. Cumulatively,
such evidence of variation, contextualization, and misunderstanding
points against a source glossary.

Nor is there any standardization of Romance orthography. The
contemporary stage of the IACTARE > *echar* development is variously

spelt: *Sil.*53 *relictis* "jectatis", *Sil.*43 *transmiserit* "zetare corri", *Sil.* 102 *inici* "por jactare", *Em.*45 *respuit* "geitat". The *puisca* of *Sil.*22 above is the *posque* of *Sil.*44. We can compare *Sil.*62 *cadabera* "corpora" and *Sil.*327 *cadabera* "elos cuerpos"; *Sil.*55 *per poculum* "por la bebetura", *Sil.*68 *poculum* "vevetura de la ierba"; *Em.*17 **"verecundia"** and *Sil.*171 "vergoina" (mentioned above) with the verb "se bergudian" of *Em.*78 (> Sp. (*a*)*verguenzan*, glossing *erubescunt*); *quomodo* glosses four separate words in *Em.*25, 50, 52, 83, but *quemo* appears twice in *Em.*115. *Uęmne, uamne* and *huamne* (<HOMINEM) appear in *Em.*130, 68 and 128. Indeed, many of the glosses are in ordinary Latin spelling, a fact which previous discussion of these glosses has overlooked; if these indeed came from a "Latin-Romance" glossary, the "Romance" side was totally inconsistent.

It seems clear that the theory of a pre-existing glossary — which, if true, would put the discussion of these centuries into enormous difficulties — has no firm evidence to support it; like *latín vulgar leonés*, it was a reasonable hypothesis once, but has fossilized far beyond its credibility. Only one variant of a "source" theory can survive; that these glosses are modernizations of pre-existing Latin glosses on other manuscripts of the same text, now lost. This theory can be invalidated by consideration of some of the most interesting glosses, in which the same lexical item is used in a different form. This rearrangement is at times due to the morphology; e.g. *Sil.*189 *promiserit* "prometieret", *Sil.*268 *arserit* "ardieret", where lost strong perfects are replaced by weak regular forms; *Em.*103 *et tu ibis* "etujras", with the Romance future (*et tu ib̲* is an interlinear explanatory gloss in any case); *Sil.*331 *ab eo non inquinetur* "non siegat jnquinata polu" (> *no sea "inquinada" por ello*), where the synthetic present passive is replaced by the participle and the auxiliary (SEDEAT > [sjeja] *siegat* > *sea*: *g* for [j] is normal here); *Sil.*111 *auguria* "agueros" replaces a neuter plural by the vernacular masculine; *Em.*133 *flos* "flore" replaces an imparisyllabic nominative. Four others, less explicably, respell the same form: *Sil.*218 *habeat* "ajat", *Sil.*251 *saltare* "sotare", *Sil.*277 *sicitates* "seketates", *Em.*121 *ubi* "obe". The first three are perhaps explicable as unusual letter-sound correspondences; *-be-* was not often [j], *-al-* was only [o] before some cases of [t], *-ci-* was usually [tsi] or [tse] rather than [ke] (Sp. *haya*, O. Sp. *sotar*, Sp. *sequedad*, O. Sp. *o*). These examples serve to overthrow the theory of the existence of orthodox Latin glosses on the manuscript from which the texts are copied, for noone would e.g. gloss *saltare* as "saltare". They remain interesting even so; we can hardly claim that the spelling of the glosses is in general meant to be

Romance in phonetic script in the light of such extreme variations as *corpora/cuerpos, quomodo/quemo*, but some, at least, of the glosses must represent such an attempt to approximate speech.

The usual assumption that the spelling of many of them is consciously devised in order to approximate vernacular phonetics is tenable provided we do not assume that they are in as rigorous a "phonetic" script as is the *Eulalia*. The gloss is meant to facilitate recognition of lexical items, rather than of their sound. In general, there is reason to suppose that non-Latin orthography in the glosses is usable as evidence of evolved speech, but no reason to suppose that Latinate orthography represents unevolved speech. *Em.*2 *repente* "lueco", for example, is evidence that [o] > [we] has happened in the Navarre/ East Castille region; it is not evidence of a vernacular [k] rather than [g] in this word (*luego* < LOCO), for written *c* would often be read aloud as [g], *t* as [d], *p* as [b]. There is confirmation of this in *Sil.*134 *ignorans* "non sapiento", *Sil.*341 *ignoranti* "[non] sapiento", which is spelt in three other glosses as *sapiendo* (17, 32 and 339); this was always [d] (SAPIENDUM > *sabiendo*); similarly *Sil.*38 *incendii* "de lo incentitu" is a word in which the first *t* represents a sound which was always [d] (INCENDIUM > *incendio*; this is the participle *encendido*). In this respect the spelling is as unrevealing as that of the cheeses. The consciously reformed spelling in the Rioja is far more revolutionary, though; e.g. Romance diphthongs are explicitly represented (*lueco, uemne, cuerpos, puisca, siegam*, above, etc.), Romance [j] is represented, usually by *i* or *g* (e.g. *siegam*; *Em.*112 "gelemo" = *yelmo* < HELM) — as in the *Eulalia* — or both (*Em.*26 *caracterem* "seingnale", which = [seɲa], < SIGNA, plus the suffix *ale*, and becomes Spanish *señal*); and a variety of inventions such as *Em.*115 "spillu" (SPECULUM > [espéʎo] > Sp. *espejo*), *Em.*138 "tueleisco" (< TU ILLE IPSE), etc. The morphology of the glosses tends also to be that of vernacular; nouns are nearly always in the form derived from the accusative, futures are the Romance ones derived from the infinitive plus HABEO, passives are rephrased analytically or with *se*, etc. That this is at times the result of a determined attempt at new representation of vernacular is clear in the only extended gloss, *Em.*89:

> *adIubante dño nro ihu xpo cui est honor et Imperiũ cum patre et spu sco In scla sclor⁺ Amen* "cono aiutorio de nuestro dueno dueno xpo dueno salbatore qual dueno get ena honore e qual duenno tienet eIa mandatione cono patre cono spu sco enos sieculos de lo sieculos. Faca nos ds ompts tal serbitio fere ke denante ela sua face gaudioso segamus Amen."

The final sentence corresponds to nothing in the text. *Cono* (< CUM ILLO) and *ena*, *enos* (< IN ILLA, IN ILLOS) are further evolved than normal Old Spanish, and presumably attest current forms without [l]. *Sieculos* attests the diphthongization and the Romance masculine plural, the original Latin being neuter SAECULA, but is no evidence of [kul] nor [kəl] nor [kl] rather than ordinary vernacular [gl] (cp. *secli* in Jimeno's colophon, above). The whole represents an attempt to write in some non-Latin way; and the question that remains is, why?

One of Menéndez Pidal's many achievements in the *Orígenes* (1926) was to show the way in which scribes spelt non-Romance (particularly Germanic) names with non-Romance sounds: e.g. *gg* for [tʃ] in *Sanggez* (Sánchez), *Oggobiz* for the Basque *Ochoiz* (para.8.2). This attempt at spelling words coming from other languages is added to in these glosses by the need to write a few words derived from Arabic: *Em.*48 *pauperibus reddet* "qui dat alosmisquinos" (Arabic *miskîn* > Sp. *mezquino*); *Em.*110 *donec* "ata quando", *Sil.*201 *usque in finem* "ata que mueran", *Sil.*226 *quandium* "ta mientre", *Sil.*240 *quousque reconciliet* "ata ke pacifiket", *Sil.*328 *usque dum mazerentur* "ata ke se monden". Arabic *háttà* > Sp. *hasta* is earliest attested in 945, as *adta*. *Mozlemos* turn up in *Sil.*51, being the Arabic *muslim*, given (like *miskîn*) a Romance ending. More urgent in the Rioja/East Castille area than Germanic or Arabic may have been a desire to write Basque. Two of the glosses are in Basque: *Em.*31 *incolumes inveniri meruimur* "jzioqui dugu", *Em.*42-43 *non nos sufficit* "guec ajutuezdugu" and "nos nonkaigamus" (Alvar 1976: 19-26; Guiter 1979 showed that Menéndez Pidal probably attached the Basque glosses to the wrong Latin words). We do not have to follow Rico's whimsy (1978) that the MS is a Basque schoolboy's Latin-learning text to find these interesting. The area may have had a large number of Basque speakers; Saralegui (1977) implies that they might have been a majority in Navarre. Yet it seems reasonable to speculate that, in addition to the impulse from creating writing for Basque, the presence of creative enterprise in writing Romance (e.g. in representing diphthongs) may have something to do with the experiments going on at the same time north of the Pyrenees. Even if the glosses are tenth-century, there is ample evidence of some unsystematic contacts in the Rioja with Carolingian scholarship, and the circle of Vigila at Albelda is no less linguistically adventurous than that of Hucbald at St Amand seventy years earlier, even if less well-informed. One of Gotescalc's entourage, for example, could well have mentioned the possibility of reformed spelling. If the Glosses date from 1020-45, as Díaz y Díaz (1978) suggests, the hypothesis of French contacts is indisputable in itself, since that is near the start of the age of increasing cultural interchange, when Cluniac monks are occasionally to be found in Northern Spain and the Santiago routes become more crowded. If so, the motive may have been to imitate a current French fashion using native words; since the contents of both texts are in the Old Visigothic Church tradition we cannot visualize that the glossers had learnt Medieval Latin or the Roman liturgy. The idea that the spelling of the glosses is designed to aid oral performance, particularly in preaching the sermons in the San Millán folios — an idea of which Díaz y Díaz is sceptical (1978: 31) —, would be reinforced by the hypothesis that the idea of changing the spelling came from France, since that is precisely the point of the contemporary French experiments.

The traditional view of these glosses contains yet one more misconception; that they represent "Navarro-Aragonese". Elcock (1975: 418) declared that:

> among consonants, intervocalic voiceless plosives are preserved (*salbatore, patre, faca, sieculos*) as they still are in certain localities. Thus in this earliest specimen of northern Hispano-Romance, the stamp of the region of Navarre is quite unmistakeable.

Voicelessness is certainly not here attested, as we saw above; Díaz y Díaz suggests that the glosses were probably added to the San Millán MS in the Castilian end of the region (1978: 30); these "certain localities" are in fact way up in the Aragonese Pyrenees, some 150 miles from the Silos/San Millán area; Elcock's argument is circular, since our knowledge of early Navarrese speech is based on these glosses; but more importantly, it seems anachronistic to see the isoglosses bundled together at this time into distinct dialect areas with clear boundaries. The evidence does not support that view. Nor does it support the view that Navarrese and Aragonese form a unit (Saralegui 1977; Líbano 1977). Even if the glosses were phonetic script — which they are not — they would represent the speech of one or two scribes in East Castile or the Rioja, not the consensus of a large and delimitable region.

In sum, many of the traditional comments on the glosses (in e.g. Olarte 1976) are ill-founded. They are probably not tenth-century but eleventh. They are not phonetic transcriptions of "Navarro-Aragonese", but the result of intelligent *ad hoc* inventions by one or two individuals. They are not derived from known glossaries; nor do they seem to derive from lost "Latin-Romance" glossaries. They are not evidence that Latin and Romance are conceptually distinct. They are not the occasion of the "birth of Spanish". Unreformed spellings therein do not attest unevolved spoken forms. The glossing is not done by ignorants who could not cope with Latin, but by scholars in a spirit of enterprise. This means that very little remains of the standard assessment except the undoubted facts that they are of exceptional interest and that they deserve a more serious and detailed study than I have been able to give them here.

### Conclusion

The conclusion is simple. In non-Catalan Northern Spain up to the eleventh century there existed in each place its own vernacular. That was all. This theory — which in itself is hardly revolutionary — means that we no longer have to believe in such chimeras as *latín vulgar leonés*, Medieval Latin pronunciation, lost precocious Latin-Romance glossaries, and a multitude of experts in phonetic script.

European culture begins to impinge in the later eleventh century. The slow absorption of Medieval Latin, and the consequential need for written Spanish Romance, took two more centuries, and forms the substance of the next chapter.

# 5

## LATIN AND ROMANCE IN SPAIN, 1050-1250

### The Council of Burgos (1080)

The central years of the eleventh century saw a growth in Christian confidence in Spain, which culminated in the recapture of Toledo in 1085. Contacts increased with trans-Pyrenean Europe. At the Council of Burgos in 1080 it was decreed that the Roman liturgy should replace the old Visigothic liturgy. This reform led to a need for educational change, including the training of clerics in Medieval Latin, but it took two centuries for the general level of Latinity to improve greatly.

The decision to change the liturgy was not caused by popular demand, nor would it have been predictable in the 1050s. Fernando I of León, after defeating the Navarrese at Atapuerca in 1054, was the leader of the North-Western Christians and a firm believer in continuing the Visigothic traditions. Bishops came from all of his lands to the reforming Church Councils of Coyanza (1055) and Santiago de Compostela (1056), which consciously modelled themselves on the great Toledo councils of the seventh century (Maldonado and Toro 1942-43; García Gallo 1950; Martínez Díez 1964). The preface to the canons of Coyanza state the Council's desire to reestablish the glories of their church's Visigothic past:

> pro corrigendis ac dirigendis regulis vel tramitibus Ecclesie, ut mos est antiquorum patrum, ac sumendis tramitibus.
>
> (*Prefatio* 6, García Gallo 1950: 287)

(Cp. also pp.312, 319, 364-66, 380, 442, 557, 560, 572, 580-81, 596-97, 622, 630-33.)

Many details of church life are specified, but nothing is said about the oral nature of the liturgy other than that essential parts are to be known by heart (III xvii p.294; V iii p.296). In the original version of the canons, the *goticista* nature of the Council is obvious. Unfortunately, Bishop Pelayo of Oviedo, in the early twelfth century, sponsored a revised version which removed this emphasis ("el falsario Don Pelayo que siempre, siempre, siempre falsificó . . .", Sánchez Albornoz 1980: 589), and this revised version was thought to be the original until García Gallo argued the contrary (Grassotti 1977 still thinks so)[1]. It is clear, however, that there was no idea in 1055 of altering the Visigothic liturgy. The Pope was not yet worrying about it, the ecclesiastical life of the Kingdom was based on it, and García Gallo (1950: 454, 557) decided not even to consider the liturgy in all the 358 pages of his article. Fernando I is said by the *Historia Silense* to have liked to visit monasteries and join in the traditional rite with the monks, apparently knowing part of it by heart (Pérez de Urbel and González 1959: 204-09). When the new church of St Isidore was consecrated in León on December 21st 1063, freshly endowed with the body of the greatest of all the Spanish Visigothic saints, the symbolic affirmation of contact with the former glories of the native church was obvious. These are the years of the preparation of excellent manuscripts of Visigothic rites, such as those of Silos (1039, 1053, 1067, 1072), Compostela (1055), León (1066), San Millán (1073), etc. (Férotin 1912: XLIII; Díaz y Díaz 1979: 184). The idea of abandoning the old liturgy for some alien French version unintelligibly pronounced was not likely to attract Fernando I.

Unfortunately for the national pride of the Leonese, both the Papacy and the French were at this time in expansionist mood. Bishko has charted the complex diplomacy of these years in a study (1968-69) that clarifies the picture and should eventually clear away several misconceptions. In 1063 the Aragonese King was encouraging the Papacy to support the arrival of a French army to help invade Moslem Zaragoza, on Aragón's southern border; these negotiations are credited with the first use of the concept of a "crusade", a march of the cross against its enemies. Zaragoza, however, was a tributary ally of León, and Fernando wished to prevent his lucrative tributary from being attacked by the French. His method was to ally himself formally with the monks of Cluny, perhaps in the hope that they could use their influence in Rome to dissuade the Pope from supporting any French-Aragonese attack; in return he arranged to send Cluny 1000 gold pieces annually, money which was welcome to Cluny and originated in the tribute paid from Zaragoza, with the implication that if the Leonese lost control of

1. The view that the Council recommended the Benedictine Rule stems from this difference of opinion – e.g. Linage (1973a: 1005), Cocheril (1966: 24, 82); Moreta (1971: 146) refers to García Gallo in support of the view García is in fact arguing against.

Zaragoza Cluny would in turn lose its money. Fernando died in 1065, after that threat had receded, and the payment lapsed; the King of Aragón upstaged that alliance by becoming the personal vassal of the Papacy in 1068.

Bishko's analysis leaves little room for doubt; the alliance with Cluny was based at least partly on the King's desire to have a fifth column in Rome. Unfortunately, the opposite view is still widely held, that the monks of Cluny were the Papacy's fifth column in León, and were instrumental, even before the change, in the Papal plan to introduce the Roman liturgy (e.g. by Cantarino 1977, who – as Lomax 1979 pointed out – has read little recent research). There were a few Cluniacs in San Juan de la Peña in Aragón in 1032; they probably left in 1035, and that monastery kept the Visigothic rite until the 1070s. There was a Catalan, Pons de Tavernoles, appointed Bishop of Oviedo in 1023; he was said to be *romano more degens*, a phrase which San Martín (1942: 4) suggested meant that he performed the Roman rite. This phrase comes from a document of 1059 in Palencia cathedral, which goes on to declare that Pons was instrumental in reviving that see; Palencia cathedral, founded in 1033, seems to have had a few Catalan and French priests from 1035. The first Cluniac monk in León can only be definitely located in 1053. They were not widespread before the 1070s, and were happy to use the Visigothic liturgy (and script). Indeed, the extant documents from Sahagún, which came to be their eventual headquarters, show that Visigothic script was normal there until at least 1120. The idea that the Cluniacs were Europeanizing zealots is not supported by evidence; for present purposes, there is no reason at all to suppose that in Spain they generally advocated or even used either the Roman liturgy or the Medieval Latin required to perform it before 1080. These may have been used at (non-Cluniac) Palencia in the 1030s, but there is no evidence for their continued subsequent use there either.

On Fernando I's death, there was a civil war between his children, eventually won by Alfonso VI in 1072, partly, so he thought, because of Cluniac intercession in heaven on his behalf. Over the next few years (1072-77) he granted the Cluniacs four monasteries. Alfonso VI wished to call himself "Emperor", but the Papacy was also feeling imperialist. Pope Alexander II was interested in abolishing the Visigothic liturgy from 1070, and his successor Gregory VII felt even more strongly about it. In 1073, soon after his accession, Gregory sent a letter to all the Spanish rulers, saying so. San Juan de la Peña had adopted the Roman rite in 1071, and the rest of Aragón adopted it in

1074. Since Aragón was a temporal fief of the Papacy, this was a logical step (Kehr 1945; Cowdrey 1970: 228 believed that the changes were made "for the convenience of pilgrims"!). Navarre adopted it in 1076 (Ubieto 1948). The Papacy then stepped up pressure on León, coupling demands for liturgical change with demands for temporal overlordship.

The Leonese church leaders rejected the view that their ancient liturgy was heretical, but they had no wish to be excommunicated. Alfonso VI followed his father's example, and reestablished the alliance with Cluny at double the price, this time in gold largely from Moslem Toledo. The Cluniacs were delighted with the money, set about using it to rebuild their Burgundy headquarters, and had prayers said on Alfonso's behalf. But even though Gregory VII was himself connected with the Cluniacs, they were less able to influence the Papal mind in 1077-80 than they had been in 1063. Gregory envisaged Europe as "Christendom" and one corner could not be allowed to be heretical. Abbot Hugh of Cluny mediated on the Spaniards' behalf, to the Pope's displeasure, and eventually a compromise was reached: as a result Alfonso VI was able to reject Gregory's claim to temporal authority, but agreed to change the liturgy. The reform was eventually decreed at the Council of Burgos in the spring of 1080 (Fita 1906a).

The motivation for the change was thus political expediency. It was not theological nor even ecclesiastical. The consequent immediate need for expertise in Latin *litterae*, new educational techniques, new pronunciation methods and a new script, was, it seems, neither foreseen, expected, demanded nor desired by the Spanish church. Indeed, the reform as a whole was not universally welcome. Alfonso VI wrote to Hugh of Cluny to the effect that his country was pretty fed up with the Roman rite that Hugh had made them accept: "De romano autem officio, quod tua iussione recepimus, sciatis nostram terram admodum desolatam esse"; but continued nevertheless to ask for a Cardinal to reform whatever needed reforming, "ut ea quae sunt emendanda emendet, et ea quae sunt corrigenda corrigat"[2]. The vagueness of this phrase suggests that he had no clear idea of what was going to be involved. In the event the reforming task was then taken over largely by the Cluniacs.

The dioceses of Coimbra and Braga initially refused to accept this decision, and it was a factor in the subsequent decision of the county of Portugal to secede from Alfonso's realms; the unrevised

---

2. Fita (1906a: 382). Hitchcock, however, dated this letter to 1077 (1973: 29), and Rivera (1962: 14-16) thought it was written in 1081 to Gregory.

version of the Council of Coyanza's canons only survives in Coimbra (cp. Bishko 1965). Elsewhere, the following years saw the arrival of many French clerics. Sahagún was made the Cluniac headquarters. This inflow is so well-documented that no modern historian seems to find it surprising. French historians tend to see it as a self-evident case of a superior culture being gratefully imitated by barbaric neighbours. But it is indeed surprising. Alfonso VI wanted to call himself "Emperor" of Spain and raise his realms to a respected place in Europe; he was proudly determined to recover Spain for the Gothic Leonese, and sure he was going to succeed until the disasters of 1086. Even though this is a period of modernization and Europeanization, Alfonso might not have been expected to allow the ancient national church to become submissive to foreigners. If, however, the hypothesis is correct that Medieval Latin did not exist in Spain until it was suddenly required for the performance of the Roman liturgy in 1080, the arrival of French clerics is in part explicable as a response to the practical need for priests trained in Medieval Latin performance of that liturgy. There happened at the time to be a boom in Latin-teaching fervour in France: for example, the two *Artes Lectoriae* of Aimericus and Siguinus date, probably, to 1086 and 1088 (see below); Guibert of Nogent, in the preface to his *Gesta Dei per Francos* (1104-12), says "cum enim passim videamus fervere grammaticam . . ." (*PL* CLVI 681D; cp. Sancho 1914: 54). In his *De Rebus Hispaniae* VI 26, Ximénez de Rada (ed. 1968: 140) called the newcomers "iuvenes dociles et litterati".

The stress on the need for *litterae* in Church leaders, and its apparent limitation to foreigners, is made explicit in a letter from Gregory VII to Alfonso VI (published by Mansilla 1955: 36-38) which congratulates the King on changing to the Roman rite, and goes on to say that Alfonso's (unnamed) choice as Archbishop (*in archiepiscopum*) is unacceptable:

> Discipline fundamento, videlicet litteralis scientie peritia indiget. Que virtus quam sit non modo episcopis, verum etiam sacerdotibus necessaria, ipse satis intelligis, cum nullus sine ea aut alios docere aut sese possit defendere.

> He lacks any expertise in the foundations of Church education, i.e. the knowledge of *litterae*. As you know, this knowledge is essential, not merely for bishops, but also for priests, since without it noone can teach others nor (?) perform adequately himself.

Mansilla and many other scholars (including myself, Wright forthcoming) have assumed that in this the Pope referred to the see of Toledo, still nominally the archbishopric for the whole of Castille. Toledo was still in Moslem hands, however, until 1085, and although the letter is undated Mansilla found it in the Vatican register for 1081. 1081 is a more likely date for congratulating Alfonso on changing the rites (in 1080) than 1085-6, and should probably be accepted. (There is also a reference in the letter to Bishop Simeon, presumably the Bishop of Burgos who died in 1082.) It is conceivable that Alfonso was already looking ahead to the capture of Toledo and wishing to have a candidate ready to jump into the metropolitan see, although in the event the new archbishop of Toledo was appointed more than a year after the capture of the city; Serrano (1935: I 309-10), however, concluded that after 1080 Alfonso wanted to appoint an existing bishop as the metropolitan, with authority over Castille and León, as was normal in other countries. This is not unlikely. The rejected candidate, in Serrano's view, could well have been Bishop Simeon of Burgos. If so, this would explain the Papal preference not to name the candidate outright, since Simeon was in the party carrying the letter to Alfonso. This would be a sensible choice from Alfonso's viewpoint: Burgos was the capital of Castille and the home of the 1080 Council, so its bishop might be expected to be the new archbishop. Burgos was not, however, a centre of *letras*. The Pope goes on to suggest that they look around for a more suitable candidate, and, as Serrano points out, it looks as if the Bishop of Palencia (Bernardo II) was chosen. There are at least four documents from 1083 to early 1085 that call Bernardo "Archbishop"; after the capture of Toledo (1085) he stopped calling himself "Archbishop" and changed his name to Raimundo — perhaps to avoid confusion with the new Archbishop Bernard of Toledo. If this is the right interpretation of the events of these years, it makes excellent sense; the new liturgy required expertise in *litterae*, and Palencia was in the late eleventh century the centre of education in the Kingdom, with established French and Catalan connections[3]. Whoever Gregory is writing about, however, the need for *litterae* in the new archbishop is an explicit and overriding criterion; and this cannot refer to the simple ability to read at all, since any existing Spanish bishop would do that when performing the old liturgy. It refers to the newly-essential Medieval Latin pronunciation.

### Toledo

The same consideration applies in Toledo; on 18th December 1086 Alfonso VI and his Council appointed as archbishop of Toledo

---

3. My mind on this matter has been changed by discussions with Derek Lomax, to whom I am most grateful.

Bernard de Sédirac, already in charge of the Cluniacs' Spanish head-quarters at Sahagún, already actively involved in educating the Spanish church in the *scientia litteralis*, and probably therefore better qualified than any native Spaniard to suit the Papal instructions. 150 years later Ximénez de Rada said that Bernard was *ab infantia litteratus* (VI 23; 1968: 137); he was in the Cluniac monastery at Auch as an adolescent, and then at Cluny itself during some part of the 1060s and 1070s, where he was a colleague of the future Pope Urban II. Similarly, the monastery of San Servando in Toledo was reopened with a staff from Marseilles (Fita 1906b); Bernard recruited other bishops from France, such as Jerome, who became bishop of Valencia (1098-1102) and of Salamanca (1102-20) (Fletcher 1978: 37-38) and is described in the *Poema de Mio Cid* as "bien entendido es de letras e mucho acordado" (l.1290). *Litterati*, "letrados", in the period 1080-1100, seems to entail "Frenchmen".

Those modern scholars who approve of Cluny *a priori*, such as Cowdrey (1970) and Rivera (1962), think Bernard was a good choice; noone else does. Mundó (1965) is particularly harsh. The capture of Toledo had been almost bloodless, for the Christian community had aided Alfonso's entry and expected to prefer his rule; but Bernard had no sympathy with their ancient traditions and dealt with Christian *mozárabe* and Moslem *mudéjar* with the same lack of sensitivity. The Mosque was desecrated, against the King's wishes. The mozarabic community, initially exhilarated at the prospect of Christian rule, found that Bernard wished to destroy the old Visigothic manuscripts and customs. It has been suggested that they had difficulty in achieving social equality with the Northern immigrants, although this view has recently been severely criticized (González 1978), and in practice it seems that the twelfth-century mozarabs, who included many immigrants from further south, had a protected position. Díaz y Díaz (1975) and Mundó have established that the Toledan *mozárabes* acquired and copied several northern manuscripts of the Visigothic rites, anxious to preserve their heritage. A few churches were permitted to continue using them.

The investigations of Van Koningsveld (1977) confirm that there was in twelfth-century Toledo a community of Christians literate in Arabic, who were responsible for the Arabic glosses on some religious manuscripts. The large Latin-Arabic glossary at Leiden is not, as was once thought, a proselytizing work for Latin-speakers in Moslem territory, but an aid for Arabic-speakers eager to understand both Latin biblical texts and Isidore of Seville's *Etymologiae*[4]. (One source of this

4. Díaz y Díaz (1978: 25 n.45) redates the MS to 1250, without explaining why.

glossary is Toledo MS 15.8 – now Madrid BN MS *Vitr.* 14.3 –, a manuscript of Isidore containing over 1,500 Arabic glosses (facsimile in Beer 1909); others are preexisting Arabic translations of Christian gospels.) Meanwhile there is no doubt that Bernard's entourage at Toledo knew and practised *litterae*. Ximénez de Rada's history (of the thirteenth century) includes the following poem in hexameters celebrating the capture of Toledo (VI 22):

O  Obsedit secura suum Castella Toletum,
P  Castra sibi septena parans, aditumque recludens.
P  Rupibus alta licet, amploque situ populosa,
I  Circundante Tago, rerum virtute referta,
D  Victu victa carens, invicto se dedit hosti.
A  Huic Medina Caelim, Talavera, Conimbria plaudat.
C  Abula, Secobia, Salmantica, Publica Septem,
A  Cauria, Cauca, Colar, Iscar, Medina, Canales,
P  Ulmus, et Ulmetum, Magerit, Atentia, Ripa,
T  Osoma cum Fluvio lapidum, Valeranica, Maura,
A  Ascalona, Fita, Consocra, Maqueda, Butracum
Victori sine fine suo modulantur ovantes:
Aldefonse, tui resonent super astra triumphi.

This poem has been ascribed to one Alo "Grammaticus" who appears in royal documents and wrote epitaphs in Caroline script for Queen Costanza, who may or may not also be the author of the so-called *Historia Silense*, and/or the brief *Chronicon Compostellanum*, and who may or may not be the Alo who was bishop of Astorga (1123-31) (Martínez 1975: 272-73; Fletcher 1978: 46; Quintana 1978). Whoever it is, it is a recognizable attempt at hexameters, and the present tense of the last two lines led Amador (1862: II 212) and others to date it to soon after 1085; if so, it is perhaps written by a Frenchman.

Another unquestionably "Medieval Latin" production is the famous *Garcineid*, *Garsuinis*, or *Tractatus Garsiae Toletani Canonici de Albino et Rufino* (the recent edition by Thomson 1973 is no improvement on Sackur 1892). This is a satirical account in prose of the visit of Bernard to Pope Urban II in 1099, probably at the council celebrated on 24th-30th April. The author has apparently adopted "García" as a pseudonym; Thomson makes no reference at all to the Spanish context in either his edition (1973) or his subsequent article (1978), which may be a justified omission as the background is clearly not Iberian (although Webber 1958 took the opposite view). "García" quotes and constructively misquotes the Bible, patristic and Roman liturgical works, proverbial and Classical sources (in particular Terence). The author was undoubtedly with Bernard at Rome in 1099, and more likely therefore to be French than Spanish; Ximénez de Rada gives the impression that all the senior staff at Toledo were French *litterati*: "hos inquam prae-dictos viros litteratos, providos, et honestos Primas Bernardus per Gallias transiens, in Hispaniam secum duxit, et eos in Toletana Ecclesia Canonicos ordinavit" (VI 27). (Bernard brought in, from Moissac and Agen, teachers of ecclesiastical chant, the technique based on note-syllable equivalence as in the sequence, which necessarily involved Medieval Latin and thus non-Hispanic instructors; Rico (1969: 29-30) prints a sequence in this style from twelfth-century Toledo itself.) "García" might even have been a Roman; he seems to know both about Italy – referring, for example, to the Monte Gargano (Thomson 1973: l.265) – and about France – referring, for example, to the Rhone (l.371) – without referring to anything Hispanic other than superficially to Toledo. The four surviving manuscripts come from twelfth-century Germany, thirteenth-century France, and two from twelfth-century England, so there is little intrinsic support for postulating a Spanish author. Lida de Malkiel (1953), however, basing her argument on the hostility expressed towards Bernard, believed the author to be a native Toledan despite his untypical knowledge of Classical culture. In fact, the tone is not hostile so much as that of a disrespectful colleague poking fun; the portrayal of hypocrisy and corruption does not ne-cessarily imply hostility or resentment. The *tensó* tradition of insulting one's friends has been a fertile genre for millennia. García Villoslada's edition (1975: 307-16) presents the whole composition as a joke. Rico (1969: 89) added to the permutations by suggesting that the author was a *toledano* living abroad. No doubt someone will soon ascribe it to Alo. Whoever he was, though, we are justified in seeing this composition as evidence that a high level of Latin literacy was brought into Toledo with Bernard. A community had been imported into Toledo which knew European culture better than the Hispanic, and among which foreign scholars were going to be able to stay without feeling in too alien an environment. If the general two-norm image of an apartheid between a Latinate élite and a Romance-speaking mass has any validity anywhere, Toledo under Bernard might qualify as the most suitable example; although even here the Romance-speaking *mozárabes* are not illiterate in the modern sense, and there is in addition an important community of Castilian immigrants.

Much of southern Spain remained in Moslem control. The only indication that anyone in Moslem Spain might perhaps have known of a distinction between Latin and Romance comes in a vast botanical handbook, written (c.1100) in Arabic apparently by the head gardener of the Seville *alcázar*, partly edited by Asín Palacios (1943) under the title *Glosario de voces romances registradas por un botánico anónimo hispano-musulmán*; so far as I can tell it has not been seriously studied since. The author studies several hundred plants and their names in Arabic, Romance and assorted other languages. On sixteen occasions (out of Asín's 726 excerpts) he uses the word *latiniyya*, "Latin", sometimes distinguished from *ʿaȳamiyya*, which means here "Romance vernacular" and is often further specified to apply to terms used in Galicia, Castille, Aragón, Toledo, Catalonia, or even France. Other languages mentioned include Greek and Persian, so he is immensely well informed. This work ought to be of crucial interest to Hispanic philologists, but unfortunately the transcription of Romance terms in Arabic script presents so many cases of lack of equivalence that many details are lost. There are, for example, only three vowel symbols, each with long and short versions, of which the short are often omitted, and this system has to cope with a Romance five-vowel system without a length distinction. It is impossible, therefore, to be certain about distinguishing Romance [a] from [e], [u] from [o]; similarly, one symbol serves for Romance [b], [v] and [p]. Conversely, three Arabic symbols compete for Latin or Romance [t], three for [d], and two for [k]. Asín has, fortunately, printed the Arabic, for his Spanish transcription usually contains an amount of interpretation on his part in order to facilitate the reader's recognition of the lexical items.

There are sixteen explicit mentions of "Latin" forms. The following transcriptions are taken from Asín's printed Arabic text: "-" stands for an indeterminate vowel. Three of these uses of *latiniyya* seem to be explicitly referring to a form also referred to in the same place as *ʿaȳamiyya*:

18 (repeated, 234, 630) "buqtur" (twice), cp. Sp. *buitre*, from Latin VULTUR(EM)

393 "b-llit-", O. Sp. *bellida*, derived from Latin BELLA

679 "y-n-j- wartayra", Sp. *yunco*, Lat. *juncea*; *wartayra* presumably derived from *\*huarto* (= *huerto*), from Latin HORTUM.

It seems that in these cases *latiniyya* means *ladino*, i.e. a synonym of *ʿaȳamiyya*, "Romance".

On seven occasions an *ʿaȳamiyya* form is explicitly contrasted with a *latiniyya* form; suggesting that here *latiniyya* means "Latin":

186 Latin "kwārks" (*quercus*), Romance "jārk-" (*?chirca*)

350 Latin "šišanburu" (*sisymbrium*), Romance "manta" (*menta*)

517 Latin "š-mīny- m-wr-" (*seminium maurum*), Romance "šamn-m-wr-" (*?siemne moro*)

521 Latin "tūš" (*tus*), Romance "šānsiy-" (*incienso*)

583 Latin "burmānty" (*frumentum*), Romance "ṭriḍco" (*trigo*)

592 Latin "ʔurdiʔwu" (*hordeum*), Romance "waryu" and "warsu", presumably derived from HORDEUM.

One pair points to morphological variation:

362 Latin "mrw-" (*maurum*), Romance "m-wrān-" (the derived adjective *moreno*).

In five uses of *latiniyya* it is not explicit in context whether it refers to *ladino* or to *latín*:

1 "lyn" (*linum*); contrasted to "abartal", which is presumably Romance, although the author does not say so.

290 "ʔūly astīr" (*oleaster*); elsewhere Romance "labāśtar" for the same plant.

387 "-l-y" (*oleum*); elsewhere, Romance "ūl-yya".

In view of the Romance forms adduced on other folios, *latiniyya* would seem to mean *latín* in these instances.

520 "šānbar" (twice, *semper*), "bību" (*vivus*), "b-yba" (*viva*).

There is no Romance alternative, and either Latin or Romance forms could be those meant here.

The remaining case is confusing. Asín translates the text (393) as "*yabrūh* is called *elorios* in Greek, which means 'ears' in Latin; singular *orella*, i.e. ear". A closer transcription of this latter form is "ʔurilla"; presumably this is a mozarabic *orella* from Latin AURICULAM, i.e. *ladino*.

The result is *latín* 10, *ladino* "Romance" 4, indeterminate 2.

The above does not present a clear picture. The author can hardly be used to encountering Latin as well as Romance at Seville, or he would mention it more often and with more consistency. Some of his informants have met Latin, in Christian Spain or France; either his transcription follows their pronunciation of it, or his information was in written Latin and he has provided his own phonetic equivalent. There is not sufficient reason here to postulate that Medieval Latin was used in Moslem Spain at that time.

Twelfth-century Toledo after Bernard's death has acquired a reputation for being a multi-cultural intellectual centre. There is some truth in this. Subsequent bishops were less hostile to the *mozárabes* than Bernard had been. Northern and southern traditions learnt to live together and be intrigued by each other. Other cities in the north saw Arabic-Latin translation ventures (Burnett 1977), but under bishop Raimundo (1125-51) Toledo became the main centre (González Palencia 1942). Spanish scholars were involved in the translations (e.g. Hugo de Santalla at Tarazona) but at this time all written translations from

Arabic were converted into Latin (or Hebrew) rather than into any Romance form. Similarly, native Toledans wrote works inspired by Northern culture, also in Latin; for example, Domingo Gundisalvo's *De divisione philosophiae*, of the mid-century, includes recognizably European theories of grammar and metrics based on Bede (Rico 1969: 18-22). The advantage of writing Latin lay in its international validity (in the *respublica litterarum*), so it is hardly surprising that none of the early Toledo scholars were impelled to create a new orthography approximating to a transcription of Toledo Romance[5]. In this century, writing in Latin was often left to foreigners, but the skill in Arabic was provided by natives of Toledo. Rico (1969: 90) quotes the instructive example of Peter the Venerable, abbot of Cluny, who came to Toledo in 1142-43 and hired a "maestro Pedro de Toledo" to translate an anti-islamic treatise written in Arabic. Pedro, however, although being a *maestro*, was also a *toledano*, and better at reading Arabic than writing Latin, so he cooperated with one of Peter's companions in producing the final version. In Peter's words:

> Sed quia lingua latina non adeo ei familiaris vel nota erat ut Arabica, dedi ei coadiutorem doctum virum . . ., qui verba latina impolite vel confuse plerumque ab eo prolata poliens et ordinans . . ., libellum . . . perfecit.

This cultural cooperation, involving reading in Arabic, speaking in Spanish, and writing in Latin, would have heightened linguistic consciousness, if nothing else. It is possible that one of the earliest works in Spanish romance comes out of this mixed community. The dramatic *Auto de los Reyes Magos* was probably composed by a Gascon priest living in Toledo at the end of the twelfth century. Lapesa (1967) suggested this; Deyermond (1971: 209) agrees; but Corominas (1958: 75) preferred an ascription to Aragón or Navarre, Solá-Solé (1975) to a *mozárabe*, and Kerkhof (1979) to a Catalan, so the answer is far from clear. The manuscript dates from c.1200. The drama seems to have been transcribed for use in the Epiphany service, and is thus another text in the tradition going back to the Eulalia sequence, a work written in vernacular spelling in order to specify a vernacular pronunciation for a written text in Church. The method of transcription suggests that the author knows of contemporary practice north of the Pyrenees, and is attempting to apply it to Spanish. Whoever wrote this, and wherever, it may well be the first surviving written Spanish literary work; this

5. Deyermond (1971: 84-85) is surely right to suggest that the Spanish prose *La Fazienda de Ultramar* is a later translation of a Latin original from Raimundo's Toledo.

extract is Herod's soliloquy (Menéndez Pidal 1900: 460-61):

¿Quin uio numquas tal mal,
sobre rei otro tal!
Aun non so io morto
ni so la terra pusto!
rei otro sobre mi?
numquas atal non ui!
El seglo ua a çaga,
ia non se que me faga:
por uertad no lo creo
ata que io lo ueo.
Uenga mio maior do[ma]
qui mios aueres toma.
Idme por mios abades
i por mis podestades
i por mios scriuanos
i por meos gramatgos
i por mios streleros
i por mios retoricos;
dezir m' an la uertad, si iace in escripto
o si lo saben elos o si lo an sabido.

(ll.107-26)

If this indeed comes from Toledo, it is fitting that that linguistically sophisticated and cosmopolitan environment should have been the one to inspire connected written Spanish vernacular texts.

### Santiago

A cultural change also came over Santiago de Compostela at the end of the eleventh century. In earlier centuries Santiago had been in the diocese of Iria Flavia, but under the energetic leadership of Diego Gelmírez it eventually became an archbishopric and a centre of *litterae*. The *Historia Compostellana* of c.1137 (Flórez 1765), subtitled *sive de rebus gestis D. Didaci Gelmirez, primi Compostellani archiepiscopi*, and composed by three Frenchmen and one French-trained Spaniard, is designed to glorify the individual, in the tradition also exemplified by the near-contemporary Eastern *Historia Roderici* on the Cid (?1144-50; Menéndez Pidal 1947: 919-69) and the Leonese *Chronica Adefonsi Imperatoris* on Alfonso VII (1147-49; Sánchez Belda 1950). This history is thus an excellent source for the period, but tends to play down the rôle played by Santiago in previous years. One comment in particular has been interpreted to mean that noone in Santiago before Gelmírez was literate:

... cum tunc temporis tota fere Hispania rudis & illiterata esset. Nullus equidem Hispanorum Episcopus Sanctae Romanae Ecclesiae matri nostrae servitii aut obedientiae quidquam tunc reddebat. Hispania Toletanam, non Romanam legem recipiebat. Sed post-quam A. rex bonae memoriae Romanam legem Romanasque con-suetudines Hispanis contradidit, ex tunc utcumque obliterata quadam nebula inscientiae Sanctae Ecclesiae vires in Hispanis pullulare coeperunt. Quid enim memorem rudes & imperitos anteriores Ecclesiae B. Jacobi fuisse prelatos?

(II i; Flórez 1765: 253)

The Spanish translators of the *Historia* insert an indignant footnote here (Suárez and Campelo 1950: 241), pointing out that it is ridiculous to call the church before Gelmírez illiterate, since the Visi-gothic rite is complex and was regularly performed. If this really were the import of the author's comment, the indignation would be justified; all that Giraldo is doing here, however, is pointing out that in per-forming the *Toletanam legem*, the Visigothic rite, clerics did not need to be *literati*, since, unlike the Roman rite regularly used in the 1100s, that rite did not require to be performed in the European Carolingian manner of giving one sound to each written *littera*. These bishops were not illiterate in the modern sense, for several of them, at least, could certainly read their liturgy, and write also; after *A. rex bonae memoriae* (Alfonso VI) had changed the rite, they had to start learning *litterae* in order to do it. Campelo and Suárez stoked their own fires by translating *inscientia* as "ignorancia" and *imperitos* as "ignorantes". This passage simply states that Medieval Latin (*litterae*) came to Santiago at the same time as the Roman rites.

The nature of clerical education in preceding centuries is not clear. The bishop's household probably taught those entrusted to it; Díaz y Díaz (1971: 188) quotes a document printed by López Ferreiro (1899: app.177) concerning a noble child being entrusted to the bishop *ad nutriendum*. All *monasterios* had liturgical books; García Alvarez's (1965) 387 texts mentioned in Galician documents seem to imply that many clerics could read; the presence of the documents themselves implies that some could also write. Literacy may not have been inno-vating but it did exist. López Ferreiro, however, who is not given to underestimating the worth of his predecessors, has harsh words for the Galician clergy's educational standards before 1080, apparently being misled by the *Historia Compostellana*. The *Compostellana* suggested that the clergy followed no monastic rule ("nullius ordinis regulam nec saltem habitu observantes", III 36 p.543), which López interpreted as a reference to general indiscipline and ignorance. However this is to be understood, we have no reason to criticize Bishop Cresconio. He re-vitalized the community, repelled the Normans (with greater success than the English), and was one of the organizers of the 1056 Council of Santiago de Compostela, which introduced the canons of the 1055 Council of Coyanza into Galicia. López said (1899: 517) that the Council ordered the establishment of schools in every monastery and diocese, but the relevant section of the statute (II 2), as printed by Martínez Díez (1964: 128) is not clear:

> Hi autem Abbates per proprias Ecclesias canonicas faciant Scholam, et disciplinam componant, ut tales deferant ad Episcopos Clericos ordinandos.

*Schola* and *disciplina* may not mean "schools" in any modern sense, and the extent to which this canon was observed is unknown. Beltrán (1946: 316), however, proclaimed that "doubtless" all this was being done already anyway.

Some time in the years following the Council of Burgos in 1080 the study of *litterae* was introduced into Santiago. Diego Gelmírez himself, born c.1069, "bonus adolescens fuit, eruditus literis in Eclesia B. Jacobi, & adultus in curia hujus Episcopi", i.e. of Diego Peláez (II ii p.254); but, as Reilly (1968) has established, the French author of this part of the *Historia* was not in Spain before 1117 and is not always to be trusted on early details, so this cannot be taken to establish the immediate presence of reformed *litterae* in Santiago after 1080. Peláez was deposed in 1087, after which the existing canons were made to go to the same classes as new trainees, so that could well be the occasion of the introduction of *litterae* and the European liturgy. Gelmírez might have learnt his *litterae* elsewhere, however, having been at Alfonso's court and become notary to Raymond of Burgundy, Count of Galicia.

By the end of the eleventh century there is a French community in the Santiago Church. The Cluniac Dalmatius became bishop in 1094, dying, perhaps at Cluny, after attending the Papal Council of Clermont in 1095 (Biggs 1949: 236-37). Gelmírez was administrator since 1093, eventually became bishop some time in 1098-1100, and went to Cluny himself in 1104. On his return in 1105, "locato de doctrina eloquentiae Magistro & de ea quae discernendi facultatem plenius administrat, ut nos ab infantiae subtraheret rudimentis, suo nos commendavit imperio" (I 20, p.55). There cannot be much doubt that the French art of Latin letters, reading aloud included, was part of this *eloquentia*. "Quoniam Ecclesia B. Jacobi rudis & indisciplinata erat temporibus illis: applicuit animum ut consuetudines Ecclesiarum Franciae ibi plantaret" (II iii, p. 255). Teachers came to Santiago from elsewhere in Europe; he sent several of his own clerics to study in France. One of Gelmírez's clerics

(*Pedro capellanus*) went to address the Pope in 1110 and "in praesentia Domni Papae querimoniam latine ventilavit" (I 37, p.87); this achievement was one of which he was rightly proud, and represents an early Hispanic attestation of *latine* to mean "in the international spelling-pronounced standard". The Archbishop's nephew Pedro "in Francia philosophicam disciplinam adiscebat" (II 49, p.346) in 1121, which would have required Medieval Latinity. One of the authors of the *Historia* was "Girardus", *magister* of the Cathedral school, who refers to himself as such: "ego Girardus . . . Didascalus Episcopi S. Jacobi" (II 6, p.265), "Giraldus magister" (II 56, p.378): on the first occasion he is an emissary to the Pope with Bishop Diego of Orense. Rainerio of Pistoia replaced Girardus in 1134 (González 1944: 451-53).

Santiago's education became so respected that it came to supply the Royal chancery with its notaries. Most of the chancellors at the Court of Queen Urraca (1109-26) came from the Santiago cathedral chapter (Sánchez Belda 1953; Millares Carlo 1926). Reilly (1976: 257) even talked of the "traditional control of Alfonso VII's chancery by the Prelate of Santiago de Compostela" up to 1134. The *schola grammaticorum* was apparently a separate room by 1140 at the latest (Díaz y Díaz 1971: 192). Fletcher's history of the bishopric (1978: 53-61) suggests that there was a relapse in the mid-century, but this may merely be a mirage caused by the relative paucity of written historical evidence after the *Historia*. (The prose and hexameter work *De Consolatione Rationis* by "Maestro Pedro de Compostela" has been redated to the fourteenth century by Torres Rodríguez 1974-75, a reassessment accepted by Moralejo 1980: 86-87.) In July 1169, Bishop Pedro Gudésteiz offered a subsidy "ut clerici de canonica nostra nostrates et ecclesiae nostrae mansionarii ad studium litterarum anhelantes, dum juxta terminum sibi a capitulo constitutum, in litteraturae studiis honeste manserint"[6]. In the *Liber Constitutionum* of 1170, I 3, the *magister scolarum* is advised to appoint another *magister* "in facultate gramatice", who "ad nutum magistri scolarum omnes litteras capituli dirigat et componat . . . et iste debet venire in omnibus festivitatibus ad serviendum choro et legentes ibidem corrigere in sillabis et accentu" (López Ferreiro 1898-1911: IV app.106; Díaz y Díaz 1971: 193). Bishop Pedro Suárez de Deza (1173-1206) acquired the title of *magister*

6. Beltrán (1946: 321-22); Díaz y Díaz (1971: 193-95). This was reinforced in 1207, with the delightful phrasing: "quantum decoris afferat ecclesiis Dei et illis qui praecipue sunt honore praedictae litteraturae praerogativa et scientiarum excellentia, nemo est sic ignarus ut nesciat, sic nescius ut ignoret" (Beltrán 1946: 322).

in Paris; he was a former royal chancellor and bishop of Salamanca, and theologian, and his was a time of intellectual advance, even though it lacks the detailed record of its own *Historia* and the diocese was in financial trouble (Fletcher 1978: 226). Santiago continued to be a respectable centre of *litterae*.

The immediate question arises: what did Gelmírez's colleagues actually learn from their French teachers? The answer could be partly found in two surviving, and very similar, treatises entitled *Ars Lectoria*, dated to 1086 and 1088, probably from South-West France. Reijnders (1971-72) published the first, by Aimericus. Kneepkens and Reijnders have now (1979) published the second, by Magister Siguinus[7]. The editors subtitle the latter *Un art de lecture à haute voix du onzième siècle*. These treatises assume in their readers the basic knowledge of sound-letter correspondences, and concentrate on the problems a reader faces in knowing where to put the stress on polysyllables, particularly in order to distinguish between homographs in reading aloud (thereby avoiding *ipsitatem omonimorum*, p.5), and in knowing how to distinguish vowel quantity. The stress instructions are often rather odd. We are told, for example, to stress the second syllable of disyllabic prepositions (*circá, siné*, etc.: p.87). Instructions are often addressed specifically to those intending to read aloud: for example, successive paragraphs (p.91) are addressed to "quisquis epistulam, hoc est "brevem", bene vult fingere et Latine loqui decentissime" and "quis vel corde vel tabulis vel codice quidlibet edicturus, uel in populo legens uel sociis proloquens uel amicis referens . . . Lector, ne perturberis, audi".

The rules concerning vowel quantity are little more than lists, arranged in alphabetical order of consonants and the length of the preceding vowel[8]. For example E before N is short in these words, but long in these others; I before N is short in these words, but long in these others, etc., etc. Significant generalizations are not their forte. Priscian, the Bible, Horace, Vergil, Ovid, Lucan and several others, are adduced as relevant authorities when possible. Neither Siguinus nor Aimericus give the impression that they are attempting anything new. They are lists of tips (as was Bede's *De Orthographia*), representing the accumulated practice that has developed in French schools since 800. Siguinus tells us in his Prose Prologue (p.5) that he once wrote an *Orthographia* (now lost); it is made explicit that the prescriptions of

---

7. Unless otherwise stated, subsequent references are to Siguinus.
8. Since it is the preceding rather than the following vowel, this tells us nothing systematic about *ce, ci, ge* or *gi*.

spelling, accentuation and quantity are all designed to aid oral reproduction without hesitation from the reader, rather than as ends in
themselves. Some of the rules of thumb here are thus also a bit peculiar;
*gu* appears in nouns but not in verbs, for example: "item scribenda
nomina per *u* et enuncianda 'lingua/lingue, anguis/angue, unguis/ungue,
inguis/inguen/unguentum'; verba vero sine *u* 'lingo/lingis, ango/angis,
ungo/ungis, ingero/ingeris'. Aliter vero inter nomen et uerbum hesitatio
haberetur" (p.30). This means that what may look to us now like
elementary scribal errors might have been done on purpose in the hope
of clarifying recitation; it would be interesting to examine the documents of Aquitaine in the 1090s to see if such extraordinary advice was
actually followed. The prescriptions of quantity are also intended to aid
the composition of metric verse (pp.4f.); Aimericus calls himself
"Aimericus metricus metricorum semper amicus" (X 86). Siguinus' first
book (pp.6-85) also deals with grammatical points that the lector has to
know ("hec dixerim ne in talibus perturbetur Lector").

　　Siguinus tells us that he is a teacher in a religious community.
He breaks off in the "I before D" section to tell us so (p.133), and
apologizes to God for not doing it better than he is: "tu autem, Domine,
maiora quam hec et profundiora scientie litteratorie scire me voluisti";
the *scientia* of *litterae*, required at precisely this time by the Pope in the
new Archbishop of León-Castille, is here clearly the knowledge of
reading Latin aloud. Where Siguinus taught is not clear, although his
editors are happy to locate him in Aquitaine (p.XXIII). He seems once
to have gone to Spain, however. In the "E before R" section (p.170) he
tells us that ". . . Hiberus, ipse est fluvius maior Hispanie, unde ipsa
dicta est Hiberia. Hunc ego fluuium cum transirem, memini me quodam
ligneo ponte medio mortem pauisse". This snippet of reminiscence is
tantalizing. It is possible to speculate that this refers to events during
the Barbastro campaign (1064), when Aquitanian soldiers were indeed
involved, and massacred a Muslim community (Lomax 1978: 58). Barbastro is not on the Ebro, however, so one of the later campaigns in
which Aquitanian soldiers joined the Aragonese in fighting Zaragoza is
possible. Or the frightening experience may not have been a military
one; looking over the side of a rickety bridge into the Ebro could make
anyone dizzy. Maybe Siguinus was assisting in Aragón or Navarre when
those kingdoms were coming under Papal authority in the 1070s,
adopting the Roman rite and in need of Latin teachers. Perhaps he was
a pilgrim to Santiago itself. In general, it seems quite probable that he
and Aimericus and those they taught had some kind of connection with
the Europeanizing movements of late eleventh- and early twelfth-century

Northern Spain; the clerics of Santiago might well have been taught a *scientia litteraturae*, which was normal practice in at least some of the more professional French schools, but not generally taught in Santiago previously.

Other areas than Santiago were touched by the intellectual expansion (González 1944: 447-64; Fletcher 1978). Bishop Pedro Seguin of Orense (1157-69) was probably a French *magister* associated with the Poitevin community in El Bierzo; his successor Adán (1169-73 or 74) had been royal chancellor (1166-67), and a letter announcing his election in 1169 confirms that he "non deest in peritia litterarum". Lugo had a French bishop from 1135 to 1152, and a royal clerk became bishop there briefly in 1181-82. The bishop of nearby Astorga (subject, in fact, to the archbishop of Braga) from 1144 to 1152 or 53, Arnaldo I, had connections with Montpellier and Barcelona, and may well have been the author of the *Chronica Adefonsi Imperatoris* and the *Poema de Almería* (Martínez 1975: chap.3; see below). The bishop of Mondoñedo from 1112-36, Nuño Alfonso, was a pupil at Diego Gelmírez's Compostela, part author of Book I of the *Historia Compostellana*, and worked in the royal chancery even after his promotion. The continuing connection between the archdiocese, French clerics and the chancery, between knowledge of *litterae* and the suitability to run a bishopric, and the lack of other Spanish nobles in episcopal office, led Fletcher to ask "was the royal hold so strong that aristocrats were excluded, passed over in favour of the incoming Frenchmen or the ubiquitous chancery servants?" (1978: 85); the answer to Fletcher's question may lie not in such antibaronial scheming but at least partly in the simple fact that chancery officials and French clerics knew the *litterae* which it was essential, as the Pope had said, for a bishop to know, and the reason for this is that *litterae*, Medieval Latin, was required for the new Roman rite.

The spread of Europeanizing centres stops in the middle of the twelfth century, as the influence of Cluny wanes and other currents of thought less obsessed with liturgy take their place. There is no need to assume that more than a few places in the Kingdom of León were practising the reformed Medieval Latin. When the Papal legate Jean d'Abbeville came in 1228-29 to see if the educational decrees of the fourth Lateran council (1215) were being carried out, he found much to displease him (Linehan 1971). The church had other urgent tasks, such as keeping the Moslems at bay and reorganizing reconquered dioceses, which relegated linguistic niceties to lower priority; "neither do we know anything at all about the steps taken (if any) by bishops to ensure that the lower clergy had a modicum of education" (Fletcher 1978: 175). It seems generally true that the intellectual reforms were more enthusiastically followed in 1100 than in 1200; the only Leonese bishops of the end of the century to win any approval from Fletcher for intellectual achievement are Suárez de Deza at Santiago and his pupil Martín Arias, bishop of Zamora (1193-1217).

Galicia was the home in the twelfth century of a flourishing vernacular lyric tradition (see Deyermond 1971: 10-20). Presumably native vernacular verses had always been sung there, but the polyglot advent of pilgrims to Santiago brought Galicia into contact with twelfth-century Occitan and French traditions (e.g. Bouza Brey 1965). It is possible that many of the Galician *cantigas* were written down in a vernacular manner in that century, but unfortunately no early manuscripts survive at all and there is no way of knowing whether, if they were written down then, their orthography was the same as the largely fifteenth-century evidence that we have. It would not be at all surprising to discover that Galicia was indeed the first part of the Iberian peninsula to have its vernacular imitated consciously in orthographic technique; Santiago was a centre in which there were heard many languages, and undoubtedly there were people there skilled in writing French or Occitan who could have applied some skill to the task of writing Galician. (A charming thirteenth-century document has been printed in facsimile by Pensado (1960) which includes instructions for guides on talking to pilgrims in Occitan, Italian, Spanish and Breton.) A Galician *juglar* called Palla was apparently at the court of Alfonso VII in 1136 (Otero 1976: 82; Martínez 1975: 60), probably performing in Galician; this tradition of court interest in Galician lyric eventually flowers in the *cantigas* of Alfonso X himself (1252-84).

The *Historia Compostellana*, *Chronica Adefonsi Imperatoris* and *Historia Silense* are evidence that some people, at least, acquired reasonably good *litterae* in North-Western Spain. The *Historia Silense* (which has no connection with Silos; Díaz y Díaz 1979: 165 locates the author in the community of St John the Baptist in León) demonstrates its knowledge of European culture in its markedly anti-French tone (Horrent 1973-74; West 1975); the French inflow inspired resentment as well as a desire for emulation. The inscriptions on the main altar at Santiago, said to be finished in 1105, are three metrically "secure" elegiac couplets with leonine rhyme (Díaz y Díaz 1971: 189-90). Probably the most interesting of these North-Western compositions is the *Poema de Almería* at the end of the *Chronica Adefonsi Imperatoris*, where the author switches into verse for the purpose of exalting Alfonso

VII's attack on Almería (1147) and the forces that took part[9]. This poem is in rhythmic hexameters. It may be that the author took a conscious decision not to use metrics, but it is as likely that he had never learnt them. In the event, several lines do not seem to fit either system particularly well. There are hints in the prose chronicle that the author would have preferred not to have to use Latin anyway; words that have no obvious written Latin equivalent are liable to appear as follows:

> turres, quae lingua nostra dicunt alcazares    (102, 150, 158, 189)
>
> magnae turbae militum, quod nostra lingua dicitur algaras    (36)
>
> civitatem opulentissimam, quam antiqui dicebant Tuccis, nostra lingua Xerez    (37)

*Lingua nostra* as used here is said by Martínez (1975: 101) to mean Castilian or mozarabic; since the author, possibly French, had Catalan connections, and a Leonese bishopric in the Braga (Portuguese) archdiocese, those two dialects would seem less plausible than several others. In fact it surely means "Romance vernacular" without specifying any one dialect. This twelfth century is the only time when two types of pronunciation coexisted with only the one Latin writing system; in the next century historians who felt ill at ease in Latin had a written vernacular alternative (which happened to correspond to Castilian, owing to the political advances of Castile in the intervening years).

One other remark in the *Poema* has been generally misunderstood to contain a reference to contemporary consciousness of dialectal division:

> Armorum tanta stellarum lumina quanta,
> Sunt et equi multi ferro seu pane suffulti.
> Illorum lingua resonat quasi tympanotriba.
> Sunt nimis elati, sunt divitiis dilatati.
> Castelle vires per secla fuere rebelles.
> Inclyta Castella sitiens saevissima bella
> Vix cuiquam regum voluit submittere collum.
> Indomite vixit, celi lux quamdiu luxit.
> Hanc cunctis horis domuit sors imperatoris.
> Solus Castellam domitavit sicut asellam
> Ponens indomito legis nova federa collo.    (ll.147-57)

---

9. This is a common purpose of occasional verse; cp. the contemporary (1147) *De Expugnatione Lyxbonensi* written by an Englishman on the capture of Lisbon (see Martínez 1975: 128). References to the Chronicle are to the edition by Sánchez Belda (1950); to the Poem to that in Gil (1974). The edition by Martínez (1975: 22-51) has different line numbers and includes a modern Spanish translation. It was previously edited by Rodríguez Aniceto (1931). Also from this area was the first *Crónica anónima de Sahagún*, now lost, only surviving in a fourteenth-century Spanish translation.

At a time when Castilian nationalism dominated Hispanic philology, 1.149 was understood to mean that the Castilian dialect was already stronger and preparing to dominate the other Romance forms (and Lapesa 1980: 197 still thinks it does). The line refers to the loudness and arrogance of the way Castilians talk. The whole work is in praise of the Leonese King Alfonso VII, and here he is being praised for having kept under control the perennially fractious and self-important Castilians, Castille being at the time just one county in his "Empire" (formerly having seceded in the tenth century, and about to do so again, 1158-1230). The sixteenth-century translation (printed by Rodríguez 1931) seems to omit 1.149 altogether, unless it is subsumed in the comment "son muy soberbios".

These lines can also serve as a sample of the rhythmic technique adopted, which betrays in part the influence of vernacular stress patterns: *imperatoris* (1.155), for example, is not *īmpĕrātŏris* but *impĕrátóris*, on the vernacular pattern of *émpèràdór*; *dilatati* (1.150) is not *dīlātātī* but *dilàtáti* on the vernacular pattern of *dilàtádós*; etc. The leonine rhyme is sometimes full and sometimes homoteleutic. The most obvious idiosyncrasy is the avoidance of elision. In the written "rhythmic" tradition elision was avoided by the simple expedient of having hiatus instead, counting each written vowel as a syllable; yet in the 385½ extant lines of the *Poema* there are (in Gil's edition) no occasions at all when a word ending in a vowel or in -*m* precedes in the same line a word beginning with a vowel. This suggests that the author consciously preferred not to raise the question, since *litterae* required full vocalic status for all written vowels in performance, but elision was a natural feature of spoken Spanish. The language of the Chronicle as a whole is described by Martínez as "un latín sumamente corrompido", but – as the references to *lingua nostra* suggest – it is surely "una vernácula muy latinizada", as is almost everything else written down at the time.

### Twelfth-Century Castille

Eastern Castille and the Rioja continued to be important cultural centres. The Riojan monasteries adopted the European rites, but they also preserved their Visigothic manuscripts and heritage in other respects, meticulously recopying many of their ancient volumes in c.1200. The centre of Castilian letters between Silos and León continued to be Palencia, which had a high reputation from the eleventh to the thirteenth century (Deyermond 1969) and became at the start of the thirteenth century the seat of the first Iberian "University" (see below). In the late twelfth century the Castilian court, now independent from

León, often resided there. The royal chancellor in the later part of Alfonso VII's reign had been Nicolás, archdeacon of Palencia. Under Sancho III (1157-58) of Castille the chancellor was Bernardo, also archdeacon of Palencia. Under Alfonso VIII, Raimundo II, bishop of Palencia (c.1148-84), perhaps the King's great-uncle, was said by Millares Carlo (1926: 269-71) to be the Raimundo who was chancellor from 1164 to 1178; Lomax (1965) discounts this, and shows that the bishop Raimundo may have been a Catalan. In any event he introduced Catalan clerics. Santo Domingo, the founder of the Dominicans, studied there in the 1180s. But until the thirteenth century this is not as prolific a literary centre as Toledo or Santiago.

One literary product of twelfth-century Castille was the *Historia Najerense* (Ubieto 1966), dated by Lomax (1974-79) to after 1174. Nájera was politically in Navarre from 1162 to 1176 and in Castille after; the monastery of Santa María de Nájera was a Cluniac house from 1079. The history includes a perceptibly rhythmical passage on the death of King Sancho II of Castille (1065-72), which Entwistle (1928) bravely suggested was the reworking of a lost Latin leonine hexameter poem, which he "reconstructed" partly on the analogy of the *Poema de Almería*. Rico's comparison (1969: 83-4) with the attested prose shows that the reconstructed verses are much less similar to the prose than Entwistle's followers seem to believe; there is no reason to suppose that Latin poems were radically rewritten when being used in Latin histories — Ximénez de Rada seems to have quoted the poem on the capture of Toledo verbatim (see above); nor is there any reason to suppose that laments for dead kings took the form of lengthy leonine hexameters — the death of Sancho III of Castille in 1158 inspired nine lines of simple octosyllables in alternate rhyme set to music, and that of his brother Fernando II of León in 1188 was celebrated in another brief musical lament in heptasyllabic form with alternate rhyme (García Villoslada 1975: 132-34); if such a Latin poem was composed in the 1070s, it was probably composed by someone with French (or Catalan) training, and the Cluniacs, at least, were allies of Sancho II's victorious brother Alfonso VI; in short, there is no advantage of Entwistle's theory over the straightforward view that the author of the *Najerense* realized that the subject was one that deserved a high style, and adopted the generally available techniques of prose rhyme and the varieties of the rhythmical *cursus* regularly sought after in elevated style without having to write a poem first. The writer had probably heard some of the popular verses on the death of Sancho II, but there is no need to reconstruct those out of his words either; we can leave the credit for his own work to himself.

Smith is one of Entwistle's followers. In his review (1977b) of Chalon's book (1976) on Castilian history and epic, he is scathing about Chalon's ignoring Entwistle's reconstructions in favour of a postulated vernacular (epic) *cantar*: ". . . what literary prose and narrative verse we have in writing from twelfth-century Spain is all in Latin . . . and it is the supposition of vernacular verse in that century that has to be argued." As we saw in the last chapter, there need be no argument; all communities have vernacular verses, there were songs if not epics on historical events, such as the Çorraquín Sancho verses printed by Rico (1975), and if there is nothing written down before c.1200 in anything other than Latin – or attempts to write Latin – that is because the subsequent orthographical reforms had not yet happened. Castille is naturally the prime battleground for these arguments since Menéndez Pidal put his enormous authority behind a date of c.1140 for the vernacular Castilian *Poema de Mio Cid*; even if that is right as an approximate date of composition, it is unlikely to be right as the date of its first being written down. (The only surviving manuscript is a fourteenth-century copy of an original probably dated 1207).

Ruy Díaz, "El Cid", died in 1099 as ruler of Valencia. The literature he inspired is at the centre of the argument concerning Latin and Romance in twelfth-century Spain. In his lifetime he inspired the long rhythmic sapphic hymn *Carmen Campi Doctoris*, probably written by someone at or from Ripoll in Catalonia c.1083 (Wright 1979). The *Historia Roderici* was probably written in North-Eastern Spain in the late 1140s (Ubieto 1961), and follows the same general tradition of interest in his Eastern exploits as the *Carmen*. In Castille the historiographical tradition is well exemplified by Ximénez de Rada's thirteenth-century history (ed. 1968; see Lomax 1977). The epic *Poema de Mio Cid* is concerned with the end of his career (Menéndez Pidal 1911; Michael 1976; Smith 1972). The fourteenth-century poem *Mocedades de Rodrigo* (Deyermond 1969), and many ballads that may or may not have arisen subsequently (Smith 1964), deal with his youth. Other popular verses deal with his participation in the siege of Zamora at which Sancho II died in 1072. There seem, in effect, to be at least five surviving strands of material deriving from him, each including material not included elsewhere. The normal attempt to date this material along a chronological line from "sober" to "fanciful" is a failure; the *Carmen* is less accurate than the *Historia Roderici* because the latter is written by a historian and the former by a poet, regardless of their dates. Menéndez Pidal claimed that the factual aspects of the *Poema* showed it had an early date; Smith claimed that the fictional aspects of the *Poema* showed that it had a late date; neither argument holds much water. If they did, we could be committed to believing that Lomax's *Reconquest of Spain* (1978) was less to be trusted than Pedro del Corral's *Cronica Sarracina* of c.1430; or that the daily newspapers of World War II were more accurate than modern accounts. Factual "sobriety" depends on the attitude of the author and little else.

The earliest apparent reference to literature about El Cid occurs in the *Poema de Almería*. After mentioning Roland and Oliver, the author compares them to Alvar Fáñez and his companion Ruy Díaz, el Cid (Alvar Fáñez was historically a more significant figure than the Cid). The lines concerning the Cid run as follows:

> Ipse Rodericus, Meo Cidi sepe vocatus,
> De quo cantatur quod ab hostibus haud superatur,
> Qui domuit Mauros, comites domuit quoque nostros . . .
> (ll.233-35)

What does *cantatur* refer to? Laza Palacio's view (1964: 35, 68-69) that the author of both the *Poema de Mio Cid* and the *Poema de Almería* had met the *Carmen Campi Doctoris* has received ridicule. His argument is certainly absurd, and the *Poema de Mio Cid* undoubtedly has no connection with it at all, but it is in fact possible that Arnaldo of Astorga, the likely author of the *Poema de Almería*, had met the *Carmen*. He was "sent on embassies to the counts of Barcelona and Montpellier late in 1146 or early in 1147" (Fletcher 1978: 46); it seems likely that the author of the *Historia Roderici* had found the *Carmen* as an available source in c.1147, and, although Arnaldo was not perhaps looking for sources, he was interested in rhythmic Latin verse, and might conceivably have also found the *Carmen* just before going on the campaign to Almería. Lines 234-35 are a summary of what happens in the *Carmen*, *comites nostros* referring to the Christian Spanish Counts (as *nostra lingua* refers to Spanish Romance) García Ordóñez of Nájera and Berenguer Ramón II of Barcelona; Rodrigo's invincibility is the theme of the *Carmen* — it may even be true that he never lost a battle, *ab hostibus haud superatur* — and the *Carmen* seems in form to be a hymn meant to be sung. However, even if Arnaldo had met the *Carmen*, the use of *cantatur* probably also refers to something else. Alvar Fáñez and the nickname *Cid* (given to Ruy Díaz in Valencia) do not appear in the *Carmen*, but do play a star rôle in the *Poema de Mio Cid*. Since it is certain that popular legends and tales of some kind were circulating in the mid-twelfth century, it seems reasonable to suppose that Arnaldo is referring to these. There is, however, no need at all to assume that the reference is to a long epic poem. The verses of c.1158 comparing

Çorraquín Sancho to Roland and Oliver do so in four pithy lines; there may not have been any more than four on Çorraquín, nor, in 1147, on Ruy Díaz.

The existence of poems on the Cid in the century seems assured. How far the corpus was at that time amalgamated into a long unit is enjoyable to consider, as Martínez (1975: chap.8) shows, but is little more than speculation. What really does stand out about the surviving 1207 version of the *Poema de Mio Cid* is its astonishing length, 3733 lines. Nothing like that is attested in writing previously in Spain, and the theory is attractive, if unprovable, that the composer of the surviving version worked as a collator of earlier traditions to produce something comparable in length to a French epic, whether or not he was copying such epic in detail. The memory of the Cid as Christian hero was strong enough to be officially exploited, after the defeat at Alarcos in 1195, as that of a national model to inspire the troops; a long poem might be elaborated to give such inspiration then, but is (in my view) harder to envisage before. Even so, it must be conceded that the majority of scholars have succeeded in envisaging this[10].

Vernacular verse of some kind existed; it does not seem to have been written down in the twelfth century. The Latinate disguise could not have seemed much use. Those trained to read the new Latin *litterae* would not have reproduced it as vernacular in any case. Eventually, as in Carolingian France, the frustrations introduced by Medieval Latin pronunciation, i.e. the inability to write material for oral reproduction in vernacular, lead to the eventual decision to elaborate and spread vernacular writing systems. Whoever composed the *Poema*, wherever and whenever, its physical recording on manuscript must have been done by an educated man.

### Script

Indirect evidence for the existence or absence of Medieval Latin in various parts of Spain may be found in the gradual replacement of Visigothic by Carolingian script. Lucas of Tuy (*el Tudense*), writing in the 1230s, was under the impression that a special Council of León in 1090 decreed the abolition of the old script in favour of the new:

> Statuerunt etiam ut scriptores de cetero Gallicam litteram scriberent et pretermitterent Toletanam in officiis ecclesiasticis et nulla esset divisio inter ministros Ecclesie Dei. (David 1947: 433)

---

10. This necessarily sketchy outline does no justice to the lakes of scholarly ink expended on the subject; for further details see Deyermond (1977).

Ximénez de Rada, in the 1240s, picked this up, but phrased it in a different way:

> Interfuit autem Renerius legatus et Romane Ecclesie cardinalis, ibidemque celebrato concilio multa de officiis Ecclesie statuerunt, et etiam de cetero omnes scriptores, omissa litera Toletana quam Gulfilas episcopus adinvenit, Gallicis litteris uterentur.
>
> (VI 29; David 1947: 434)

David is very sceptical of the existence of this decree (1947: 431-39), and certainly if there was such a decree few took much immediate notice of it. On the other hand, there was such a Council, whose acts are now lost (Fletcher 1978: 206), so Lucas may be right; he must have had some source. Even if he is wrong, the comments of these two thirteenth-century clerics are significant, because it seems natural to them that it should be the Church, even a Papal legate (Rainerius, the future Pope Paschal II), that decreed the French script, specifically to standardize the offices of the Church. The same idea is repeated in the vernacular histories of later in the century; e.g. the author of *Primera Crónica General* chapter 872 takes it for granted that the new script and rites go together, commenting that nowadays "al comun, el de Francia anda por toda la tierra, et aquel usan al comun en la escriptura de las letras et en ell officio" (Menéndez Pidal 1955: II 543); the previous reference to "ell officio frances, tanbien en el Salterio como en las otras leendas" reinforces the view that the new script was explicitly connected with the new rite, making the *leendas* easier to *leer* correctly. This connection of liturgy and script is not generally to be expected. That a hard-worked Papacy should express firm views on Leonese handwriting is in itself improbable. Yet if the correct pronunciation of the new *litterae* in church depended on easily recognizable individual letters, each to be given its sound in turn, with a minimum of recognizable abbreviations and ligatures, the connection is simple to understand.

Replacing the script may not have been strictly necessary, other than for the French and French-trained clerics. It is not merely a question of neatness; earlier Visigothic liturgical manuscripts are often in large legible non-cursive script for the same practical purpose of avoiding confusion, and the plates at the end of Férotin's (1912) edition of the Visigothic texts, for example, show how neat mid eleventh-century Visigothic calligraphy could be. The problem was probably one concerning unfamiliar abbreviations and such confusing phenomena as the Visigothic *a*, which is not easily distinguished from *u*. That the new script was originally confined to the production of performing manuscripts in French-dominated centres seems likely. The Cluniac documents at Sahagún are in Visigothic script until the 1120s, and the only one of Gelmírez's own Santiago documents to survive in the original form, one of 1122 concerning the cathedral water supply, is in what Fletcher called "unusually pure Visigothic script" (1978: 116). Outside the main centres of French influence there are even examples of early manuscripts of parts of the Roman rites themselves in Visigothic script; one from Braga in Portugal, one from San Millán dated 1095, and two from Silos (David 1947: 438; Díaz y Díaz 1979: 201-02; Whitehill 1976). In the Kingdom of León both scripts are used until the 1150s, when gradually a generation of French-trained clerics phase out the Visigothic. Fletcher has found a private charter in Visigothic script from 1155 (León: Archivo de San Isidoro, 298) which contains at the foot a kind of conversion table of the two scripts, as if to aid readers unused to the older form. The last royal Leonese charter to have Visigothic script comes from 1158 (Fletcher 1978: 115). French script is used earlier for non-ecclesiastical matters also; Fletcher (1978: 118-19) reproduces an attractive document of 1132 in French script from Lugo (AHN 1325C/21 bis), a see that had close relations with Rome. The conclusion seems to be that the presence of French script means that its writer has encountered Medieval Latin (*litterae*) and the Roman liturgy; that those who have not been taught the Roman liturgy or Medieval Latin used Visigothic script; but that some people in the first half of the century used both Visigothic script and the Roman rites.

The middle of the century seems to be the time when Visigothic script falls into disuse in León, perhaps as the result of a conscious decision. The same applies to Aragón. In the first half of the twelfth century Aragonese church centres used Caroline script and the chancery used Visigothic; Balaguer (1954) identified the first document in Caroline script from the Aragonese chancery as one dated May 1147, in which the French script is used by a scribe who had previously used the Gothic. This is therefore presumably the result of a conscious decision to extend the French script, previously only used in the church, into all official documents (cp. also the plates in Usón 1935). It is reasonable to see this as an administrative consequence of the union of Aragón and Catalonia in 1137, to form the *Corona de Aragón*. Balaguer sensibly draws no conclusions, from this date of 1147 for the official introduction of French script, as regards the death of the Gothic, pointing out that some of the documents of Alfonso II of Aragón (1162-96) are in Visigothic script, although by the end of that reign the Caroline had become standard; Ubieto (1961) apparently misunderstood Balaguer's evidence on this point.

By the end of the century, and probably earlier, the only remaining area using Visigothic script was Toledo. Mundó (1965) established that it was used there until the second half of the thirteenth century, not only for manuscripts but for the signatures of witnesses. This survival is mainly due to the Christian exiles who came to Toledo from Moslem areas in the twelfth century, when Moslem rule was markedly less tolerant than it had been earlier; these would not have been trained in any reformed method. So the fact that the old hand decays in Toledo in the years following the end of the main part of the Reconquest (c.1250) is probably no coincidence. The spread of knowledge of Medieval Latin and the use of French handwriting are different phenomena, but closely linked.

It has been implied that the change of script made the old native Visigothic culture inaccessible (e.g. Jackson 1972: 57). This is an exaggeration. Even now, those who can read Caroline script have no serious problem in reading Visigothic script, once a few simple equivalences have been grasped, and had it not been for the view that standardization of practice on European lines was desirable the change might never have been undertaken. In San Millán, around 1200, many of the old Visigothic manuscripts were copied in French script, but even then the old ones were often preserved carefully enough to be still here. Some of the old liturgical texts were lightly "carolinized", presumably to continue in use (Díaz y Díaz 1979: 106-07). San Millán continued to preserve its Visigothic traditions and reverence for Visigothic saints to such an extent that the notary, Gonzalo de Berceo, wrote some of the greatest works in praise of those saints between the 1220s and the 1250s, even though he used a poetic form probably taught to him by Frenchmen (see below). After the city of Valencia was recaptured from the Moslems in 1238, the archbishoprics of Toledo and of Tarragona both claimed authority over the see of Valencia, and the neutral arbitrators examined many ancient manuscripts in Visigothic script in close detail when assessing the evidence (Díaz y Díaz 1979: 167-68). In, or just before, 1270 Alfonso X borrowed from the Riojan monasteries of Albelda and Nájera the oldest available manuscripts they could lend him (*libros de letra antigua*), seeking the most authoritative sources for his historians[11]. And for many centuries the veneration of local saints, and even some services, such as the baptism,

---

11. The receipts are published in *Memorial histórico español* I (Madrid 1851) pp. 257-58.

continued with hardly a change. The culture did not die as a consequence of the change of script.

### Vernacular Writing

*a) Navarre*

The earliest written completely Romance text in the peninsula is often ascribed to Navarre. Elcock (1975: 425), for example, declared that it was the *Fueros de la Novenera*; but his dating of this legal code from the North-East Rioja to the reign of Sancho el Sabio (1150-94) can only have been based on a misunderstanding of Tilander's introduction to his edition (1951). Tilander established that the manuscript he edited was a copy of one which came from the reign of Teobaldo I (Thibault de Champagne, King of Navarre 1234-53), and although most of the material dates from considerably earlier there is no reason to suppose that that material was not originally in Latin. Saralegui (1977: 51) declared that a document of 1169 was in Romance, but that document is a thirteenth-century copy (Lacarra 1965: I no.175). The *Liber Regum*, a historical text probably copied in Teobaldo's reign, may originate from the 1190s, but the original could well have been in Latin (Serrano y Sanz 1919). The earliest "Romance" document printed by Ciérvide (1972) is taken from Arigita (1900: 158-59) and dated 1198; but even if that is the original form, it is in fact still somewhat Latinized, as are the two dated to 1202; it is considerably earlier than Lacarra's (1933) suggested date of 1220 for the official introduction of written Romance in Navarrese legal texts. It seems on balance most probable that the fragmentary *corónicas navarras* (Ubieto 1964: 31-35) of 1206-09 are the oldest extant Navarrese text intentionally in Romance script throughout; even though the surviving manuscript is a fourteenth-century copy, their experimental and awkward appearance supports this view, e.g.:

> Quando morio Diaz Layniz – el padre de Rodic Diaç – priso el rey don Sancho de Castieylla a Rodic Diaz, et criolo et fizolo cavayllero, et fo con eyll en Çaragoça.
> Et quoando se combatio el rey don Sancho con el rey don Romiro en Grados, no ovo migor cavayllero de Rodic Diaz. Vino al rey don Sancho a Castieylla, et amolo muyto et dioli su alferizia, et fo muyt bon cav[all]ero.

There are several *fueros* (local legal codes) produced in the following years. It looks as if the Occitan model was influential in elaborating the details of the orthography, in particular of the *Fuero*

*General de Navarra*[12]. This is hardly surprising in view of Navarre's position on the frontier; but if the conservative estimate of c.1206-09 is right for the experiment of writing complete texts in vernacular Navarrese, developments further west may be of greater significance.

### b) Castille

The treaty of Cabreros between León and Castille was signed on Palm Sunday, March 26th 1206; what seems to be one of the original versions survives in the Cathedral Archive at León (MS 27), bearing the seals of the Kings of Castille and León. It is in Romance. Cabreros is in the Tierra de Campos area around Palencia, just on the Leonese side of the Leonese-Castilian border. At this time Alfonso VIII was King of Castille and Alfonso IX King of León. González has edited the surviving documents of both (1960: Cabreros, no.782; 1944: Cabreros, no.205; cp. Lomax 1971). No other Leonese document is totally in Romance till 1230, when Fernando III of Castille (1217-52) became King of León as well, reuniting the realms. It may be also true that no other Castilian document was in Romance before San Fernando's accession in 1217, although if so his reign saw the change to Romance writing initiated at once; for example, the *Fuero de Zorita de los Canes* seems to have been translated into Romance in 1218 (González 1960: no.339. All other Romance documents are translations, except conceivably 1944: no.254, of 1209, which is from Portugal). This long treaty of Cabreros is thus left standing alone as an official document wholly in Romance script. It looks remarkably professional and non-experimental; this is just a brief extract (González 1960: 368, ll.14-24):

> Et, si el rei de León fizer fer omenage de suo regno ad algún otro omne fora a suo filio, nieto del rei de Castella, ho alguna part enagenare ques pierda del sennorio del regno, uiuendo alguno filio del rei de León, nieto del rei de Castella, et non lo enmendare fasta sex meses, pierda destos quinque castellos, Monreal, Carpio, Castrouerde, Castro Gonzaluo, Valentia, el seruicio que end deuia auer, et fáganlo a suo filio, filio de la reina donna Berenguela, nieto del rei de Castella; pero los castellos finquen en manos de los fieles en toda uida del rei de León por fer complir todas las otras conuenenzas quomodo en esta carta dize; et guerreen al rei de León de todos los otros fasta que lo emiende.

12. See Líbano (1977). The Occitan model extends further west too, e.g. in the *Fuero de Avilés*. The *Fuero de Avilés* is often said to date to 1155; the original charter of this Asturian town was granted in 1155, but the surviving version is undatable and almost certainly a Romance translation of a Latin original (facsimile in Fernández Guerra 1865). It is less Latinized than the average notarial document, but still not independent. It too has a Provençal writer bringing over his own habits into an attempt to reproduce Asturian dialect (Lapesa 1948; cp. also Lapesa 1972).

The whole treaty runs for 239 lines in González's edition, with several important signatories from each kingdom; since it is the Leonese original that survives, the chancelry servants at the end are Ferando, dean of Compostela, chancellor of the King of León, and Pedro Pérez, notary of the King. But since this treaty represents in part a capitulation of the Leonese to Castilian wishes, many of the details of language as well as content could have come from Castille. The presence of the seals seems to ensure that this is an original.

Apart from the words *quomodo*, *quinque* and *sex* (which are always written like this throughout the treaty), this document is in thirteenth-century Old Spanish similar to the forms used through the rest of the century. It seems to present unavoidable evidence that by 1206 someone, at least, had decided with care and consistency how vernacular could be represented on paper. The reason why it was not written in Latin may be comparable to that which probably underlay the format of the Strasbourg Oaths: to ensure that all concerned appreciated the details. There is no reason to suppose that Alfonso VIII or Alfonso IX actually read it aloud themselves, but since it was a document of vital importance for the future relationship of the two Kingdoms, intended to solve a long-running dispute, it was essential both that the details of the wording should be fixed in advance and that the assembled company should have those details accurately fixed in their minds. Someone probably read it aloud from the written text. If he reproduced the text following the Latin system of the production of a specific sound per letter, the result might have sounded more like Castilian than any other variety of vernacular; the *ch* ([tʃ]) in *ocho* (< OCTO), for example, was a development apparently unique to Castille, but on the other hand the *-li-* in *filio* has more in common with Leonese than with the [ʒ] of O. Cast. *fijo* (> *hijo*). It might perhaps represent the vernacular of the Tierra de Campos, in which case the orthographic moving spirit probably came from Palencia (whose bishop was the second Castilian dignitary to sign, after the Archbishop of Toledo); the Castilian chancellors themselves had close links with the diocese of Palencia. The Catalan Pedro de Cardona was chancellor from 1178 to 1182, and abbot of Santa María de Husillos, in the Palencia diocese, for example. The current chancellor Diego García (author of the Latin *Planeta* in 1218) was born in the Tierra de Campos. A later Castilian copy of the treaty of Cabreros (now in the Archivo de la Corona de Aragón: Cirot 1918) states explicitly that their copy was not drawn up by Diego García but by "Dominicus regis notarius", who was apparently abbot of Valladolid (a Palencian dependency) from 1207 or earlier. Diego García's *Planeta*, commenting on the state of the church, describes most of his contemporaries in the church as "a bunch of philistines" (Linehan 1971: 30): "et ita prelati, proh pudor, penas quas deberent exsolvere inferentes: honestatem et litteras quas in se non reperiunt in aliis persecuntur" (Alonso 1943: 405). Diego seems to identify himself as *litteratus*; the most Latinate circle in Castille or León was probably the one to prepare the first long Romance document.

Chancellor Diego García's *Planeta* is odd (and Alonso's edition (1943) is odder). It is not always a reliable historical source. Ximénez de Rada, for example, is said to speak seventy languages (173); but Rada also "emendat vel commendat gallecos in loquela, legionenses in eloquencia ... provinciales in rithmis, turonenses in metris" (178), which, though hyperbolic (and not sarcastic), is of interest in suggesting *inter alia* that the *provençales* were thought the specialists in rhythmic verse, and those from Tours in metric. Other interesting comments include the view that when angels sing they fit one note per syllable: "celeuma angelicum o quam alte reboat, set nec sub phonasco vocalium neumas protrahit, nec achroama intonat, nec invigilat protractionibus neumarum set consonancie sillabarum" (385); that Paul read his epistles and John his gospel *gramatice*: "Paulus epistolam, et iohannes evvangelium sine barbarismo et soloecismo ita gramatice perlegerunt" (385-86); that the abbreviated names of Jesus Christ, *ihc* and *xpc*, may be *illegibile: per linguam* (i.e. unpronounceable as [ihc], [xpc]), but that is all right because he is said to be *ineffabile* anyway (415); and that some *studiosus* has assured him that in "primitive" Latin there were exactly 4,484 words (159); etc. At least in his old age his mind was wandering, but the evidence is unmistakeable in many comments that he knew well the Medieval Latin pronunciation techniques; and his chancery produced the Cabreros treaty.

As in Navarre, so at Cabreros: 1206 is the earliest date for "official" vernacular writing of which we can be sure. The Toledan *Auto de los Reyes Magos* is of uncertain date, but the manuscript is approximately contemporary; the earliest written Romance literature from Castille also seems to have been first written down around then, if the date of 1207 at the end of the only manuscript of the *Poema de Mio Cid* (a fourteenth-century copy) is to be taken seriously. This epic, and the treaty of Cabreros, do not seem to be hesitant (although the fourteenth-century copyist of the epic may have regularized many details, for all we can tell); the reason for this could well lie in the way that a kind of vernacular writing system seems to have been in use for many years, hidden under a veneer of Latinity.

The practical writing represented in the cheeses, the experimentation of the glosses, had not just disappeared; no manuscripts
written entirely and selfconsciously in Romance writing survive from
before 1200, but many of those ostensibly in Latin seem to have had,
in Elcock's phrase (1975: 424), a "camouflage of Latin" fitted onto the
vernacular. From the outside, these documents sometimes seem to be in
bizarre Latin, as if their writers had gone to great lengths to a) learn
Latin and b) then get it wrong; Fletcher's comments (1978: 229) on his
twelfth-century documents from Santiago seem to carry this implication. From a Hispanic viewpoint, it seems more likely that the writers
of such documents as the following had never learnt Latin at all; they
had just learnt a few tricks for making their vernacular seem Latinate
on paper. This sample document is also dated 1207, and comes from
the capital of Old Castille (Menéndez Pidal 1966: no.158):

> [in Dei no*min*e, am*e*n. Notu]m sit homnib*us* hominib*us* tamp*re*-
> sentib*us* q*u*am fut*u*ris, quod [ego] don Armengot debono anj |² mo
> [& de] *pro*pria uoluntade, iecto inpign*us* Soto & elmonesterio de
> *san*c*t*i Martinj & Baluas & q*u*anto hamj hi *per*te |³nece in sol[ares],
> terras, molino*s*, montes, fontes, ualles, & in ualles prado*s*, hauos
> prior de Uilla [m]ediana & hatodo elcon|⁴uento, p*or* .cccc.
> [cie]nto*s* & .xxv. mor*a*bedis bono*s* alfonsis, derecto*s* deauro &
> decuno & depeso; [et s]o pagado; & p*or*hatal |⁵ plecto & p*or*hatal
> *con*benencia, que ista heredat nonsaque sinon fore p*or*amio corpo;
> & q*u*anta renda seleuantare |⁶ dista hered[at], dolo p*or*mia anima
> halahuebra des*an*c*t*a Maria de Uilla mediana, & sihio Don Armen-
> got pasare |⁷ dest sieglo antes que esta heredat saque, dolo p*or*
> mia anima halacasa de Uilla mediana por heredat & fa|⁸ [ciant] de
> [h]eo quecumque uoluerint & *p*restent ej inuita & inmorte; &
> filio ninfilia non sea pod*er*oso d[e]s[a]carlo |⁹ nindedemandarlo.
> Siquis homo u*e*l femina dep*ro*ienie mea u*e*l deextranea qui ista
> ca[r]ta infr[ingere] uolue|¹⁰rit, hab[ea]t [ir]am Dei omnipotentis,
> & sup*er* ipsum pectet incoto mil mor*a*bedis, mediaetate rege &
> medieta[te] |¹¹ mo[nes]te[rij] des*an*c*t*a [Maria] de Uilla mediana.
> Facta carta inBurgos, inmense iulij, septimo kalendas |¹² hagustij,
> era M.ª CC.ª XL.ª V.ª, regnante rege Aldefonso cumregina
> Alionor in Toleto & in |¹³ Castella. Vnde sunt testes: elabat don-
> Martino de sant Pelagio deCerato; Garcia Gilez; Gil Gilez; Diago
> Ximenez; Martin |¹⁴ Romeo; Peidro Gustioz, suo erno; Tel
> Ramirez; Peidro Peidrez, suo maiordomo, quilosmetihio enella;
> Lop Diaz delaserna; Lop |¹⁵ Gonzaluez deFrias; Hienego Lopez;
> donMateo deCortes; don Ioan, erno dedonGarcia el moninero;
> Martin de Uila meio; |¹⁶ Remont, elbufon; Peidro Campsino;
> *Pere* Ponz, elalcalde; Estefan*us* scripsit & ocsignu*m* fecit +.

Esteban, the notary, has learnt the set phrases for such documents; they
are recognizably formulae, as "In dei nomine ... ego" at the start, "si
quis homo ...", "facta carta ...", "unde sunt testes". Otherwise, he is

attempting to reproduce on paper what the depositor is saying, in as official-looking a manner as he can.

One of the tricks of this trade is to use initial *h*-. He knows that a "silent" *h*- often occurs in official orthography; sometimes the *h*- indeed has a Latinizing effect, as in *heredat* (lines 5, 6, 7) for [eɾedad], although since the Latin was in fact HEREDITATEM the result is less than convincing. Esteban also does it consistently before *a* (*ha*, lines 2, 3 etc.), even spelling O. Sp. *pora* as *porha* (< PRO AD ; > *para*). Spelling *yo* as *hio* (1.6) extends his enthusiasm into semivowels: *hio* would look odd in comparison with the formulaic *ego* (1.1) if we seriously thought that this document represented a single "semiculto" register. The *h*- is available for the Latin formulae as well, which were as likely to be learnt by rote as to be faithfully copied, so that for example in the introductory formula not only *hominibus* but also *homnibus* (i.e. "all") acquires the *h*-, thereby spoiling the effect. We can probably deduce from this that [h-] was often not used in Latin pronunciation either. There is no sign yet of any tendency to use *h*- for the [φ] common in some parts of Castille for words originally beginning with a Latin *f*- (e.g. FACERE > O. Sp. *fazer* [φadzeɾ] > Mod. Sp. *hacer* [aθeɾ]). At the end, in his final formula, Esteban refrains from putting an *h*- on *oc*; *omnis* and *hoc* have both fallen from the spoken vocabulary long since, of course, so to Esteban it was all a question of guesswork. If he used the sounds [φ-] or [h-] himself, he did not connect them with the letter *h*: *faciant, filio, femina, bufon* have the *f* (Sp. *hagan, hijo, hembra, buhón*). The tendency to add *h*- is visible in the *Poema de Mio Cid* as well (e.g. *hyo, hido*, ll.1435, 1439, and passim). Sometimes it survived in the standard orthography of later Castille: *huebra*, for example (< OPERA), 1.6, is still spelt as Esteban spelt it here, and has never had any initial consonant or aspiration at all.

Similarly, Esteban knows that medial [d] is often represented by an official letter *t*. Hence the use of -*t*- in e.g. *Toleto* and *vita* (ll.12, 8); we can be sure that he and Don Armengot used [d] from e.g. *pagado* (1.4)[13]. He knows that [we] is often written with the letter *o*, as in *corpo* (1.5), *morte* (1.8), etc. (Spanish *cuerpo, muerte*) but does not always apply that rule of thumb in dictation conditions, e.g. in *huebra*. The case of [je] is more awkward for him; the rule of thumb is that [je] ought to be written *e*. We can be sure that Esteban and Armengot used [je] from *sieglo* (1.7), although he usually remembers the trick, as in *terras* (TERRAS > *tierras*), 1.3. This trick is not infallible, however;

---

13.  Armengot seems to be a Catalan name (Lapesa 1975: 20).

whereas *ue* is not a common Latin spelling, *ie* is, so that spelling Sp. *conveniencia* as *conbenencia* (1.5) with a simple *e* is in fact wrong, because the Latin was CONVENIENTIA with the *ie*. A more illuminating case is that of *erno*, the spelling twice used here for Sp. *yerno* "son-in-law" (ll.14, 15) which comes from Latin GENERUM. *Conbenencia* might be representing a monophthongized vernacular [e], since the *-encia* ending is occasionally found elsewhere in selfconsciously vernacular works (e.g. in the extract from the treaty above; cp. also *mantenençia*, *Libro de Alexandre* 2105c, 2380a), and although the change of Latin [je] > Sp. [e] might seem to be impossible in the face of the regular [e] > [je], dissimilation of palatal [j]s at the time of the [e]~ [je] "free" variation is at least conceivable (i.e. [jentsja > entsja]). *Erno*, however, is inexplicable except as a result of the scribal technique of writing *e* for [je]. Since it appears twice, it is presumably not a slip. (Otherwise, according to Oelschläger 1940, this form only seems to be attested once, in a document of 1204.) *Erno* ([erno]) does not seem to be the spoken form in any dialect; the GE- > *ye* development, which is fairly common but not quite regular in Castille, is in itself unusual, and the *ye-* > *e* development only happens in pretonic position (e.g. GER- MANUM > *iermano* > *hermano*), whereas a postulated change *yerno* > *erno* would happen in the tonic syllable. *Yerno* is the Castilian. The Cid's sons-in-law are often mentioned in the *Poema*; according to the facsimile of the *Poema*, on twenty-two occasions they are *yerno*, on two they are *hyerno*. The lawyer, unlike the poet, felt the need to Latinize the Castilian sound [je] as written *e*; often he was right, but on this occasion he was wrong. Such forms as *terras* are thus no more evidence that the scribe knew Latin than is *erno*.

Other similar forms corroborate this argument. *Yermo*, for example, (< EREMUM) appears in the *Poema*, and in the slightly later works of Berceo, as *yermo*, *iermo*, *hyermo*; these, and also the written forms with simple *e*, *ermo* and *hermo*, appear in prose documents. *Yerbas* (< HERBAS) appear in the *Poema*, and *yerba*, *Ierva*, *Yerva* in Berceo: Gloss *Em.*134 is *jerba*. In prose, as well as *ierba*, there is *erba*. *Erno*, (*h*)*ermo* and *erba* only occur in documents, where trained notaries operate the trick of spelling [je] as *e*. Latinate spelling in prose is not necessarily, therefore, evidence of knowledge of Latin, even in a community where Latin pronunciation is being taught to some people.

Another revealing example in this document is the word *pectet* (l.10). The trick of the trade is to transcribe [tʃ] as *ct*. Often this works: Spanish *derechos* turns up as written *derectos* (although the Latin was in fact DIRECTOS), for [kt] > [tʃ] is a regular Castilian change. *Pectet* is a perfectly good Latin word, the future of *pecto*, "comb". Unfortunately, the Spanish word in Esteban's mind is *peche*, "let him pay", the subjunctive of *pechar*, which in fact comes from Latin PACTET. We know now that [akt] $>$ [etʃ] is the normal development – cp. FACTA $>$ *hecha* – but Esteban's rules of thumb are not that sophisticated[14].

Esteban is happy to use non-Latinate vocabulary, such as Arabic *morabedis*, *alcalde* and Germanic *sacar*; and non-Latinate syntax, such as the reflexive future subjunctive in *selevantare*. Apart from his own, he transcribes names in vernacular form; as *Peidro* is the western and *Pere* the eastern form of *Pedro* ($<$ PETRUM). The evidence supports Elcock's suggestion of a thin coating of Latinity on a vernacular base, rather than the view that documents of this type are Latin with Romance interference. Esteban is thus in a similar position to that of the scribes of Sabatini's pre-Carolingian documents, of the cheeses in San Justo y Pastor, and of Esplendonio's sale deeds; he knows that the vernacular needs to be spelt in peculiar ways to be respectable, and as far as he can he does so. Yet, as Dutton (1980) showed, such documents were largely understood when read aloud to the witnesses, so presumably could be read aloud as Spanish (apart from the formulae). This analysis implies that the innovations used by the Riojan glossers and others were not lost; Esteban knows how to write *ie* in *sieglo*, *ue* in *huebra*, etc. There is, therefore, an inherited body of scribal technique that the man who drew up the treaty of Cabreros and the man who recorded the *Poema de Mio Cid* were able to draw on; maybe not standardized nor consistent, but not non-existent either. The decision to write in vernacular without its disguise is thus a decision to cast off clothes and come out topless rather than a decision to form an embryo.

This analysis also implies that works of semi-Latinate appearance such as this document are written by those who do not know Latin, whereas completely and emancipatedly vernacular writing – such as that at Cabreros, or that of Berceo, who read Latin sources – implies a skilled level of Latinity in the writer until such time as, in the late thirteenth century, writers are explicitly trained in the writing of naked Castilian. If so, the old assumption that the level of "Latinity" in a text corresponds to the level of "Latinity" of the author's speech has no more legs to stand on.

---

14. *Plecto* (1.5) is odd. Castilian *pleito* is said to be borrowed from French or Aragonese ($<$ PLACITUM); perhaps the trick of *ct* for [jt] was also known.

**Literature**

In two important articles Dutton (1967, 1973) claimed to have established the birthplace and initial procedures of much early written Spanish literature. The place is Palencia; the literature is that of the *mester de clereçía*, a Spanish form calqued on French models of composing verse in Latin. As we have seen, there had long been a good school at Palencia, and it seems reasonable to suppose that the scholars might have trained the Castilian notaries who composed the Treaty of nearby Cabreros for Alfonso VIII; in any event, at some time in the next few years (probably c.1210) its school was elevated by the King to the status of *studium generale* or University, the first in Castille. Bishop Tello Téllez, elected bishop in 1207, consecrated in office in 1212, ran it until his death in 1246. Ximénez de Rada, archbishop of Toledo, was a patron. Teachers were imported from Paris and Bologna; Rico has suggested that one of these teachers was Peter of Blois (not the poet of the same name, who died in London in 1212), who described Tello in the following glowing terms[15]:

> ... ad onorem tamen domini Tl venerabilis episcopi Pallentini, per quem Palencie virgineus elicon vigere studium gratulatur, cuius meribus, liberalitate et eloquencia, largitate, magnanimitate et magnificencia ceterisque virtutibus, non solum commemorata civitas, set tota Hispania a primis cunabulis ipsius floruit, floret in perpetuum et florebis (*sic*).

Tello's *studium* was selfconsciously *litteratum*. *Litterae* still seem to be the preserve of an élite; Tello described his parish clergy as *inscii litterarum*, and the Pope granted Palencia the right to use part of the tithes to help pay for the teaching of these rural *inscii litterarum* in 1225. Pupils were specifically trained in order to help celebrate the mass (*qui missam celebrent*) in their new skill (San Martín 1942: 89; Linehan 1971: 31; González 1960: I 628).

Dutton argued impressively that the *mester de clereçía* verse form was inspired by the education of the intellectual élite of the Spanish church at or near Palencia. (López Estrada 1978 has also shown that it is only in this initial phase that the word *clereçía* is narrowly identified with the church.) Berceo wrote prolifically in the form, adapting Latin prose sources into Spanish verse. Berceo's references to Palencia and its environs are additions to those sources; he refers in knowing tones to "todos los maestros de Francia" (*Duelo que fizo la*

---

15. This comes from folio 1r of the fourteenth-century Ripoll MS 122 in the *Archivo de la Corona de Aragón* in Barcelona. I am grateful to Professor Rico for checking the manuscript on my behalf.

*virgen* 6d), and to Tello himself in a cryptic comment that sounds like
a scholarly in-joke (all quotations are from Dutton 1967-):

> Nin ardió la imagen     nin ardió el flabello,
> Nin prisieron de danno     quanto val un cabello:
> Solamiente el fumo     non se llegó a ello
> Nil nució más qe nuzo     yo al bispo don Tello.
>
> (*Milagros* 325)

The Latin original has no comparable phrase. Dutton suggests that
Berceo was probably at the University between 1222 and 1227, which
is the period of Papal interest in its educative ventures. (In 1225 the
Pope refers to the church as one "que consuevit litteratis clericis venu-
stari"; San Martín 1942: 94.) Thereafter he was notary and perhaps
administrator at San Millán. He had learnt to read and understand Latin
fluently, since his works adapt Latin ones, and to draw up documents.
He never seems to have considered writing Latin verse, however. Maybe
this was because he wished his verse to be read aloud and generally
understood. At the start of his *Martirio de San Lorenzo* he says he is
writing "en romanz que la pueda saber toda la gent" (1b); in the second
stanza of his *Vida de Santo Domingo de Silos* he says the same:

> Quiero fer una prosa     en romanz paladino,
> en qual suele el pueblo     fablar con so vezino
> ca non só tan letrado     por fer otro latino:
> bien valdrá, como creo,     un vaso de bon vino.

Whether his modesty topos – that he cannot write Latin verse – is true
or not, the distinction between the *romanz* in which people talk to each
other, and the latin used by *letrados*, is clear. *Letrado* means "Latinate"
still, not simply "literate", although we are here witnessing the early
stages of the conceptual break between Latin and Romance in Spain.
This conscious conceptual distinction could also have been inspired by
the French scholars coming from an area where the distinction was by
now usual. San Millán itself, however, remained largely untouched by
French culture in general.

    Berceo has sometimes been claimed to be the author of the ano-
nymous *Libro de Alexandre*, a life of Alexander the Great in 10,700
lines, inspired by the Latin *Alexandreis* of Walter of Châtillon (which
may well have been on the University curriculum) and the French
*Roman d'Alexandre*[16]. This may be the earliest work in the form, and
starts as follows:

---

16. Nelson's edition (1979) confidently proclaims Berceo as author on the cover;
    the edition by Cañas Murillo (1978), from which quotations here come,
    wisely does not. Ware (1965) dated it to 1204, but not many scholars agree
    with him. On the inspiration see Willis (1934, 1935).

1 Señores, si queredes mi serviçio prender
querríavos de grado servir de mi mester;
deve de lo que sabe home largo seer,
si non, podrié en culpa e en riebto caer.

2 Mester traigo fermoso, no es de joglaría,
mester es sin pecado, ca es de clerezía;
fablar curso rimado por la cuaderna vía,
a sílabas contadas, ca es grant maestría.

These stanzas have given the verse form the name *mester de clereçía*, "metre of the educated". They explain that the form is a consciously elaborated one. Unlike previous Spanish verse, *joglaría*, it is *rimado*; the popular metres, such as ballads or epics, tended to use assonance alone, and consistent consonant rhyme is new. The *mester* has regular four-line stanzas, *cuaderna vía*, with AAAA rhyme. The *grant maestría* of counting syllables is a new achievement, unless we are not prepared to believe that vernacular verse was previously stress-based rather than syllable-based; even if rhythm leads to syllabic similarity, it is hard to visualize *juglares* actually counting syllables (*a sílabas contadas*). What this stanza omits to mention is that the definition of a vernacular syllable to mean each written vowel, accepted vernacular diphthongs apart, is also new in vernacular (see below). *Pecado*, meaning "sins against strict metrics", is an ancient European cliché, and line 2b is a pedantic joke (Deyermond 1965; Rico 1979). The word *fablar* is also given prominence, since (pace Gybbon-Monypenny 1965) these verses are designed for oral reproduction.

The contrast with *joglaría* here is literary and metrical rather than sociological, but that *juglares* were not thought to be suitable company for clerics can be seen from ordinance 5 of the Council of Valladolid in 1228 (see below):

Item establecemos, que los Clerigos no sean en compañas do estan Joglares, et trashechadores, et que escusen de entrar en las tabiernas, salvo con necesidat, et con priesa, non lo podiendo escusar, yendo en camino, en non joguen los dados, nin las taulas.

The wording does not imply that there was no previous contact, nor does the edict seem to have been observed. There may be an echo of the edict in Berceo's *Santo Domingo* 89c:

Si *ad opera manuum* los mandavan exir,
bien sabié el bon omne en ello abenir;
por nulla joglería non lo farién reír,
nin liviandat alguna de la boca decir.

A later contrast (*Santo Domingo* 701b) shows that *juglaría* is more or less by definition not written down:

> Peidro era su nomne    de esti cavallero,
> el escripto lo cuenta,    non joglar nin cedrero.

(A *cedrero* is a musician.) Berceo calls himself a *trobador* at the end of *Los Loores de Nuestra Señora* (232a):

> Aun merced te pido    por el tu trobador,
> que est romance fizo    fue tu entendedor . . ..

*Escripto* can be Romance, but *letras* remain Latin. Cañas (1978: 404) pointed out that in stanza 10 of the *Alexandre*, which comes from the Latin work, the author calls his source *letras*, but in stanza 11, which comes from the French, the author calls his source *escripto*:

> 10   En tierras de Egipto,   — en letras fue trobado —,
> fabló un corderuelo    que era rezient nado,
> parió una gallina    un culebro irado;
> era por Alexandre    tod'esto demostrado.

> 11   Aún avino al    en el su naçimiento:
> fijos de altos condes    naçieron más de çiento,
> fueron pora servirle    todos de buen taliento,
> — en escripto yaz'esto,    sepades, non vos miento —.

(In *Santo Domingo* 609c, the source is "mala letra, encerrado latino" — *latino* as a noun.) Alexander's own education in the poem came from Aristotle — *home bien letrado*, 51a — whom he addresses as follows:

> Maestro, tú me crieste    por tí se clerezía . . .    (38a)
> . . . que m'enseñest las artes    todas a entender.    (39d)

> Entiendo bien gramática    se bien toda natura
> bien dicto e versifico,    conosco bien figura,
> de cor se los actores,    de livro non he cura,
> mas todo lo olvido,    ¡tant'he fiera rencura!    (40)

His education, called in general *clerezia*, includes versification and prose composition; *dicto* presumably refers to the *Ars Dictaminis* (Faulhaber 1972: 64, 75). Dutton does not mention this stanza, but it seems to support his view that versification was part of the education of thirteenth-century *clerezia*.

So we have a group of early thirteenth-century poems written in Spanish, probably by writers who had learnt the form while studying at Palencia, but not necessarily forming a "school" in any other sense. The most interesting feature in the metre is the fact that the counting of syllables is carried out according to the same principles that had already been used for centuries in the composition of Medieval Latin rhythmic verse. In the *mester de clereçía* each line has fourteen syllables, each syllable being a written vowel or vernacular diphthong, and the line is divided into two heptasyllabic hemistichs with stress on the sixth syllable; Dutton (1973: 84) pointed out that this stress position comes from the French version of the metre rather than the Latin, which tended to have fifth-syllable stress (so far as we can tell). This model therefore excludes elision and requires hiatus instead; unlike contemporary compositions in Latin it makes no effort to avoid the question. In *Alexandre* 10-11 (reproduced above), therefore, there is hiatus in *de Egipto, fabló un, que era, parió una, culebro irado, avino al*; the apparent exceptions *tod* and *yaz* are in fact commonly-found thirteenth-century forms (for *todo* and *yaze*) even in prose. Native Spanish speech almost certainly involved eliding such pairs of vowels then as now – e.g. *que era* [keɾa] – so this is an artificial requirement.

Dutton's most interesting discovery concerned the procedure followed for the syllabification of new borrowings from Latin; he found "a carefully established rule that *new* Latinisms were to be given their Latin syllable value" (1973: 89), i.e. one syllable per written vowel, in the time-honoured fashion. Dutton went carefully through the works of Berceo looking at words ending in *-ión*, to see whether the *i* was a semivocalic [j] as in vernacular Spanish, thereby forming a monosyllable with the diphthong [jo], or whether it was a fully syllabic [i] as in Medieval Latin. The results are striking.

He found 32 words requiring a syllabic [i]; of these, 25 always required it, e.g. *afflicción, devoción, dissensión, lisión* and ubiquitously *visión*, and all these 25 are borrowings from Latin (except, in Dutton's view, *pipión*, a coin of little value). This list includes none of the common normal Romance words in *-ación*, which are often (e.g. Pattison 1975: 93), but in my view wrongly, classified as Latinisms (see Chapter 1, under *Doublets*). The remaining seven words attested with full syllabic value are also found with semivocalic value elsewhere; of these, two are reclassifiable as always syllabic, and a further two as always semivocalic, given the simple and plausible textual emendations suggested by Dutton. The other three are *condición*, which has syllabic value only once, when used in a specialized Latin context (*Sacrificio de la Misa* 116d); *missión*, which is only, but consistently, syllabic in the phrase *a muy grand missión*; and *lección*, which includes the diphthong in all uses other than a liturgical sense, when it can be trisyllabic. There is, then, in this large group of words, a regular pattern: the many words current in vernacular Romance speech which end in *-ión* have this syllable treated by Berceo as a diphthong; the many words borrowed from Latin which end in *-ión* have that ending treated as two separate syllables, as in the normal pattern of Latin rhythmic verse, where it was the number of written vowels (with specified exceptions not including *io*) that determined the mathematics of isosyllabicity.

Inspired by the clarity of this discovery, Dutton extended his investigation to the *ie* pair. Of words containing these two vowels together, he discovered that *sapiencia, paciencia, obediencia, obedient, audiencia, orient, ciencia, sociedat* and *propriedat* always had full syllabic value for the *i*, and these are all taken by Berceo from Latin words containing the written letters IE. Other words in which the vernacular *ie* represents [je], corresponding to an original Latin E, have a diphthong and never a disyllable – e.g. *ardiente, reciente*; and [je] also appears in *suciedat* etc., where the [e-] of a suffix is added to a stem in [-j] (here *sucio*).

This pattern is remarkable enough in a single author. When Dutton extended his analysis to the *Libro de Apolonio*, *Libro de Alexandre* and *Poema de Fernán González*, he found the same pattern there involving the same words: "when Berceo and the thirteenth-century *mester de clereçía* in general felt the need to use a Latinism, they did so fully in the sense that the Latin syllabic value was maintained in the imported Latin word" (1967: 58-59). We can consequently be certain both that these writers pronounced their Latin by giving a syllable to each vowel on the European pattern, and also that they pronounced their Romance in the normal vernacular fashion.

Spanish poets also composed Latin poems on similar lines. One of these is the *Carmen in honorem Roscidee Vallis*, a poem in praise of the Navarrese monastery of Roncesvalles, recently edited by Martínez (1980) and attributed by him to Ximénez de Rada (who was Navarrese by birth); Martínez suggests that he composed it at Roncesvalles in the spring of 1210. This consists of 42 four-line stanzas with AAAA rhyme. The length of line is consistently 7 + 6 syllables, although Martínez claims erroneously that they are dodecasyllabic (1980: 281). The author calls his composition *rimi* in the final stanza. The last five stanzas (ll.149-168) run as follows:

> Domus dicte sepius fratres et sorores
> Predictorum omnium sunt dispensatores;
> Vitam regulariter ducunt atque mores.
> Seculum despiciunt et ejus honores.

> Custos horum omnium dicitur Martinus
> Vir vite laudabilis, velut alto pinus,
> Erga Christi pauperes lare pandens sinus;
> Ejus implet viscera spiritus divinus.

> Servat, auget pauperum has possessiones,
> Sibi pro pauperibus prebens passiones,
> Nam celestis patrie gratulationes,
> Habentur per maximas tribulationes.

Dedit ei Dominus villicationem,
Petiturus siquidem de hoc rationem:
Cum bene reddiderit commutationem
Dignamque recipiet retributionem.

Bona prestat plurima domus pretaxata
Que presenti pagina non sunt declarata,
Nisi rimi series foret fini data
Auditori tedium daret protelata.

From the rhyme words of the two penultimate stanzas it is clear that the [i] in e.g. *rationem* is fully syllabic; similarly the [u] in *seculum* (1.152; also 1.19). This is an expertly arranged rhythmic Latin poem on the traditional model based on counting written vowels without interference from vernacular counterparts such as *razón* or *sieglo*. We can also tell that it was recited in Medieval Latin rather than Spanish from the fact that the rhythm of the Latin words is approximately trochaic (/ . / . / . . || / . / . / .) throughout. We know little for certain about the way in which a thirteenth-century Spaniard put stresses into Latin verse, but this pattern is more plausible than most; the final line – *aúditóri tédium dáret próteláta* – for example, granted that secondary stress qualifies for the purpose, fits such a system. Ximénez de Rada, the likely author of this *Carmen*, had studied in Paris, and was one of the patrons of the nascent University of Palencia. Presumably a similar tradition was available there, although the decision to lengthen the Spanish *mester* by one syllable (7 + 7) from the normal Latin (7 + 6) is probably caused by the French predilection for accentuating Latin words oxytonically, thereby requiring the last tonic Spanish syllable to be the sixth of the hemistich and thus, normally, the last but one in the line, given that most Spanish words are and were paroxytonic.

This pattern of Latin verse stanzas survives into the central part of the century. The capture of Seville from the Moslems in 1248, for example, was celebrated in verse by Guillermo Pérez de la Calzada; he sent his poem (of 106 stanzas) to Prince Alfonso, the future Alfonso X, in 1250, expressing in a preface the hope that the latter could include it in the histories: "si placet predictos rithmos cum hac epistola in cronicis annotari, ob memorie perpetue nutrimentum." The first three stanzas run as follows (Catalán and Gil 1968):

1 G lorior in gloria urbis, Ispalensis
    Quam natura diligens opibus immensis
    Ditauit ut fieret ensis inofensis
    Et lustrari debeat cereis accensis

2 V  rbis orbis urbium nomen immutatur
      Dum Iulia Romula nomine uocatur
      Insignito nomine dum sic illustratur
      Eius nomen celebre ubique laudatur
3 I  nsigni(i)s preconiis urbs preconizetur
      Fertilis et utilis quam sit declaretur
      Et referta mercibus quantum fecundetur
      Vt ex his et aliis quanta sit probetur

Pérez de la Calzada wrote from the Cluniac house of San Zoilo de Carrión (in the diocese of Palencia); he had previously been abbot of Sahagún. This extraordinary poem was apparently intended for incorporation in *cronica*; Alfonso's histories were to be in Spanish and did not reach 1248 in his lifetime, so there is no way of knowing if Alfonso planned to accede to this request[17]. Such Latin *rithmi*, however, remained a cultivated genre throughout the time of the strict syllabic *mester de clereçía* poetry in vernacular. Latin poems are composed in metric genres as well; for example, some time before 1213, a poem of 758 lines in metric elegiacs was written at the monastery of Santa María de Benevivere, also in Carrión, in praise of the monastery's founder Diego Martínez. Its modern editor suggests that the author was a Gascon (Fernández Martín 1961).

The spelling of Berceo's poetry is sufficiently consistent for us to deduce that it was consciously decided. Features that appear strange to Castilians include *-ss-* (for Castilian *-x-*), *lh* (for *ll*), *-i* (for *-e* in e.g. *li*, *esti*), *qe qi qa* (for *que qui ca*, [k]) and *que* (for *cue*, [kw]). This is also different from the usage of the treaty of Cabreros, which spells *que* for [ke], *x* for [ʃ], *ll* for [ʎ], and scholars may be right to ascribe some of these orthographic features to a conscious attempt by Berceo to approximate the speech of the Rioja (e.g. Gulsoy 1969); the *lh* and the *q-* forms, however, are only orthographic variants and are probably inspired by Occitan usage. *Qe*, in fact, is normal in San Millán until the 1270s (Dutton 1967: 77-79). As we have seen, the *clereçía* poets did not have to invent their orthography *ex nihilo*, as whoever drew up the treaty signed a few miles away at Cabreros in 1206 was already using the system that became the standard; but, in general, the Palencia scholars were those that laid the way for that standard.

Not all the literature written in Spanish before 1240 is in *mester de clereçía*, of course. Other compositions were inspired by other elements of French culture, such as the probably Toledan *Auto*

---

17. The study of the poem announced by Catalan and Gil is still awaited. The MS is Bodleian Holkham misc.26. One prothetic [e-] is required, in 16b (*stiterunt*).

*de los Reyes Magos* referred to above, and the debate poems, of which
the earliest (and least orthographically standardized) is the *Disputa del
alma y el cuerpo* found on the back of a document of 1201 from San
Salvador de Oña in Castille. These thirty-seven lines include *que* for
both [ke] and [kwe] (*quende* represents a diphthongized variant of
*conde*, [kwende] ; Menéndez Pidal 1900: 449-53):

> que tu fu[este] tan rico, agora eres mesquinu!
> dim, o son tos dineros que tu mi[sist en] estero?
> o los tos morauedis azaris et melequis
> que solies manear et a menudo contar?
> .o son los pala[fres] que los quendes ie los res
> te solien dar por to loseniar?

(ll.26-31)

There is also, inevitably, the *Poema de Mio Cid*. As Ian Michael
observed (1976: 61), "the orthography of the manuscript is chaotic in
some aspects, and may often reflect the habits of the fourteenth-century
copyist rather than those that applied at the time of composition of the
Poema". The thirteenth-century scribe may well have been the Per
Abbat "quien escrivio este libro" at the end (l.3731). Whether or not he
was also the author, or "refundidor", is unclear; Smith is sure that he
was (1977a: Chap.I), identifying him with one Per Abbat attested at
Santa Eugenia de Cordobilla (in the north-east of Palencia province) in
1223. Riaño (1971) identifies him with one attested at Fresno de
Caracena, near Gormaz, in 1220. Whoever wrote it down is likely to
have been trained at Palencia (before its elevation to *studium generale*)
and may have acquired the difficult technique of vernacular transcription there. Perhaps the structural awkwardness of some lines is
attributable to the newness of this technique as much as to the problems of following dictation or of copying French epic (as Harvey 1963
and Smith 1979 respectively suggest).

One argument against the view that the scribe was also the
author could be based on this line (already discussed in Chapter 4):
"un moro latinado bien ge lo entendió" (l.2667). This is the only
use in the Poem of *latin-* as a lexical entity, and it has the normal
pre-reform meaning of "Romance-speaking". In context it specifically
must mean "able to understand Spanish", and if this was open to
misunderstanding the point of the episode would be dangerously
weakened. The Latinate bishop Jerome is *letrado*; the author of this
poem seems to use the vernacular meaning of *latin-* rather than that
current in Latinate circles (e.g. in Berceo's *Santo Domingo* 2c quoted
above; the apparently suggestive final comment in the *Poema* – "el
romanz es leído", l.3733 – is a later addition). The orthography of the

*Poema* also shares the uncertainties of the notarial tradition rather than the comparative clarity of the Cabreros treaty; it tends, for example, to add unnecessary *h-*, and has no fixed graph for [ʎ], which is often merely *l*. As Adams (1976: 6) established, "there is no reason why there should be any general consistency between spelling and sound" in the *Poema*, although on the whole there is such a consistency in the early *mester* poetry. So although the scribe must have been educated somewhere, and quite probably at Palencia, that must have been before the systematic establishment of vernacular orthographies on the pattern subsequently to become the standard; even if he is also the "author" of the surviving version, it seems unlikely that he knew much about academic Latin poetry.

The theory that the native Spanish verse tradition was based on stress, and thus not isosyllabic, and that this helps to explain the lack of syllabic regularity in this poem, remains acceptable. Such echoes of French epic as there may be in the *Poema* are echoes rather than translations. There is no need to suppose that anyone knew anything at all about Germanic culture, but a native pattern of rhythmic vernacular verse, allied to an early attempt to expand the existing *ad hoc* notarial orthographical practices into extended use before the more professional attempts made at and near Palencia, seems on balance to be the view of the *Poema*'s written form best supported by the evidence adduced here.

### The Spread of the Reforms in the 1220s

The *studium generale* of Palencia led an uncertain existence as an institution; some details can be found in the examples in its 1222 *Ars Dictandi* manuscript (Barrero García 1976). It was singled out by the Papal legate Jean d'Abbeville in 1228 as having been a respectable centre of letters, but now in need of revitalization. Jean was sent to Spain to see if the reforms prescribed in the Fourth Lateran Council of 1215 were being carried out (Linehan 1971). On the whole, they were not. Ximénez de Rada, head of the Castilian church at the time, described the visit as follows:

> Eo tempore erat in Hispaniis legatus Romanae Ecclesiae Ioannes de Abbatis villa, quae est in Comitatu Pontini, Sabinensis Episcopus Cardinalis, vir bonus, sapiens, litteratus, qui celebratis in singulis regnis Conciliis, postquam monita salutis proposuit, ad Sedem Apostolicam est reversus, tribus annis legationis expletis.

(IX xii)

Jean was described by Ximénez de Rada as *litteratus* (like Bernard de Sédirac): "concerned with the effective practice of Medieval Latin" (astonishingly translated as "out of touch" by Linehan 1971: 48). The

Council of Valladolid which he summoned in the autumn of 1228, valid
for the ecclesiastical province of Toledo, put prominent emphasis on
the ability to speak Latin and the need to set up schools for that
purpose. The original ordinances have not survived, but a Castilian
translation made subsequently was preserved in a Leonese manuscript.
The second and third of these ordinances run as follows (Tejada 1849-
62: III 325):

### DE MAGISTRIS

Item establecemos, que en cada Eglesia Cathedral sean escogidos
dos varones los maes idoneos, et maes letrados que hi fueren, para
predicar la palabra de Dios, et para oir las confesiones generalmiente.

Item establecemos, que en todas las Eglesias conventuales por el
Obispo sea escogido uno de los maes idoneos, y maes letrados que
hi fueren para predicar et para oir las confesiones generalmiente.

### DE BENEFICIATIS ILLITERATIS

Stablecemos, que todos Beneficiados que non saben fablar latin,
sacados los viejos, que sean constreñidos que aprendan, et que
non les den los Beneficios fasta que sepan fablar latin.

Otrosi dispensamos con todos aquellos que quisieren estudiar, et
aprovechar en Gramatica, que hayan los Beneficios bien et entregamiente en las escolas, de la fiesta de San Luchas fasta tres años,
se hi oviere otros Clerigos porque la Eglesia sea servida. Et se fasta
este termino non sopieren fablar latin, non hayan los Beneficios,
fasta que emienden la sua negligencia por estudio, et fablen latin.

Porque muchos cobdician traer corona porque hayan libertad de
la Clerecia, et non quieren aprender, firmemiente mandamos, que
los que non quisieren aprender, non sean ordenados de Corona, et
que non sean de quatro grados fasta que sepan fablar latin.

Item porque queremos tornar en so estado el estudio de Palencia,
otorgamos que todos aquellos que fueren hi Maestros, et leieren
de qualquier sciencia, et todos aquellos que oieren hi Theologia,
que hayan bien et entregamiente sos Beneficios por cinco años,
asi como se serviesen a suas Eglesias.

The specified tasks of the *maestros* in the second ordinance,
preaching and confession, involved the use of the vernacular. In the
third, however, it is unambiguously Latin that is prescribed for the
*illiterati*; more precisely, the ability to speak it, *fablar latín*, is essential.
*Gramática* is prescribed to make them suitably able to read Latin aloud
and thus perform acceptably. This ability to pronounce the written text
remains an essential requirement; in 1260, for example, the synod of
Calahorra ordered each archdeaconry to provide two masters of
grammar, "e ansí non podrán haber excusas que non saben fablar latín
e pronunciar" (Faulhaber 1972: 32). A similar Council was called by

Jean in March 1229 in Lérida (Lleida), valid for Aragón. These records survive in Latin; the following are ordinances VI and VII (Tejada 1849-62: III 331-32; Chapman 1976: 28-29):

> Cum in generali concilio pia fuerit constitutione provisum ut non solum in cathedralibus ecclesiis, sed etiam in aliis, in quibus suppetunt facultates, magistris, qui ibidem laborant in doctrina, provideantur in beneficio competenti: nos attendentes quod in partibus Hispaniae ex defectu studiorum et literaturae multa et intolerabilia detrimenta animarum proveniunt, non solum in locis statutis praedictam constitutionem praecipimus observare, verum etiam ad multiplicem ignorantiam extirpandam eatenus scholas multiplicari statuimus, ut per singulas dioceses in quolibet Archidiaconatu in certis locis, si ad haec loca idonea inventa fuerint, per provisionem Episcopi scholae de Grammatica statuantur, et magistri collocentur. Quibus de ipsius Episcopi provisione vel ordinatione, si ipsius loci, in quo scholae fuerint, non sufficiat ecclesia, de aliis ecclesiis circa positis secundum singularum facultates competentes praecipimus provideri: ne ex defectu magistrorum illiterati suam possint ignorantiam excusare.
>
> Statuimus quoque ut omnes beneficiati et promovendi in ecclesiis parochialibus, qui latinis verbis loqui nesciunt, exceptis illis de quorum profectu propter aetatem non est sperandum, in studio ab Episcopo et Archidiacono loci, ubi tale jus consuevit habere Archidiaconus, per subtractionem beneficiorum quoad usque latinis verbis loqui sciant, addiscere compellantur. Illis autem, qui studere in Grammatica, et proficere voluerint, misericorditer indulgemus, ut beneficia sua integre in scholis habeant a proximo festo sancti Ioannis usque ad triennium, ac si in suis ecclesiis deservirent. . . . Qui vero infra hunc terminum non tantum proficere curaverit, ut latinis verbis loqui sciat quia suam juvare, vel vincere neglexerit ignorantiam, donec talem negligentiam per subsequens studium correxerit, beneficio suspendatur eodem.

The English translation in Chapman's article vaguely translates *qui latinis verbis loqui nesciunt* as "ignorant of the Latin tongue", but from the continual use of *loqui* in VII it is clear that here too speaking, rather than understanding or composing, Latin is the essential requirement of a *literatus*.

The Aragonese reform was in practice carried out after 1239 with some sense of purpose under the Archbishop of Tarragona, Pere d'Albalat, who had been sacristan at Lérida at the time of the Council (Linehan 1969; 1971: Chap.4). In a useful unpublished thesis on Aragonese education, Winterbottom (1974: 97) observed that the reaction to the Council of Lérida was mainly that of "preparing local candidates for orders in the essentials of Latin grammar necessary for the exercise of clerical functions, ultimately for the priesthood".[18] In Albalat's *Summa Septem Sacramentorum* of 1241, under *De Ordinibus Clericorum* he decreed that candidates for ordination *ad acolitatum* (the fourth grade) should be examined to see whether they could sing, read, and speak Latin words: "utrum cantent, vel legant, vel sint legitimi, vel loqui sciant latinis verbis ... qualiter in domo Domini conversari debeant"; noone can be admitted "nisi loqui sciat verbis latinis" (Linehan 1969). The Aragonese extended this requirement to Valencia; in 1258 a synod of Valencia also decreed that noone should apply for the same fourth level of orders "nisi loqui sciat latinis verbis"; and, when reading aloud in church, "punctantes sine sincopa legant psalmos ac etiam lectiones".

In Castille the church leaders were less enthusiastic. Such cathedral schools as existed in León-Castille after the Council had existed before it also, and it was not until the reign of Alfonso X (1252-84) that education seems to have been widely given a high priority. Jean d'Abbeville's comment on Palencia at the end of Canon III of the Council of Valladolid is suggestive, however, and it seems that that *studium* was at the same time the main centre of both Latin knowledge and vernacular Spanish writing. This is no coincidence, for only a Latinate scholar would be likely to feel the need for a distinctive consistent Romance orthography in addition to the traditional one. The essential connection between the new pronunciation (Latin) and the new orthography (Romance) becomes clearer if we look at the career of Juan, abbot of Valladolid in 1228 and eventually Chancellor at the court of Fernando III (Lomax 1971; Serrano 1941).

Juan Díaz (Serrano 1941) or Domínguez (Millares Carlo 1926: 282-83) was probably from Soria, and apparently a cousin of Ximénez de Rada. He was at the Lateran Council of 1215 as abbot of Santander; from 1217 he was appointed to the Castilian chancery to replace Diego García. From 1219 to 1231 he was abbot of Valladolid, and presumably host of the 1228 Council; subsequently he became Bishop of Osma (1231-40), sang the first mass in reconquered Córdoba (1236), was appointed tutor to Fernando III's son Felipe, and became Bishop of Burgos (1240-46). The professional skills of bishop and chancellor remain as united as they had been in the previous century. By the time of his death in 1246 Juan's chancery had developed the habit of emitting most of the documents for internal consumption in Romance

---

18. I am grateful to the Liverpool University Library for permission to quote from this thesis.

rather than in Latin. The reason was that documents that had to be read to and understood by excisemen and local officials, or participants in boundary disputes, needed to specify vernacular pronunciation since the recipients would not understand Latin (Lomax 1971). In earlier days when all documents were given vernacular pronunciation anyway (Dutton 1980), Romance script would have been as unnecessary for such documents as phonetic script would be in Modern England; this change, which is only noticeable after 1230, implies that at court the prescriptions of the Council of Valladolid (1228) were taken seriously, that written Latin would have been read in the European manner as Latin rather than Spanish by at least some officials, and that simultaneously several officials were becoming practised in reading Romance writing. The same reasoning applies to the redaction of the *fueros* and other declarations of legal rights and duties that needed to be explained aloud in public. The translation in 1218 of the *fuero* of Zorita de los Canes into written Romance is likely to have been a consequence not only of the accession of Fernando III but of the chancellorship of Juan Díaz in the same year. There is no inconsistency in suggesting that the spread of Romance writing was patronized by the man who was at the same time urging the learning of Latin pronunciation; the new writing and the new pronunciation are here, as elsewhere, connected. Juan's contemporary Lucas of Tuy called Juan "vir sapiens et valde litteratus", and he may have been among the first in Castille to consider Latin and Romance to be distinct languages. The techniques evolved by notaries, elaborated under Diego García's aegis for Cabreros, and used for poetry at Palencia and elsewhere, come quite soon to be given official blessing by an expert Latinist. (It has also been proposed that Juan was the author of the so-called *Chronique Latine des rois de Castille*, on Spanish history from the tenth century to 1236: see Cirot 1912-13, Lomax 1963. This chronicle calls Jean d'Abbeville "virum providum et discretum et literatum"; Cirot 1913: 272.)

By the end of Juan's chancellorship vernacular is the normal written mode; under Alfonso X (1252-84) Latin was reserved for foreign letters, and not even always then. Juan died on the 1st October 1246, having three days earlier issued a final testament at Palencia, witnessed by the Bishops of Toledo, Astorga and Compostela, and the bishop-elect of Palencia, of which the original survives in Burgos Cathedral Archives vol.25 fol.351 (Serrano 1941: 37-40). This will has the first two paragraphs in Latin; the third — which details specific debts — in Castilian; the witnesses in Latin; seven subsequent detailed paragraphs in Castilian. Each section is strictly in one language with no visible interference from the other. Notarial documents — such as Esteban's of 1207, discussed above — used to present an apparent mixture of norms; Juan's will presents a juxtaposition of two separable and separate written (and spoken) norms, identifiable and identified as two languages. It is the attestation of a consciously "bilingual" literate community.

Juan Díaz may have been the prototype for the ideal chancellor described in Alfonso X's *Siete Partidas* (c.1260; ed. 1807). Among other things, "et leer et escrebir conviene que sepa en latin et en romance, porque las cartas quel mandare facer sean dictadas et escriptas bien et apuestamente" (II ix 4). In the *Siete Partidas* the existence of two languages is accepted. In section I xxxvii, *De las cosas que debe ser sabidor el perlado*, the second requirement of the prelate is a knowledge of *gramatica*, defined as "que es arte para aprender el lenguaje del latin". As regards Church education, the first word under the heading *Quales deben ser los clerigos que hobieren de ser beneficiados en santa eglesia* is *Letrados* (I xvi 2), which is subsequently explained as follows: "que sean letrados que entiendan Latin, et que sean sabidores del uso de la eglesia que es cantar et leer". As usual, the point of latinity is seen in the performance of church singing and reading. The same skills are conjoined again in the description of the duties of the teacher, the *maestrescuela* (I vi 7):

> Maestrescuela tanto quiere decir como maestro et proveedor de las escuelas: et pertenesce a su oficio de dar maestros en la eglesia que muestren a los mozos leer et cantar, et el debe emendar los libros en que leyeren en la eglesia, et otrosi al que leyere en el coro quando errare: et otrosi a su oficio pertenesce de estar delante quando probaren los escolares en las cibdades do son los estudios, si son tan letrados que merescan ser otorgados por maestros de gramatica, o de logica o de alguno de los otros saberes; et a los que entendiere que lo merescen puédeles otorgar que lean asi como maestros.

The essential requirement of *leer et cantar* in *litterae* in the mid-thirteenth century is further attested in stanza 354 of Berceo's *Milagros de Nuestra Señora*; the Latin source has the simple phrase *litteris instruebatur*, which is expanded into:

> Tenié en essa villa    ca era menester
> Un clérigo escuela    de cantar et leer;
> tenié muchos criados    a letras aprender,
> fijos de bonos omnes    qe qerién más valer.

The phrase *ca era menester* suggests that Berceo had in mind the Council of Valladolid's edict on schools; the *Siete Partidas* confirm that in Alfonso's reign that ideal is being actively pursued.

The long gestation is over. Medieval Latin at last exists in Spain as a conceptually separate language from Spanish Romance. From the time of Alfonso X there are people literate in Spanish without necessarily being at the same time literate in Latin. Pérez de la Calzada celebrated the capture of Seville in Latin; at about the same time someone else lamented the capture of Jerusalem in Spanish in the equally isosyllabic *¡Ay Jerusalén!* (Pescador 1960: 244-46). The poets had a choice.

## CONCLUSION

The changing relationship between Late Latin and Early Romance in Spain and Carolingian France can be presented schematically.

**STAGE A**

*France*: up to c.800
*Spain*: up to 1080

ONE LANGUAGE ("Proto-Romance")

*Written*: in the traditional way
*Spoken*: in different evolving ways in different places ("vernacular").

**STAGE B**

*France*: c.800 to c.842
*Spain*: 1080 to c.1206

ONE LANGUAGE IN EACH COMMUNITY
(Old French, Old Spanish, etc.)

*Written*: in the traditional way
*Spoken*: in two distinct ways
    a) in ordinary vernacular
    b) reading aloud in church in the new method of *litterae*, producing one sound for each written letter.

**STAGE C** (Unstable)

*France*: c.842 to c.1000
*Spain*: c.1206 to c.1228

ONE LANGUAGE IN EACH COMMUNITY

*Written*: in two distinct ways
    a) the traditional way
    b) the new "Romance" way, with one letter for each existing vernacular sound; different in different places.
*Spoken*: in two distinct ways
    a) in ordinary vernacular
    b) *litterae* in Church.

**STAGE D**

*France*: since c.1000
*Spain*: since c.1228

TWO LANGUAGES

*Written* in the traditional way, *spoken* in the new way: LATIN
*Written* in the new way, *spoken* in the normal way: ROMANCE

The conceptual separation follows, rather than precedes, the inventions of new "Latin" pronunciation and new "Romance" writing.

This hypothesis is supported by a wide variety of disparate facts, philological, linguistic, textual and historical. It cannot be said to have been proved, but it does appear to be more compatible with established evidence than the generally accepted view that Latin and vernacular Romance are independent from the end of the Roman Empire. And Latin, as we have known it for over a thousand years, really does seem to have been introduced into Romance Europe by the Carolingian scholars.

Dante said that *grammatica* was an invented international language (Marigo and Ricci 1968: 72):

> Hinc moti sunt inventores gramatice facultatis; que quidem gramatica nihil aliud est quam quedam inalterabilis locutionis idemptitas diversis temporibus atque locis.
>
> (*DVE*: I. IX. II)

Modern scholars have laughed at him. But Dante was right.

# APPENDIX

## Suggested translations of quotations from Grammarians

Page
55-56          *Velius Longus*                    (Keil VII 54.1-13)
When I started on the rationale of writing it struck me straight-
away that some people have thought that we should write in the same
way as we speak and hear others speak. For the way we ought to pronounce is quite often such that some of the letters included in the
spelling are not audible when pronounced. For example, when we say
*illum ego* and *omnium optimum*, both *illum* and *omnium* end in an *m*
which is not noticeable in pronunciation ... we have to admit that it is
written one way and pronounced in another ... often we ought to
write one thing and pronounce another ....

57          *Consentius*                    (Keil V 394.16-22)
There will be inconsistency in Roman speech concerning this,
such that its sound is weak when a word begins in it, as *ite*, or fatter
when a word ends in it, as *habui, tenui*; it has a sound halfway between
*e* and *i* when in the middle of a word, as in *hominem*. It seems to me
that when it is long it is fuller, or sharper, but when it is short it ought
to have a middling sort of sound — as the examples above can show you.

58          *Pompeius*                    (Keil V 102.13-18)
Should *o* be long or short? If it is long, the sound should come
from within the palate, as when you say *orator* it sounds as if it is
inside, inside the palate. If it is short, the sound should come from the
outer lips, as if from the edges of the lips, as when you say *obit*. You
have this rule expressed in Terentianus; *when you want to say it short,
it sounds on the outer lips: when you say it long, it sounds inside the
palate.*

          *Sergius*                    (Keil IV 520.27-31)
There are five vowels. They do not all have more than one
sound; two do, *e* and *o*. For when *e* is short, it sounds like a diphthong,
as in *equus*; when it is long, it sounds like an *i*, as in *demens*. Similarly
with *o*; when it is long, it sounds inside the palate, as in *Roma, orator*;
when it is short, it is said on the outer lips, as in *opus, rosa*.

59          *Servius*                    (Keil IV 421.16-21)
There are five vowels; *a, e, i, o, u*. Two of these, *e* and *o*, sound
different when long from when short. For when *o* is long, it sounds
from the top of the mouth, as in *Roma*; when it is short, it sounds from
the lips, as in *rosa*. It is the same when *e* is long, it is close to the sound
of the letter *i*, as in *meta*; but when it is short, it is close to the sound
of a diphthong, as in *equus*.

59          *Pompeius*                           (Keil V 285,5-9)
     There is another barbarism of pronunciation; we often pro-
nounce badly, and make a mistake, so that a short syllable is given a
long pronunciation, or a long one a short pronunciation; if we wished
to say *Ruoma*, or wished to say *aequus* instead of *equus*, that would be
this barbarism of pronunciation.

60          *Pompeius*                           (Keil V 286,6-33)
     There are some mistakes that we ought to avoid. You should
avoid these five; iotacism, labdacism, myotacism, collision, hiatus.
Iotacisms are mistakes over the letter *i*, as if one said *Titius* for *Titsius*,
*Aventius* for *Aventsius*, *Amantius* for *Amantsius*. So how is the mistake
made? Let us define it, and then we will see how we ought to take care.
This mistake is made whenever a vowel follows *ti* or *di* and there is no
sibilant. For whenever a vowel follows *ti* or *di*, that *ti* or *di* should become a sibilant. We ought not to say *Titius* as it is written, but as
*Titsius*; that middle syllable becomes a sibilant. So if you should want
to say *ti* or *di*, do not pronounce it in the way it is written, but pronounce it with a sibilant. You ought to know that, so that then you
ought to do that, if it is in the middle of a word. If, however, it is at the
start of the word, even if there is a following vowel, then it does not
turn it into a sibilant. E.g. *dies* has a vowel after the *di*; we should say
*dzies*, but we do not. Add a first part to that word, and you do say
*meridzies*; we are unable to say *meridies*; so you should know that this
happens to *ti* and *di* when it is in the middle, but not when it is at the
beginning . . ..

79          *Cassiodorus*                        (*PL* 1245C)
     *Tamtus* and *quamtus* should have an *m* in the middle, for they
are *quam* and *tam*, from which come *quamtitas*, *quamtus*, *tamtus*. Do
not worry because the sound is an *n*; I told you earlier that *n* should
be the sound, even though the written form has an *m*.

                                                (*PL* 1243B)
     So if there are two consecutive words of which the first has an
-*m* at the end and the second begins with a vowel, an -*m* is written, even
though it sounds harsh and wrong if pronounced.

                                                (*PL* 1267C)
     If the letter *m* is next to a vowel at the start of the next word,
we will not pronounce it.

                                                (*PL* 1244D)
     Yet it is better, both in pronouncing and writing, to put *i*
rather than *u*, as has become normal.

                                                (*PL* 1245B)
     We will decide when this is to happen and when it is not from
the sound: *accedo* has two *c*s, *attuli* two *t*s . . . the consonants change
not only for the smoothness of the sound, but also because a *d* could
not be pronounced. It does sound, and is also written, next to an *f*; as
in *adfluo*, *adfui*, *adfectus*; it does not sound next to a *b*, as in *offui*,
*offero*, *offendo*.

80         *Cassiodorus*                    (*PL* 1241C)
    . . . so what you start to learn well you should carry through to
the end with a blameless delivery. For if you want to be understood,
what you once sought to achieve through slowness you will subsequently
run through with exemplary speed. It is well worth studying . . . how to
write accurately what you ought to say, and to read what has been
written without any uncertainty or mistake.

                                            (*PL* 1242A)
    I particularly thought you should be advised that you should
carefully examine where to insert pauses as the sense requires, without
which we cannot manage to read or understand anything.

80-81                                       (*PL* 1128C)
    In cases where words can be either in the accusative or the
ablative case after prepositions, look carefully to see if it is place or
motion, because copyists who do not know their grammar are particularly liable to get this wrong. For if you put on or take off a letter
*m* inappropriately, the whole phrase gets muddled.


84         *Isidore*                        (I 27.12)
    For as grammar deals with word-endings, so *orthographia* deals
with expertise in writing; for example *ad*, when it is a preposition, has
a letter *d*, and when it is a conjunction it has a letter *t*. *Haud*, when it is
an adverb of negation, finishes in *d* and has an *h* at the start; when it is
the disjunctive conjunction, it is written with a letter *t* and without an *h*.

                                            (I 27.12)
    *Id*, when the pronoun of neuter gender, is written with a *d*,
being a part of *is*, *ea*, *id*, because that gives *idem*. If it is the third-person
verb it will be written with a *t*, being a part of *eo*, *is*, *it*, because that
gives *itur*.

85                                          (I 27.28)
    For although *iustitia* is pronounced with a letter *z*, it should be
written with a *t*, because it is a Latin word. Similarly *militia*, *malitia*,
*nequitia*, etc.

86                                          (I 32.1)
    A barbarism is a word pronounced with a wrong letter or sound.
With a wrong letter, e.g. *floriet* when we should say *florebit*; with a
wrong sound, if the first syllable is stressed (lengthened?) rather than
the middle one, e.g. in *latebrae*, *tenebrae*. It is called a *barbarismus*
from the *barbari*, who do not completely appreciate the proper nature
of our speech.

87                                          (I 32.3-8)
    Barbarism of pronunciation can be committed through mistakes
in length, stress, the use of *h*, and the other following ways. In length, if
a short syllable is uttered instead of a long, or a long syllable instead of
a short; in stress, if the accent is moved to another syllable; in the use
of *h*, if an *h* is put onto where it should not be, or removed where it
should be. Hiatus, whenever a verse is cut short in speech before it
is finished, or when a vowel follows another, as in *Musae Aonides*.

Barbarism can also happen through *motacism*, *iotacism*, and *labdacism*. It is a *motacism* when an *m* is followed by a vowel, such as *bonum aurum*, *iustum amicum*; we avoid the mistake by suspending or removing the *m*. It is an *iotacism* when the sound is doubled in a letter *i*, as sometimes happens in *Troia, Maia*; where the pronunciation of the letters should be so slight that one *i* rather than two should seem to be uttered. It is a *labdacism* if two *l*s are pronounced instead of one, as the Africans do, saying *colloquium* for *conloquium* (or when we pronounce one *l* too weakly or two *l*s too strongly).

88                                                                            (*De Ecclesiasticis Officiis* II 11)

Concerning readers.

1. The order of readers took its nature and origin from the prophets. So those are readers who preach the word of God, to whom it is said; "Cry aloud, spare not, lift up thy voice like a trumpet" (Isaiah 58). When these are ordained, the bishop first speaks about their new duties to the congregation. Then he publicly gives them the manuscript of the most holy words for them to read out the word of God.

2. Whoever reaches this level will be imbued with learning and books, adorned with the knowledge of senses and words, so that he understands in the punctuation of sentences where a clause should end, where a clause is still continuing, where the end of the sentence has a rhythmic *clausula*. And he will be so prepared with the technique of delivery that he will move the minds and senses of all to understanding, by distinguishing the kinds of delivery and expressing suitable tones for the sentences, now with a matter-of-fact voice, now sad, now rebuking, now encouraging, or other such modes according to the kinds of suitable delivery.

3. In this it is particularly important to be aware of ambiguities in sentences. For there are many such in the Scriptures, which, unless they are delivered in the right way, change the meaning of the sentence into its opposite; for example, "Who shall lay anything to the charge of God's elect? It is God that justifieth" (Romans viii 33-34). If this is said in a positive way, not respecting the kind of delivery that is suitable, misunderstanding arises. It must therefore be delivered as if it were saying "is it God who justifieth?", so that *no* is understood.

4. So it is essential to have perception and understanding of so many things, so that every individual passage is delivered appropriately and suitably. So the reader should know the force of stresses also, so that he knows which syllable of a word the reader should accentuate. For many inexperienced readers get the stresses wrong on words, and then those who do seem to understand are likely to mock us and disparage us and swear that they have no idea what we are saying.

5. The reader's voice should also be straightforward, clear, adaptable to all kinds of delivery, full of virility and strength, avoiding boorishness or rudeness; not humble, nor excited, nor broken, nor tender, and with no feminine sounds, nor moving the body, but just with an expression of *gravitas*. For the reader should be addressing himself to the ears and the heart, not to the eyes of his audience, and

he should not make them his spectators rather than hearers. It is an old precept that readers should have taken special care of their voice for the sake of delivery, so that they might be heard amid a disturbance; which is why readers used to be called criers or proclaimers.

92-93 (IX 1.6-7)
Some people have said that there have been four Latin languages, i.e. Ancient, Latin, Roman, and Mixed. It was Ancient as used by the very ancient people of Italy under Janus and Saturn, as in the songs of the Salii. Latin was spoken under Latinus and the Kings by the Tuscans and others in Latium, in which the Twelve Tables were written. Roman began once the Roman people drove out the Kings, eloquently used by the poets Naevius, Plautus, Ennius and Vergil, and the orators Gracchus, Cato, Cicero, etc. Mixed came in once the Empire spread more widely, when new customs and peoples came into the Roman state, corrupting the proper nature of words with solecisms and barbarisms.

97 *Julian of Toledo* (II V 1)
In a verb ending in *a*, is it long or short? In all moods, numbers, persons, tenses and conjugations, if it ends in *a* it is long, as in *ama*.

(II I 6)
How many letters are vowels? Five.
Which? *a, e, i, o, u.*
Are they always vowels? *a*, *e*, and *o* are always vowels; *i* and *u* have different uses.
In what way? Because sometimes they are vowels, and sometimes they acquire the value of consonants, sometimes they are doubled, sometimes they are joined with other vowels, sometimes they are between vowels, sometimes a *u* is put between a *q* and a vowel, and then it is neither a consonant nor a vowel, sometimes a *u* is put in for a digamma (w), when two are written together, sometimes an *i* is put between two vowels in one word and takes the place of two consonants.

116 *Rabanus Maurus (De Clericorum Institutione* III 18)
Concerning grammar, and its varieties.
The first of the liberal arts is grammar, the second is rhetoric, the third dialectic, the fourth arithmetic, the fifth geometry, the sixth music, the seventh astronomy. Grammar took its name from *litterae*, as the derivation of that word shows. This is the definition of it: Grammar is the discipline of interpreting poets and historians, and the rationale of correct writing and speaking. This is the origin and source of the liberal arts. So it is essential to read this in the Lord's schools, because the knowledge of correct speaking and the manner of writing consists of this. How can anyone appreciate the force of spoken words or the values of letters and syllables if he has not first learnt it in grammar? Or how does he know the distinct value of feet, accents and punctuation, if he has not first found the knowledge of it in this discipline? Or how does he know the value of parts of speech, the decorative value of *schemata*, the point of *tropi*, the reasons of ety-

mologies, and correct *orthographia*, if he has not first learnt the art of grammar? For he learns this art blamelessly, nay, praiseworthily, who likes not to make an empty jumble of words out of it but seeks to acquire the knowledge of correct speaking and the skill of writing.

118          *Admonitio Generalis*                    (Canon 72)
     And there should be set up reading schools for boys. Carefully correct the psalms, *notae*, chants, *computus* [the method of calculating dates of Church festivals], grammar and Church books in each monastery or cathedral; because often, when some people want to pray properly to God, they pray wrong because the text has not been corrected. And do not let your pupils make mistakes when reading or writing them; and if it is necessary to write the gospel, psalms and missal, grown men should write them with all care.

                                             (Canon 82)
     ... that the priests that you send through your parishes to preach in church and organize the God-fearing parishioners, should preach correctly and accurately; and do not let them make up and preach to the people anything new or uncanonical from their own initiative, not in accord with holy Scripture.

122          *Council of Mainz*                       (Canon 2)
     (incorporating Canon 17 of the Council of Tours, p.120)
     Concerning Church teaching.
     Although all the conciliar canons that are handed down are supposed to be read and understood by the priesthood, and they ought to live and preach according to them, we thought it necessary that those that concern the Faith, and deal with the rooting out of vices and implanting of virtues, should be particularly studied by them, and well understood, and preached publicly. And every bishop should have the homilies that contain the necessary advice with which to instruct their subjects in the Christian faith, as far as they can understand it, concerning the eternal reward for the good and eternal damnation for the evil, as well as about the future resurrection, and the last judgement, and what actions can promote or deny a state of grace; and they should all take care consciously to transfer to ordinary Romance or German when reading these homilies, so that everyone can find it easier to understand what is being said.

137          *Abbo*          (*Quaestiones Grammaticales*, § 10)
     When an *e* or an *i* follows a *c* in the same syllable, there are three normal ways of pronouncing it. Sometimes it sounds rather like a *g*, particularly when there is an *s* in front of it, as in *suscipio*, *suscepi*, *suscepit*. Sometimes it has a sibilant sound, as if there were an *s* in there somewhere, as in *civis*, *cepit*; this is commoner when a *t* is pronounced like a *z* as the start of a syllable, as in *laetitia*, *justitia*. Some people, finally, add a third variety with the sound as of *quae* or *qui*, and say that that is how it should be pronounced, as *susquipio* rather than *suscipio*, *susquepit* rather than *suscepit*, *quivis* rather than *civis* — but anyone who knows anything about it can see how ridiculous that is.

150          *Council of Tarragona, 1233*          (Canon 2)
Likewise, it is decreed that nobody should have books of the
Old or New Testament in Romance. If anyone does, within eight days
from the time of publication of this decree he should give them to the
bishop of the area to be burnt. If he does not do so, whether he is a
cleric or a layman, he should be as if under suspicion of heresy until he
redeems himself.

153-54          *Julian of Toledo*          (*Ars Grammatica* II xx 2-4)
If apart from these forms anyone writes, or reads something
written by another, that is not based on the fixed rules of metric feet,
but on the counting and measurement of rhythmical patterns, he
should realize that that is not a *metrum* but a *rhythmus* . . . the *rhythmus* is subjected to the judgement of the ears by the number of
syllables, in the same way as are the songs of ordinary poets. Give an
example of this: *Lupus dum ambularet viam incontravit asinum*. Can a
*metrum* be without rhythm, or a *rhythmus* without metre? A *metrum*
cannot be without rhythm, but a *rhythmus* can be without metre.
Why? Because a *metrum* is a calculation plus speech-patterns, whereas
a *rhythmus* is a speech-pattern with no further calculations.

225          *Siguinus*          (p.30)
Nouns should be written and pronounced with a *u* – e.g. *lingua/
lingue*, *anguis/angue*, *unguis/ungue*, *inguis/inguen/unguentum* – but
verbs without the *u* – e.g. *lingo/lingis*, *ango/angis*, *ungo/ungis*, *ingero/
ingeris*. Otherwise there would be hesitation over whether it was a noun
or a verb.

256          *Council of Lérida, 1229*          (Canons 6 and 7)
Since it was agreed at the Fourth Lateran Council that sufficient
resources should be made available for *magistri* who are teaching
*doctrina*, not only in cathedrals but in other churches where the resources exist, and we are aware that in Spain there is great harm and
damage done to souls from insufficient study and *litterae*, we not only
decree that this decision should be carried out in the places mentioned,
but that more schools should be founded in order to root out the
ignorance on many matters, so that in each diocese – in every archdeaconry in some places if suitable places can be found – schools of
*Grammatica* should be set up and teachers brought in from the Bishop's
funds. We decree that if the Bishop's resources are not sufficient for
these schools, then other nearby churches should contribute according
to their ability to do so, to prevent those without *litterae* from claiming
their ignorance is due to the non-existence of *magistri*.
We also decree that all those with benefices and due to be sent
out to parish churches but who do not know how to speak words in the
Latin way – except for those who are too old to be expected to learn –
should be made to learn to do so, by the bishop – or the Archdeacon,
where the Archdeacon has traditionally such powers –, and to forgo
their benefice until they do know how to speak in Latin words. We
look with favour on those who have wished to study and become

proficient in *Grammatica*, and grant that they can enjoy their benefices completely in the *scholae* for three years from next St John's Day, as if they were working in their parishes ... but if any of them after this time has not been sufficiently conscientious to become proficient and know how to speak Latin words, because he has not bothered to improve or overcome his lack of knowledge, he should be suspended from that benefice until he has corrected that negligence by later study.

# BIBLIOGRAPHY

*Abbreviations used*

| | |
|---|---|
| *AEF* | Anuario de Estudios Filológicos |
| *AEM* | Anuario de Estudios Medievales |
| *AH* | Analecta Hymnica |
| *AHDE* | Anuario de Historia del Derecho Español |
| *ALMA* | Archivum Latinitatis Medii Aevi |
| *BAH, BRAH* | Boletín de la (Real) Academia de la Historia |
| *BBMP* | Boletín de la Biblioteca Menéndez Pelayo |
| *BH* | Bulletin Hispanique |
| *BHS* | Bulletin of Hispanic Studies |
| *BRAE* | Boletín de la Real Academia Española |
| *CC* | Corpus Christianorum |
| *CCM* | Cahiers de Civilisation Médiévale |
| *CHE* | Cuadernos de Historia de España |
| *CLHM* | Cahiers de Linguistique Hispanique Médiévale |
| *EEMCA* | Estudios de Edad Media de la Corona de Aragón |
| *EHR* | English Historical Review |
| *ELH* | Enciclopedia Lingüística Hispánica |
| *FL* | Foundations of Language |
| *HR* | Hispanic Review |
| *HS* | Hispania Sacra |
| *JEH* | Journal of Ecclesiastical History |
| *JHP* | Journal of Hispanic Philology |
| *KRQ* | Kentucky Romance Quarterly |
| *MCV* | Mélanges de la Casa de Velázquez |
| *MGH* | Monumenta Germaniae Historica |
| *MJ* | Mittellateinisches Jahrbuch |
| *MLR* | Modern Language Review |
| *NRFH* | Nueva Revista de Filología Hispánica |
| *PL* | Patrologia Latina |
| *PLLS* | Papers of the Liverpool Latin Seminar |
| *PMLA* | Publications of the Modern Language Association of America |
| *RABM* | Revista de Archivos, Bibliotecas y Museos |
| *RF* | Romanische Forschungen |
| *RFE* | Revista de Filología Española |
| *RLiR* | Revue de Linguistique Romane |
| *RPh* | Romance Philology |
| *SM* | Studi Medievali |
| *TPS* | Transactions of the Philological Society |
| *TraLiLi* | Travaux de Linguistique et de Littérature |
| *VR* | Vox Romanica |
| *ZRPh* | Zeitschrift für Romanische Philologie |

Adams, J.N. (1977a). *The Vulgar Latin of the Letters of Claudius Terentianus*. Manchester.
-    (1977b). 'The Vocabulary of the *Annales Regni Francorum*', *Glotta* LV pp.257-82.
Adams, K. (1976). 'The Yugoslav model and the text of the *Poema de Mio Cid*', *Medieval Hispanic Studies presented to Rita Hamilton*, pp.1-10. London.
Aherne, C.M. (1949). *Valerio of Bierzo*. Washington.
Alfonso el Sabio (1807). *Las Siete Partidas*. 3 vols. Madrid.
Allen, W.S. (1970). *Vox Latina*. Cambridge.
Alonso, M. (ed.) (1943). *Planeta* by Diego García. Madrid.
Alvar, M. (1976). *El dialecto riojano*. Madrid.
Amador de los Ríos, J. (1862). *Historia Crítica de la Literatura Española*. 7 vols. Madrid. (Reprint, Hildesheim/ New York 1970).
Andersen, H. (1973). 'Abductive and Deductive Change', *Language* XLIX pp.765-93.
Anderson, J.M. (1973). *Structural Aspects of Language Change*. London.
Antolín, G. (1910). *Catálogo de los Códices Latinos del Escorial. I.* Madrid.
Arigita y Lasa, M. (1900). *Colección de documentos inéditos para la historia de Navarra*. Pamplona.
Ariza Viguera, M. (1979). 'Notas sobre la lengua de las glosas y de su contexto latino', *AEF* II pp.7-18.
Asín Palacios, M. (1943). *Glosario de voces romances registradas por un botánico anónimo hispanomusulmán*. Madrid.
Avalle, D'A.S. (1965). *Latino "circa romançum" e "rustica romana lingua"*. Padua.

Badía Margarit, A. (1951). *Gramática histórica catalana*. Barcelona.
-    (1972). 'Por una revisión del concepto de "Cultismo" en Fonética Histórica', *Studia Hispanica in Honorem R. Lapesa*, 3 vols. Vol.I pp.137-52. Madrid.
Balaguer, F. (1954). 'Una nota sobre la introducción de la letra carolina en la cancillería aragonesa', *Cuadernos de Historia Jerónimo Zurita* III pp.155-61.
Balaguer, J. (1974). *Apuntes para una historia prosódica de la métrica castellana*[2]. Santo Domingo.
Baldinger, K. (1980). *Semantic Theory*. Oxford.
Barnett, F.J. (1961). 'Some notes to the Sequence of St. Eulalia', *Studies in Medieval French presented to Alfred Ewert in Honour of his 70th birthday* pp.1-25. Oxford.
Barrero García, A.M. (1976). 'Un formulario de cancillería episcopal castellano leonés del siglo XIII', *AHDE* XLVI pp.671-711.
Bassols i Climent, M. (1976). *Fonética Latina*. Madrid.
Bastardas y Parera, J. (1960). 'El latín medieval', *ELH* I pp.251-90. Madrid.
-    (1977). 'El català pre-literari', *Actes del Quart Col·loqui*

*internacional de llengua i literatura catalanes*. Montserrat.
Battisti, C. (1960). 'Secoli illetterati', *SM*³ I pp.362-96.
Beaulieux, C. (1927). 'Essai sur l'histoire de la prononciation du latin en France', *Revue des Etudes Latines* V pp.68-82.
Beer, R. (1907-08). *Die Handschriften des Klosters Santa Maria de Ripoll*. Vienna.
–   (1909). *Codices Graeci et Latini photographice depicti duce Scatone de Vries* XIII. Leiden.
Beeson, C.H. (1924). 'The *Ars Grammatica* of Julian of Toledo', *Miscellanea Francesco Ehrle* I pp.50-70. Rome.
Beltrán de Heredia, V. (1946). 'La formación intelectual del clero en España durante los siglos XII, XIII y XIV', *Revista Española de Teología* VI pp.313-57.
Berger, M. (1899). *Die Lehnwörter in der französischen Sprache ältester Zeit*. Leipzig.
Biggs, A.G. (1949). *Diego Gelmírez, First Archbishop of Compostela*. Washington.
Bischoff, B. (1959). 'Ein Brief Julians von Toledo über Rhythmen, metrische Dichtung und Prosa', *Hermes* LXXXVII pp.247-56.
–   (1961). 'The study of foreign languages in the Middle Ages', *Speculum* XXXVI pp.209-24.
Bishko, C.J. (1948). 'Salvus of Albelda and frontier monasticism in Tenth-Century Navarre', *Speculum* XXIII pp.559-90. (Now reprinted in *Studies in Medieval Spanish Frontier History*. 1980. London.)
–   (1951). 'Gallegan Pactual Monasticism in the Repopulation of Castille', *Estudios Dedicados a Menéndez Pidal* II pp.513-31. Madrid.
–   (1965). 'The Cluniac Priories of Galicia and Portugal: their acquisition and administration, 1075 - ca.1230', *Studia Monastica* VII pp.305-56.
–   (1968-69). 'Fernando I y los orígenes de la alianza castellano-leonesa con Cluny', *CHE* XLIII-XLIV pp.31-135; XLV-XLVI pp.50-116. (Reprinted in *Studies in Medieval Spanish Frontier History*. 1980. London.)
Blair, P.H. (1970). *The World of Bede*. London
Blaylock, C. (1973). 'Observations on sound change, especially loss, with particular reference to Hispano-Romance', in B.B. Kachru et al (eds), *Issues in Linguistics: Papers in Honor of Henry and Renée Kahane* pp.48-57. Urbana.
Blume, C. (ed.) (1897). *Analecta Hymnica* XXVII. Leipzig. (Reprinted 1961. Frankfurt.)
Bonnaz, Y. (1977). 'La Chronique d'Alphonse III et sa 'continuatio' dans le manuscrit 9.880 de la Bibliothèque Nationale de Madrid', *MCV* XIII pp.85-101.
Boussard, J. (1972). 'Les influences anglaises sur l'école carolingienne des VIIIe et IXe siècles', *Settimane di studio del centro italiano di studi sull'alto medioevo* XIX pp.417-52.

Boutemy, A. (1946-47). 'Le scriptorium et la bibliothèque de Saint Amand', *Scriptorium* I pp.6-16.
— (1949). 'Le style franco-saxon, style de Saint Amand', *Scriptorium* III pp.260-64.
Bouza Brey Trillo, F. (1965). 'Fortuna de las Canciones de Gesta y del héroe Roldán en el románico compostelano y en la tradición gallega', *Compostellanum* X pp.663-85.
Bradley, H. (1921-23). 'On the text of Abbo of Fleury's *Quaestiones Grammaticales*', *Proceedings of the British Academy* X pp.173-80.
Bresnan, J., Halle, M., Miller, G.A. (eds) (1978). *Linguistic Theory and Psychological Reality*. London.
Brou, L. (1951). 'Séquences et tropes dans la liturgie mozarabe', *HS* IV pp.27-41.
Brou, L. and Vives, J. (1959). *Antifonario visigótico mozárabe de la catedral de León*. Barcelona-Madrid.
Bullough, D. (1964). 'Le scuole cattedrali e la cultura dell'Italia settentrionale prima dei Comuni', *Italia Sacra* V pp.111-43.
— (1970). '*Europae Pater*; Charlemagne and his achievement in the light of recent scholarship', *EHR* LXXXV pp.59-105.
— (1973a). *The Age of Charlemagne*.² London.
— (1973b). 'Alcuino e la tradizione culturale insulare', *Settimane di studio del centro italiano di studi sull'alto medio evo* XX pp.571-600.
Burger, A. (1943). 'Pour une théorie du roman commun' in *Mémorial des Etudes Latines offert a J. Marouzeau* pp.162-69. Paris.
Burger, M. (1978). 'Paraulla grezesca — lengua serrazinesca', *TraLiLi* XVI pp.55-60.
Burnett, C.S.F. (1977). 'A group of Arabic-Latin translators working in Northern Spain in the mid-twelfth century', *Journal of the Royal Asiatic Society* pp.62-108.
Bustos Tovar, J.J. de (1974). *Contribución al estudio del cultismo léxico medieval*. Madrid.
Bynon, T. (1977). *Historical Linguistics*. Cambridge.

Cantarino, V. (1977). *Entre monjes y musulmanes*. Madrid.
Cantera Orive, J. (1948-49). 'Un ilustre peregrino francés en Albelda (Logroño) (Años 950-951)', *Berceo* III pp.421-42; IV pp.107-21, 299-304, 329-41.
— (1950-63). 'El primer siglo del monasterio de Albelda', *Berceo* V pp.13-23, 313-26, 509-21; VI pp.175-86, 531-41; VII pp.293-308; XVI pp.81-96, 437-48; XVII pp. 201-06, 327-42; XVIII pp.7-20, 377-86; now dormant, perhaps extinct.
Cañas Murillo, J. (ed.) (1978). *Libro de Alexandre*. Madrid.
Cappuyns, D.M. (1949). 'Cassiodore' in A. Baudrillart, A. de Meyer, E. van Cauwenbergh (eds), *Dictionnaire d'Histoire et*

*de Géographie Ecclésiastiques* XI cols. 1349-1408. Paris.

Castellani, A. (1978). 'Nouvelles remarques au sujet de la langue des Serments de Strasbourg', *TraLiLi* XVI pp.61-73.

Castro, A. (1936). *Glosarios Latino-Españoles de la Edad Media*. Madrid.

Catalán, D. and Gil, J. (1968). 'Guillelmi Petri de Calciata, Rithmi de Iulia Romula seu Ispalensi Urbe (a. 1250)', *AEM* V pp.549-58.

Cela, C.J. (1969). *Diccionario Secreto* vol.II. Madrid.

Chalon, L. (1976). *L'Histoire et l'épopée castillane du moyen âge*. Paris.

Chambers, J.K. and Trudgill, P. (1980). *Dialectology*. Cambridge.

Chapman, J.A. (1976). ' "I lerned never rethoryk": a problem of apprenticeship', *Medieval Hispanic Studies presented to Rita Hamilton* pp.21-30. London.

Chen, M.Y. (1972). 'The Time Dimension: contribution toward a theory of sound change', *FL* VIII pp.457-98.

Chen, M.Y. and Wang, W.S-Y. (1975). 'Sound Change: Actuation and Implementation', *Language* LI pp.255-80.

Ciérvide, R. (1972). *Primeros documentos navarros en Romance (1198-1230)*. Pamplona.

Cirot, G. (1912-13). 'Une chronique latine inédite des rois de Castille (1236)', *BH* XIV pp.30-46, 109-18, 244-74, 353-74; XV pp.18-37, 170-87, 268-83, 411-27.

— (1918). 'Traité entre Alphonse VIII de Castille et Alphonse IX de León', *BH* XX pp.172-80.

Cocheril, M. (1966). *Etudes sur le monachisme en Espagne et au Portugal*. Paris-Lisbon.

Codoñer, C. (1966). 'Estudio de fuentes del manuscrito 99.30 de la Catedral de Toledo', *Archivum* XVI pp.67-90.

Colbert, E.P. (1962). *The Martyrs of Córdoba (850-59)*. Washington.

Collinge, N.E. (1978). 'Exceptions, their nature and place – and the Neogrammarians', *TPS* pp.61-86.

Collins, R. (1977). 'Julian of Toledo and the Royal Succession in Late Seventh-Century Spain' in P.H. Sawyer and I. Wood (eds), *Early Medieval Kingship* pp.30-49. Leeds.

— (1980). 'Mérida and Toledo: 550-585' in E. James (ed.), *Visigothic Spain: New Approaches* pp.189-219. Oxford.

Contini, G. (1966). 'La Posizione di Eulalia', *Studi in onore di Italo Siciliano* I pp.241-53. Florence.

Corominas, J. (1954-57). *Diccionario Crítico Etimológico de la Lengua Castellana* 4 vols. Madrid. (Enlarged, 1980-).

— (1958). Review of T. Navarro Tomás, *Documentos Lingüísticos del Alto Aragón*, *NRFH* XII pp.65-75.

— (1961). *Breve Diccionario Etimológico de la Lengua Castellana*. Madrid.

— (ed.) (1967). *Libro de Buen Amor*, by Juan Ruiz. Madrid.

— (1976-77). *Entre dos Llenguatges*. 3 vols. Barcelona.

Corriente, F. (1978). 'Los fonemas /p/, /č/ y /g/ en árabe hispánico', *VR* XXXVII pp.214-18.

Coseriu, E. (1977). 'Vulgärlatein und Rumänisch in der deutschen

Tradition', in *Homenaje a Rodolfo Grossmann* pp.337-46. Frankfurt.

Cotarelo Valledor, J. (1933). *Alfonso III el Magno*. Madrid.

Cousin, P. (1954). *Abbon de Fleury-sur-Loire*. Paris.

Cowdrey, H.E.J. (1970). *The Cluniacs and the Gregorian Reform*. Oxford.

Crystal, D. and Davy, D. (1969). *Investigating English Style*. London.

d'Abadal i de Vinyals, R. (1969-70). *Dels visigots als catalans* 2 vols. Barcelona.

David, P. (1947). *Etudes historiques sur la Galice et le Portugal du VI^e au XII^e siècle*. Lisbon.

Défourneaux, M. (1949). 'Carlomagno y el reino asturiano', *Estudios sobre la monarquía asturiana* pp.259-76. Oviedo.

De Marco, M. (ed.) (1968). *Tatuini Opera Omnia*. Turnholt. (= CC CXXXIII and CXXXIIIa).

De Poerck, G. (1956). 'Le sermon bilingue sur Jonas du Ms. Valenciennes 521 (475)', *Romanica Gandensia* IV pp.31-66.

−      (1963). 'Les plus anciens textes de la langue française comme témoins de l'époque', *RLiR* XXVII pp.1-34.

−      (1964). 'Le ms Clermont-Ferrand 240 (anc. 189), les *scriptoria* d'Auvergne et les origines spirituelles de la *Vie* française de Saint Léger', *Scriptorium* XVIII pp.11-33.

Devoto, D. (1979). 'Sobre la métrica de los romances según el Romancero Hispánico', *CLHM* IV pp.5-50.

−      (1980). 'Leves o aleves consideraciones sobre lo que es el verso', *CLHM* V pp.67-100.

Deyermond, A.D. (1965). '*Mester es sen pecado*', *RF* LXXVII pp.111-16.

−      (1969). *Epic Poetry and the Clergy*. London.

−      (1971). *The Middle Ages* (in the series *A Literary History of Spain*). London.

−      (1977). 'Tendencies in *Mio Cid* scholarship, 1943-1973', in A.D. Deyermond (ed.) *Mio Cid Studies* pp.13-47. London.

Díaz y Díaz, M.C. (1951-52). 'Sobre formas calificadas de vulgares o rústicas en glosarios. Contribución al estudio de *Vulgo*', *ALMA* XXII, pp.193-216.

−      (1954). 'Los prólogos del antiphonale visigothicum', *Archivos Leoneses* XV-XVI pp.226-57.

−      (1957). 'Movimientos fonéticos en el latín visigodo', *Emerita* XXV pp.369-86.

−      (1958). *Anecdota visigotica* I. Salamanca.

−      (1959). *Index scriptorum latinorum medii aevi hispanorum*. Madrid.

−      (1960). 'Ruta crítica por la lexicografía latina medieval', *Helmántica* XXXVI pp.497-518.

−      (1965). 'El latín de la liturgia hispánica' in J. Rivera Recio (ed.), *Estudios sobre la liturgia mozárabe* pp.55-87. Toledo.

– (1969). 'La circulation des manuscrits dans la Péninsule Ibérique du VIIIe siècle', *CCM* XII pp.219-41, 383-91.
– (1971). 'Problemas de la cultura en los siglos XI-XII: la escuela episcopal de Santiago', *Compostellanum* XVI pp.187-200.
– (1975). 'La transmisión de los textos antiguos en la península ibérica en los siglos VII-XI', *La Cultura Antica nell'Occidente Latino dal VII all' XI secolo* pp.133-75. Spoleto.
– (1976a). *De Isidoro al siglo XI*. Barcelona.
– (1976b). 'Sobre las series de voces de animales', in J.J. O'Meara, B. Naumann (eds), *Latin Script and Letters, A.D. 400-900* pp.148-55. Leiden.
– (1978). *Las primeras glosas hispánicas*. Barcelona.
– (1979). *Libros y Librerías de la Rioja altomedieval*. Logroño.
– (1981a). 'Vigilán y Sarracino', *Festgabe für Walther Bulst zum 80. Geburtstag* pp.60-92. Heidelberg.
– (1981b). 'El cultivo del latín en el siglo X', *AEF* IV pp.71-81.
Díaz Jiménez, J.E. (1892). 'Inmigración mozárabe en el reino de León: el monasterio de Abellar o de los santos mártires Cosme y Damián', *BRAH* XX pp.123-51.
Dick, A. (ed.) (1969). *Martianus Capella*. Stuttgart.
Dronke, P. (1965). 'The Beginnings of the Sequence', *Beiträge zur Geschichte der deutschen Sprache und Literatur (Tübingen)* LXXXVII pp.43-73.
– (1968). *The Medieval Lyric*. London.
– (1979). 'The Interpretation of the Ripoll love-songs', *RPh* XXXIII pp.14-42.
Dutton, B. (1967). 'Some Latinisms in the Spanish *Mester de Clereçía*', *KRQ* IV pp.45-60.
– (ed.) (1967-). *Gonzalo de Berceo: Obras Completas*. London. I (1967): La Vida de San Millán de la Cogolla; II (1971): Milagros de Nuestra Señora; III (1975): El Duelo de la Virgen, Los Himnos, Loores de Nuestra Señora, Los Signos del Juicio Final; IV (1978): La Vida de Santo Domingo de Silos; V (forthcoming): El Sacrificio de la Misa, La Vida de Santa Oria, El Martirio de San Lorenzo.
– (1973). 'French influences in the Spanish *Mester de Clereçía*' in B. Dutton et al. (ed.), *Medieval Studies in Honour of R.W. Linker* pp.73-93. Madrid.
– (1980). 'Legal formulae in medieval literature', *Studies in Honor of John Esten Keller* pp.13-28. Newark.
Dworkin, S. (1975). 'Therapeutic Reactions to excessive Phonetic Erosion', *RPh* XXVIII pp.462-72.
– (1978). 'Derivational Transparency and Sound Change: the two-pronged growth of -ÍDU in Hispano-Romance', *RPh* XXXI pp.605-17.

Elcock, W.D. (1961). 'La pénombre des langues romanes', *Revista Portuguesa de Filologia* II pp.1-19.
 —    (1975). *The Romance Languages.*[2] London.
Entwistle, W.J. (1928). 'On the *Carmen de morte Sanctii Regis*', *BH* XXX pp.204-19.
 —    (1962). *The Spanish Language.*[2] London.
Ewert, A. (1933). *The French Language.* London.
 —    (1935). 'The Strasbourg Oaths', *TPS* pp.16-35.
Fábrega Grau, A. (1951-52). 'Un glosario del siglo X', *ALMA* XXII pp.217-37.
Faulhaber, C. (1972). *Latin Rhetorical Theory in 13th and 14th Century Castile.* California.
Felix, S.W. (1979). 'Anatomy of a Sound Change in Canarian Spanish', *ZRPh* XCV pp.358-81.
Ferguson, C.A. (1959). 'Diglossia', *Word* XV pp.325-40.
Fernández Guerra, A. (1865). *El Fuero de Avilés.* Madrid.
Fernández Martín, L. (1961). 'Un poema latino medieval', *Humanidades* XIII pp.275-321.
Férotin, M. (ed.) (1904). *Le Liber Ordinum.* Paris.
 — (ed.) (1912). *Le Liber Mozarabicus Sacramentorum.* Paris.
Fischer, B. (1957). *Die Alkuin Bibel.* Freiburg/Breisgau.
Fita, F. (1906a). 'El Concilio nacional de Burgos en 1080: nuevas ilustraciones', *BRAH* XLIX pp.337-84.
 —    (1906b). 'El monasterio toledano de San Servando en la segunda mitad del siglo XI. Estudio crítico', *BRAH* XLIX pp.280-331.
Fletcher, R.A. (1978). *The Episcopate in the Kingdom of León in the Twelfth Century.* Oxford.
Flórez, H. (ed.) (1765). *Historia Compostellana* (= *España Sagrada* vol. XX). Madrid. (Reprinted 1965.)
Floriano Cumbrero, A. (1951). *Diplomática española del período astur.* 2 vols. Oviedo.
Fontaine, J. (1959). *Isidore de Seville et la culture classique.* 2 vols. Paris.
Fought, J. (1979). 'The "medieval sibilants" of the *Eulalia-Ludwigslied* manuscript and their development in Early Old French', *Language* LV pp.842-58.
Franquesa, A. (1959). 'El códice emilianense 60 y sus piezas litúrgicas', *HS* XII pp.423-44.

Gaeng, P.A. (1968). *An Inquiry into Local Variations in Vulgar Latin.* Chapel Hill.
Galmés de Fuentes, A. (1977). 'El dialecto mozárabe de Toledo', *Al-Andalus* XLII pp.183-206, 249-99.
 —    (1980). 'El mozárabe de Sevilla según los datos de su repartimiento', *Homenaje a Samuel Gili Gaya* pp. 81-98. Barcelona.
Ganshof, F.L. (1947). 'La révision de la bible par Alcuin', *Bibliothèque d'Humanisme et Renaissance* IX pp.7-20.

—  (1971). *The Carolingians and the Frankish Monarchy*.
London.

García Alvarez, M.R. (1965). 'Los libros en la documentación gallega de
la alta edad media', *Cuadernos de Estudios Gallegos* XX
pp.292-329.

García de Cortázar, J.A. (1969). *El dominio del monasterio de San
Millán de la Cogolla (Siglos X a XIII)*. Salamanca.

—  (1977). 'La ordenación económica y social de la Rioja Alta
en el siglo X', *Homenaje a Don José María Lacarra de
Miguel* I pp.97-120. Zaragoza.

García de Diego, E. (1933). *Glosarios latinos del Monasterio de Silos*.
Murcia.

García Gallo, A. (1950). 'El Concilio de Coyanza', *AHDE* XX pp.275-
633 (sic).

García y García, A., Cantelar Rodríguez, F. and Nieto Cumplido, M.
(1976). *Catálogo de los manuscritos e incunables de la
catedral de Córdoba*. Salamanca.

García Villada, Z. (1914). 'Poema del Abad Oliva en alabanza del
monasterio de Ripoll', *RFE* I pp.149-61.

García Villoslada, R. (1975). *La Poesía Rítmica de los Goliardos
Medievales*. Madrid.

Garrod, H.W. and Mowat, R.B. (eds) (1915). *Einhard's Life of
Charlemagne*. Oxford.

Garvin, J.N. (1946). *The Vitas Sanctorum Patrum Emeretensium*.
Washington.

Germán Prado, P. (1928). *Historia del rito mozárabe y toledano*. Burgos.

Gibson, M. (1975). 'The Continuity of Learning circa 850-circa 1050',
*Viator* VI pp.1-13.

Gil, J. (1971). 'Apuntes sobre la morfología de Albaro de Córdoba',
*Habis* II pp.199-206.

— (ed.) (1973a). *Corpus Scriptorum Muzarabicorum*. 2 vols.
Madrid.

—  (1973b). 'Para la edición de los textos visigodos y
mozárabes', *Habis* IV pp.189-234.

—  (1974). 'Carmen de Expugnatione Almariae Urbis', *Habis*
V pp.45-64.

Goetz, G. (ed.) (1888-1923). *Corpus Glossariorum Latinorum*. 6 vols.
Leipzig.

Gökçen, A. (1977). 'The language of *Homílies d'Organyà*' in *Catalan
Studies. Volume in Memory of Josephine de Boer* pp.
59-69. Barcelona.

Gómez Moreno, M. (1932). 'Las primeras crónicas de la Reconquista',
*BAH* C pp.562-628.

González, J. (1944). *Alfonso IX*. 2 vols. Madrid.

—  (1960). *El reino de Castilla en la época de Alfonso VIII*.
3 vols. Madrid.

—  (1978). 'Los mozárabes toledanos desde el siglo XI hasta el
cardenal Cisneros' in *Historia mozárabe. Congreso internacional de estudios mozárabes* pp.79-90. Toledo.

González Palencia, A. (1942). *El Arzobispo don Raimundo de Toledo*. Barcelona.

Grassotti, H. (1977). 'La iglesia y el estado en León y Castilla de Tamarón a Zamora (1037-72)', *CHE* LXI-LXII pp.96-144.

Grundmann, H. (1958). 'Litteratus – illitteratus', *Archiv für Kulturgeschichte* XL pp.1-65.

Guilmain, J. (1976). 'Some observations on mozarabic manuscript illumination', *Scriptorium* XXX pp.183-91.

Guiter, E. (1979). 'Nota sobre el vascuence de las "Glosas Emilianenses" ', *Cuadernos de Investigación Filológica* V pp.145-48.

Gulsoy, J. (1969). 'The *-i* words in the Poems of Gonzalo de Berceo', *RPh* XXIII pp.172-87.

Gybbon-Monypenny, G. (1965). 'The Spanish *Mester de Clereçía* and its intended public: concerning the validity as evidence of passages of direct address to the audience', *Medieval Miscellany presented to Eugène Vinaver* pp.230-44. Manchester.

Gysseling, M. (1949). 'Les plus anciens textes français non littéraires en Belgique et dans le nord de la France', *Scriptorium* III pp.190-210.

Hagerty, M.J. (1978). *Los Cuervos de San Vicente*. Madrid.

Hall, R.A. (1950). 'The Reconstruction of Proto-Romance', *Language* XXVI pp.6-27. (Reprinted in A.R. Keiler (ed.) *A Reader in Historical and Comparative Linguistics*, 1972, pp.25-48. New York.)

– (1965-66). 'Old Spanish stress-timed verse and Germanic superstratum', *RPh* XIX pp.227-34.

– (1974). *External History of the Romance Languages*. New York.

– (1976). *Proto-Romance Phonology*. New York.

Harlow, S. (1975-76). 'Competing models of Linguistic Change', *Proceedings of the University of Newcastle-upon-Tyne Philosophical Society* II pp.77-87.

Harris, R. (1967). Review of Avalle (1965), *Medium Aevum* XXXVI pp.52-54.

Hartman, S.L. (1980). 'La etimología de *dulce*: ¿realmente una excepción?', *NRFH* XXIX pp.115-27.

Harvey, L.P. (1963). 'The metrical irregularity of the *Cantar de Mio Cid*', *BHS* XL pp.137-43.

Harvey, R. (1945). 'The Provenance of the Old High German *Ludwigslied*', *Medium Aevum* XIV pp.1-20.

Hillgarth, J.N. (1958). 'St Julian of Toledo in the Middle Ages', *Journal of the Warburg and Courtauld Institutes* XXI pp.7-26.

– (1962). 'Visigothic Spain and early Christian Ireland', *Proceedings of the Royal Irish Academy* LXII pp.167-94.

– (ed.) (1976). *Sancti Iuliani Toletanae Sedis Episcopi Opera*

*(Pars I)*. Turnholt. (= *CC* CXV).
Hilty, G. (1978). 'Les Serments de Strasbourg et la Séquence de Sainte Eulalie', *VR* XXXVII pp.126-50.
Hitchcock, R. (1973). 'El rito hispánico, las ordalías y los mozárabes en el reinado de Alfonso VI', *Estudios Orientales* VIII pp. 19-41.
—   (1977). *The Kharjas: a critical bibliography*. London.
—   (1978). 'El supuesto mozarabismo andaluz', *Actas del I Congreso de Historia de Andalucía, Andalucía Medieval I* pp.149-51. Córdoba.
—   (1980). 'The Kharjas as Early Romance Lyrics: a Review', *MLR* LXXV pp.481-91.
Hohler, C. (1957). Review of G. Ellard, *Master Alcuin, Liturgist: a Partner of our Piety*, *JEH* VIII pp.222-26.
Holtz, L. (1981). *Donat et la tradition de l'enseignement grammatical.* Paris.
Hooper, J.B. (1974). *Aspects of Natural Generative Phonology*. Indiana.
Horrent, J. (1973-74). 'L'Histoire Silense ou Seminense', *Marche Romane* XXIII-XXIV pp.135-50.
Hubert, M. (1972). 'Le vocabulaire de la "ponctuation" aux temps médiévaux', *ALMA* XXXVIII pp.57-167.

Jackson, G. (1972). *The Making of Medieval Spain*. London.
Janson, T. (1979). *Mechanisms of Language Change in Latin*. Stockholm.
—   (1981). Review of Pulgram (1975), *RPh* XXXIV (special issue) pp.*323-25.
Jiménez Delgado, J. (1961). 'El *De Ortographia* isidoriano del Códice Misceláneo de León', *Isidoriana* pp.475-93. León.
Jones, A. (1980). 'Romance Scansion and the Muwassahat', *Journal of Arabic Literature* XI pp.36-55.
Jones, C.W. and King, H. (eds) (1975). *Bedae Venerabilis Opera VI.* Turnholt. (= *CC* CXXIIIA).
Kehr, P. (1945). 'Cómo y cuándo se hizo Aragón feudatario de la Santa Sede', *EEMCA* I pp.285-326.
Keil, H. (ed.) (1855-80). *Grammatici Latini*. 7 vols. Leipzig. (Reprinted 1961. Hildesheim.)
Kerkhof, M. (1979). 'Algunos datos en pro del origen catalán del autor del *Auto de los Reyes Magos*', *BH* LXXXI pp.281-88.
Kneepkens, C.H. and Reijnders, H.F. (1979). *Magister Siguinus: Ars Lectoria*. Leiden.
Kramer, J. (1976). *Literarische Quellen zur Aussprache des Vulgärlateins*. Meisenheim.
Krishnamurti, Bh. (1978). 'Areal and Lexical Diffusion of a Sound Change: Evidence from Dravidian', *Language* LIV pp.1-20.

Lacarra, J.M. (1933). 'Notas para la formación de las familias de fueros navarros', *AHDE* X pp.203-72.

- (1945). 'Textos navarros del códice de Roda', *EEMCA* I
  pp.193-283.
- (ed.) (1965). *Colección Diplomática de Irache*. Zaragoza.
Laistner, M.L.W. (1957). *Thought and Letters in Western Europe A.D.
  500-900*.[2] London.
Lambert, E. (1953). 'Le voyage de Saint Euloge dans les Pyrénées en
  848', *Estudios dedicados a Menéndez Pidal* IV pp.557-67.
Lanchetas, R.J. (1900). *Gramática y vocabulario de las obras de Gonzalo de Berceo*. Madrid.
Lapesa, R. (1948). *Asturiano y provenzal en el Fuero de Avilés*. Salamanca.
- (1967). 'Sobre el *Auto de los Reyes Magos*: sus rimas
  anómalas y el posible origen de su autor', in *De la Edad
  Media a nuestros días* pp.37-47. Madrid.
- (1972). 'Los provenzalismos del Fuero de Valfermoso de las
  Monjas (1189)', *PQ* LI pp.54-59.
- (1975). 'De nuevo sobre la apócope vocálica en castellano
  medieval', *NRFH* XXIV pp.13-23.
- (1980). *Historia de la Lengua Española*.[8] Madrid.
Lavaud, R. and Machicot, G. (eds) (1950). *Boecis*. Toulouse.
Law, V. (1982). *The Insular Latin Grammarians*. Ipswich.
Laza Palacio, M. (1964). *La España del Poeta de Mio Cid*. Málaga.
Le Bras, G. (1931). 'Pénitentiels espagnols', *Revue historique de droit
  français et étranger* X pp.115-31.
Le Coultre, J. (1905). 'La prononciation du latin sous Charlemagne',
  in *Mélanges Nicole* pp.313-34. Geneva.
Lehmann, P. (1913). 'Cassiodorstudien. IV. Die Abhängigkeit Isidors
  von Cassiodor', *Philologus* LXXII pp.504-17.
Leonard, C.S. (1980). 'Comparative Grammar' in J. Green and R. Posner
  (eds) *Trends in Romance Linguistics and Philology* I
  pp.23-43. The Hague.
Leonard, W.E. (1931). 'The recovery of the metre of the *Cid*', *PMLA*
  XLVI pp.289-306.
Lesne, E. (1938). *Histoire de la Propriété Ecclésiastique*. vol.IV. Lille.
- (1940). *Les écoles de la fin du VIII^e siècle à la fin du XII^e*
  (=*Histoire . . .* vol.V). Lille.
Lewis, A.R. (1965). *The Development of Southern French and Catalan
  Society*. Texas.
Líbano Zumalacárregui, A. (1977). *El romance navarro en los manu-
  scritos del Fuero Antiguo del Fuero General de Navarra*.
  Pamplona.
Lida de Malkiel, M.R. (1953). 'La Garcineida de García de Toledo',
  *NRFH* VII pp.246-58.
Linage Conde, A. (1973a). *Los orígenes del monacato benedictino en la
  península ibérica*. 3 vols. León.
- (1973b). *Una Regla Monástica Riojana Femenina del Siglo
  X: El "Libellus a Regula Sancti Benedicti Subtractus"*.
  Salamanca.
- (1976). 'Un testimonio de la europeización riojana en el

siglo X', in Olarte (1976) pp.85-105.
Lindley Cintra, L.F. (1978). 'Langue parlée et traditions écrites au
     moyen âge (Péninsule Ibérique)', *XIV Congresso Inter-
     nazionale di Linguistica e Filologia Romanza (1974):
     Atti* I pp.463-72. Naples.
Lindsay, W.M. (ed.) (1962). *Etymologiae sive Origines* of Isidore of
     Seville.³ Oxford.
Linehan, P.A. (1969). 'Pedro de Albalat, Arzobispo de Tarragona, y su
     "Summa Septem Sacramentorum" ', *HS* XXII pp.9-30.
—   (1971). *The Spanish Church and the Papacy in the Thir-
     teenth Century*. Cambridge.
Linskill, J. (1937). *Saint Léger. Etude de la langue du manuscrit de
     Clermont-Ferrand*. Paris.
Livermore, H. (1971). *The Origins of Spain and Portugal*. London.
Lloyd, P. (1979). 'On the definition of Vulgar Latin', *Neuphilologische
     Mitteilungen* LXXX pp.110-22.
Löfstedt, B. (1959). 'Zur Lexicographie der Mittellateinischen Ur-
     kunden Spaniens', *ALMA* XXIX pp.5-89.
—   (1965). *Der Hibernolateinische Grammatiker Malsachanus*.
     Uppsala.
—   (1976). 'Zum spanischen Mittellatein', *Glotta* LIV pp.117-
     57.
Löfstedt, E. (1959). *Late Latin*. Oslo.
Lomax, D.W. (1963). 'The Authorship of the *Chronique Latine des
     Rois de Castille*', *BHS* XL pp.205-11.
—   (1965). 'Don Ramón, Bishop of Palencia (1148-84)', *Home-
     naje a Jaime Vicens Vives* I pp.279-91. Barcelona.
—   (1971). 'La lengua oficial de Castilla', *Actes du XIIe Congrès
     International de Linguistique et Philologie Romanes*
     pp.411-17. Bucharest.
—   (1974-79). 'La fecha de la crónica najerense', *AEM* IX
     pp.404-06.
—   (1977). 'Rodrigo Jiménez de Rada como historiador',
     *Actas del Quinto Congreso Internacional de Hispanistas*
     pp.587-92. Bordeaux.
—   (1978). *The Reconquest of Spain*. London.
—   (1979). Review of Cantarino (1977), *MLR* LXXIV pp.961-
     63.
López, C-M. (1961). *Leyre*. Pamplona.
López Estrada, F. (1978). 'Mester de Clereçía: las palabras y el con-
     cepto', *JHP* II pp.165-74.
López Ferreiro, A. (1898-1911). *Historia de la Santa Apostólica Metro-
     politana Iglesia de Compostela*. 11 vols. Santiago.
Lorenz, E. (1963). 'Das altfranzösische Eulalialied und die Sequenz',
     *RF* LXXV pp.22-38.
Lot, F. (1931). 'A quelle époque a-t-on cessé de parler latin?', *ALMA*
     VI pp.97-159.
Lüdtke, H. (1968). *Geschichte des romanischen Wortschatzes*. Frei-
     burg.

–     (1978). 'Tesi generali sui rapporti fra i sistemi orale e scritto del linguaggio', *XIV Congresso Internazionale di Linguistica e Filologia Romanza (1974): Atti* I pp.433-43. Naples.

Lyovin, A. (1977). 'Sound Change, Homophony, and Lexical Diffusion', in Wang (1977) pp.120-32.

Mackay, A. (1975). *Spain in the Middle Ages*. London.

Macpherson, I. (1975). *Spanish Phonology*. Manchester.

Maestre Yenes, M.A.H. (1973). *Ars Iuliani Toletani Episcopi. Una gramática latina de la España visigoda*. Toledo.

Magnotta, M. (1976). *Historia y Bibliografía de la Crítica sobre el Poema de Mio Cid (1750-1971)*. Chapel Hill.

Mahn, J.B. (1949). 'El clero secular en época asturiana (718-910)', *Estudios sobre la monarquía asturiana* pp.259-76. Oviedo.

Maldonado, J. and Toro, F. (1942-43). 'Las relaciones entre el derecho canónico y el derecho secular en los concilios españoles del siglo XI', *AHDE* XIV pp.226-381.

Malkiel, Y. (1963-64). 'The Interlocking of Narrow Sound Change, Broad Phonological Pattern, Level of Transmission, Areal Configuration, Sound Symbolism; Diachronic Studies in the Hispano-Latin Consonant Clusters *cl-*, *fl-*, *pl-*', *Archivum Linguisticum* XV pp.144-73; XVI pp.1-33.

–     (1968). 'The inflectional paradigm as an occasional determinant of sound change', in W.P. Lehmann and Y. Malkiel (eds), *Directions for Historical Linguistics* pp.21-64. London.

–     (1975a). 'Some late twentieth-century options open to Hispanic Philology and Linguistics', *BHS* LII pp.1-11.

–     (1975b). 'En torno al cultismo medieval: los descendientes hispánicos de DULCIS', *NRFH* XXIV pp.24-45.

–     (1979). 'Problems in the Diachronic Differentiation of Near-Homophones', *Language* LV pp.1-36.

–     (1980a). 'The Fluctuating Intensity of a Sound Law', *Papers from the Fourth International Conference on Historical Linguistics* pp.321-30. Amsterdam.

–     (1980b). 'Old Spanish *maraviella* "marvel", Late Old Spanish *Sierta* "Syrtis" ', *RPh* XXXIII pp.509-10.

Manitius, K. (ed.) (1958). *Gunzo, Epistola ad Augienses (= MGH, Quellen zur Geistesgeschichte des Mittelalters II)* pp. 1-57. Weimar.

Mansilla, D. (1955). *La documentación pontificia hasta Inocencio III*. Rome.

Marigo, A. and Ricci, P.G. (eds) (1968). *Dante Alighieri: De Vulgari Eloquentia*. Florence.

Marsili, A. (ed.) (1952). *Alcuini Orthographia*. Pisa.

Martínez, H.S. (1975). *El "Poema de Almería" y la epica románica*. Madrid.

– (1980). *'Carmen in honorem Roscidee vallis*: edición crítica y estudio', *Etudes de philologie romane et d'histoire littéraire offertes à Jules Horrent* pp.279-93. Liège.

Martínez Díez, G. (1964). 'El concilio compostelano del reinado de Fernando I', *AEM* I pp.121-38.

Maurer, T.H. (1962). *O Problema do Latim Vulgar*. Rio de Janeiro.

McKitterick, R. (1977). *The Frankish Church and the Carolingian Reforms (789-895)*. London.

McNeill, J.T. and Gamer, H.M. (1938). *Medieval Handbooks of Penance*. Columbia. (Reprint, New York 1965).

Menéndez Pidal, G. (1954). 'Mozárabes y asturianos en la cultura de la alta edad media', *BRAH* CXXXIV pp.137-291.

– (1958). 'Sobre el escritorio emilianense en los siglos X a XI', *BRAH* CXLIII pp.7-19.

Menéndez Pidal, R. (1900). ' "Disputa del alma y el cuerpo" y "El auto de los Reyes Magos" ', *RABM* IV pp.449-62.

– (1904). *Manual de Gramática Histórica Española*. Madrid. (Much reprinted; expanded till 6th ed. 1940.)

– (ed.) (1911). *Poema de Mio Cid*. Madrid. (Much reprinted.)

– (1926). *Orígenes del Español*. Madrid. (7th ed. 1972.)

– (1944). *Cantar de Mio Cid: Texto, Gramática y Vocabulario*. 3 vols. Madrid.

– (1947). *La España del Cid*.[2] 2 vols. Madrid.

– (1951). 'Cantos románicos andalusíes, continuadores de una lírica latina vulgar', *BRAE* XXXI pp.187-270.

– (ed.) (1955). *Primera Crónica General de España*. Madrid.

– (1966). *Documentos Lingüísticos de España* I.[2] Madrid.

Messenger, R. (1946). 'Mozarabic hymns in relation to contemporary culture in Spain', *Traditio* IV pp.149-77.

Meyer, W. (1936). *Gesammelte Abhandlungen zur Mittellateinischen Rythmik* vol.III. Berlin.

Meyer-Lübke, W. (1935). *Romanisches Etymologisches Wörterbuch*.[3] Heidelberg.

Michael, I. (ed.) (1976). *Poema de Mio Cid*. Madrid.

Miles, G.C. (1950). *The Coinage of the Umayyads in Spain*. New York.

Millares Carlo, A. (1926). 'La Cancillería Real en León y Castilla hasta fines del reinado de Fernando III', *AHDE* III pp.227-306.

Mohl, F.G. (1899). *Introduction à la chronologie du latin vulgaire*. Paris.

Mohrmann, C. (1952). 'La latinité de Saint Benoît', *Revue Bénédictine* LXII pp.108-39.

– (1961a). 'Les formes du latin dit "vulgaire" ', *Etudes sur le latin des chrétiens* 4 vols, II pp.135-53. Rome.

– (1961b). 'Notes sur le latin liturgique', *Etudes sur le latin des chrétiens* 4 vols, II pp.93-108. Rome.

– (1961c). 'Medieval Latin and Western Civilization', *Etudes sur le latin des chrétiens* 4 vols, II pp.155-79. Rome.

Monroe, J.T. (1975). 'Formulaic Diction and the common origins of Romance lyric traditions', *HR* XLIII pp.341-50.

—    (1979). 'Prolegomena to the Study of Ibn Quzman: the Poet as Jongleur', *El Romancero hoy* vol.IV pp.77-120. Madrid.

Moralejo, J.L. (1980). 'Literatura hispano-latina', in J.M. Díez Borque (ed.), *Historia de las literaturas hispánicas no castellanas* pp.15-137. Madrid.

Moralejo Laso, A. (1978). 'Para la etimología de la palabra *jerigonza*', *RFE* LX pp.327-31.

Moreta Velayos, S. (1971). *El Monasterio de San Pedro de Cardeña. Historia de un dominio monástico castellano (902-1338)*. Salamanca.

Morin, D.G. (ed.) (1953). *Caesarius Arelatensis, Sermones*. 2 vols. Turnholt. (= *CC* CIII and CIV).

Muller, H.F. (1945). *L'Epoque mérovingienne*. New York.

Muller, H.F. and Taylor, P. (1932). *A Chrestomathy of Vulgar Latin*. Boston.

Mundó, M. (1965). 'La datación de los códices litúrgicos visigóticos toledanos', *HS* XVIII pp.1-25.

Mynors, R.A.B. (ed.) (1937). *Cassiodorus "Institutiones"*. Oxford. (Reprint 1963.)

Nelson, D.A. (ed.) (1979). *Gonzalo de Berceo; Libro de Alexandre*. Madrid.

Nelson, H.L.W. (1966). 'Die Latinisierungen in den Strassburger Eiden', *VR* XXV pp.193-226.

Nicolau D'Olwer, L. (1920). *L'Escola poètica de Ripoll en els segles X - XIII*. Barcelona.

Norberg, D. (1952). 'L'Origine de la versification latine rythmique', *Eranos* L pp.83-90.

—    (1954). *La Poésie latine rythmique du haut moyen âge*. Stockholm.

—    (1958). *Introduction à l'étude de la versification latine médiévale*. Stockholm.

—    (1965). 'La récitation du vers latin', *Neuphilologische Mitteilungen* LXVI pp.496-508.

—    (1968). *Manuel pratique de latin médiéval*. Paris.

—    (1977). 'Latin scolaire et latin vivant', *ALMA* XL pp.51-63.

O'Donnell, J.R. (1976). 'Alcuin's Priscian', in J.J. O'Meara and B. Naumann (eds), *Latin Script and Letters A.D. 400-800*. London.

Oelschläger, V.R.B. (1940). *A Medieval Spanish Word-List*. Wisconsin.

Olarte Ruiz, J.B. (ed.) (1976). *San Millán de la Cogolla*.[2] Madrid.

—    (1977). *Glosas Emilianenses*. Madrid.

Otero, C.P. (1976). *Evolución y revolución en Romance* vol.II. Barcelona.

Palmer, R.B. (1959). 'Bede as textbook writer: a study of his *De Arte Metrica*', *Speculum* XXXIV pp.573-84.

Paris, G. (1909). 'Les mots d'emprunt dans le plus ancien français',

*Mélanges Linguistiques* pp.315-52. Paris.
Parkes, M.B. (1978). 'Punctuation: or Pause and Effect' in J.J. Murphy (ed.), *Medieval Eloquence* pp.127-42. Berkeley.
Pattison, D.G. (1975). *Early Spanish Suffixes*. Oxford.
Penny, R.W. (1972). 'The re-emergence of /f/ as a phoneme of Castilian', *ZRPh* LXXXVIII pp.463-82.
    — (1976). 'The convergence of B, V, and -P- in the Peninsula: a reappraisal', *Medieval Hispanic Studies presented to Rita Hamilton* pp.149-60. London.
Pensado, J.L. (1960). 'Aspectos lingüísticos de la Compostela medieval', *VR* XIX pp.319-40.
Penzl, H. (1973). 'Orthography and Phonology in the Old High German *Ludwigslied*' in B.B. Kachru et al (eds), *Issues in Linguistics: Papers in Honor of Henry and Renée Kahane* pp. 759-85. Urbana.
Peña, J. (1972). *Páginas emilianenses*. Salamanca.
Pérez de Urbel, J. (1926). 'Origen de los himnos mozárabes', *BH* XXVIII pp.5-21.
    — (1950). 'La conquista de la Rioja y su colonización espiritual en el siglo X', *Estudios dedicados a Menéndez Pidal* I pp.495-534. Madrid.
    — (1952). *Sampiro: su crónica y la Monarquía leonesa en el siglo X*. Madrid.
Pérez de Urbel, J. and González Ruiz-Zorrilla, A. (eds) (1959). *Historia Silense*. Madrid.
Pescador del Hoyo, M.C. (1960). 'Tres nuevos poemas medievales', *NRFH* XIV pp.242-50.
Platelle, H. (1962). *Le Temporel de l'Abbaye de Saint-Amand des origines à 1340*. Paris.
Politzer, R.L. (1961). 'The Interpretation of Correctness in Late Latin Texts', *Language* XXXVII pp.209-14.
Pope, M.K. (1934). *From Latin to Modern French*. Manchester.
Porter, L.S. (1960). 'The *Cantilène de Sainte Eulalie*; phonology and graphemics', *Studies in Philology* LVII pp.587-96.
Posner, R. (1974). 'Ordering of Historical Phonological Rules in Romance', *TPS* pp.98-127.
Priebsch, J. (1895). 'Altspanische Glossen', *ZRPh* XIX pp.1-40.
Pujol, P. (1917). 'L'acte de consagració i dotació de la catedral d'Urgell, de l'any 819 o 839', *Estudis Romanics* II pp.92-115.
Pulgram, E. (1950). 'Spoken and Written Latin', *Language* XXVI pp. 458-66.
    — (1975). *Latin-Romance Phonology: Prosody and Metrics*. Munich.
Purczinsky, J. (1965). 'Germanic influence in the *Santa Eulalia*', *RPh* XIX pp.271-75.

Quintana Prieto, A. (1978). 'Sampiro, Alón y Arnaldo, tres obispos de Astorga, cronistas del reino de León', *León medieval. Doce estudios* pp.59-68. León.

Rabanal Alvarez, M. (1970). 'La lengua hablada en tiempos de San Isidoro', *Archivos Leoneses* XXIV pp.187-201.
Raby, F.J.E. (1934). *A History of Secular Latin Poetry in the Middle Ages*. 2 vols. Oxford. (Reprinted 1957.)
Rand, E.K. (1931). 'A preliminary study of Alcuin's Bible', *Harvard Theological Review* XXIV pp.323-96.
Reijnders, H.F. (1971-72). 'Aimericus, Ars Lectoria', *Vivarium* IX pp. 119-37; X pp.41-101, 124-76.
Reilly, B.F. (1968). 'Santiago and Saint Denis: the French Presence in Eleventh-Century Spain', *Catholic Historical Review* LIV pp.467-83.
    — (1976). 'The Chancery of Alfonso VII of León-Castilla', *Speculum* LI pp.243-61.
Reynolds, L.D. and Wilson, L.G. (1968). *Scribes and Scholars*. Oxford.
Riaño Rodríguez, T. (1971). 'Del autor y fecha del *PMC*', *Prohemio* II pp.467-500.
Rice, C.C. (1909). *The Phonology of Gallic Clerical Latin after the sixth century*. Harvard.
Riché, P. (1962). *Education et culture dans l'occident barbare, VIe-VIIe siècles*. Paris.
    — (1973). *La Vie quotidienne dans l'empire carolingien*. Paris.
Rickard, P. (1974). *A History of the French Language*. London.
Rico, F. (1969). 'Las letras latinas del siglo XII en Galicia, León y Castilla', *Abaco* II pp.9-91.
    — (1975). 'Corraquín Sancho, Roldán y Oliveros: un cantar paralelístico castellano del siglo XII', *Homenaje a la memoria de D. Antonio Rodríguez Moñino (1910-1970)* pp.537-64. Madrid.
    — (1978). 'El cuaderno de un estudiante de latín', *Historia 16*, III no.25 pp.75-78.
    — (1979). 'Sylva XI. El "pecado" del "mester" ', *RPh* XXXIII pp.143-44.
Rivera Recio, J.F. (1940). *Elipando de Toledo; nueva aportación a los estudios mozárabes*. Toledo.
    — (1962). *El Arzobispo de Toledo Don Bernardo de Cluny (1086-1124)*. Rome.
Robson, C.A. (1955). 'Literary Language, Spoken Dialect, and the Phonological Problem in Old French', *TPS* pp.117-80.
    — (1963). 'L'*Appendix Probi* et la philologie latine', *Le Moyen Age* LXIX pp.39-54.
Rodríguez Aniceto, C. (1931). 'El Poema latino *Prefacio de Almería*', *BBMP* XIII pp.140-75.
Rodríguez Pantoja, M. (1974). 'Notas de ortografía isidoriana', *Habis* V pp.65-92.
Roger, M. (1905). *L'Enseignement des lettres classiques d'Ausone à Alcuin*. Paris. (Reprinted 1968. Hildesheim.)
Russell-Gebbett, P. (1965). *Medieval Catalan Linguistic Texts*. Oxford.
    — (1973). 'Medieval Catalan Literature' in P.E. Russell (ed.),

*Spain. A Companion to Spanish Studies* pp.247-63. London.

Ryle, S.F. (1976). 'The Sequence: Reflections on Literature and Liturgy', *PLLS* I pp.171-82.

Sabatini, F. (1965). 'Esigenze di realismo e dislocazione morfologica in testi preromanzi', *Rivista di Cultura Classica e Medievale* VII pp.972-98.
—   (1968). 'Dalla *scripta latina rustica* alle *scriptae* romanze', *SM³* IX pp.320-58.
—   (1978). 'Lingua parlata, scripta, e coscienza linguistica nelle origini romanze', *XIV Congresso Internazionale di Linguistica e Filologia Romanza (1974): Atti* I pp.445-54. Naples.

Sackur, E. (ed.) (1892). 'Tractatus Garsiae', *MGH, Libelli de Lite* II pp. 423-35. Hanover.

Sage, C.M. (1943). *Paul Albar of Córdoba: Studies on his life and writings*. Washington.

Salrach i Marés, J.M. (1978). *El procés de formació nacional de Catalunya, segles VIII - IX*, vol.I. Barcelona.

Sampson, R. (ed.) (1980). *Early Romance Texts, an Anthology*. Cambridge.

Samuels, M.L. (1972). *Linguistic Evolution*. Cambridge.

San Martín Payo, J. (1942). *La Antigua Universidad de Palencia*. Madrid.

Sánchez Albornoz, C. (1944). 'Nota sobre los libros leídos en el reino de León hace mil años', *CHE* I-II pp.222-38.
—   (1980). *Historia de España VII. La España cristiana de los siglos VIII al XI: el reino astur-leonés*. Madrid.

Sánchez Alonso, B. (1941). *Historia de la Historiografía Española*. Madrid.

Sánchez Belda, L. (ed.) (1950). *Chronica Adefonsi Imperatoris*. Madrid.
—   (1953). 'La cancillería castellana durante el reinado de Doña Urraca (1109-26)', *Estudios dedicados a Menéndez Pidal* IV pp.587-99. Madrid.

Sanchis y Sivera, J. (1921). *Diócesis Valentina*. Valencia.

Sancho, H. (1914). 'La enseñanza en el siglo XII', *Ciencia Tomista* IX pp.52-76.

Saralegui, C. (1977). *El dialecto navarro en los documentos del monasterio de Irache (958-1397)*. Pamplona.

Savage, J.J. (1928). 'Lingua romana', *Speculum* III p.405.

Schuchardt, H. (1866-68). *Der Vokalismus des Vulgärlateins*. 3 vols. Leipzig.

Scudieri Ruggieri, J. (1959). 'Correnti esotiche e impronte dimenticate nella cultura ispanica dell'alto medio evo', *Cultura Neolatina* XIX pp.173-214.

Serdá, L. (1955). 'Inicios de la liturgia romana en la Cataluña vieja', *HS* VIII pp.387-94.

Serrano, L. (1925). 'Tres documentos logroñeses de importancia',

        *Homenaje a Menéndez Pidal* III pp.171-79. Madrid.
-  (1935). *El obispado de Burgos y Castilla Primitiva*. 3 vols. Madrid.
-  (1941). 'El Canciller de Fernando III de Castilla', *Hispania* I pp.3-40.
Serrano y Sanz, M. (1919). 'Cronicon Villarense (Liber Regum)', *BRAE* VI pp.192-220.
Shailor, B.A. (1979). 'The scriptorium of San Pedro de Cardeña', *Bulletin of the John Rylands University Library of Manchester* LXI pp.444-73.
Sholod, B. (1966). *Charlemagne in Spain*. Geneva.
Simonet, F. (1888). *Glosario de voces ibéricas y latinas usadas entre los mozárabes*. Madrid.
-  (1903). *Historia de los mozárabes de España*. Madrid. (Reprint 1967. Amsterdam.)
Smith, C.C. (ed.) (1964). *Spanish Ballads*. Oxford.
-  (1971). 'Latin Histories and Vernacular Epic in Twelfth-Century Spain: Similarities of spirit and style', *BHS* XLVIII pp.1-19. (= 1977a: chap.4).
- (ed.) (1972). *The Poem of the Cid*. Oxford.
-  (1977a). *Estudios Cidianos*. Madrid.
-  (1977b). Review of Chalon (1976), *BHS* LIV pp.336-38.
-  (1979). 'La métrica del *Poema de Mio Cid*: nuevas posibilidades', *NRFH* XXVIII pp.30-56.
Sofer, J. (1930). *Lateinisches und Romanisches aus den Etymologiae des Isidorus von Sevilla*. Göttingen.
-  (1937). '*Vulgo*: Ein Beitrag zur Kennzeichnung der lateinischen Umgangs- und Volksprache', *Glotta* XXV pp.222-29.
Solá-Solé, J.M. (1975). 'El *Auto de los Reyes Magos*: ¿impacto gascón o mozárabe?', *RPh* XXXIX pp.20-27.
Southern, R.W. (1953). *The Making of the Middle Ages*. London.
Suárez, M. and Campelo, J. (1950). *Historia Compostelana*. Santiago.
Suárez Fernández, L. (1970). *Historia de España: Edad Media*. Madrid.
Szövérffy, J. (1971). *Iberian Hymnody*. Wetteren.
Tagliavini, C. (1972). *Le origini delle lingue neolatine*.[6] Bologna.
Tejada y Ramiro, J. (1849-62). *Colección de Canones de la Iglesia española*. 7 vols. Madrid.
Terry, A. (1972). *Catalan Literature*. London.
Thomson, R.M. (1973). *Tractatus Garsiae*. Leiden.
-  (1978). 'The origins of Latin satire in twelfth-century Europe', *MJ* XIII pp.73-83.
Thorsberg, B. (1962). *Etudes sur l'hymnologie mozarabe*. Stockholm.
Tilander, G. (ed.) (1951). *Los Fueros de la Novenera*. Uppsala.
Torres Rodríguez, C. (1974-75). 'El maestro Pedro Compostelano. Un compostelano olvidado', *Cuadernos de Estudios Gallegos* XXIX pp.65-101.
-  (1976). 'La era hispánica', *RABM* LXXIX pp.733-56.

Ubieto Arteta, A. (1948). 'La introducción del rito romano en Aragón
        y Navarra', *HS* I pp.299-324.
    – (1960). *Cartulario de Albelda*. Valencia.
    – (1961). 'La *Historia Roderici* y su fecha de redacción',
        *Saitabi* XI pp.241-46.
    – (1964). *Corónicas Navarras*. Valencia.
    – (ed.) (1966). *Crónica Najerense*. Valencia.
Ullmann, S. (1967). *Semantics: An Introduction to the Science of
        Meaning*. Oxford.
Unterkircher, F. (1969). *Alkuin-Briefe*. Graz.
Usón y Sesé, M. (1935). 'El libro gótico o cartulario de San Juan de la
        Peña', *Revista de la Universidad de Zaragoza* XII pp.3-55.

Valdeavellano, L. (1952). *Historia de España* I. Madrid.
Van Der Vyver, A. (1947). 'Hucbald de Saint-Amand, écolâtre, et l'in-
        vention du Nombre d'or', *Mélanges Auguste Pelzer* pp.
        61-79. Louvain.
Van Koningsveld, P.S. (1977). *The Latin-Arabic Glossary of the Leiden
        University Library*. Leiden.
Vicuña Ruiz, J.A. and F.J. (1971). 'La Rioja, tierra de contacto entre los
        reinos hispánicos (923-1134)', *Berceo* XXIII pp.127-48.
Vincent, N. (1978). 'Is sound change teleological?', in J. Fisiak (ed.),
        *Recent Developments in Historical Phonology* pp.409-
        30. The Hague.
    – (1980). 'Words versus morphemes in Morphological Change',
        in J. Fisiak (ed.), *Historical Morphology* pp.383-98. The
        Hague.
Vives, J. (1946). *Oracional Visigótico*. Barcelona.
    – (1955). 'En torno a la datación del antifonario legionense',
        *Hispania Sacra* VIII pp.117-24.
    – (1969). *Inscripciones Cristianas de la España Romana y
        Visigoda*.[2] Barcelona.
Vollmer, F. (ed.) (1895). *MGH Auctores Antiquissimi* XIV. Berlin.
Von Winterfeld, P. (1901). 'Rhythmen- und Sequenzenstudien', *Zeit-
        schrift für Deutsches Alterthum* XLV pp.133-49.

Waldron, R.A. (1967). *Sense and sense development*. London.
Wallace-Hadrill, J.M. (1967). *The Barbarian West, 400-1000*.[3] London.
Wallach, L. (1959). *Alcuin and Charlemagne*. Ithaca.
Wang, W. S-Y. (1969). 'Competing Changes as a cause of residue',
        *Language* XLV pp.9-25.
    – (ed.) (1977). *The Lexicon in Phonological Change*. The Hague.
Wanner, D. and Cravens, T.D. (1980). 'Early Intervocalic Voicing in
        Tuscan', *Papers from the Fourth International Con-
        ference on Historical Linguistics* pp.339-48. Amsterdam.
Ware, N.J. (1965). 'The Date of Composition of the *Libro de Alex-
        andre*', *BHS* XLII pp.252-55.
Webber, E.J. (1958). 'Comedy as Satire in Hispano-Arabic Spain', *HR*
        XXVI pp.1-11.

West, G. (1975). 'Una nota sobre la *Historia Silense* y la *Ilias* Latina', *BRAE* LV pp.383-87.

Whinnom, K. (1980). 'Creolization in Linguistic Change' in A. Valdman and A. Highfield (eds), *Theoretical Orientations in Creole Studies* pp.203-12. New York.

Whitehill, W.M. (1976). 'The manuscripts of Santo Domingo de Silos', *Homenaje a Fray Justo Pérez de Urbel* I pp.271-303. Silos.

Willis, R.S. (1934). *The Relationship of the Spanish Libro de Alexandre to the Alexandreis of Gautier de Châtillon*. Princeton. (Reprint, 1965. New York.)

— (1935). *The Debt of the Spanish Libro de Alexandre to the French Roman d'Alexandre*. Princeton. (Reprint, 1965. New York.)

Winterbottom, M. (1977). 'Aldhelm's prose style and its origins', *Anglo-Saxon England* VI pp.39-76.

Winterbottom, S. (1974). *Education in Aragon and Catalonia, c. 1213-1327*. Liverpool M.A. thesis.

Wright, R. (1976a). 'Semicultismo', *Archivum Linguisticum* VII pp.13-28.

— (1976b). 'Speaking, Reading and Writing Late Latin and Early Romance', *Neophilologus* LX pp.178-89.

— (1976c). 'Pretonic Diphthongs in Old Castilian', *VR* XXXV pp.133-43.

— (1979). 'The First Poem on the Cid: the *Carmen Campi Doctoris*', *PLLS* II pp.213-48.

— (1980). 'Linguistic Reasons for Phonetic Archaisms in Romance', *Papers from the Fourth International Conference on Historical Linguistics* pp.331-37. Amsterdam.

— (1981). 'Late Latin and Early Romance: Alcuin's *De Orthographia* and the Council of Tours (813 A.D.)', *PLLS* III pp.343-61.

— (forthcoming). 'El Concilio de Burgos (1080) y sus consecuencias lingüísticas', *Actas del XVI Congreso de Lingüística y Filología Románicas*. Palma.

Ximénez de Rada, R. (1968). *Opera*. Valencia.

Zaal, J.W.B. (1962). *"A lei francesca" (Sainte Foy v. 20)*. Leiden.

Zamora Vicente, A. (1970). *Dialectología Española.*² Madrid.

Zonneveld, W. (1978). *A Formal Theory of Exceptions in Generative Phonology*. Lisse.

# INDEXES

## WORD-INDEXES

gavilla, 9
gazmoño, 9
gaznate, 9
gazpacho, 9
gazuza, 9
geitat, 203
gelemo, 204
gente, 14
gerranza, 202
gota, 15
grado, 74
gramática, 255, 259
guacamayo, 33
guacho, 33
guadafiones, 32
guadamecí, 31, 32
guadaña, 32
guadanyar, 32
guadapero, 32
Guadalajara, 32
Guadalquivir, 32
Guadiana, 32
guagua, 33
guano, 33
guante, 32
guardar, 31, 32
guarir, 32
guarnir, 32
guasanga, 33
guasasa, 33
guasca, 33
guaso, 33
guay, 32
guayaba, 33
ha, 242
haba, 21
hace, 10
hacer, 39, 168, 242
hacia, 14
hagan, 242
hasta, 14, 205
haya, 203
hecha, 244
hembra, 242
heredat, 242
hermano, 13, 31, 243
hermo, 243
hice, 39
hido, 242

hielo, 13
hija, 10
hijo, 239, 242
hinojo, 20, 21
hio, 242
hombre, 12, 57
honra, 13
horca, 93
hoy, 85
hoz, 35
huamne, 203
hube, 57
huebos, 59
huebra, 29, 242, 244
huerto, 217
huir, 74
huyo, 26
hyermo, 243
hyerno, 243
hyo, 242

id, 57
ierba, 243
iermano, 13, 31, 243
iermo, 243
ierva, 243
iglesia, 76
ignorancia, 221
ignorantes, 221
igual, 60
incendio, 204
incentitu, 204
incienso, 217
inquinata, 203
-ión, 249
irás, 39, 203

jactare, 203
jectatis, 203
jerba, 243
jerigonza, 94
jet, 202
joglaría, 247
juez, 35
juglares, 247
julgar, 167
junctatione, 202

kaigamus, 205

TEXT AND AUTHOR INDEX

## SUBJECT INDEX

Diego of Orense, 223
Diglossia, 2
Diphthongization, 9, 28, 51, 58-
60, 168
Douai, 136
Doublets, 23-30, 249
Drama, 219-20
Dulcidio, 187

Ebreuil, 141
Ebro, 188, 225
Ecclesiastical pronunciation, 3,
25, 31, 48, 70, 82, 99,
102, 104-22, 164, 171,
211, 233, 261
Elision, 69, 153-54, 229, 249
English, 46, 50, 64, 138, 165
Enneco, 189
Epic, 185, 231, 233, 253
Esteban (notary), 241-44, 259
Eudes, 128
Eulalia, 129-35
Evaluation, 11
Exceptions, 17, 40

Fáñez, Alvar, 232
Felipe, Prince, 257
Ferando of Compostela, 239
Fernando I of León-Castille,
183, 208-10
Fernando II of León, 230
Fernando III of Castille-León,
238, 257-58
Fleury, 136-39, 142
France, 7, 45, 62, 70, 96, 103,
217-18
French, 36-7, 51, 111, 150, 209
*Fueros*, 237-38, 258
Future, 39, 42-3

Galicia, 145, 165, 177, 188,
195, 217, 220-30
Gascon, 219, 252
Gelmírez, Diego, 220-24, 226,
235
German(ic), 30, 51, 99, 107,
111, 120-26, 129-30,
141, 184, 205, 254
Girona, 146, 150

Glides, 70
Glosses: see in Text Index
Gormaz, 253
Gotescalc of Le Puy, 190-91,
195, 205
Gothic, 82, 111, 131, 184
Gozlin, 128
Grammarians, 41, 51, 54-61, 78-
103, 108, 111
Greek, x, 30, 33, 89, 93, 108,
110-11, 117, 138, 156,
174, 217
Gregory V, 144
Gregory VII, 210-13
Gudésteiz, Pedro, 223

Hadrian I, 164
Hebrew, 156, 161, 219
Hiatus, 68, 87, 229, 249, 264-65
Homonymic Clash, 20-23
Homonymy, 20-30
Hostegesis, 159-60
Hugh of Cluny, 211
Hugo de Santalla, 218

Iambics, 69
Indian languages, 33
Iria Flavia, 181, 220
Irish scholars, 98-9, 103
Isolative changes, 14, 21
Italian, 79, 99-100, 102, 107,
148, 227
Italy, 70, 103, 108, 143-44

Jaume I of Aragon, 150
Jean d'Abbeville, 226, 254-58
Jerome de Périgord, 214, 253
Jerusalem, 260
Jonah, 135
Juan I of Castille, 167

Lateran Council, 4th, 150, 226,
254-57
Learnèd borrowings, 5-6, 13-16,
23-4, 28, 172, 249-50
Legal language, x, 42, 61-6, 125,
144, 148, 166-73, 241-
44, 253
Leocritia, 163

# ARCA Classical and Medieval Texts, Papers and Monographs

(ISSN 0309-5541)
General Editors: Francis Cairns, Robin Seager.

1. **THE BISHOPS' SYNOD ("THE FIRST SYNOD OF ST. PATRICK").** A Symposium with Text, Translation and Commentary. M.J. FARIS (Editor). vi + 63pp. + 11 plates. 1976. 0 905205 01 4. Pback. *Contributors to the Symposium*: W.C. Kerr, A.B. Scott, M.J. Faris, G.B. Adams, M.J. McGann, R.H.M. Dolley.

2. **PAPERS OF THE LIVERPOOL LATIN SEMINAR 1976. Classical Latin Poetry/Medieval Latin Poetry/Greek Poetry.** FRANCIS CAIRNS (Editor) vi + 310 pp. 1977. 0 905205 00 6. Pback. Contents. *Classical Latin Poetry*: Christopher Tuplin (Liverpool), 'Cantores Euphorionis'; I.M.LeM. DuQuesnay (Birmingham), 'Vergil's Vourth Eclogue'; E.L. Harrison (Leeds), 'Structure and Meaning in Vergil's *Aeneid*'; Alex Hardie (FCO), 'Horace *Odes* 1,37 and Pindar *Dithyramb* 2'; C.W. MacLeod (Oxford), 'Propertius 4,1'; *Summary*: R. Seager (Liverpool), 'Horace and the Parthians'. *Medieval Latin Poetry*: P.G. Walsh (Glasgow), '*Pastor* and Pastoral in Medieval Latin Poetry'; S.F. Ryle (Liverpool), 'The Sequence: Reflections on Literature and Liturgy'; Mark Davie (Liverpool), 'Dante's Latin *Eclogues*'; *Summaries*: A.B.E. Hood (Edinburgh), 'The Cambridge Songs'; Michelle Levy (Oxford), 'The Poetic *Persona* in Twelfth Century Latin Lyric'; R.B. Kevin Maguire (Liverpool), 'The Revision of the Breviary Hymnal under Urban VIII'. *Greek Poetry*: J.G. Howie (Edinburgh), 'Sappho *Fr.* 16 (LP): Self-Consolation and Encomium'; Giuseppe Giangrande (London), 'Three Alexandrian Epigrams: *APl.* 167; Callimachus *Epigram* 5 (Pf.); *AP* 12,91'; *Id.*, 'Aspects of Apollonius Rhodius' Language'; Francis Cairns (Liverpool), 'The Distaff of Theugenis – Theocritus *Idyll* 28'.

3. **PAPERS OF THE LIVERPOOL LATIN SEMINAR SECOND VOLUME 1979. Vergil and Roman Elegy/Medieval Latin Poetry and Prose/Greek Lyric and Drama.** FRANCIS CAIRNS (Editor) viii + 360 pp. 1979. 0 905205 03 0. Pback. Contents. *Vergil and Roman Elegy*: E.L. Harrison (Leeds), 'The Noric Plague in Vergil's Third *Georgic*'; H.D. Jocelyn (Manchester), '*Vergilius Cacozelus* (Donatus *Vita Vergilii* 44)'; Tilman Krischer (Berlin), 'UnHomeric Scene-Patterns in Vergil'; J.C. Yardley (Calgary), 'The Door and the Lover: Propertius 1,16'; J.C. McKeown (Cambridge), 'Ovid *Amores* 3,12'. *Medieval Latin Poetry and Prose*: William Barr (Liverpool), 'Claudian's *In Rufinum*: An Invective?'; J.E. Cross (Liverpool), 'Popes of Rome in the *Old English Martyrology*'; Roger Wright (Liverpool), 'The First Poem on the Cid: The *Carmen Campi Doctoris*'; Keith Bate (Reading), 'Twelfth-Century Latin Comedies and the Theatre'; John Margetts (Liverpool), '*Christus Vitis, Praedicator 'quasi Vitis'*: Some Observations on Meister Eckhart's Latin Sermon Style'; Jonathan Foster (Liverpool), 'Petrarch's *Africa*: Ennian and Vergilian Influences'. *Greek Lyric and Drama*: J.G. Howie (Edinburgh), 'Sappho *Fr.* 94 (LP): Farewell, Consolation and Help in a New Life'; W. Geoffrey Arnott (Leeds), 'Time, Plot and Character in Menander'.

4. **FORM AND UNIVERSAL IN ARISTOTLE**                          A.C. LLOYD
vi + 89 pp. 1981. 0 905205 05 7. Pback.
This volume offers the first full-length case against a conventional picture which presents Aristotle as holding an in re theory of universals. It argues that forms as such are not universals but particular and identical with particular things and explains how Alexander of Aphrodisias filled some gaps in this theory and was followed by the Neoplatonic commentators. Excursuses suggest a bearing of this approach on other philosophical difficulties in Aristotle, such as the nature of thought, the extent of God's thought, and the functions of matter. There is an appendix of translated illustrative texts.
"Lloyd's discussion is throughout intelligent and interesting . . . It is clearly an important contribution to the subject." (*Classical Review*)

*Continued overleaf*

5. **COURT AND POET**. Selected Proceedings of the Third Congress of the International Courtly Literature Society (Liverpool 1980)
GLYN S. BURGESS (Editor)
xiv + 364 pp. 1981. 0 905205 06 5. Hback.

*Court and Poet* contains thirty two papers by leading American and European scholars on a wide range of topics in Provençal, French, German, Spanish and English courtly poetry from the twelfth to the fifteenth centuries.
The contributors are: Charles Muscatine, Alan Deyermond, John F. Benton, F.R.B. Akehurst, Michael J. Bennett, Fanni Bogdanow, Constance Bullock-Davies, Martin Camargo, Marie Collins, Dafydd Evans, Luciano Formisano, Peter Frenzel, Albert Gier, Martin Gosman, Carol Heffernan, Tony Hunt, Margaret Jennings C.S.J., Mary Coker Joslin, Alfred Karnein, Erik S. Kooper, Lise Lawson, Marie-Noelle Lefay-Toury, John Margetts, Alan R. Press, Jacques Ribard, V.J. Scattergood, Nathaniel B. Smith, Robert Taylor, Brigitte Uhde-Stahl, Marc Vuijlsteke, Gregory J. Wilkin, Charity Cannon Willard.

6. **THE FRAGMENTARY CLASSICISING HISTORIANS OF THE LATER ROMAN EMPIRE: EUNAPIUS, OLYMPIODORUS, PRISCUS AND MALCHUS** R.C. BLOCKLEY
xii + 196 pp. 1981. 0 905205 07 3. Hback.

The fragmentary fifth-century Greek historians of the later Roman Empire are important sources for a period which is attracting increasing interest among ancient historians. This monograph, which is the first of a two-volume set devoted to them, offers a detailed examination of each author, with particular attention to the differences between them, their individual value as sources for the period, and their contributions to its historiography, together with an annotated conspectus of their fragments. A full text of the fragments, with translation and notes, will appear subsequently in the ARCA series.

7. **PAPERS OF THE LIVERPOOL LATIN SEMINAR, THIRD VOLUME 1981** FRANCIS CAIRNS (Editor)
vi + 423 pp. 1981. 0 905205 08 1. Hback.

Contents. Elaine Fantham (Toronto), 'Plautus in Miniature: Compression and Distortion in the *Epidicus*'; I.M. LeM. DuQuesnay (Birmingham), 'Vergil's First *Eclogue*'; Matthew W. Dickie (Illinois), 'The Disavowal of *Invidia* in Roman Iamb and Satire'; E.L. Harrison (Leeds), 'Vergil and the Homeric Tradition'; Paolo Fedeli (Bari), 'Elegy and Literary Polemic in Propertius' *Monobiblos*'; Robert Maltby (Sheffield), 'Love and Marriage in Propertius 4,3'; Frederick Williams (Southampton), 'Augustus and Daphne: Ovid *Metamorphoses* 1,560-64 and Phylarchus *FGrH* 81 F 32 (b)'; Harry Hine (Edinburgh), 'The Structure of Seneca's *Thyestes*'; H.D. Jocelyn (Manchester), 'Difficulties in Martial, Book I'; K.-D. Fischer (Berlin), 'Pelagonius on Horse Medicine'; Judith McClure (Oxford), 'The Biblical Epic and its Audience in Late Antiquity'; C. Codoñer (Salamanca), 'The Poetry of Eugenius of Toledo'; Roger Wright (Liverpool), 'Late Latin and Early Romance: Alcuin's *De Orthographia* and The Council of Tours (AD 813)'; Paul Gerhard Schmidt (Marburg), 'Elias of Thriplow — A Thirteenth-Century Anglo-Latin Poet'; Birger Bergh (Lund), 'A Saint in the Making: St Bridget's Life in Sweden (1303-1349)'; J.W. Binns (Birmingham), 'Biblical Latin Poetry in Renaissance England'; Brief notes by W.A. Camps (Cambridge), William Barr (Liverpool), K.-D. Fischer (Berlin), Francis Cairns (Liverpool).

8. **LATE LATIN AND EARLY ROMANCE. In Spain and Carolingian France** ROGER WRIGHT
xii + 322pp. 1982. 0 905205 12 X. Hback.

*Forthcoming 1982/83*

9. **STATIUS AND THE *SILVAE*. Poets, Patrons and Epideixis in the Graeco-Roman World** ALEX HARDIE
approx. 200 pp. 0 905205 13 8. Hback.

Statius was, by origin and training, a Greek poet, and the *Silvae* are a Roman extension of contemporary trends in Greek display poetry. Dr. Hardie reconstructs the professional background to the *Silvae*, and considers Statius' performances as a Neapolitan poet at Rome, his portrayal of his own society and his friends, and his attitudes to his Latin predecessors. The study includes several new interpretations of individual *Silvae*, and makes an important contribution to the current debate on the relationship between poetry and rhetoric in the Classical world.

*Further volumes in preparation.*